The Junior Illustrated Encyclopedia of Sports

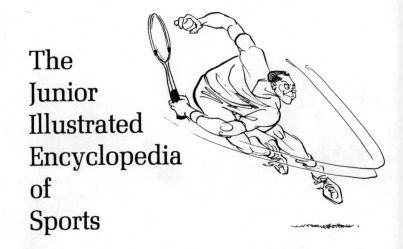

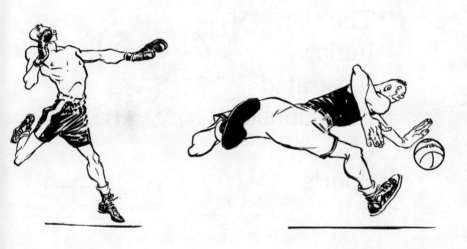

The Junior Illustrated Encyclopedia Of Sports

WILLARD MULLIN
Illustrator

HERBERT KAMM
Editor

THE BOBBS-MERRILL COMPANY, INC.
INDIANAPOLIS · NEW YORK

Auto Racing, Surfing, and Winter Skiing drawings
by MURRAY OLDERMAN

The Bobbs-Merrill Company, Inc.
A Subsidiary of Howard W. Sams & Co., Inc.
Publishers / Indianapolis • Kansas City • New York

Acknowledgments

The compilation of a book such as this is never the sole work of its editors. It is rather a distillation of the spirit, the encouragement, and the patient help of a great many people who share an affection for sports and a respect for the influence athletic competition has on our lives, whether we be players or spectators.

Particular gratitude is due the late Don Schiffer, himself the author of numerous sports books, who provided the inspiration for this one.

Contents

Boxing

Football

Auto Racing

The History of Automobile Racing

For all its complexity, millions of Americans are devoted to auto racing. In the United States it attracts a yearly paid attendance of more than 40 million, second only to horse racing, which has the advantage of pari-mutuel betting. Still, the auto-racing crowd shells out generously for the privilege of chills, thrills and spills. Seats at the Indianapolis 500 in 1969, for instance, cost up to $35 each. Even at less glamorous races tickets cost $25 and there is as much as a $5 charge for standing room.

The sport has made tremendous gains in the United States, as is reflected by the scramble to build speedways. By 1969, auto racing had become a major industry. New tracks were springing up over land which was once cow pasture in such obscure places as Cambridge Junction, Michigan; Ontario, California, and Talladega, Alabama, just to mention a few. And they all were making money.

The bigger the tracks the bigger the purses, naturally. Purse money had reached such heights that by 1969 over $7 million

3

had been paid out to the daredevils on wheels. With the money and resultant publicity, race car drivers were better known in some parts of the United States than major league ballplayers. Only the Kentucky Derby winner (the horse, not the jockey) was better known than other sports heroes in 1969.

With the growth came turmoil in auto racing. There is an excess of racing organizations, each with its own roster of champions. There is confusing overlap as one racing group moves into areas previously considered private. There are road circuits, oval tracks, dirt tracks, paved tracks, hill climbs, endurance races, sprints, 500-milers, and drags. New words like prototype, displacement, double overhead cams, homologation, and stock block confuse most of the fans, but still they flock to watch the races.

Auto racing is even more popular in Europe. The Le Mans 24-hour grind attracts as many as 400,000 persons. Since the sport is so universal, with many U.S. drivers taking part in European races and many manufacturers competing, international control is necessary. The organization in complete charge is called the Fédération Internationale de l'Automobile, based in Paris. The FIA is a voluntary association of the national automobile clubs of 70 countries. Drivers and manufacturers win world championships by competing in races recognized by the FIA.

The United States has four major organizations, and numerous minor ones, that sanction competition. The big four are the Sports Car Club of America, the National Association for Stock Car Auto Racing, the United States Auto Club, and the National Hot Rod Association.

Indeed, auto racing is big-pie industry and everyone, it appears, wants a slice.

The earliest races in America were staged over public roads, the first competition being in 1895 when Charles Duryea won the 52-mile Chicago-to-Evanston-and-return race. Duryea averaged 7.5 miles per hour. In 1896 auto racing spread to Narragansett, Rhode Island, where the fastest 5-mile heat of 26.2 miles per hour was recorded on a horse-racing track.

William K. Vanderbilt, to encourage automobile manufacturing in the United States, started the Vanderbilt Cup race in 1904. The only stipulation was that the car, its parts and tires had to be made in the nation from which it came.

George Heath, driving a 90-horsepower Panhard-Levassor, won the first Vanderbilt Cup after completing the 284.4 miles over Long Island, New York, roads at 52.2 miles per hour. The Vanderbilt races lasted until 1916, when the war ended them.

Another early race to capture worldwide attention was the 1908 New York-to-Paris "Round the World" race. Six cars entered, with an American entry, a Thomas Flyer, winning. George Schuster and Montague Roberts drove, pushed, and pulled it over 12,000 miles in 170 days.

Barney Oldfield became America's first auto-racing hero with his famous Stutz soaring over the dirt roads. In 1914 Barney won the Cactus Derby, a three-stage dash from Los Angeles to Phoenix.

Track racing was secondary in the early days, people preferring to line the roads as the early drivers sputtered along. The Indianapolis Speedway held its first race in 1911 and was not an immediate great success. But after World War I, road

5

racing took a downward trend. The public now preferred the dirt ovals and banked tracks, and the Indianapolis Speedway caught on. The crowd liked being confined to the grandstand with all the action in front of it.

But road racing refused to die. It was revived in 1934 when the Automobile Racing Club of America was formed and races were held over privately owned roads in the East.

As the cars got better and faster more and more people came out to watch the speed demons of the road. The Sports Car Club of America was formed in 1944 and held its first major race four years later at Watkins Glen, New York. Frank Griswold won it in an Alfa Romeo, averaging 63.7 miles per hour for 52 miles. The 6.6-mile circuit was laid out over public roads.

Racing returned to Bridgehampton, New York, after a lapse of twenty-nine years, and the first major airport race was held at Linden, New Jersey. In 1950 the Sebring, Florida, Six Hour was started, and road racing spread to Palm Springs and Pebble Beach, California.

Road racing was firmly established in 1952 when the SCCA and Strategic Air Command agreed to a series of charity races over SAC airports.

Professional road racing made a great advance in 1959 with the Grand Prix of the United States, counting toward the World's Driver Championship, at Sebring. Bruce McLaren was the first winner, averaging 98.87 miles per hour for 218 miles.

The SCCA kept growing and in 1962 began sanctioning professional road races. In 1968, it held more than 270 weekends of racing and sanctioned 90 percent of the road races held in the United States. In that same year, the SCCA awarded $1,079,820 in prize money, including $356,020 in accessory awards. The club, with 102 chapters spread across the country, conducted 1,800 amateur and 43 professional races.

Types of Racing Cars

CHAMPIONSHIP CARS

The average championship car weighs 1,400 pounds without fuel, oil, or driver, and has an engine developing from 500 to 600 horsepower. The driver operates the car from what is commonly called the "lay-down" position. Actually, it is a supine position with the driver's legs extended into the body of the car and his head held at windshield level. Most of the cars are built like bullets in an effort to eliminate wind resistance.

There are a few big championship cars which weigh close to 2,000 pounds and are driven by massive super-charged engines. The championship car is limited to an engine size of 255-cubic-inch Racing or 305-cubic-inch Stock Block and a minimum weight of 1,350 pounds.

The championship cars which compete at Indianapolis have changed from the big front-engined roadsters to sleek, snug, and speedy rear-engined cars.

500 driver A. J. Foyt in a new rear-engine Offenhauser.

LATE-MODEL STOCK CARS

The late-model stock cars are the racing version of the latest factory models from Detroit. Mostly Fords, Chevrolets, Pontiacs, Dodges, and Plymouths make up this popular branch of auto racing.

Engine limits on these cars are 430 cubic inches for regular sedans and 405 cubic inches for the smaller wheel-base models. Their outward appearance must remain absolutely stock. Only minor engine changes, suspension adjustments,

Driver Rodger Ward brings his racer onto the track.

and safety equipment can be changed from the original Detroit model. The cars weigh about 4,000 pounds.

SPORTS CARS

Many types and varieties of machinery are included in the broad classification of sports cars. Basically, a racing sports car is a production automobile with traditional sports-car lines that is used on the various road courses of the nation such as Sebring, Florida; Elkhart Lake, Wisconsin; or Riverside, California.

These cars include such machines as the Cobra, Corvette, Mustang, Ferrari, Jaguar, Lotus, and Sunbeam Tiger. Prototype sports cars such as the Chaparral and Ford GT, stream-

10

lined sports cars designed specifically for racing, are also included.

DRAGSTERS AND HOT RODS

The many classifications and types of hot rods are unique in that they race in acceleration tests down a straight course, usually a quarter mile long. This is commonly known as drag racing.

The many classifications of drag racing enable all types of cars to compete against each other according to horsepower and body design. This is racing's most popular participant sport; thousands each weekend try their cars at local quarter-mile strips.

Automobile Racing Associations

NASCAR

The National Association for Stock Car Racing, with head-quarters in Daytona Beach, Florida, was started following World War II by Bill France, its current president. During the past decade stock-car racing has risen to be the most popular form of racing in the United States.

The form of NASCAR's Grand National division are five southern superspeedways of a mile or more: Daytona, Florida, Darlington, South Carolina, Charlotte, North Carolina, Atlanta, Georgia, and Rockingham, North Carolina. NASCAR sanctions stock-car races all over the United States under strict rules and regulations. NASCAR has done much to advance safety in this form of racing.

1968 NASCAR Champions

(A total of $3,121,104 in prize money was paid out in 1968 by NASCAR in the 1,027 races sanctioned by the organization.)

Race	Driver	Car	Speed
Riverside 500	Dan Gurney	'68 Ford	100.598*
Daytona 500	Cale Yarborough	'68 Mercury	143.251
Atlanta 500	Cale Yarborough	'68 Mercury	125.564
Charlotte 500	Charles Glotzbach	'68 Dodge	135.324
Darlington 500	Cale Yarborough	'68 Mercury	126.132
Rockingham 500	Richard Petty	'68 Plymouth	105.06 *

*Record

USAC

The United States Auto Club is located in Indianapolis, Indiana, where the famous "500" is run under its banner. Formed in 1957 following the drop of the AAA's racing flags, USAC has been instrumental in the forming of the famed national championship circuit, which also includes Phoenix, Arizona; Trenton, New Jersey; Langhorne, Pennsylvania; Milwaukee, Wisconsin; and Sacramento, California.

USAC has developed an extensive "feeding" ground for Indianapolis with the sprint and midget circuits. It also includes a stock-car circuit.

SCCA

The Sports Car Club of America is located in Westport, Connecticut. The main sanctioning body involved in sports-car racing in this country, SCCA lists over 19,000 members in America. However, it also conducts a professional road-racing series called the United States Road Racing Championship (USRRC). SCCA has made road racing one of the most popular forms of auto racing in the nation.

(Total membership in this group is 19,802 with more than 5,000 special competition license holders.)

Race	Driver	Car	Speed	Time
Continental Divide, Castle Rock, Colo.	Lou Sell	Eagle-Chevrolet	80.85	1:31:43.2
Road America, Elkhart, Wis.	Jerry Hansen	Lola-Chevrolet	98.16	1:13:21.0
Lime Rock, Conn.	George Winter	Eagle-Chevrolet	97.57	1:12:06.11
Laguna Seca, Calif.	Lou Sell	Eagle-Chevrolet	99.8	1:37:42.0
Bridgehampton Double 500	Skip Scott	Lola-Chevrolet	107.868	1:35:29.8

NHRA

The National Hot Rod Association has grown into one of the four major racing associations in the United States and has added tremendous prestige to quarter-mile drag racing throughout the country. NHRA has taken drag racing off the highway and put it onto the race track in a professional and safe way.

Others

In addition to the Big Four, there are various other sanctioning racing bodies in the United States, including the American Hot Rod Association, the Bonneville Racing Association, Auto Racing Club of America, the United Racing Club, the International Motor Contest Association, and many more.

1968 National Racing Champions

DAVID PEARSON

NASCAR Stock-Car Champion

At thirty-four, curly-haired David Pearson ranks as one of the ten best drivers in the United States. In nine seasons, Pearson has won 46 of 281 NASCAR Grand Nationals. In 1968, Pearson won sixteen races and his second Grand National Championship, although only one of these, the Rebel 400, was a superspeedway event. Pearson was a major factor in Ford's racing program with plenty to say about design and fuel injectors.

BOBBY UNSER

USAC National Champion

Bobby Unser was magnificent in 1968. Not only did he win the Indianapolis 500 but the chunky, fearless driver also won USAC races on the Las Vegas Road Course, at Phoenix, Trenton and Pike's Peak. Unser, though only in his early

30's, has a reputation for making moves expected only of more experienced veterans.

A. J. FOYT

USAC Stock-Car Champion

A. J. Foyt, a rangy Texan, has cut back his racing in recent years but he was still good enough to drive away with the top stock-car honors, just nosing out Mario Andretti, who went on to win the 1969 Indianapolis 500. Foyt appears to win when he wants to and his record on dirt tracks is almost legendary. He shows a definite preference for dirt, but those ovals appear to be on the way out.

MARK DONOHUE

U.S. Road Racing Champion

This was the second year in a row that Mark Donohue was acclaimed as the road-racing king. Donohue, of Media, Pa., won every race he finished (15). That's because he is a careful, systematic driver who usually wears down his opponents. He has great stamina and an unusual capacity for concentration. He is easily one of the very best American drivers on the racing scene.

Grand Prix Racing

In 1909 the world's major auto race was the James Gordon Bennett Cup. It was governed by racing's first formula, a set of specifications covering the motor, body, and race. From that race came the first Grand Prix race.

The first two Bennetts were won by French cars, but after the French lost the third race they proposed entries be in proportion to a country's auto production. The idea was rejected. Finally, plans were accepted for a Grand Prix in which competition would be between factory teams and not nations.

The first "formula" called for a weight limit of 2,200 pounds. With no limit on engine size, an 18,279-cubic-centimeter Panhard-Levassor raced but a smaller 12,970-cubic-centimeter Renault won.

When the Fédération Internationale de l'Automobile (FIA) became racing's chief governing body in 1946, its first act was to set a formula for sports-car racing. Four classes were defined according to displacement ; there were no weight limits and all cars had to use pump gas.

Here are current formulas:

FORMULA I—engines limited to 3 liters (183 cubic inches) not supercharged or 1.5 liters supercharged. Minimum weight 1,102.3 pounds without fuel, which must be pump gas. Self-starter required with rollover bars, seat belts, and rupture-proof gas tanks. Cockpit and wheels must be open.

FORMULA II—maximum engine size is 1 liter (61 cubic inches) for a four-cylinder engine. Minimum weight is 924 pounds in running order, including lubricant and coolant but without fuel.

FORMULA III—maximum engine size is 1 liter; minimum weight, 880 pounds in running order. Engine must be from a series-produced touring car; that is, a four-seat touring car that is used for business and pleasure, with no modifications for racing.

Under these rules Grand Prix racing has been brought under strict control and has gained popularity throughout the world.

1968 GRAND PRIX WINNERS

Country	Winner	Car	Speed	Time
South Africa	Jim Clark (Scotland	Lotus-Ford	107.42	1:53.56.0
Spain	Graham Hill (England)	Lotus-Ford	84.408	2:15.20.1
Monaco	Graham Hill (England)	Lotus-Ford	77.82	2:00.32.3
Belgium	Bruce McLaren (New Zealand)	McLaren-Ford	147.138	1:40.02.1
Holland	Jackie Stewart (Scotland)	Matra-Ford	84.659	2:46.11.26
France	Jacky Ickx (Belgium)	Ferrari-V12	100.45	2:25.40.9
Great Britain	Jo Siffert (Switzerland)	Lotus 49B-Ford	104.83	2:01.20.3
Germany	Jackie Stewart (Scotland)	Matra-Ford V8	86.495	2:19.03.2
Italy	Denis Hulme (New Zealand)	McLaren-Ford	145.415	1:40.14.8
Canada	Denis Hulme (New Zealand)	McLaren-Ford	97.25	2:27.11.2
United States	Jackie Stewart (Scotland)	Matra-Ford	124.89	1:59.20.29
Mexico	Graham Hill (England)	Lotus-Ford	107.24	1:56.43.95

1968 FINAL POINT STANDINGS

(Best 5 finishes of first 6 races and best 5 finishes of last 6 races; score points on a 9-6-4-3-2-1 scale)

Driver	Points	Driver	Points
1—Graham Hill	48	6—Pedro Rodriguez	18
2—Jackie Stewart	36	7—Jo Siffert	12
3—Denis Hulme	33	7—John Surtees	12
4—Jacky Ickx	27	9—Jean-Pierre Beltoise	11
5—Bruce McLaren	22	10—Chris Amon	9
		10—Jim Clark	9

1968 CANADIAN-AMERICAN CHALLENGE CUP

Race	Driver	Car	Speed	Time
Road America Elkhart Lake	Denis Hulme	McLaren-Chevrolet	95:54	2:06.55.8
Bridgehampton (199.5 Miles)	Mark Donohue	Sunoco McLaren-Chevrolet	111.32	1:47:43.3
Edmonton, Alberta, Can.	Denis Hulme	McLaren-Chevrolet	103.15	1:57:36.7
Laguna Seca, Calif.	John Cannon	McLaren-Chevrolet	85.6	1:46.24.6
Riverside Calif.	Bruce McLaren	McLaren-Chevrolet	114.353	1:46:36.1
Las Vegas	Denis Hulme	McLaren-Chevrolet	113.1	1:52:15.38

1968 FINAL POINT STANDINGS

Driver	Points	Driver	Points
1—Denis Hulme	35	6—John Cannon	10
2—Bruce McLaren	24	7—George Follmer	6
3—Mark Donohue	23	8—Jerry Titus	5
4—Jim Hall	12	9—Chuck Parsons	5
5—Lothar Motschenbacher	11	9—Sam Posey	5

The Indianapolis 500

The Indianapolis Motor Speedway is the most famous automobile race track in the United States and perhaps in the world. Every Memorial Day some 250,000 people pack the 2.5-mile track to watch the world's best championship drivers in the traditional 500-mile race.

Parnelli Jones streaks across the finish line to win the 47th Indianapolis 500.

Jim Clark of Scotland, after winning the pole position for the 1964 Indianapolis 500.

This has been going on since 1909, when a 300-mile race was run on a soft macadam surface. The 500-mile events began in 1911, when the track was paved with bricks. The race begins at 11 A.M., when thirty-three cars are sent off on the fast drive to nowhere. To many people it is the most exciting sports spectacle anywhere.

A FEW INDIANAPOLIS GREATS

Peter De Paolo: First driver to exceed 100 miles per hour at Indianapolis with victory in 1925. Began racing following a two-year apprenticeship with his uncle Ralph De Palma, 1915 Indianapolis winner.

Louis Meyer: First three-time winner—1928, 1933, and 1936. Established speed records in last two victories.

Wilbur Shaw: Finished fourth in 1927, his rookie year, but won in 1937, 1939, and 1940. He was second in 1933, 1935, and 1938.

Mauri Rose: Competed in fifteen 500 races. Won in 1947, 1948, and was co-winner with Floyd Davis in 1941. Finished second in 1934, third in 1940 and 1950.

Rodger Ward: Won in 1959 and 1962. In his six races he has finished first, second, third, first, fourth, and second.

A. J. Foyt: Won in 1961 and 1964 and finished third in 1963. In 1964 he was first driver ever to win without a tire change.

Parnelli Jones: Won in 1963 and was second in 1965.

Jimmy Clark: 1965 winner was first driver to average more than 150 miles per hour. He did it without a tire change, too. He was second in his rookie year, 1963, and was leading in 1964 before car trouble forced him out.

Bobby Unser: 1968 winner set a record of 152.882 mph in a turbocharged Eagle-Offenhauser. However, Mario Andretti broke that when he won the Indy the next year in 156.867.

INDIANAPOLIS 500 WINNERS

Year	Driver	Car	Time	Av. Speed	Cyl.
1911	Ray Harroun	Marmon	6:42:08	74.59	6
1912	Joe Dawson	National	6:21:06	78.72	4
1913	Jules Goux	Peugeot	6:35:05	75.93	4
1914	René Thomas	Delage	6:03:45	82.47	4
1915	Ralph De Palma	Mercedes	5:33:55.51	89.84	4
1916*	Dario Resta	Peugeot	3:34:17	84.00	4
1919	Howard Wilcox	Peugeot	5:40:42.87	88.05	4
1920	Gaston Chevrolet	Monroe	5:38:32.00	88.62	4
1921	Tommy Milton	Frontenac	5:34:44.65	89.62	8
1922	James A. Murphy	Murphy Special	5:17:30.79	94.48	8
1923	Tommy Milton	H.C.S. Special	5:29:50.17	90.95	8
1924	L. L. Corum– Joe Boyer	Duesenberg Special	5:05:23.51	98.23	8
1925	Peter De Paolo	Duesenberg Special	4:56:39.46	101.13	8
1926**	Frank Lockhart	Miller Special	4:10:14.95	95.904	8
1927	George Souders	Duesenberg	5:07:33.08	97.545	8
1928	Louis Meyer	Miller Special	5:01:33.75	99.482	8
1929	Ray Keech	Simplex Piston Ring Special	5:07:25.42	97.585	8
1930	Billy Arnold	Miller-Hartz Special	4:58:39.72	100.448	8
1931	Louis Schneider	Bowes Seal Fast Special	5:10:27.93	96.629	8
1932	Fred Frame	Miller-Hartz Special	4:48:03.79	104.144	8
1933	Louis Meyer	Tydol Special	4:48:00.75	104.162	8
1934	Bill Cummings	Boyle Products Special	4:46:05:20	104.863	4
1935	Kelly Petillo	Gilmore Speedway Special	4:42:22.71	106.240	4
1936	Louis Meyer	Ring Free Special	4:35:03.39	109.069	4
1937	Wilbur Shaw	Shaw-Gilmore Special	4:24:07.80	113.580	4
1938	Floyd Roberts	Burd Piston Ring Special	4:15:58.40	117.200	4
1939	Wilbur Shaw	Boyle Special (Maserati)	4:20:47.39	115.035	8
1940	Wilbur Shaw	Boyle Special	4:22:31.17	114.277	8
1941	Floyd Davis– Mauri Rose	Noc-Out H. C.	4:20:36.24	115.117	4
1946	George Robson	Thorne Engineering Special	4:21:26.70	114.820	6
1947	Mauri Rose	Blue Crown Spark Plug Special	4:17:52.17	116.338	4

23

Year	Driver	Car	Time	Av. Speed	Cyl.
1948	Mauri Rose	Blue Crown Spark Plug Special	4:10:23.33	119.814	4
1949	Bill Holland	Blue Crown Spark Plug Special	4:07:15.97	121.327	4
1950***	Johnny Parsons	Kurtis-Kraft Special	2:46:55.97	124.002	4
1951	Lee Wallard	Belanger Special	3:57:38.05	126.244	4
1952	Troy Ruttman	Agajanian Special	3:52:41.88	128.922	4
1953	Bill Vukovich	Fuel Injection Special	3:53:01.69	128.740	4
1954	Bill Vukovich	Fuel Injection Special	3:49:17.27	130.840	4
1955	Bob Sweikert	John Zink Special	3:53:59.13	128.209	4
1956	Pat Flaherty	John Zink Special	3:53:28.84	128.490	4
1957	Sam Hanks	Belond Exhaust Special	3:41:14.25	135.601	4
1958	Jimmy Bryan	Belond AP Special	3:44:13.80	133.791	4
1959	Rodger Ward	Leader Card Special	3:40:49.20	135.857	4
1960	Jim Rathmann	Ken Paul Special	3:36:11.36	138.767	4
1961	A. J. Foyt	Bowes Seal Fast Special	3:35:37.49	139.130	4
1962	Rodger Ward	Leader Card Special	3:33:50.38	140.293	4
1963	Parnelli Jones	Agajanian Willard Battery Special	3:29:35.40	143.137	4
1964	A. J. Foyt	Sheraton-Thompson Special	3:23:35.83	147.350	4
1965	Jimmy Clark	Lotus Ford	3:19:05.34	150.686	8
1966****	Graham Hill	Lola-Ford	3:27:52.53	144.317	8
1967	A. J. Foyt	Sheraton-Thompson Spl.	3:18:24.42	151.207	8
1968	†Bobby Unser	Eagle-Offenhauser	3:16:13.76	152.882	
1969	‡Mario Andretti	Hawk-Ford	3:11:14.71	156.867	

No race during war years—1917–1918; 1942–1945.

* 300 miles.
** 400 miles, called because of rain.
*** 350 miles, called because of rain.
**** Accident at start; 11 of 33 cars knocked out of race.

† Turbocharged
‡ Record (Old Record: Unser—1968)

Start of the 1965 Indianapolis 500, Jim Clark in the lead.

First turn of the 1965 Indianapolis 500.

American Racing Milestones

1895

America's first auto race is won by Frank Duryea at 7.5 m.p.h. for 52 miles from Chicago to Evanston, Ill., and return.

1904

The first hill-climb in America at Mt. Washington, N.H., is won by H. S. Harkness at 19.4 m.p.h. over a twisting eight-mile course. Inaugural running of the Vanderbilt Cup. George Heath wins in a Panhard-Levassor at 52.2 m.p.h. for 284.4-mile race over Long Island roads.

1905

Forerunner of the modern rally, the Glidden Tour has its first running over 12 days and 883 miles.

1908

Montague Roberts and George Schuster, driving a Thomas Flyer, win the "Round the World Race" covering 12,000 miles from New York to Paris in 170 days.

1921

Jimmy Murphy in a Duesenberg becomes first American to win a European Grand Prix when he wins the French Grand Prix.

1934

Revival in road racing marked with races over public roads in Briarcliff, N.Y.

1936 and 1937

The Vanderbilt Cup Races are renewed at Roosevelt Raceway, N.Y. Tazio Nuvolari and Bernd Rosemeyer win the events which are financial failures and discontinued.

1944

Sports Car Club of America is formed by a group of New England enthusiasts. SCCA supplants the pre-World War II Automobile Racing Club of America.

1947

Sports-car racing begins on the Pacific Coast with races against time at Palos Verdes near Los Angeles.

1948

First open road race since 1935 held at Watkins Glen, N.Y. Frank Griswold, driving an Alfa Romeo, wins at 63.7 m.p.h. for 52.8 miles over a 6.6-mile circuit.

1950

Sebring, Florida, stages its first endurance race. Fred Wacker and Frank Burrell in a Cad Allard cover 389 miles in six hours, but Fritz Koster and Bob Deshon win Index in a Crosley Hot Shot.

1959

America's first Grand Prix on the World's Driving Championship schedule race at Sebring, Florida. Bruce McLaren is the winner.

1961

Phil Hill becomes first American to win the World's Driving Championship.

1965

Shelby-American is first U.S. firm to win division of World Manufacturers' Championship.

1968

Firestone Tire and Rubber Company stopped competing with Goodyear in financing racing teams. Sports Car Club of America formed department exclusively for professional racing.

1969

Turbine engines outlawed at Indianapolis 500. Also recommended: No four-wheel drive cars for the 1970 race.

Baseball

The History of Baseball

Baseball is America's great game. It is part of our way of life. Every youngster in the land, and just about every grown-up, too, has his favorite team, his favorite player.

Nothing can compare with going to a big-league game. It is like a picnic, a drama, and a circus all rolled into one, with enough action, thrills, peanuts, hot dogs, and soda pop to satisfy the hungriest appetite.

The twenty-four teams that make up the two major leagues now pull some twenty-five million fans a season through the gates. Millions more follow the game on television and radio, so that on some afternoons and evenings, especially at World Series time, it would seem that the whole country has gone baseball mad.

All this represents the fruits of more than one hundred years of development. And, just as a boy experiences growing pains, so did baseball go through its share of miseries before it became the healthy giant it is today.

How did it all start? We have to go back to ancient history to find the origins of the game we know as baseball. As

The fans pack Yankee Stadium.

a matter of fact, there is evidence that the Egyptians of five thousand years ago engaged in batting contests with club and ball and that the Greeks and Romans also played ball. For many years these games were part of religious ceremonies.

But it remained for the British to bring to our shores, early in the 1880's, the infant form of the game. The contest they played was called rounders and is still played today in girls' schools in England. Wooden posts were used, rather than bases; the batter would strike the ball and run around the posts, with the defending team trying to put him out by hitting him with the ball as he ran.

Some history books credit Abner Doubleday with having started the game of baseball in the United States by laying out the first playing field at Cooperstown, New York, in 1839.

34

The first formal game in the U.S.—Elysian Fields, 1846.

So widely supported is the legend, that baseball celebrated its one-hundredth anniversary in 1939 in Cooperstown. Further, baseball's shrine, the Hall of Fame, is located at Cooperstown, and an exhibition game between major league teams is played there as part of an annual celebration.

On the basis of more careful research, however, credit for establishing the game in this country belongs to Alexander Joy Cartwright, Jr. In 1845 he organized the first formal team, the New York Knickerbockers, and headed a committee that drew up the first set of playing rules.

The Knickerbockers played their first opponent on June 19, 1846, but it was not a very happy occasion for them. No field was available to them in New York, so the game was played in Hoboken, New Jersey, on a site called the Elysian Fields.

The game went four innings, and the Knickerbockers were beaten, 23–1, by a team called the New York Nine.

As one-sided as the contest was, it excited tremendous interest in the sport, and by 1858 so many teams were playing that a meeting to organize a league was called. Twenty-five clubs responded and set up the first league in history, the National Association of Base Ball Players.

The hottest rivalry was between teams representing New York and Brooklyn, later to become the game's most bitter foes as the Giants and Dodgers, and even then the sponsors realized that money could be made. As a result, when New York and Brooklyn met in the league opener on Long Island, on July 20, 1858, an admission fee of fifty cents was charged, although the players were all amateurs. Fifteen hundred patrons paid their way in to see New York defeat Brooklyn, 22–18.

By now baseball had attracted national attention, and even the Civil War, which lasted from 1861 to 1864, could not smother it. On the contrary, baseball talk was popular among soldiers of both sides, and when the war ended, the country had an even stronger thirst for baseball competition.

The National Association of Base Ball Players expanded to 100 teams in 1866 and to 237 the following year. City after city, eager to boast a team of its own, organized clubs; national tours were arranged; fans flocked to the playing fields to cheer for their heroes. And then trouble set in.

So popular was the game that betting became widespread; there were numerous cases of players being bribed to lose games on purpose. Actually, many players were paid salaries, even though the game still was supposed to be amateur, but

36

the first to admit it was Al Reach, whose name is still famous today in the manufacture of sporting goods.

In 1869 the first professional team, the Cincinnati Red Stockings, made its appearance and became the talk of the country. It won 65 games and tied 1 in a cross-country tour. In 1870 the Red Stockings won 26 more games in a row, making an unbeaten string of 92 games, before they lost to the Brooklyn Atlantics in eleven innings, 8–7.

The success of the Red Stockings wrecked the amateur league and paved the way for formation, in 1871, of the first professional league, the National Association of Professional Base-Ball Players.

The nine charter teams were the Philadelphia Athletics, the Bostons, the Chicago White Stockings, the Troy (New York) Haymakers, the Washington Olympics, the Forest City Club of Rockford, Illinois, the Fort Wayne (Indiana) Keki-ongas, the New York Mutuals, and the Forest City Club of Cleveland. In August of that year Fort Wayne was replaced by the Brooklyn Eckfords.

In the first professional league game on record, Fort Wayne defeated Cleveland, 2–0, and the first championship went to Philadelphia.

The league continued to play for five seasons, even though its team membership changed each year. Its brightest star was another noted name in the manufacture of sporting goods, A. G. Spalding, who pitched the Boston Red Stockings to four straight pennants. In 1872 curveball pitching was permitted for the first time, but Spalding relied entirely on control and a tricky change of pace.

But the same factors that wrecked the first amateur league

combined to ruin the first professional league—betting and bribery. In 1876 a new professional league, the National— the same National League we have today—was founded under the leadership of William A. Hulbert, a Chicago businessman.

The original teams were New York, Philadelphia, Boston, Hartford, Chicago, St. Louis, Cincinnati, and Louisville. Chicago, with Spalding as pitcher-manager, swept to the first championship.

In its second season, the National League was shaken by its worst scandal. Four members of the Louisville team were banned for life for taking bribes to lose games. But the league bounced back and had banner years from 1880 to

Albert G. Spalding

Hall of Fame

His plaque in the Hall of Fame.

Hall of Fame

1882. The famous Cap Anson, who finished his career with 3,528 hits, led the Chicago White Stockings to three straight pennants as player-manager.

The year 1882 also saw the National League threatened by a rival circuit called the American Association. But the AA collapsed after the 1891 season.

Another league, the Union Association, cropped up in 1884, and still another, the Players League, was organized in 1890, but each lasted only one year.

From 1892 to 1900 the National League alone was the world of baseball in America. It had the field all to itself, and its most colorful team was the Baltimore Orioles. Led by such stars as John McGraw, Willie Keeler, and Hughie Jennings, the roughhouse Orioles won three straight pennants starting in 1894.

With the turn of the century, the increase in baseball interest and the country's growing population had made the time ripe for another league. The American League took the field in 1901 in eight cities, Chicago, Boston, Detroit, Philadelphia, Baltimore, Washington, Cleveland, and Milwaukee. Its chief founder and first president was Byron (Ban) Johnson.

The National refused to have anything to do with the new league, and for two seasons the two circuits were in a state of war. In 1903, however, they reached an agreement, and baseball seemed on its way to lasting peace as well as prosperity. At the end of the 1903 season, Boston's American League champions defeated Pittsburgh's National League champions, five games to three, in a best-of-nine series.

Bitterness set in again in 1904. Still angry over the success of the American League in the 1903 playoff, John T. Brush, owner of the New York Giants, and their manager, John Mc-Graw, refused to let their National League champs meet the Boston Red Sox after the 1904 season. So there was no series.

But in 1905 the World Series, as we know it today, came into being. It has been played every year since and is the greatest sports event in the United States.

McGraw's Giants, having won the National League pennant again, defeated Connie Mack's Philadelphia Athletics, four games to one, in that memorable 1905 series. Each game was a shutout, with the great Christy Mathewson pitching three of them for the Giants.

The three names—McGraw, Mack, Mathewson—became among the most famous in baseball history and have been enshrined in the Hall of Fame, which was set up in 1936.

Many new stars have blazed across baseball's heavens in the drama-filled seasons since 1905. The game also has had its share of goats and its share of problems, but the story is one largely of heroes and heroic performances.

The Chicago Cubs set the all-time major league record for games won in one sea-

A New York player of 1888— Timothy J. Keefe, pitcher.

Harper's Weekly

son—116—when they captured the pennant in 1906. But they lost the World Series, four games to two, to their city rivals, the White Sox, the team known as the Hitless Wonders because their batting average for the season was only .228.

The 1908 season was famous for, among other things, a strange piece of drama known as "Merkle's boner." It was the last half of the ninth inning of a late-season game between the Cubs and Giants, battling bitterly for the pennant. The score was tied 1–1. With two out, the Giants had Moose McCormick on third base and Fred Merkle, only nineteen years old, on first.

Al Bridwell singled cleanly to center, scoring McCormick with what should have been the winning run. But Merkle, instead of touching second base, headed for the clubhouse, and the Cubs claimed that his failure to touch second nullified the run.

After a long wrangle, the game was declared a 1–1 tie and was ordered replayed. This time the Cubs defeated the Giants, 4–2, as Mordecai (Three-Finger) Brown won a duel with Christy Mathewson, who had pitched 37 victories that season. So the

A New York player of 1888—
William Ewing, catcher.

Harper's Weekly

The Championship Cubs of 1910.

Cubs won the pennant again and went on to whip Detroit in the World Series.

It was during this period that two of the all-time greats were making baseball history at bat and in the field—Ty Cobb for the Detroit Tigers in the American League, and Hans Wagner for the Pittsburgh Pirates in the National.

In 1911 both leagues adopted a ball with a cork center, and the change introduced what is generally considered the modern era of baseball.

A feature of the 1914 season was the excitement and frenzy produced by the Boston Braves "miracle team" in the National League. In last place on July 19, they launched a drive that swept them past the Giants for the pennant and carried them to a World Series victory in four straight games over the Athletics.

The outbreak of World War I and the formation of a third league, the Federal, dealt baseball two blows in 1914. But the Federal League lasted only two years, and the return to world peace in 1918 found the country's millions more eager than ever for baseball.

The year 1919 was the blackest for baseball since the National and American Leagues were established as rivals, but it also marked a vital turning point.

The 1919 regular season ended with the Chicago White Sox and the Cincinnati Reds as pennant winners, and the country was poised for the World Series, to be decided on a five-out-of-nine basis.

Cincinnati won the Series, five games to three. But it was discovered that eight players on the favored White Sox, soon to be scorned as the "Black Sox,"

Christy Mathewson

Hall of Fame

Babe Ruth

had been bribed by gamblers to lose. The eight players—Shoeless Joe Jackson, Eddie Cicotte, Chick Gandil, Lefty Williams, Swede Risberg, Buck Weaver, Happy Felsch, and Fred McMullin—were barred from baseball for life, and public confidence in the game fell to rock bottom.

But in 1920, two men—one seated at a desk, the other waving a powerful bat at the plate—not only gave baseball new life, but put it on the road to its greatest glory.

Kenesaw Mountain Landis, a federal judge, was appointed high commissioner of baseball with full power to run the game as he saw best. And Babe Ruth, greatest home-run hero of all time, started the batting bombardment that was to revolutionize the game and send attendance soaring to new, undreamed-of highs.

Further, Sunday baseball was made legal in New York, and the city became baseball's capital.

John McGraw, who gave the Giants ten National League pennants in twenty-one years, led them to four in a row from 1921 through 1924, while over in the American League, the Yankees, with Miller Huggins at the helm and Ruth smashing records, swept to three straight.

The Babe's 59 home runs in 1921 captivated the nation and set the Yankees up as the most exciting and powerful baseball organization in the business, eighteen years after they came into being by taking over the franchise of the old Baltimore Orioles. When they built Yankee Stadium in 1923, they not only had the best team, the best front office, and the best attendance, but they also had the best and most famous ball park.

The Washington Senators, with Stanley (Bucky) Harris, the "boy wonder" manager, and Walter Johnson, still a great

45

pitcher though past his prime, broke the Yankee reign by winning pennants in 1924 and 1925.

But the Yankees took charge again in 1926 and once more drove to three straight pennants under Huggins. Their Murderers' Row of hitting featured Ruth, Lou Gehrig, Bob Meusel, and Tony Lazzeri. The 1927 team, still ranked the greatest in the game's history, took the flag on the wings of the Babe's 60 home runs and crushed the Pittsburgh Pirates in four straight games for the world championship.

Both leagues now were turning out stars and thrills by the bundle, and historians were hard put to find adjectives that would do justice to them.

The Philadelphia Athletics, with Lefty Grove the pitching star and Jimmy Foxx the spark plug at the plate, gave Connie Mack the last three of his nine American League pennants in 1929, 1930, and 1931, and his fourth and fifth world titles.

In 1932 the Yankees returned to power under Joe McCarthy, who was to manage them to nine pennants and seven World Series conquests. After their 1932 sweep, the Yanks ran into three lean years; but, beginning in 1936, when Joltin' Joe DiMaggio joined the team and started rewriting a good part of the record book, the Bronx Bombers nailed seven pennants to the mast in eight years and took four straight world championships.

Since 1948 the story of the American League, and much of baseball, has been the Yankees all over again. Between 1948 and 1962, the Yanks were stopped only three times, twice by Cleveland and once by the White Sox.

In 1948 the Indians and the Boston Red Sox finished in a tie for the pennant, and the first title playoff in the league

records decided the winner. Manager-shortstop Lou Boud-
reau was the star of both the season-long scramble and the
playoff for the Indians, who went on to defeat the Boston
Braves in the World Series.

In 1954 the Indians had to win 111 games, a record in the
American League, to beat out the Yankees, but this time the
Tribe suffered four straight defeats in the World Series at
the hands of the New York Giants and their rampaging Willie
Mays.

Bucky Harris was the Yankee manager when the Yanks
failed in 1948. In
1949 Casey Stengel
was given charge of
the club, and had
it not been for that
loss to Cleveland
in the 1954 pen-
nant race, he would
have captured ten
straight flags. But
his record as a man-
ager of the Yankees
is unique—ten pen-
nants and seven
world championships
in twelve years, in-
cluding a record five
world crowns in a
row, 1949 through
1953.

United Press International

*Don Larsen hurling the final pitch of
his perfect Series game in 1956.*

All of those Yankee victories were filled with drama, but the one that held the most people breathless was Don Larsen's perfect no-hitter against the Brooklyn Dodgers in the 1956 World Series. In the fifth game of the Series, the big right-hander, using no windup, retired all 27 batters he faced in a 2–0 victory. Perfect games are rare enough, but one in the World Series was never dreamed of.

Another feature of American League history in the 1950's was the transfer of two clubs to new cities. The St. Louis Browns became the Baltimore Orioles in 1953, and the Philadelphia Athletics moved to Kansas City in 1954.

To turn again to the National League, three clubs, the St. Louis Cardinals, the Brooklyn Dodgers, and the New York Giants, shared the greatest successes after the McGraw reign was ended in 1925 by the Pittsburgh Pirates. And the man who had the greatest influence on the league was not a player, not a manager, but a front-office executive—Branch Rickey.

Between 1926 and 1946, the Cardinals won nine pennants, and they all could be traced to Rickey's genius, even though he had moved to Brooklyn in 1943.

In 1919, Rickey came up with the idea of establishing a farm system of minor league clubs through which the Cardinals could develop their own players. In 1926 the plan— since adopted by every other major league team in baseball —paid its first dividends. Leading a team of young players who had been brought up through the farms, player-manager Rogers Hornsby saw his charges not only win the flag but also beat the Yanks in the World Series.

Casey Stengel as a Giant star of 1922.

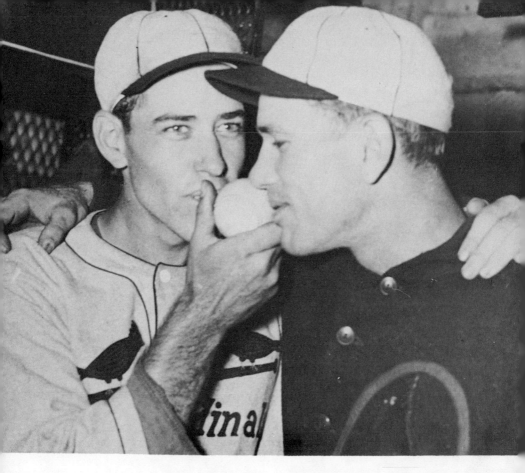

The pitching brothers—Paul (left) and Dizzy Dean.

Most colorful of the Cardinal pennant teams was Frankie Frisch's Gashouse Gang of 1934. Dizzy Dean pitched 30 victories, his brother Paul racked up 19 and Pepper Martin ran wild on the bases as the rough-riding Cards beat out the Giants for the flag on the last day of the season. In the World Series, the Cards bested the Detroit Tigers, four games to three, with Dizzy winning two games and Paul the other two.

It was in this same year that night baseball won approval. The originator of night ball was Larry McPhail, then general manager of the Cincinnati Reds, who later moved on to

Branch Rickey and Jackie Robinson

the Dodgers and Yankees. The first night game was played at Cincinnati on May 29, 1935, the Reds defeating the Phillies, 4–1.

The Dodgers had won a pennant in 1941, before Rickey took command of the club, but they enjoyed their best years under his leadership after World War II, winning four pennants between 1946 and 1953. Of far greater significance, Rickey was the man who wiped out the color line in baseball. In 1945 he signed Jackie Robinson as the first Negro in the game, bringing him up to the Dodgers in 1946 after Robinson had spent one sparkling season with Montreal in the International League.

Brooklyn had large quantities of glory in the Rickey regime —and it also had its hours of despair. In 1946 the Dodgers finished in a tie for the pennant with the Cardinals and then lost two straight in a two-out-of-three playoff.

And in 1951 the Dodgers led the league by 13½ games in mid-August, only to fall apart before the stretch drive of the Giants, led by Leo Durocher, a former Brooklyn manager. Again a playoff was required. The teams split the first two games. In the deciding battle, the Dodgers led 4–1 going

into the last of the ninth, when the Giants put on a fairy-tale finish.

With the score 4–2, one man out, two men on base, Bobby Thomson lined a home run into the left-field stands, against relief pitcher Ralph Branca, to win the game and the pennant for the Giants. Because so much was riding on it, Thomson's homer went into the books as the most famous in baseball history.

For the next five years the Dodgers and Giants continued to occupy the spotlight. Brooklyn won flags in 1952 and 1953. The Giants were on top in 1954. And the Dodgers took the prize again in 1955 and 1956, finally winning their first world title in 1955 by beating the Yankees in the Series, four games to three.

In 1957 a completely new name graced the list of National League pennant winners, the Milwaukee Braves. The club had been shifted from Boston to Milwaukee in 1953, setting new attendance records for the league in its first two seasons, and it didn't take long to reward the fans with a flag.

Bobby Thomson crosses the plate after his pennant-winning homer in the 1951 playoff.

United Press International

The Braves went on to beat the favored Yankees, four games to three, in the 1957 World Series, with Lew Burdette pitching three of the Milwaukee victories.

The year 1958 found the Braves winning the pennant again and the Yanks turning the tables in the Series. But the year will be remembered—and not too fondly by New York fans —as the one in which New York lost the Giants and Dodgers.

The great rivalry between them was transferred 3,000 miles as major league baseball reached the West Coast for the first time. The Giants made their new home in San Francisco, the Dodgers in Los Angeles. Thus baseball became a national game, geographically as well as spiritually.

The Dodgers, who had finished seventh in their first season at Los Angeles, lost little time in bringing a world title to the West Coast. The Giants led the 1959 National League pennant race until the last seven games of the season, then went into a tailspin. Both the Dodgers and Milwaukee Braves passed them, finished in a tie for the flag, and forced the third playoff in NL history.

The Los Angeles club, under Manager Walter Alston, swept the playoff series in two straight games. Larry Sherry, an unheralded young relief pitcher, hurled 7⅔ innings of 4-hit, no-run ball to give the Dodgers a 3–2 decision in the first game. In the second, the Dodgers won in twelve innings, 6–5, after rallying for 3 runs in the last of the ninth to tie the score at 5 all.

Thus the Dodgers faced the Chicago White Sox in the World Series. Al Lopez, manager of the Sox, carried an unusual record into the Series. In nine seasons as a big-league pilot, he had never finished worse than second. Twice he had won pennants to stop the Yankees—with Cleveland, in 1954, and now with the White Sox.

But, as was the case in 1954, Lopez couldn't bring his team out on top in the World Series. The villain to Lopez—and the hero to the Dodgers—was Larry Sherry, more brilliant in the Series than he was in the playoff.

Sherry was the winning pitcher in two battles and helped win the other two as the Dodgers conquered the White Sox, four games to two. In 12⅔ innings of relief pitching, the hard-working right-hander allowed only 8 hits and 1 earned run.

The 1959 Series was notable, too, in that it smashed all attendance records. Crowds of 92,394, 92,650, and 92,706 witnessed the three games played in the Dodgers' temporary home park, the huge Los Angeles Coliseum, and the total for the six games was 420,784.

Pitching was responsible for two other magnificent entries in 1959's "book of memories," both of them authored by members of the Pittsburgh Pirates—Harvey Haddix and Elroy Face.

On May 26, in a night game at Milwaukee, Haddix turned in a performance hailed by baseball historians as one of the greatest of all time, surpassing even the two successive no-hit games hurled by the Cincinnati Reds' Johnny Vander Meer on June 11 and June 15, 1938.

Haddix, a slim southpaw, pitched twelve innings of perfect ball, retiring thirty-six batters in a row.

The irony of it is that Haddix lost the game in the thirteenth inning, 1–0, on a home run by Joe Adcock.

The winning pitcher was Lew Burdette, although he had

allowed 12 hits—the same Lew Burdette who had pitched three victories over the Yankees in the 1957 World Series.

Face, a relief pitcher, set a new record for consecutive victories—17—and finished the season with an all-time-high percentage of .947, with 18 won and 1 lost.

The Yanks, in Casey Stengel's final season as their manager, won the 1960 flag. But they lost the World Series to the Pittsburgh Pirates when Bill Mazeroski, a light-hitting second baseman, lashed a home run off Ralph Terry in the last of the ninth inning of the seventh and deciding game to give the Pirates a 10–9 victory.

Sixty-one was the magic number in '61, as Yankee outfielder Roger Maris belted 61 home runs in a display of batting power that put him in the record books alongside Babe Ruth.

Maris and Mickey Mantle, smashing a record 115 homers between them, led the Yanks to the pennant; and the New Yorkers, under rookie manager Ralph Houk, smothered the Cincinnati Reds in the World Series, four games to one.

Two new American League clubs, the Los Angeles Angels and the Minnesota Twins, made their debut in 1961, and when the New York Mets and the Houston Colt .45's joined the National in 1962, both leagues had ten teams on the field.

Casey Stengel returned to the managerial wars in 1962 as pilot of the Mets, but even his genius couldn't keep them from finishing in last place.

The Los Angeles Dodgers, with Maury Wills stealing a record 104 bases, led the National League pennant race most of the way but were tied on the last day of regular play by the San Francisco Giants, while the Yankees cruised to their twenty-seventh American League championship.

Associated Press

As Maris poked his 61st.

The inspired Giants seized the NL pennant by defeating the Dodgers in a playoff series, two games to one, and carried the Yankees to seven games in the World Series. Ralph Terry may have been the "goat" of the 1961 Series, but he was the hero of 1962 as he pitched a 1–0 victory in the deciding game to give the Yanks their twentieth world title.

The Dodgers made few mistakes in 1963. With Sandy Kou-

57

fax posting a 25–5 record and Tommy Davis batting .326, both tops in the NL, they won the pennant by six games. Ron Perranoski was another Los Angeles hero as he posted a 16–3 record and a league-leading 1.67 earned-run average. In the American League, the Yankees coasted to their twenty-eighth pennant, then were overwhelmed in the World Series. With Sandy Koufax winning two games, Los Angeles destroyed the Bombers in four straight.

The Yankees, with new manager Yogi Berra at the helm, won the pennant again in 1964; the Dodgers finished sixth. The NL was a three-way dogfight between St. Louis, Cincinnati, and Philadelphia. The Cards won it with only two days to go in the regular season and went on to beat the Yankees in the World Series, four games to three. A strange turn of events took place right after the Series: Berra was fired, and Cards manager Johnny Keane resigned and was hired to manage the Yankees in 1965.

Sandy Koufax compiled a brilliant 26–8 record as the Dodgers bounced back to win the NL flag. Koufax recorded the fourth no-hitter (a perfect game) of his career, first man in baseball history ever to pitch four no-hitters, and broke Bob Feller's record of 346 strikeouts by fanning 382. Los Angeles finished one game ahead of the Giants to win the flag. In the AL the Minnesota Twins picked up the pennant, and carried the Dodgers to seven games before losing the World Series on a 2–0 three-hitter by Koufax in the seventh game.

The 1965 season also brought overtones of the Space Age to baseball. The Houston club changed its name from Colt 45's to Astros and moved into a new indoor stadium called the Astrodome. This was the year, too, when the Los Angeles Angels changed their billing to California Angels.

As the 1966 season opened, the Braves—originally of Boston, later of Milwaukee—transplanted themselves to Atlanta. The Dodgers retained the National League flag but were crushed in the World Series by the Baltimore Orioles, who took four straight games—the last three by shutouts.

In 1967, the Boston Red Sox won their first American League pennant in twenty-one years, only to have a gallant bid for the world championship denied in the seventh game of the Series by the Cardinals.

Another team long absent from the World Series—the Detroit Tigers—ended a drought of twenty-three years in 1968 as Denny McLain led the way to the pennant by pitching thirty-one victories. But the Series hero was Mickey Lolich, who won three games as the Tigers defied the percentages and conquered the Cardinals in seven games after losing three of the first four.

The 1969 season was notable for many things and could prove one of the most significant in the history of the game.

Harking back to the fact that the first professional baseball team made its debut in 1869, the major leagues designated 1969 as the game's centennial year. A new commissioner, a New York lawyer with the unlikely name of Bowie Kuhn, was in command. Four new teams joined the majors: the San Diego Padres and the Montreal Expos in the National, and the Seattle Pilots and the Kansas City Royals in the American. Kansas City thus returned to the game after having seen its franchise transferred to Oakland in 1967.

That wasn't all.

With twelve teams in each league, they were divided into four divisions of six teams each, and divisional playoffs were introduced. Further, the pitching mound was lowered and the strike zone was narrowed, both moves designed to favor the hitter and put more life in the game.

Despite these drastic steps, the season opened with gloomy predictions by many that baseball's popularity was on the wane, that football, especially pro football, was the sport America really loved the most.

But no one counted on the saga of the New York Mets.

Since coming into the National League in 1962, the Mets had finished in last place five times and next-to-last twice. But in 1969, everything came together for them. With a late rush, they won the Eastern Division title and then swept three straight from the Atlanta Braves, the Western Division winner, to become NL champion.

Their World Series opponents were the slugging Baltimore Orioles, who not only had made a shambles of the Eastern AL race but had won three straight over the Western winners, the Minnesota Twins, in the divisional playoffs.

Few gave the Mets much of a chance against the Orioles in the Series, and Baltimore promptly showed its muscle by taking the opening game. Just as abruptly, the tide turned. The Mets, a national joke as the losingest team in baseball during their first seven seasons, now were the national darlings.

They took the second game of the Series. And the third. And the fourth. And the fifth. The New York Mets, champions of the baseball world! The adoring fans of New York went wild, and much of the country glowed over the incredible achievement.

Baseball thus gained a new lease on life. The new leadership, the new structure, the new rules all contrived to produce long-needed changes for the better. But it's what hap-

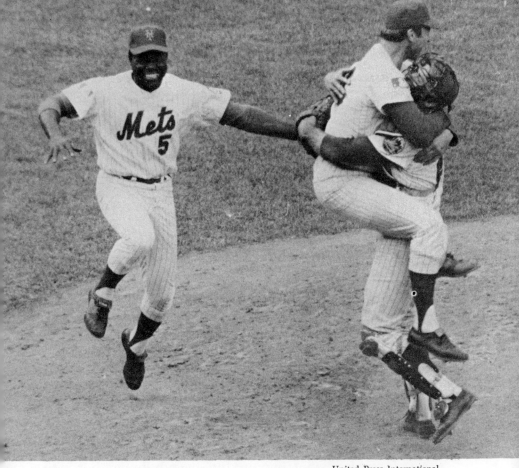

New York Met third baseman Ed Charles jumps with joy as pitcher Jerry Koosman and catcher Jerry Grote hug each other after the Mets down the Baltimore Orioles, 5–3, in the fifth and final game of the 1969 World Series.

pens on the field that counts most, and there the amazin' Mets, as people loved to call them, lifted the national pastime back into the nation's hearts.

Great Names in Baseball

GROVER ALEXANDER

It was the seventh and deciding game of the 1926 World Series between the St. Louis Cardinals and the New York Yankees, the Yankees of Ruth, Gehrig, and the rest of the Murderer's-Row sluggers.

The Cards led 3–2 going into the seventh inning, but with two out the Yanks filled the bases against Card pitcher Jess Haines. New York fans, sensing victory, rocked Yankee Stadium with cheers as Tony Lazzeri, later to become one of the few players to hit a World Series home run with the bases loaded, strode to the plate.

Out of the bullpen came the familiar figure of Grover Cleveland Alexander—Alexander the Great, Old Pete. At thirty-nine he already had hurled two victories over the Yanks in this Series.

With his typical effortless pitching motion, Alex set Lazzeri down, swinging, on four pitches, shut out the Yanks in the eighth and ninth, and gave the Cards their first world title.

No one ever speaks of Alexander without recalling that storybook performance against the Yanks. But it was only one of the epic chapters he wrote into the books in a big-league career that ran from 1911 to 1930.

With 373 victories, he shares the all-time National League record with Christy Mathewson. He had more shutouts than any other National Leaguer (90), and no other pitcher has equaled his mark of 16 shutouts in one season (1916) or 4 one-hitters in one season (1915). Twice he won both ends of a double-header, pitching the full distance in each game.

Alex toiled with Philadelphia, Chicago, and St. Louis, winning a total of 94 games for the Phillies from 1914 through 1916. There were five seasons when he had 200 or more strikeouts, and his career total was 2,227, including 29 in three World Series.

He was forty-three when his name faded from the roster—forgotten in the later years of his life, but never to be forgotten for the drama he contributed to the game.

TY COBB

No one ever picked an all-time baseball team without including Ty Cobb. If he wasn't the greatest player of them all, he was as great as any you can mention.

Name anything a ballplayer is supposed to do, and the Georgia Peach, Tyrus Raymond Cobb, did it. Hit, run, field, fight, think—Cobb was superb through twenty-four hectic seasons (1905–1928) that produced almost as many fireworks off the diamond as on. He was a battler, a brawler with a ferocious temper, and he is still spoken of today as the most hated as well as the most respected competitor the game has known.

But for all his fights and feuds, Cobb never lost sight of the fact that his job was to play ball, to stop the enemy, to win. You have to read the statistics slowly to fully appreciate how well he did his job.

In twenty-two seasons with the Detroit Tigers—the last six as player-manager—and two with the Philadelphia Athletics, he set the all-time record for both base hits (4,191) and lifetime average (.367). He also played more games (3,033), went to bat more times, scored more runs (2,244), and stole more bases (892) than any other player in history.

For twenty-three consecutive seasons he batted better than .300—in fact, never worse than .320—and topped the .400 mark three times. He captured the American League batting title twelve times in thirteen years. Even when he missed, his average was .371.

But, as with Babe Ruth, statistics tell only part of the Cobb story. He was a master at bunting, at place-hitting, and at predicting every move of the opposition when it came to taking an extra base or stealing. He ran the bases like a demon, ready to cut down with spikes anyone in his path, and if he was challenged, he fought—with teammates, with opponents, with umpires, with fans.

One fight with a fan in 1912 led to his suspension and the only players' strike in the game's history. His teammates had no love for him, but they knew his worth to the club and refused to take the field again until he was reinstated.

The more the pressure, the higher the stakes, and the more the fans hooted him, the harder Cobb played. It was the only way he knew. He died in 1961 at the age of seventy-four.

JOE DIMAGGIO

With the exception of Babe Ruth, no player was more the idol of America's baseball-loving millions in his time than Joe DiMaggio. Like the Babe, his name by any name—DiMag, Joe D, Joltin' Joe, the Yankee Clipper—spells baseball magic.

From his rookie year with the Yankees in 1936 until he retired from the game after the 1951 season, Joseph Paul Di-Maggio was the star of the high drama that unfolded on big-league diamonds. He was a thrill to watch, with his wide-spread picture stance, his clutch hitting, his loose, easy style in the outfield as he pulled in fly balls that seemed far out of reach, his rifle arm that cut down base runner after base runner.

The son of a San Francisco fisherman, Joe was twenty-one years old when he came to the Yankees after three spectacu-

lar seasons with the San Francisco Seals of the Pacific Coast League. He was a shy fellow, not very good at conversation. He did his talking with heroic deeds on the ball field.

In fourteen seasons with the Yanks, DiMaggio compiled a lifetime batting average of .325, smashed 361 home runs and batted in 1,537 runs. He twice led the league in percentage, homers, and runs batted in. Three times he was voted the league's most valuable player. He played in ten World Series and in eleven All-Star games. It was icing on the cake when he was elected to the Hall of Fame in 1955.

DiMag probably will be remembered best for his feat of hitting safely in 56 consecutive games in 1941. The streak ran from May 15 to July 16. During that stretch, the Yankee Clipper batted .408, collected 15 homers, 4 triples, 16 doubles, and drove in 55 runs. No other player has even come close to such a streak.

Joe DiMaggio

United Press International

There is no telling what other heights DiMag would have reached had he not spent three years in the Army at the peak of his career and had he not been troubled by stomach ulcers and a bone spur in his heel.

When he announced his retirement on December 11, 1951, the judgment of the baseball world was that Joe still had plenty of big-league ball in his system. But DiMaggio felt he no longer could give his best. Champion that he was, he refused to settle for less.

BOB FELLER

No ballplayer in modern times broke into baseball as sensationally as Robert William Andrew Feller, the Iowa farm boy who could fire the ball as hard as a cannon.

Rapid Robert was a mere seventeen when the Cleveland Indians put him under contract in 1936. High school ball and the sand lots had been his only experience. Yet, in his first effort in a big-league uniform—three innings against the St. Louis Cardinals in an exhibition game—the baby-faced right-hander struck out eight batters.

It was a sign of what was to come. Before he delivered his last pitch in 1956, Bob Feller was to give baseball some of its most exciting and historic moments.

Feller struck out 15 St. Louis Browns in his first complete game in August 1936. Three weeks later he fanned 17 Philadelphia Athletics to tie the major league record for a nine-inning game, set by Dizzy Dean in 1933, and in 1938 he took the record all to himself by whiffing 18 Detroit Tigers. The

67

Bob Feller

feat went unequaled until Sandy Koufax of the Los Angeles Dodgers struck out 18 San Francisco Giants in 1959.

Through the early years of his career, Feller drew so much attention he could hardly sneeze without making headlines. It was a lot of pressure for a youngster, but he kept getting better and growing more mature with each turn on the mound.

He pitched three no-hitters (1–0 against Chicago in 1940, 1–0 against the Yankees in 1946, and 2–1 against Detroit in 1951) and holds an all-time major league record of 11 one-hitters. He won 266 games against 162 losses, and led the American League in strikeouts seven times. He was elected to the Hall of Fame in 1962.

JIMMY FOXX

Long before Mickey Mantle came along to invent the "tape-measure" home run, James Emory Foxx propelled a ball into the top deck of the left-field stand at Yankee Stadium. Nobody had done it before. No one has done it since.

Mr. Double XX went on that season (1932) to explode 58 home runs for the Philadelphia Athletics, against some of the game's outstanding pitchers. In twenty big-league seasons, the muscular, jovial Jimmy beat a steady bombardment against the fences. When his career ended in 1945, he stood without challenge as the most powerful right-handed slugger the American League had ever known.

In fact, the game has produced few players more versatile (he played all nine positions), more powerful, and more colorful than the Maryland strong boy the players fondly called "The Beast."

He had a lifetime average of .325, with twelve straight seasons of 30 or more home runs. Only Babe Ruth and Mickey Mantle exceeded his league total of 534 homers. There were thirteen seasons in succession—seven with the Athletics, six with the Boston Red Sox—when he drove in more than 100 runs. In three World Series for the Athletics, he had 22 hits, including 4 homers, and an average of .344.

He is one of three players in the game's history to have been named the American League's most valuable player three times, and he made the All-Star team seven times.

The tragedy of Foxx' career is that it ended with his being almost broke and bouncing around from job to job as a coach. But baseball remembers its heroes for their brightest performances, as it should, and moon-faced, good-natured Jimmy Foxx had more than enough of these when he was voted into the Hall of Fame in 1951.

LOU GEHRIG

The most durable player in all baseball history was Henry Louis Gehrig, the Iron Horse of the Yankees. He also was one of the true greats, but he holds a special place as the man who played in 2,130 consecutive games.

Gehrig held down first base for the Yanks from June 1, 1925, when he replaced Wally Pipp, until May 2, 1939, when he turned over the position to Babe Dahlgren, never to appear in the lineup again. Yet, remarkable as that record is, it does not even begin to tell the story of Gehrig, the player and the man.

Larrupin' Lou and Babe Ruth gave the Yankees the most fearsome one-two punch of their era. Despite the fact that Lou spent much of his career in the shadow of the Babe, he stood out in bold relief as a murderous hitter and an inspiring team leader.

Born and raised in New York, Gehrig was not a natural ballplayer, as so many are. Though powerfully built and capable of smashing a ball even farther than Ruth, he had to learn to hit curveball pitching and to field. No player ever worked harder. Even at his peak, Gehrig never stopped polishing his talent.

His lifetime average was .340. He hit 494 home runs. He led the league twice with 49 and another year tied Ruth with 46, missing number 47 only because the runner in front of him

Lou Gehrig

Associated Press

failed to touch home plate. His runs-batted-in total was 1,991 —phenomenal considering that the Babe, batting ahead of him, frequently cleared the bases. In seven World Series, he hit 10 homers, drove in 35 runs, and batted .361.

The greatest baseball day in Gehrig's life was June 3, 1932, against Connie Mack's Athletics in Philadelphia. He hit four home runs in four consecutive times at bat—and missed another his next time up when the drive struck the top of the scoreboard.

When, on that 1939 day in Detroit, Gehrig took himself out of the lineup for the first time in fifteen seasons, the disease that was to cost him his life—a rare form of paralysis—already had robbed him of his skills.

He died June 2, 1941, but he lived long enough to see himself voted into the Hall of Fame and to be honored with a memorable day at Yankee Stadium. Tears choking his voice, he stood before the hushed stadium throng and said: "I consider myself the luckiest man on the face of the earth."

Small wonder they called him "The Pride of the Yankees."

LEFTY GROVE

Of all the pitchers elected to the Hall of Fame, Robert Moses Grove holds the best lifetime percentage—300 won, 141 lost, for .680. And he established the record during a time when some of the most murderous sluggers in the game were knocking the lively ball lopsided.

In fact, Lefty Grove is the only southpaw in the American League to have won 300 games since the so-called rabbit ball came into use. He always argued he would have won 500 had he been pitching with the dead ball.

In any case, Old Man Mose, as he became known in the

latter stages of his seventeen-year career (1925–1941), had no reason to view his achievements with regret.

After nine seasons with the Philadelphia Athletics and eight with the Boston Red Sox, Grove could boast these feats: He led the American League three straight seasons in both earned runs and won-lost percentage (1929, 1930, 1931); he led the league in earned runs nine times in all and in won-lost five times. No pitcher in this century has topped his 1931 record of 31 wins, 4 losses—this after he had won 28 and lost only 5 the year before. He was the league champion in strike-outs for seven years in a row, and he shares the league record of having won 16 straight games in one season.

In three World Series with the A's, Grove had 4 wins against 2 losses, but his earned-run average was 1.75 and his strikeout total was 36, 10 of them in a stretch of only 6⅓ innings.

Grove joined the A's in 1925 after winning 108 games and losing only 36 in four seasons with the Baltimore Orioles of the International League. He came up to the majors with one of the most blistering fast balls ever seen. But in his final days on the mound Lefty was a curve-ball artist. His fast ball gone, he knew he had to change his style to snare his 300th victory. Great competitor that he was, he hung on until he got it— when he was forty-one years old.

ROGERS HORNSBY

Rogers Hornsby, a fiery figure on major league diamonds for more than twenty years, is generally thought of as the game's greatest right-handed hitter.

He was the major league batting champion from 1920 through 1925—six straight seasons—with averages of .370,

73

.397, .401, .384, .424 (still the modern record), and .403. He was the league champion again in 1928 with .387, and his lifetime average of .358 is topped only by Ty Cobb's .367.

The Rajah won his richest glories with the St. Louis Cardinals, with whom he spent the first twelve years of his career. His crowning achievement came in 1926 when, as player-manager, he led the Cards to the pennant and then to victory in the World Series over a Yankee team everyone thought unbeatable.

When he was traded to the Giants the next season, St. Louis fans did everything but stage riots in protest, but it turned out to be only the first of a number of trips the rugged and outspoken Rajah was to make around the majors.

Before his playing days ended, he wore the uniform of the Chicago Cubs, the Boston Braves, and the St. Louis Browns. He was well-traveled as a manager, too. In addition to the Cards, he piloted the Braves, Cubs, Browns, and Cincinnati Reds.

Hornsby's conduct on and off the field kept him in constant hot water, but few ever played the game more fiercely or more scientifically. He could hit to any field, and his fielding made him one of baseball's greatest double-play men at second base.

Curiously, it was on the strength of his fielding that Hornsby won a shot at the big leagues. But it was his talent at the plate that carried him into the Hall of Fame.

CARL HUBBELL

Carl Owen Hubbell, the lean left-hander who literally pitched his arm out for the New York Giants, had his finest hour in a game that had nothing to do with a pennant race or a World Series. But what a perfect setting it was.

The 1933 season had seen the Meal Ticket, as Hubbell was called, pace the Giants to the National League flag with 23 victories. In the World Series, Hub again was the hero, pitching 2 more victories—twenty innings without allowing an earned run—as the Giants crushed the Washington Senators in five games.

It was only natural, then, for the stylish screwball artist to be the starting pitcher for the National League in the 1934 All-Star game. The American League lineup featured the five most feared batsmen in many a day—Babe Ruth, Lou Gehrig, Jimmy Foxx, Al Simmons and Joe Cronin. They came up to the plate in that order. They went down in that order—all on strikes.

Both before and after that mighty effort Hubbell made glittering entries in the record book. In sixteen major league seasons (1928–1943), all with the Giants, he racked up 253 victories and a lifetime earned-run average of 2.98.

There were five straight seasons when he won 21 or more games. He won 16 games in a row in 1936—24 straight if you count the 8 he won at the start of the 1937 season.

Also notable is his streak of 46⅓ scoreless innings in 1933, a no-hitter, a one-hitter in which he faced the minimum twenty-seven batters, and his career average of less than 2 walks per game.

Had the screwball not put such strain on his arm, Hubbell likely would have gone on for several more seasons. As it was, he achieved enough fame to earn a place among the all-time pitching greats.

Walter Johnson

WALTER JOHNSON

Youngsters who marvel at today's speedball pitchers would have been sent out of this world by Walter Perry Johnson, the Big Train of the Washington Senators.

In Johnson's heyday, from 1907 to 1928, statisticians never thought of clocking the speed of his pitch, as they have Bob Feller's and others' of more recent times. But those who saw the big right-hander in action say no one could possibly throw faster.

So blinding was his side-arm delivery and so perfect his

control that he won more games (414) than any other hurler in baseball's modern history, despite the fact that he pitched for a club that was never a pennant contender until his career was almost over.

By all odds, Johnson was the American League's greatest pitcher. Aside from his victories, he posted all-time records for strikeouts (3,497), innings pitched (5,923), complete games (531), and shutouts (113). In 1913 there was a stretch when he went fifty-six consecutive innings without being scored on—still a record.

He had winning streaks of 16 games in 1912, 14 straight in 1913 and 13 in a row in 1914. He was the league's winningest pitcher six times and its strikeout leader ten times. There were twelve seasons when he won 20 or more games and two when he topped 30.

Johnson was thirty-seven years old and long past his prime when the Senators developed a team good enough to win pennants. So his record for the 1924 and 1925 World Series was only 3 victories and 3 defeats.

But by then the Big Train had roared to so many records that when the Hall of Fame was established in 1936, he was among the first five chosen to enter.

SANDY KOUFAX

As a youngster Sanford Koufax wanted to be an architect, not a baseball player.

Considering the record he built with his southpaw pitching arm, he was a sparkling success at both.

When the classy Brooklyn-born hurler retired after the

77

Sandy Koufax

1967 season because of a damaged elbow, he had assured himself a place among the all-time great left-handers. Take the 1965 season as an example. Sandy had a 26 and 8 record which helped the Dodgers win the 1965 National League pennant. The won-lost mark was great, but sandwiched in between were two records no other man in baseball has touched.

On September 9, 1965, Sandy pitched a perfect game against the Chicago Cubs to give him the fourth no-hitter of his career. He stands alone in that department. On that day he struck out 14. By the time the season was over he had a total of 382 strikeouts, erasing Bob Feller's record of 346 set in 1946.

Born December 30, 1935, the 6-foot 2-inch Koufax had natural blazing speed and worked hard to develop brilliant control. He got his first no-hitter on June 30, 1962, winning 5–0 over the Mets. The following year, on May 11, Sandy blanked the Giants, 8–0. On June 4, 1964, Sandy made it three no-hitters when he stopped the Phils, 3–0. His perfect game the next year was a 1–0 job over the Cubs: four no-hitters in four years.

Sandy was a workhorse. In 1965, for example, he pitched the most innings (336) and faced the most batters (1,297) in the NL. He finished with a 2.04 earned-run average, the fourth straight year he led the league in that department. He was 1.74 in 1964, had a 1.88 ERA in 1963 and 2.54 in 1962.

He was voted the National League's Most Valuable Player of 1963, when he started 40 games, posted a brilliant 25–5 record, and set an NL strikeout record (at that time) of 306. In addition to the MVP he received the coveted Young Award as baseball's top pitcher. He won the Cy Young Award again in 1965.

In World Series competition Sandy won 4 games and lost 3. He beat Whitey Ford and the Yankees twice in 1963, and in 1965 he pitched two shutouts against the Twins.

A product of the Brooklyn sand lots, Sandy came up to the Brooklyn Dodgers in 1955 when he was not yet twenty. He spent most of the time on the bench, learning the batters, and trying to control his great speed. He did not hit his peak until the team moved to Los Angeles.

In 1966, his last season, Koufax rang up twenty-seven victories and an earned run average of 1.73, tops in the majors that year. It therefore came as a shock when Koufax, thirty years old and seemingly in his prime, announced his retirement. But the injury to his pitching elbow compelled him to bow out.

His career was capped when he was voted the Cy Young Award for an unprecedented third time. His feat of leading the NL in earned runs for five years in a row also was without equal.

Among his other records were these: He pitched the most games (97) with 10 or more strikeouts; he had the most seasons (3) with 300 or more strikeouts; and he had the most shutouts (11) by a left-hander in one season. He also is credited with the most strikeouts (23) in a four-game World Series—against the Yankees in 1963.

Koufax played on every NL All-Star team from 1961 through 1966 and was the winner of the '65 contest.

After his retirement, Koufax joined the National Broadcasting Company as a sportscaster.

MICKEY MANTLE

The switch-hitter—the batter who can hit from both sides of the plate—is a valuable man in big-league baseball, especially when he can do it with power.

Mickey Mantle, the muscle man of the Yankees, was such a slugger. Mantle sent many a ball bouncing into the record books, and despite frequent injuries, assured himself a place among Yankee immortals—for his batting exploits, for brilliant defensive play, and for inspirational leadership to his teammates.

80

Mickey Mantle

It was the Oklahoma Kid who introduced the "tape-measure" home run with a drive against the Washington Senators at Griffith Stadium in 1953 that is widely regarded as the longest ball ever hit.

Batting right-handed, Mickey sent the ball screaming against a sign in center field, 565 feet from the plate. It was found in a yard two blocks from the ball park and now rests in the Baseball Museum at Cooperstown, New York.

No one has ever hit a fair ball out of Yankee Stadium, but in 1956 Mantle came closer than anyone ever had before. Batting lefty this time, he lifted the ball against the top of the right-field deck. It missed clearing the park by only a couple of feet.

Mickey four times led the American League in homers and six times in runs scored. When he retired after the 1968 season, he could point to a lifetime batting average of .298 and a total of 536 homers, not counting 18 in World Series games.

Mickey joined the Yankees in 1951 but was sent to Kansas City, then a minor league club, after hitting .267 in 96 games. He came back in 1952 to develop into one of the brightest stars in baseball. He was voted Most Valuable Player in 1956, 1957, and 1962, and was runner-up to teammate Roger Maris for that honor in 1960 and 1961 by narrow margins. He hit 54 homers in 1961, but 1956 must be considered his best year—a .353 average, 52 home runs, 130 runs batted in and 132 runs scored, all league-leading figures.

Mickey was particularly effective in the World Series. He holds the Series record for homers (18) and shares the Series record for most runs scored in a seven-game series (8). He played in twelve World Series.

Mickey was a speedboy on the bases and in the field—and also, early in his big-league career, was very much a little boy at times. The camera once caught him blowing bubble gum in center field during a game.

ROGER MARIS

When Roger Maris was traded to the Yankees by the Kansas City Athletics after the 1959 season, there was little in his

Roger Maris and Sal Durante, who retrieved the ball in the right-field stands of Yankee Stadium, after Maris hit his 61st home run of the season on October 1, 1961.

Photo by William C. Greene

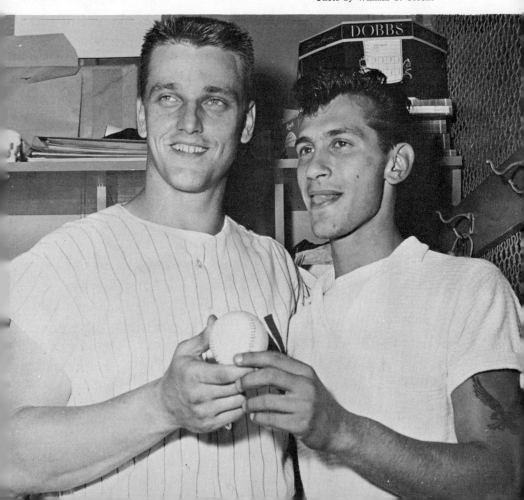

record to suggest he would soon become the most talked about player in baseball.

In three seasons as a major-leaguer, he had struck a total of only 58 home runs—14 with Cleveland in 1957, 28 with the Indians and Athletics in 1958 and 16 with the A's in 1959.

But in his first season as a Yankee, the southpaw slugger batted .283, his best average in the big leagues, hit 39 homers, led the American League in slugging percentage and runs batted in with 112, and nosed out Mickey Mantle in the voting for the Most Valuable Player award.

As brilliant as Maris was in 1960, his feats were only a prelude of what was to come.

In 1961 Maris captivated the sports world. Through much of the season, his production of home runs was well ahead of Babe Ruth's record pace of 1927, when the Babe hit 60 in a schedule of 154 games.

As the pressure and tension mounted, Maris fell slightly behind, and he came up to the Yanks' 154th game needing two homers to tie Ruth's mark. He hit only one, and the Babe's record remained intact.

But Maris had eight more games to play, the result of a schedule lengthened by the American League's expansion to ten teams. His 60th homer came in the 158th game, and number 61 soared into the right-field stands of Yankee Stadium on October 1, in the season's final game.

Maris ended the 1961 season with a batting average of only .269. But those 61 homers, a league-leading figure of 142 runs batted in, and his sparkling defensive play in the outfield won him the Most Valuable Player award again, once more by a slim margin over teammate Mantle.

84

Christy Mathewson

United Press International

Born September 10, 1934, Maris broke into organized baseball in 1953. He retired in 1968 after two seasons with the
St. Louis Cardinals.

CHRISTY MATHEWSON

There was a time when every boy who dreamed of becoming a big-league pitcher thought of just one man as his hero—
Christy Mathewson. He was everybody's idea of pitching
perfection.

They talk about the slider, the screwball, and the knuckle-
ball today. In Matty's time—the early 1900's—it was the
fadeaway, a pitch just like today's screwball in that, thrown
by a right-hander, it broke toward right-handed batters and
away from left-handed ones.

Mathewson, also known fondly as the Big Six, sent that
pitch blazing into the record books through seventeen glorious
seasons with the New York Giants of John McGraw—from
1900 until he was traded to the Cincinnati Reds in 1916.

A master of control, with a beautiful pitching motion, Matty
pitched 373 victories (2 of them no-hitters) for a National
League record he shares with Grover Cleveland Alexander.
In 1908 he won 37 games, another league record that still
stands. There were three other seasons when he won 30 or
more games and nine when he won more than 20.

Also in 1908 he went a record sixty-eight consecutive innings without allowing a base on balls. The same season saw
him pitch 416 innings with only 42 walks—an average of less
than one per nine-inning game.

In World Series competition, Mathewson's record was 5
won and 5 lost, but he won 3 of those games in the Giants'

1905 triumph over the Philadelphia Athletics—and all by shutouts.

As brilliant as Matty's career was, he lost vital games by two of the biggest boners in the book.

In 1908 the famous "Merkle boner," the failure of teammate Fred Merkle to touch second base, cost the Giants the pennant. And in the 1912 Series, a muffed fly by outfielder Fred Snodgrass cost the Giants the world title.

But, heartbreaking though they were, those twists of fate could not detract from the feats that made Christy Mathewson a *giant* as well as a Giant. As the inscription on his Hall of Fame plaque says, "Matty was master of them all."

WILLIE MAYS

The most electrifying baseball player on any diamond for the better part of two decades was wing-footed Willie Mays, who hit, ran, and threw as if every game were for the championship of the world.

It took less than one season to make Willie Howard Mays the most talked about star in the game. He had just reached his twentieth birthday when the New York Giants summoned him to the Polo Grounds in May of 1951, after he had hit a sensational .477 in thirty-five games for Minneapolis in the American Association.

In 121 games for the Giants that year, Mays batted only .274. But his 20 homers and 68 runs batted in, plus his eye-popping play in center field and on the bases, were vital factors in the famous "little miracle" stretch run that enabled the Giants to overtake the Brooklyn Dodgers and win the pennant.

The Say-Hey Kid—the nickname came to him because he couldn't remember the other players' names and simply called out, "Say, hey!"—had played 34 games in 1952 when he was drafted into the Army.

Back in baseball uniform in 1954, he made his first full season a great one. With 195 hits, 41 homers, and 110 runs driven in, he batted a league-leading .345 and won the Most Valuable Player award as the Giants captured another flag. He won a second MVP in 1965 when he hit 52 homers, tops in the league, and closed with a .317 batting average. He drove in 112 runs with 177 hits.

In the opener of the 1954 World Series, which the Giants took from the Cleveland Indians in four games, Willie turned in a catch that has had few equals. Running out from under his cap, as he so often did, he snared a tremendous shot off the bat of Vic Wertz in front of the Polo Grounds bleachers with his back to the plate.

Even though the end of his career seemed near in 1969, as he reached his thirty-eighth birthday, Mays managed to pole thirteen home runs. They brought his career total to an even six hundred—a major league record for a right-hand hitter and second on the all-time list only to Babe Ruth's 714.

These are some of Willie's other spectacular accomplishments: He is the first player to have hit 50 or more homers (51) and to have stolen 20 or more bases (24) in the same season (1955); he tied a major league record in 1955 by hitting 7 home runs in six consecutive games; he led the league in slugging percentage five years; he tied another major league mark by leading his league in double plays by an outfielder three seasons in a row, and he hit four homers in one game in 1961.

89

Willie Mays

United Press International

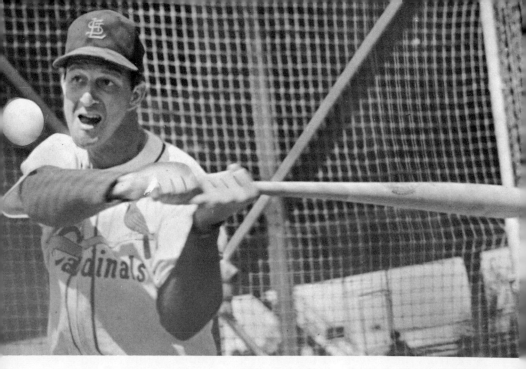

Stan Musial

He was a perennial All-Star choice, having been chosen on every team from 1954 through 1968. In 1964, in addition to his customary center-field spot, he played first base, shortstop, and third base. His lifetime batting average at the end of the 1969 season was .307.

Mays' best batting percentage, .347, was posted in 1958, the Giants' first year in San Francisco. New York's loss was San Francisco's gain in more ways than one.

STAN MUSIAL

Stanley Frank Musial, the left-handed batting magician of the St. Louis Cardinals, started out in baseball as a pitcher. And there are those who will tell you he might have become one of the best had he not injured his left shoulder during his third season in the minors (1940).

No one can be sure of that, of course, but this much is certain—that "tough break" put Musial on the path to baseball greatness. He is one of only eight players in the entire history of the game to have gathered more than 3,000 hits. When he retired in 1963, his total of 3,630 ranked him second only to Ty Cobb.

For this and many other feats, Stan the Man earned the right to be called one of the finest batters of all time. He ended his twenty-two-year career with a .331 lifetime batting average collected in 3,026 games. He also held forty records.

Musial broke into the majors late in 1941 and never batted less than .310 in any season until 1959. He led the National League in hitting seven times and won three Most Valuable Player awards. At forty-one and in his twenty-first season, he batted .330 in 1962, third best in the league.

Musial stood at the plate like a coil, his back almost to the pitcher but with his keen eye ever on the ball. He hit to any field, and with power, as evidenced by his 475 home runs and his records for extra-base hits and total bases.

In four World Series, Musial had to satisfy himself with a batting average of .256, but he was a solid standout in the All-Star games, with 6 home runs to his credit. He broke up the 1955 battle with a twelfth-inning homer. He was in twelve All-Star games.

Stan played the outfield and first base with equal polish. And both on and off the field he was one of the most popular players baseball has ever known.

MEL OTT

Like many another youngster, Mel Ott got lost on the subway the first time he went to the Polo Grounds. But when he finally found his way, he stayed for twenty-two years—to become one of baseball's all-time favorites and batting heroes.

Melvin T. Ott was a country boy of sixteen out of Gretna, Louisiana, when John McGraw, the great manager of the New York Giants, got his first look at him at a Polo Grounds tryout in 1925. Some other manager might have tried to change Ottie's style of lifting his right leg every time he swung. But McGraw left him alone, and that, along with the home run, was the mark by which Ott is best remembered.

Master Melvin made his varsity debut with the Giants in 1926. When his playing days ended in 1947, the chunky little right-fielder held more batting records than any other National Leaguer. For many years he was the league's all-time home-run champion (511). He set league records as well for runs scored, runs batted in, extra-base hits, and bases on balls.

In three World Series, the left-handed slugger had a batting average of only .295, but four of his hits were homers. In the 1933 Series he was the standout with 13 hits for .389, including one game in which he went 4 for 4. He was chosen on the All-Star team eleven consecutive years, 1934 through 1944.

The record in which Ott took greatest pride was that of having played more years with one club than any other National Leaguer—twenty-two with the Giants. He occupied right field so long, in fact, that he actually wore a bare spot in the grass.

93

Mel Ott

United Press International

Ott managed the Giants from 1942 until July of 1948, when he was succeeded by Leo Durocher. Too much of a gentleman, too easygoing, he was not too successful as a pilot. When he was fatally injured in an auto accident in November, 1958, his work as a manager was hardly recalled. But almost any fan could have mentioned at least one of Ottie's batting feats. Added together, they gave him a richly earned place in the Hall of Fame.

JACKIE ROBINSON

As the player who broke the color line in organized baseball, Jack Roosevelt Robinson holds a proud and secure place in the history of our national game. Baseball took formal recognition of this fact in 1962 with his election to the Hall of Fame.

It is no coincidence that the Brooklyn Dodgers won six National League pennants and a world championship during Jackie's career (1947–1956). Aside from his batting—he had a lifetime average of .311—Robinson was the outstanding clutch player of his day. He came through with the key hit, the key fielding play, the key move on the bases, time and time again. And there is no telling how many times his fighting spirit made the rest of the team catch fire.

Robinson, who had been an All-American football player at UCLA, was twenty-six years old when Branch Rickey, president of the Dodgers, signed him to a contract in 1945. It took only one season to convince everyone that Jackie was big-league caliber.

In his very first game with the Montreal Royals, in fact, he got four hits, including a home run, and stole two bases. For

Jackie Robinson

Photo by William C. Greene

the season, he was the International League's leader in batting (.349), its best fielding second baseman, and its base-stealing champion with 40 thefts.

When he moved up to the Dodgers in 1947, the club was badly in need of a first baseman. Robinson, brand new at the position, nevertheless filled it like a veteran. He batted .297, stole 29 bases to lead the National League, and was chosen rookie of the year.

Two years later he won the Most Valuable Player award after leading the league in both batting (.342) and stolen bases (37). He also smacked out 303 hits and drove in 124 runs.

But Robinson's highest achievement is that he made the position of the Negro permanent in baseball. In the care of a lesser figure, the "noble experiment" of Branch Rickey and Jack Roosevelt Robinson might have failed.

BABE RUTH

Baseball, somebody once said, was made for kids. It's a nice sentiment, and there is much truth in it. But it would be even nearer the truth to say that baseball—big-league baseball, as we know it today—was made *by* Babe Ruth, the biggest "kid" in the history of the game.

If ever anyone was born for baseball, it was the slugging, rollicking, fun-loving Babe. You'd run into a lot of arguments if you called him the greatest player of all time. A fellow by the name of Ty Cobb gets as many votes from the fans as Ruth, if not more. But you'll get no argument on this: when it came to color and influence on the game, George Herman Ruth was in a class by himself.

The home run was Ruth's trademark, and he changed baseball with it. Until the Babe came along with his 42-ounce bat, the standard batter choked up his grip and punched base hits through or over the infield. Ruth held the stick at the extreme end of the handle and stroked it like a wand. As he knocked down the fences with his booming drives, baseball moved into an era of power, big parks, big crowds.

Stadiums were rebuilt to accommodate the soaring attendance and the crop of home-run hitters who sprang up in hopes of challenging Ruth. The Yankee Stadium—The House That Ruth Built—was designed as an arena for the Babe's bat, and it was there that he lifted the Bronx Bombers to eminence as the number one team in the land.

Counting the 15 he clouted in World Series play (including 3 in one game) and the one he hit in the 1933 All-Star game, Ruth drove the ball out of the park 730 times in twenty-two big-league seasons. That total and the 60 homers he belted in 1927 are but two of the more than fifty records he set.

Which homer is best remembered? That's easy. In the third game of the 1932 World Series against the Chicago Cubs, the score tied at 4–4, the Babe took two strikes from Pitcher Charlie Root, pointed to the center-field bleachers, and then, on the next pitch, parked the ball where he said he would. Only the Babe could call a shot like that.

As every student of the game knows, Ruth came to the majors as a pitcher, and a great one he was. In the 1916 and 1918 World Series, he put together 29⅔ consecutive scoreless innings for the Boston Red Sox, a record which stood until the Yankees' Whitey Ford topped it in 1961. Twice he won 23 games in one season.

It was Ed Barrow, then manager of the Red Sox and later to become general manager of the Yankees, who converted Ruth from a pitcher-outfielder into a full-time outfielder in 1919. That year he led the league with 29 homers. At the end of the season, the Red Sox, who had bought him from Baltimore of the International League in 1914 for $2,900, sold him to the Yankees for $125,000 plus a $350,000 loan.

Babe Ruth being honored by New York fans, shortly before his death in 1948. This is a picture that denotes better than words the end of an era.

The Babe spent fifteen drama-packed seasons with the Yanks. He led the American League in home runs ten times and tied another time. When he called it quits in 1935, after a short stint with the Boston Braves of the National League, he left a lifetime batting average of .342 and a treasury of records and thrills.

The Babe died August 16, 1948, of cancer. The whole nation mourned his passing. But none mourned him more than the youngsters, who worshipped him as no other sports figure has ever been worshipped. To them he was, and *still* is, a hero beyond compare.

99

WARREN SPAHN

Warren Spahn was the winningest left-handed pitcher in baseball history.

Spahn closed out the 1965 season with a lifetime total of 363 victories, including two no-hitters. He holds the National League mark for shutouts by a lefty (63) and is the only left-hander in league history to win 20 games a season as many as thirteen times. Further, for seventeen seasons he

Warren Spahn

registered at least 100 strikeouts, and his career total of 2,550 strikeouts by a southpaw is first on the all-time list.

His lifetime earned-run average through 1965 was a shade under three for twenty-two years. In 1957, he was honored with the Cy Young Memorial Award as the outstanding pitcher of the year in the majors.

Spahn entered the big leagues with the Braves (then of Boston, later of Milwaukee and now of Atlanta) in 1942. After three years in military service, he began to make his mark in 1947, when he won 21 games and led the league in earned runs with an average of 2.33. He topped the league again in 1961 at the age of forty.

It was in the 1958 World Series, though, that he showed best the stuff of which champions are made. The crafty left-hander battled the Yankees through ten innings of the Series opener for a 4–3 victory. In the fourth game, he treated a crowd of 71,563 at Yankee Stadium to the most brilliant effort of his career—a 2-hit, 3–0 masterpiece.

For sheer courage, the sixth game of the Series was perhaps even more dramatic. Spahnie lost it, 4–3, again in ten innings, but he was working with only two days' rest at the age of thirty-seven. He thus ended the Series with an earned-run average of 1.88 for 28⅔ innings.

Released by the Braves, Spahn was picked up by the New York Mets in 1965. They released him in July and he finished the year with the San Francisco Giants. At forty-four his age was beginning to show. He won 4 and lost 12 for the year and was 3–4 with the Giants. The Giants released him at the end of 1965, and this time he retired.

TRIS SPEAKER

Baseball historians never will agree on the greatest player of all time, but the same names invariably tumble from their lips when they are asked to pick the three greatest outfielders —Cobb, Ruth, and Speaker.

Of the three, the name of Speaker—Tristram E. Speaker— is least familiar to the young fans of today. The Gray Eagle, as he was called, never generated the excitement and color of Cobb and Babe. But make no mistake about it, he belonged in the same company.

Speaker won the American League batting title only once (with .386 in 1916), but only because he happened to be playing at the same time as Cobb. Even in 1920 when he averaged .388, and in 1925 when he hit .389, the championship was denied him.

In nineteen full playing seasons, Tris failed to hit over .300 only once. He did .380 or better five times and ended a career of twenty-two years (1907–1928) with a lifetime mark of .344. His hit total of 3,515 is fourth on the all-time list.

Yet with all this, Speaker, who starred eight seasons with Boston and eleven with Cleveland, was admired more in his time as a fielder. No player, not even DiMaggio, patrolled center field with more daring and science. He played the position so shallow that he time and again robbed batters of hits behind second and short. Twice in one month he made unassisted double plays, something unheard of for an outfielder.

The Gray Eagle is hardly remembered as manager of the Cleveland Indians for seven and a half seasons, but it was in that capacity that he won the sweetest victory of all. In 1920 he led the Tribe to the pennant and the world title, batting .320 himself in the seven-game set against the Brooklyn Dodgers.

HANS WAGNER

To his dying day, John McGraw maintained that Hans Wagner was the greatest player who ever lived. You have only to touch the highlights of the Flying Dutchman's baseball story to appreciate why.

John Peter Wagner—they always called him Hans or Honus—did not look like a ballplayer, with his bowed legs and gnarled features. He was an "old" man, nearing the age of thirty, when he hit his stride. And he spent his entire career in the era of the dead ball, when base hits didn't come cheaply.

With a lifetime average of .329 over twenty-one seasons, he batted .300 or better for seventeen consecutive years, including a mark of better than .320 against the peerless Christy Mathewson. Between 1900 and 1911, he led the National League eight times—four times in succession. He still holds the league record for both doubles and triples.

Possessed of a powerful arm and catlike instincts, he ranks among the greatest fielding shortstops of all time, and as a base-runner he stole 720 times—fourth among all the players in history.

Wagner, who spent his early years working in the Pennsylvania coal mines, made his big-league debut in 1897 with Louisville, when the National League was composed of twelve clubs. When he joined the Pittsburgh Pirates in 1900, he had come home to stay. Not until 1917 did he hang up his spikes,

and even that year, at the age of forty-three, he batted a respectable .265.

Wagner's star shone at the same time that Ty Cobb was writing baseball history with the Detroit Tigers in the American League. They matched skills in hand-to-hand combat only once—the 1909 World Series—and the facts speak for themselves as to who came off the better man.

In the Series opener, Cobb threatened to cut Wagner to ribbons on a steal of second. He roared into the base with spikes flashing, but old Honus took the throw and rammed the ball into Cobb's face, cutting his mouth and loosening several teeth.

From that point on, it was Wagner's show. With eight safe hits and a mark of .333, he out-hit Cobb by more than 100 points. He even beat Cobb at his own specialty, base stealing, with six thefts.

John McGraw knew what he was talking about.

TED WILLIAMS

The game of baseball has produced so many great hitters that it is impossible to list them in an order that would satisfy every fan. One thing, at least, can be said for certain about Theodore Samuel Williams: He was one of the best.

He may not have had the best temperament. He frequently feuded with fans and sports writers—he drew a $5,000 fine in 1956 for unsportsmanlike conduct. But no one could argue with Ted's work from the left side of the plate.

Six times the American League batting champion; an average of .406 in 1941, highest in the league since 1922; a life-

105

Ted Williams

Associated Press

time average of .344; 521 homers—these are the jewels in Ted's collection.

One of the striking features of Williams' record is that he was so good for so long. He started in 1939 when he was twenty years old. When he won his fifth batting crown in 1957 with .388, the Splendid Splinter was thirty-nine years old. No other player in the game, not even Ty Cobb, won the title at such an advanced age. Williams' average fell off to .328 in 1958, but it still was good enough to win the title again.

Williams piled up records despite the fact that, proud man that he is, he refused to alter his batting style to get "cheap" hits. When enemy defenses shifted over to the right, he drove the ball through or past them rather than punch the ball into left field.

Williams had more great days on the diamond than he can remember, but one easily stands out. That was the 1946 All-Star game, when he hammered out 2 homers in a perfect day at bat (4 for 4), batted in 5 runs and scored 4.

Another All-Star game, in 1950, was to cost him dearly. He crashed into the outfield wall, making a catch, and fractured his left elbow. In fact, injuries hampered Williams almost every year after he returned to the Boston lineup in 1956 after three years in the Air Force during the Korean War.

But the lanky belter with the perfect batting eye and the whiplash swing overcame enough obstacles, including those he made himself, to join the greats.

He was elected to the Hall of Fame in 1966.

Photo by William C. Greene

Casey Stengel

THE GREAT MANAGERS

In the art of masterminding, as on the field of play, the New York Yankees take most of the honors. You can count the great managers of baseball on the fingers of one hand— Mack, McGraw, Huggins, McCarthy, Stengel—and three of them belong to Yankee history.

No one in all baseball managed as long as Connie Mack, who led the Philadelphia Athletics for forty-nine years, producing nine pennants and five world championships. And in the National League, none can come close to John McGraw, who brought his beloved New York Giants ten pennants and three world titles during a managerial career of close to thirty years.

But between 1921 and 1960, or in fewer years by far than Mack's career covered, the Yankee threesome of Miller Huggins, Joe McCarthy, and Casey Stengel collected the incredible total of twenty-four pennants and seventeen world championships. And the man who stands alone, from the standpoint of having won the most in the least time, is the clown-turned-genius, Charles Dillon Stengel, with ten pennants and seven world titles.

Stengel, a famous ballplayer in his day but a dismal failure as a manager before he took over the Yanks in 1949, won the pennant and the World Series in his very first year at the helm and guided the Yanks to five straight flags and world crowns from 1949 through 1953.

It took 111 victories by the Cleveland Indians, an American League record, to beat Stengel out for the pennant in 1954, after which he won four more flags in a row.

In nine seasons as a National League manager—three at Brooklyn and six at Boston—Stengel never was able to bring in a team higher than fifth place and was best known as a funny man. In fact, it came as a shock when he was hired to replace Stanley (Bucky) Harris as Yankee manager after the 1948 season.

But the double-talk for which Stengel is noted began to make sense with the Yanks. So did his knack of "platooning" players, of using them at positions new to them and of juggling his lineup with almost every game. Most important, for the first time the Ol' Perfessor had an abundance of talented players and a front office that got him more when he needed

Photo by William C. Greene

Joe McCarthy

them. The result is a record that should go unequaled for many, many years.

After the 1960 season Stengel was fired by the Yankees, presumably for being too old. When the Mets asked him to manage the club in 1962 he was reluctant, but he yielded to the pleas of old boss George Weiss and club owner Mrs. Joan W. Payson. Casey could do little with the combination of inexperienced and past-their-prime ballplayers.

On July 25, 1965, early in the morning before his seventy-fifth birthday, Casey fell and broke his hip. He retired on August 30. On March 8, 1966, baseball honored the grand old man by waiving the five-year waiting rule, and Casey was admitted into the Hall of Fame.

Little Miller Huggins, who steered the Yankees from 1918 through 1929, was the dugout leader when they came into power as baseball's mightiest club. With Babe Ruth, Lou Gehrig, and other sluggers to smash down the opposition, Hug piloted the Yanks to six pennants and three world titles between 1921 and 1928.

Joseph Vincent McCarthy, in command from 1931 through part of the 1946 season, topped that performance and gave Stengel something to shoot at. He brought the Yanks eight pennants and seven World Series conquests, including four in a row from 1936 through 1939. McCarthy also won a National League pennant—with the Chicago Cubs in 1929.

Cornelius McGillicuddy—Connie Mack—was for many years a living legend as "The Grand Old Man of Baseball." Kind and patient, he developed more stars than any other manager in the game and twice broke up championship teams because he loved the challenge of rebuilding.

Connie Mack

Photo by William C. Greene

Mr. Mack, as even the old-timers called him, led the A's from 1901 until he turned over the reins to Jimmy Dykes, one of his former stars, in 1950. He won his first pennant in 1902 and his last in 1931.

To the very last, he wore a white shirt with a high starched collar in the dugout, and could always be seen waving his scorecard to move his players to proper fielding positions. He died at the age of ninety-three on February 8, 1956, a year after the Athletics had moved to Kansas City.

As Connie Mack was gentle, so John J. McGraw was fierce—the "Little Napoleon" of the Giants. A fighter clean through and a man who made his players live baseball around the clock, McGraw took charge of the Giants in 1902 and ruled until ill health forced his retirement in June, 1932.

McGraw won his first pennant in 1904, repeated in 1905 and beat Connie Mack in the World Series, lost to Mr. Mack in the 1911 Series, and had his greatest success starting in 1921. From 1921 through 1924 the Giants swept to four straight pennants—a National League record—and beat the Yanks in the 1921 and 1922 World Series.

McGraw died February 26, 1934, at the age of sixty. Many still consider him the smartest manager who ever lived.

Associated Press

All-Time Records

Category	Lifetime
Average	Ty Cobb, .367
Hits	Ty Cobb, 4,191
Home Runs	Babe Ruth, 714
Runs Batted In	Babe Ruth, 2,209

Category	Season
Average	*Rogers Hornsby, .424 (1924)
Hits	George Sisler, 257 (1920)
Home Runs	†Babe Ruth, 60 (1927)
	‡Roger Maris, 61 (1961)
Runs Batted In	Hack Wilson, 190 (1930)

PITCHING

Category	Lifetime
Games Won	Cy Young, 511
Shutouts	Walter Johnson, 113
Strikeouts	Walter Johnson, 3,497

Category	Season
Games Won	Jack Chesbro, 41 (1904)
Shutouts	Grover Alexander, 16 (1916)
Strikeouts	Sandy Koufax, 382 (1965)

*Modern era   †154-game season   ‡162-game season

114

Hall of Fame

The Hall of Fame

The Baseball Hall of Fame is, as its name suggests, America's shrine to the heroes of its national pastime. No greater honor can come to a baseball player, manager, umpire, or executive than election to the Hall of Fame. Elections are held every two years by two groups—the Baseball Writers Association of America and the Baseball Hall of Fame Committee on Veterans.

The Hall of Fame, with its museum and library containing priceless relics and bronze plaques honoring its members, is situated in Cooperstown, New York.

It is open every day of the year except Thanksgiving Day, Christmas, and New Year's Day. Visiting hours are 9 A.M. to 9 P.M. from May 1 through October 31, and from 9 A.M. to 5 P.M. during the other months of the year. Admission is seventy-five cents for adults, and fifteen cents for boys and girls six to eighteen. Service men in uniform are admitted free.

The Hall of Fame

Member	Year Elected	Member	Year Elected
ALEXANDER, Grover Cleveland	1938	DUFFY, Hugh	1945
ANSON, Adrian Constantine (Cap)	1939	EVERS, John Joseph	1946
APPLING, Luke	1964	EWING, William B. (Buck)	1939
BAKER, J. Franklin (Home Run)	1955	FABER, Urban (Red)	1964
BARROW, Edward G.	1953	FELLER, Robert W. A.	1962
BENDER, Charles (Chief)	1953	FLICK, Elmer	1963
BRESNAHAN, Roger	1945	FOXX, James E.	1951
BROUTHERS, Dan	1945	FRICK, Ford C.	1970
BROWN, Mordecai Peter	1949	FRISCH, Frank	1947
BULKELEY, Morgan G.	1937	GALVIN, James	1965
BURKETT, Jesse C.	1946	GEHRIG, Henry Louis	1939
CAMPANELLA, Roy	1969	GEHRINGER, Charles	1949
CAREY, Max G.	1961	GOSLIN, Leon (Goose)	1968
CARTWRIGHT, Alexander J.	1938	GREENBERG, Henry	1956
CHADWICK, Henry	1938	GRIFFITH, Clark C.	1946
CHANCE, Frank LeRoy	1946	GRIMES, Burleigh	1964
CHESBRO, John Dwight	1946	GROVE, Robert Moses (Lefty)	1947
CLARKE, Fred	1945	HAINES, Jess	1970
CLARKSON, John	1963	HAMILTON, William R.	1961
COBB, Tyrus Raymond (Ty)	1936	HARTNETT, Charles Leo (Gabby)	1955
COCHRANE, Gordon (Mickey)	1947	HEILMANN, Harry	1952
COLLINS, Edward Trowbridge	1939	HORNSBY, Rogers	1942
COLLINS, James	1945	HOYT, Waite	1969
COMBS, Earle	1970	HUBBELL, Carl Owen	1947
COMISKEY, Charles A.	1939	HUGGINS, Miller	1964
CONNOLLY, Thomas A.	1953	JENNINGS, Hugh	1945
COVELESKI, Stanley	1969	JOHNSON, Byron Bancroft (Ban)	1937
CRAWFORD, Sam	1957	JOHNSON, Walter Perry	1936
CRONIN, Joseph	1956	KEEFE, Tim	1964
CUMMINGS, W. A. (Candy)	1939	KEELER, William (Wee Willie)	1939
CUYLER, Hazen (Kiki)	1968	KELLY, Michael J. (King)	1945
DEAN, Jay Hanna (Dizzy)	1953	KLEM, William J.	1953
DELAHANTY, Ed	1945	LAJOIE, Napoleon (Larry)	1937
DICKEY, William	1954	LANDIS, Kenesaw Mountain	1944
DIMAGGIO, Joseph Paul	1955	LYONS, Theodore	1955

116

Member	Year Elected	Member	Year Elected
MANUSH, Heinie	1964	RUFFING, Charles (Red)	1967
MARANVILLE, Walter (Rabbit)	1954	RUTH, George Herman (Babe)	1936
MATHEWSON, Christopher (Christy)	1936	SCHALK, Raymond	1955
		SIMMONS, Al	1953
McCARTHY, Joseph V.	1957	SISLER, George Harold	1939
McCARTHY, Thomas F.	1946	SPALDING, Albert Goodwill	1939
McGINNITY, Joseph Jerome	1946	SPEAKER, Tristram E. (Tris)	1937
McGILLICUDDY, Cornelius (Connie Mack)	1937	STENGEL, Charles D. (Casey)	1966
		TERRY, William H.	1954
McGRAW, John J.	1937	TINKER, Joseph B.	1946
McKECHNIE, William B.	1962	TRAYNOR, Harold J. (Pie)	1948
MEDWICK, Joseph (Ducky)	1968	VANCE, C. Arthur (Dizzy)	1955
MUSIAL, Stanley	1969	WADDELL, George Edward (Rube)	1946
NICHOLS, Charles A. (Kid)	1949		
O'ROURKE, James H.	1945	WAGNER, John Peter (Hans)	1936
OTT, Melvin T.	1951	WALLACE, Roderick (Bobby)	1953
PENNOCK, Herbert J.	1948	WALSH, Edward Arthur	1946
PLANK, Edward S.	1946	WANER, Lloyd	1967
RADBOURNE, Charles (Hoss)	1939	WANER, Paul	1952
RICE, Sam	1963	WARD, John M.	1964
RICKEY, Branch	1967	WHEAT, Zachariah (Zack)	1959
RIXEY, Eppa	1963	WILLIAMS, Theodore S. (Ted)	1966
ROBINSON, Jack Roosevelt	1962	WRIGHT, George	1937
ROBINSON, Wilbert	1945	WRIGHT, Harry	1953
ROUSH, Edd J.	1962	YOUNG, Denton T. (Cy)	1937

Batters Who Have Hit .400

Average	Player	Year	Average	Player	Year
.492	Tip O'Neill	1887	.408	Joe Jackson	1911
.471	Pete Browning	1887	.407	George Sisler	1920
.469	Denny Lyons	1887	.406	Sam Thompson	1887
.438	Hugh Duffy	1894	.406	Fred Clarke	1897
.432	Willie Keeler	1897	.406	Ted Williams	1941
.426	Yank Robinson	1887	.404	Harry Stovey	1884
.424	Rogers Hornsby	1924	.404	Paul Radford	1887
.423	Jesse Burkett	1895	.403	Sam Thompson	1894
.422	Nap Lajoie	1901	.403	Harry Heilmann	1923
.421	Cap Anson	1887	.403	Rogers Hornsby	1925
.420	Ty Cobb	1911	.402	Harry Stovey	1887
.420	George Sisler	1922	.402	Jesse Burkett	1899
.419	Dan Brouthers	1887	.401	Tom Burns	1887
.410	Reddy Mack	1887	.401	Ty Cobb	1922
.410	Jesse Burkett	1896	.401	Rogers Hornsby	1922
.410	Ty Cobb	1912	.401	Bill Terry	1930
.408	Duke Esterbrook	1884	.400	Ed Delahanty	1894
.408	Ed Delahanty	1899			

Pennant and World Series Winners

The annual race for the American and National League pennants starts in April, ends in September, and is climaxed by the greatest spectacle in all sports—the World Series. Actually, a postseason championship series was played as early as 1884, when Chicago of the National League and Cincinnati of the American Association played two games, each winning one. The World Series, as we know it today, was begun in 1903, two years after the founding of the American League and twenty-seven years after the National started play. The New York Yankees have won by far the most pennants and the most Series. In the National League, the New York Giants hold the record for pennants, but the St. Louis Cardinals have won the most Series.

(* Denotes World Series winner.)
(Number of Series games won shown in parentheses.)

Year	National League	American League
1969	*New York (4)	Baltimore (1)
1968	St. Louis (3)	*Detroit (4)
1967	*St. Louis (4)	Boston (3)
1966	Los Angeles (0)	*Baltimore (4)
1965	*Los Angeles (4)	Minnesota (3)
1964	*St. Louis (4)	New York (3)
1963	*Los Angeles (4)	New York (0)
1962	San Francisco (3)	*New York (4)
1961	Cincinnati (1)	*New York (4)
1960	*Pittsburgh (4)	New York (3)
1959	*Los Angeles (4)	Chicago (2)
1958	Milwaukee (3)	*New York (4)
1957	*Milwaukee (4)	New York (3)
1956	Brooklyn (3)	*New York (4)
1955	*Brooklyn (4)	New York (3)
1954	*New York (4)	Cleveland (0)
1953	Brooklyn (2)	*New York (4)
1952	Brooklyn (3)	*New York (4)
1951	New York (2)	*New York (4)
1950	Philadelphia (0)	*New York (4)
1949	Brooklyn (1)	*New York (4)
1948	Boston (2)	*Cleveland (4)
1947	Brooklyn (3)	*New York (4)
1946	*St. Louis (4)	Boston (3)
1945	Chicago (3)	*Detroit (4)
1944	*St. Louis (4)	St. Louis (2)
1943	St. Louis (1)	*New York (4)
1942	*St. Louis (4)	New York (1)
1941	Brooklyn (1)	*New York (4)
1940	*Cincinnati (4)	Detroit (3)
1939	Cincinnati (0)	*New York (4)
1938	Chicago (0)	*New York (4)
1937	New York (1)	*New York (4)
1936	New York (2)	*New York (4)
1935	Chicago (2)	* Detroit (4)

119

Year	National League	American League
1934	*St. Louis (4)	Detroit (3)
1933	*New York (4)	Washington (1)
1932	Chicago (0)	*New York (4)
1931	*St. Louis (4)	Philadelphia (3)
1930	St. Louis (2)	*Philadelphia (4)
1929	Chicago (1)	*Philadelphia (4)
1928	St. Louis (0)	*New York (4)
1927	Pittsburgh (0)	*New York (4)
1926	*St. Louis (4)	New York (3)
1925	*Pittsburgh (4)	Washington (3)
1924	New York (3)	*Washington (4)
1923	New York (2)	*New York (4)
1922	*New York (4)	New York (0)
1921	*New York (5)	New York (3)
1920	Brooklyn (2)	*Cleveland (5)
1919	*Cincinnati (5)	Chicago (3)
1918	Chicago (2)	*Boston (4)
1917	New York (2)	*Chicago (4)
1916	Brooklyn (1)	*Boston (4)
1915	Philadelphia (1)	*Boston (4)
1914	*Boston (4)	Philadelphia (0)
1913	New York (1)	*Philadelphia (4)
1912	New York (3)	*Boston (4)
1911	New York (2)	*Philadelphia (4)
1910	Chicago (1)	*Philadelphia (4)
1909	*Pittsburgh (4)	Detroit (3)
1908	*Chicago (4)	Detroit (1)
1907	*Chicago (4)	Detroit (0)
1906	Chicago (2)	*Chicago (4)
1905	*New York (4)	Philadelphia (1)
1904	New York (No series played.)	Boston
1903	Pittsburgh (3)	*Boston (5)
1902	Pittsburgh	Philadelphia
1901	Pittsburgh	Chicago
1900	Brooklyn	(No league)

(Note: The American League started play in 1901. The World Series as we know it today was played for the first time in 1903.)

The All-Star Game

The All-Star game, bringing together the best players of both leagues, was first played in 1933 as a feature of the Chicago Century of Progress Exposition. It proved so popular that it was made an annual event and is one of the season's top attractions. Two games were played each year from 1959 through 1962.

Year	Winner	Loser	Year	Winner	Loser
1969	National, 9	American, 3	1953	National, 5	American, 1
1968	National, 1	American, 0	1952	National, 3	American, 2
1967	National, 2	American, 1	1951	National, 8	American, 3
	(15 innings)		1950	National, 4	American, 3
1966	National, 2	American, 1	1949	American, 11	National, 7
	(10 innings)		1948	American, 5	National, 2
1965	National, 6	American, 5	1947	American, 2	National, 1
1964	National, 7	American, 4	1946	American, 12	National, 0
1963	National, 5	American, 3	1945	(No Game)	
1962	American, 9	National, 4	1944	National, 7	American, 1
1962	National, 3	American, 1	1943	American, 5	National, 3
1961	*National, 1	American, 1	1942	American, 3	National, 1
1961	National, 5	American, 4	1941	American, 7	National, 5
1960	National, 5	American, 3	1940	National, 4	American, 0
1960	National, 6	American, 0	1939	American, 3	National, 1
1959	American, 5	National, 3	1938	National, 4	American, 1
1959	National, 5	American, 4	1937	American, 8	National, 3
1958	American, 4	National, 3	1936	National, 4	American, 3
1957	American, 6	National, 5	1935	American, 4	National, 1
1956	National, 7	American, 3	1934	American, 9	National, 7
1955	National, 6	American, 5	1933	American, 4	National, 2
1954	American, 11	National, 9			

* Called after nine innings—rain.

121

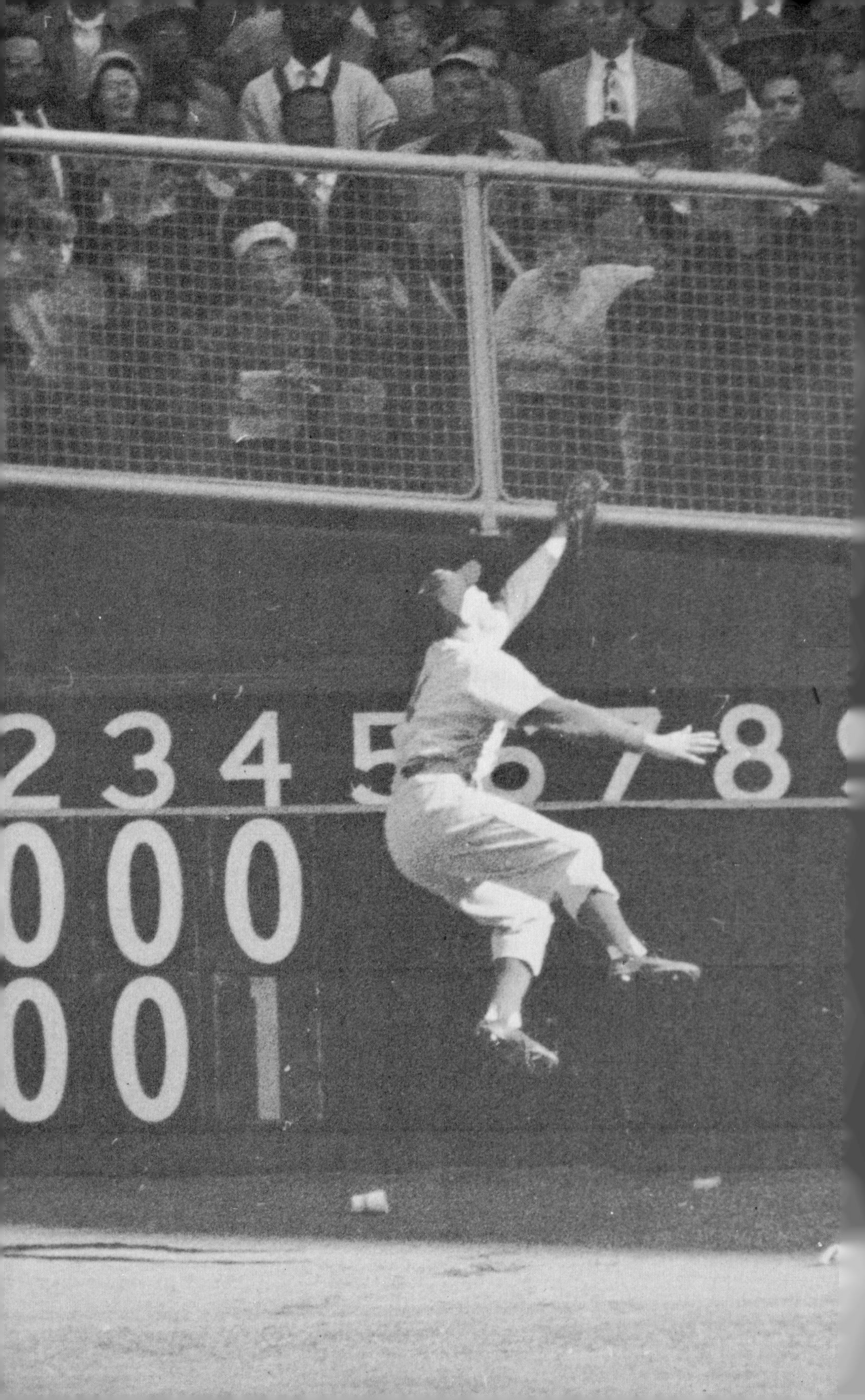
2 3 4 5 6 7 8
0 0 0
0 0 1

Batting Champions

Year	National League	Year	National League
1969	Rose, Cincinnati, .348	1934	P. Waner, Pittsburgh, .362
1968	Rose, Cincinnati, .335	1933	Klein, Philadelphia, .368
1967	Clemente, Pittsburgh, .357	1932	O'Doul, Brooklyn, .368
1966	M. Alou, Pittsburgh, .342	1931	Hafey, St. Louis, .349
1965	Clemente, Pittsburgh, .329	1930	Terry, New York, .401
1964	Clemente, Pittsburgh, .339	1929	O'Doul, Philadelphia, .398
1963	T. Davis, Los Angeles, .326	1928	Hornsby, Boston, .387
1962	T. Davis, Los Angeles, .346	1927	P. Waner, Pittsburgh, .380
1961	Clemente, Pittsburgh, .351	1926	Hargrave, Cincinnati, .353
1960	Groat, Pittsburgh, .325	1925	Hornsby, St. Louis, .403
1959	Aaron, Milwaukee, .355	1924	Hornsby, St. Louis, .424
1958	Ashburn, Philadelphia, .350	1923	Hornsby, St. Louis, .384
1957	Musial, St. Louis, .351	1922	Hornsby, St. Louis, .401
1956	Aaron, Milwaukee, .328	1921	Hornsby, St. Louis, .397
1955	Ashburn, Philadelphia, .338	1920	Hornsby, St. Louis, .370
1954	Mays, New York, .345	1919	Roush, Cincinnati, .321
1953	Furillo, Brooklyn, .344	1918	Wheat, Brooklyn, .335
1952	Musial, St. Louis, .336	1917	Roush, Cincinnati, .341
1951	Musial, St. Louis, .355	1916	Chase, Cincinnati, .339
1950	Musial, St. Louis, .346	1915	Doyle, New York, .320
1949	Robinson, Brooklyn, .342	1914	Daubert, Brooklyn, .329
1948	Musial, St. Louis, .376	1913	Daubert, Brooklyn, .350
1947	Walker, St. Louis-Phila., .363	1912	Zimmerman, Chicago, .372
1946	Musial, St. Louis, .365	1911	Wagner, Pittsburgh, .334
1945	Cavarretta, Chicago, .355	1910	Magee, Philadelphia, .331
1944	Walker, Brooklyn, .357	1909	Wagner, Pittsburgh, .339
1943	Musial, St. Louis, .357	1908	Wagner, Pittsburgh, .354
1942	Lombardi, Boston, .330	1907	Wagner, Pittsburgh, .350
1941	Reiser, Brooklyn, .343	1906	Wagner, Pittsburgh, .339
1940	Garms, Pittsburgh, .355	1905	Seymour, Cincinnati, .377
1939	Mize, St. Louis, .349	1904	Wagner, Pittsburgh, .349
1938	Lombardi, Cincinnati, .342	1903	Wagner, Pittsburgh, .355
1937	Medwick, St. Louis, .374	1902	Beaumont, Pittsburgh, .357
1936	P. Waner, Pittsburgh, .373	1901	Burkett, St. Louis, .382
1935	Vaughan, Pittsburgh, .385	1900	Wagner, Pittsburgh, .380

Year	American League	Year	American League
1969	Carew, Minnesota, .332	1967	Yastrzemski, Boston, .326
1968	Yastrzemski, Boston, .301	1966	F. Robinson, Baltimore, .316

123

United Press International

1965	Oliva, Minnesota, .321		1932	Alexander, Det.-Bost., .367
1964	Oliva, Minnesota, .323		1931	Simmons, Philadelphia, .390
1963	Yastrzemski, Boston, .321		1930	Simmons, Philadelphia, .381
1962	Runnels, Boston, .326		1929	Fonseca, Cleveland, .369
1961	Cash, Detroit, .361		1928	Goslin, Washington, .379
1960	Runnels, Boston, .320		1927	Heilmann, Detroit, .398
1959	Kuenn, Detroit, .353		1926	Manush, Detroit, .378
1958	Williams, Boston, .328		1925	Heilmann, Detroit, .393
1957	Williams, Boston, .388		1924	Ruth, New York, .378
1956	Mantle, New York, .353		1923	Heilmann, Detroit, .403
1955	Kaline, Detroit, .340		1922	Sisler, St. Louis, .420
1954	Avila, Cleveland, .341		1921	Heilmann, Detroit, .394
1953	Vernon, Washington, .337		1920	Sisler, St. Louis, .407
1952	Fain, Philadelphia, .327		1919	Cobb, Detroit, .384
1951	Fain, Philadelphia, .344		1918	Cobb, Detroit, .382
1950	Goodman, Boston, .354		1917	Cobb, Detroit, .383
1949	Kell, Detroit, .343		1916	Speaker, Cleveland, .386
1948	Williams, Boston, .369		1915	Cobb, Detroit, .370
1947	Williams, Boston, .343		1914	Cobb, Detroit, .368
1946	Vernon, Washington, .353		1913	Cobb, Detroit, .390
1945	Stirnweiss, New York, 309		1912	Cobb, Detroit, .410
1944	Boudreau, Cleveland, .327		1911	Cobb, Detroit, .420
1943	Appling, Chicago, .328		1910	Cobb, Detroit, .385
1942	Williams, Boston, .356		1909	Cobb, Detroit, .377
1941	Williams, Boston, .406		1908	Cobb, Detroit, .324
1940	DiMaggio, New York, .352		1907	Cobb, Detroit, .350
1939	DiMaggio, New York, .381		1906	Stone, St. Louis, .358
1938	Foxx, Boston, .349		1905	Flick, Cleveland, .306
1937	Gehringer, Detroit, .371		1904	Lajoie, Cleveland, .381
1936	Appling, Chicago, .388		1903	Lajoie, Cleveland, .355
1935	Myer, Washington, .349		1902	Delahanty, Washington, .376
1934	Gehrig, New York, .363		1901	Lajoie, Philadelphia, .422
1933	Foxx, Philadelphia, .356		1900	(AL not organized)

Players with 3,000 Hits

One of the fondest goals of every major leaguer is to collect more than 3,000 hits during his career, no matter how many years it may take. Only eight players have done it—and Ty Cobb alone has topped 4,000.

Hits	Player	Years	Games	Hits	Player	Years	Games
4,191	Ty Cobb	24	3,033	3,430	Honus Wagner	21	2,785
3,630	Stan Musial	22	3,026	3,313	Eddie Collins	25	2,826
3,528	Cap Anson	27	2,509	3,251	Nap Lajoie	21	2,475
3,515	Tris Speaker	22	2,789	3,152	Paul Waner	20	2,549

125

Home Run Champions

Time was when the player who hit as many as 10 homers in one season was a rare animal. In fact, Frank Baker of the old Philadelphia Athletics acquired the nickname "Home Run" because he hit 9 in 1911, 10 in 1912 and 12 in 1913. But Babe Ruth changed all that with his record-smashing bat. The Babe's mark of 60 home runs in 1927 was, of course, the all-time high for a single season until Roger Maris hammered out 61 in 1961.

Year	National League	Year	National League
1969	McCovey, San Francisco, 45	1941	Camilli, Brooklyn, 34
1968	McCovey, San Francisco, 36	1940	Mize, St. Louis, 43
1967	Aaron, Atlanta, 39	1939	Mize, St. Louis, 28
1966	Aaron, Atlanta, 44	1938	Ott, New York, 36
1965	Mays, San Francisco, 52	1937	Medwick, St. Louis, 31
1964	Mays, San Francisco, 47		Ott, New York, 31
1963	Aaron, Milwaukee, 44	1936	Ott, New York, 33
	McCovey, San Francisco, 44	1935	Berger, Boston, 34
1962	Mays, San Francisco, 49	1934	Collins, St. Louis, 35
1961	Cepeda, San Francisco, 46		Ott, New York, 35
1960	Banks, Chicago, 41	1933	Klein, Philadelphia, 28
1959	Mathews, Milwaukee, 46	1932	Klein, Philadelphia, 38
1958	Banks, Chicago, 47		Ott, New York, 38
1957	Aaron, Milwaukee, 44	1931	Klein, Philadelphia, 31
1956	Snider, Brooklyn, 43	1930	Wilson, Chicago, 56
1955	Mays, New York, 51	1929	Klein, Philadelphia, 43
1954	Kluszewski, Cincinnati, 49	1928	Bottomley, St. Louis, 31
1953	Mathews, Milwaukee, 47		Wilson, Chicago, 31
1952	Kiner, Pittsburgh, 37	1927	Williams, Philadelphia, 30
	Sauer, Chicago, 37		Wilson, Chicago, 30
1951	Kiner, Pittsburgh, 42	1926	Wilson, Chicago, 21
1950	Kiner, Pittsburgh, 47	1925	Hornsby, St. Louis, 39
1949	Kiner, Pittsburgh, 54	1924	Fournier, Brooklyn, 27
1948	Kiner, Pittsburgh, 40	1923	Williams, Philadelphia, 41
	Mize, New York, 40	1922	Hornsby, St. Louis, 42
1947	Kiner, Pittsburgh, 51	1921	Kelly, New York, 23
	Mize, New York, 51	1920	Williams, Philadelphia, 15
1946	Kiner, Pittsburgh, 23	1919	Cravath, Philadelphia, 12
1945	Holmes, Boston, 28	1918	Cravath, Philadelphia, 8
1944	Nicholson, Chicago, 33	1917	Cravath, Philadelphia, 12
1943	Nicholson, Chicago, 29		Robertson, New York, 12
1942	Ott, New York, 30		

Year	National League	Year	National League
1916	Robertson, New York, 12	1909	Murray, New York, 7
	Williams, Chicago, 12	1908	Jordan, Brooklyn, 12
1915	Cravath, Philadelphia, 24	1907	Brain, Boston, 10
1914	Cravath, Philadelphia, 19	1906	Jordan, Brooklyn, 12
1913	Cravath, Philadelphia, 19	1905	Odwell, Cincinnati, 9
1912	Zimmerman, Chicago, 14	1904	Lumley, Brooklyn, 9
1911	Schulte, Chicago, 21	1903	Sheckard, Brooklyn, 9
1910	Schulte, Chicago, 10	1902	Leach, Pittsburgh, 6
	Beck, Boston, 10	1901	Crawford, Cincinnati, 16
		1900	Long, Boston, 12

Year	American League	Year	American League
1969	Killebrew, Minnesota, 49	1934	Gehrig, New York, 49
1968	Howard, Washington, 44	1933	Foxx, Philadelphia, 48
1967	Killebrew, Minnesota, 44	1932	Foxx, Philadelphia, 58
	Yastrzemski, Boston, 44	1931	Gehrig, New York, 46
1966	F. Robinson, Baltimore, 49		Ruth, New York, 46
1965	Conigliaro, Boston, 32	1930	Ruth, New York, 49
1964	Killebrew, Minnesota, 49	1929	Ruth, New York, 46
1963	Killebrew, Minnesota, 45	1928	Ruth, New York, 54
1962	Killebrew, Minnesota, 48	1927	Ruth, New York, 60
1961	Maris, New York, 61	1926	Ruth, New York, 47
1960	Mantle, New York, 40	1925	Meusel, New York, 33
1959	Colavito, Cleveland, 42	1924	Ruth, New York, 46
	Killebrew, Washington, 42	1923	Ruth, New York, 41
1958	Mantle, New York, 42	1922	Williams, St. Louis, 39
1957	Sievers, Washington, 42	1921	Ruth, New York, 59
1956	Mantle, New York, 52	1920	Ruth, New York, 54
1955	Mantle, New York, 37	1919	Ruth, Boston, 29
1954	Doby, Cleveland, 32	1918	Ruth, Boston, 11
1953	Rosen, Cleveland, 43		Walker, Philadelphia, 11
1952	Doby, Cleveland, 32	1917	Pipp, New York, 9
1951	Zernial, Chi.-Phila., 33	1916	Pipp, New York, 12
1950	Rosen, Cleveland, 37	1915	Roth, Chicago-Cleveland, 7
1949	Williams, Boston, 43	1914	Baker, Philadelphia, 8
1948	DiMaggio, New York, 39		Crawford, Detroit, 8
1947	Williams, Boston, 32	1913	Baker, Philadelphia, 12
1946	Greenberg, Detroit, 44	1912	Baker, Philadelphia, 10
1945	Stephens, St. Louis, 24	1911	Baker, Philadelphia, 9
1944	Etten, New York, 22	1910	Stahl, Boston, 10
1943	York, Detroit, 34	1909	Cobb, Detroit, 9
1942	Williams, Boston, 36	1908	Crawford, Detroit, 7
1941	Williams, Boston, 37	1907	Davis, Philadelphia, 8
1940	Greenberg, Detroit, 41	1906	Davis, Philadelphia, 12
1939	Foxx, Boston, 35	1905	Davis, Philadelphia, 8
1938	Greenberg, Detroit, 58	1904	Davis, Philadelphia, 10
1937	DiMaggio, New York, 46	1903	Freeman, Boston, 13
1936	Gehrig, New York, 49	1902	Seybold, Philadelphia, 16
1935	Foxx, Philadelphia, 36	1901	Lajoie, Philadelphia, 13
	Greenberg, Detroit, 36	1900	(AL not organized)

No-Hit Games

Date	Pitcher, Club	Against	Score
Apr. 17, 1969	Stoneman, Mont. (N)	Phila.	7–0
Apr. 30, 1969	Maloney, Cin. (N)	Houst.	10–0
May 1, 1969	Wilson, Houst. (N)	Cin.	4–0
Aug. 13, 1969	Palmer, Balt. (A)	Oak.	8–0
Aug. 19, 1969	Holtzman, Chi. (N)	S.F.	3–0
Sept. 20, 1969	Moose, Pitt. (N)	N.Y.	4–0
Sept. 18, 1968	Washburn, S.L. (N)	S.F.	2–0
Sept. 17, 1968	Perry, S.F. (N)	S.L.	1–0
July 29, 1968	Culver, Cin. (N)	Phila.	6–1
May 8, 1968	Hunter, Oak. (A)	Minn.	4–0
Apr. 27, 1968	Phoebus, Balt. (A)	Bost.	6–0
Sept. 10,1967	Horlen, Chi. (A)	Det.	6–0
Aug. 25, 1967	Chance, Minn. (A)	Cleve.	2–1
June 18, 1967	Wilson, Houst. (N)	Atl.	2–0
Apr. 30, 1967	⎰ Barber, Balt. (A) (8⅔ innings) ⎱ Miller, Balt. (A) (⅓ inning)	Det.	1–2
June 10, 1966	Siebert, Cleve. (A)	Wash.	2–0
Sept. 16, 1965	Morehead, Bost. (A)	Cleve.	2–0
†Sept. 9, 1965	Koufax, L.A. (N)	Chi.	1–0
Aug. 19, 1965	Maloney, Cin. (N)	Chi.	1–0
°°°June 14, 1965	Maloney, Cin. (N)	N.Y.	0–1
†June 21, 1964	Bunning, Phila. (N)	N.Y.	6–0
June 4, 1964	Koufax, L.A. (N)	Phila.	3–0
°°Apr. 23, 1964	Johnson, Houst. (N)	Cin.	0–1
June 15, 1963	Marichal, S.F. (N)	Houst.	1–0
May 17, 1963	Nottebart, Houst. (N)	Phila.	4–1
May 11, 1963	Koufax, L.A. (N)	S.F.	8–0
Aug. 26, 1962	Kralick, Minn. (A)	K.C.	1–0
Aug. 1, 1962	Monbouquette, Bost. (A)	Chi.	1–0
June 30, 1962	Koufax, L.A. (N)	N.Y.	5–0
June 26, 1962	Wilson, Bost. (A)	L.A.	2–0
May 5, 1962	Belinsky, L.A. (A)	Balt.	2–0
Apr. 28, 1961	Spahn, Mil. (N)	S.F.	1–0
Sept. 16, 1960	Spahn, Mil. (N)	Phila.	4–0
Aug. 18, 1960	Burdette, Mil. (N)	Phila.	1–0
May 15, 1960	Cardwell, Chi. (N)	S.L.	4–0
‡May 26, 1959	Haddix, Pitt. (N)	Mil.	0–1
Sept. 20, 1958	Wilhelm, Balt. (A)	N.Y.	1–0
July 30, 1958	Bunning, Det. (A)	Bost.	3–0
Aug. 20, 1957	Keegan, Chi. (A)	Wash.	6–0
†Oct. 8, 1956	Larsen, N.Y. (A)	B'klyn. (N)°	2–0

Date	Pitcher, Club	Against	Score
Sept. 25, 1956	Maglie, B'klyn. (N)	Phila.	5–0
July 14, 1956	Parnell, Bost. (A)	Chi.	4–0
May 12, 1956	Erskine, B'klyn. (N)	N.Y.	3–0
May 12, 1955	Jones, Chi. (N)	Pitt.	4–0
June 12, 1954	Wilson, Mil. (N)	Phila.	2–0
May 6, 1953	Holloman, S.L. (A)	Phila.	6–0
Aug. 25, 1952	Trucks, Det. (A)	N.Y.	1–0
May 15, 1952	Trucks, Det. (A)	Wash.	1–0
June 19, 1952	Erskine, B'klyn. (N)	Chi.	5–0
Sept. 28, 1951	Reynolds, N.Y. (A)	Bost.	8–0
July 12, 1951	Reynolds, N.Y. (A)	Cleve.	1–0
July 1, 1951	Feller, Cleve. (A)	Det.	2–1
May 6, 1951	Chambers, Pitt. (N)	Bost.	3–0
Aug. 11, 1950	Bickford, Bost. (N)	B'klyn.	7–0
Sept. 9, 1948	Barney, B'klyn. (N)	N.Y.	2–0
June 30, 1948	Lemon, Cleve. (A)	Det.	2–0
Sept. 3, 1947	McCahan, Phila. (A)	Wash.	3–0
July 10, 1947	Black, Cleve. (A)	Phila.	3–0
June 18, 1947	Blackwell, Cin. (N)	Bost.	6–0
Apr. 30, 1946	Feller, Cleve. (A)	N.Y.	1–0
Apr. 23, 1946	Head, B'klyn. (N)	Bost.	5–0
Sept. 9, 1945	Fowler, Phila. (A)	S.L.	1–0
May 15, 1944	Shoun, Cin. (N)	Bost.	1–0
Apr. 27, 1944	Tobin, Bost. (N)	B'klyn.	2–0
Aug. 30, 1941	Warneke, S.L. (N)	Cin.	2–0
Apr. 30, 1940	Carleton, B'klyn. (N)	Cin.	3–0
Apr. 16, 1940	Feller, Cleve. (A)	Chi.	1–0
Aug. 27, 1938	Pearson, N.Y. (A)	Cleve.	13–0
June 15, 1938	Vander Meer, Cin. (N)	B'klyn.	6–0
June 11, 1938	Vander Meer, Cin. (N)	Bost.	3–0
June 1, 1937	Dietrich, Chi. (A)	S.L.	8–0
Aug. 31, 1935	Kennedy, Chi. (A)	Cleve.	5–0
Sept. 21, 1934	P. Dean, S.L. (N)	B'klyn.	3–0
Sept. 18, 1934	Newsom, S.L. (A)	Bost.	1–2
Aug. 8, 1931	Burke, Wash. (A)	Bost.	5–0
Apr. 29, 1931	Ferrell, Cleve. (A)	S.L.	9–0
May 8, 1929	Hubbell, N.Y. (N)	Pitt.	11–0
Aug. 21, 1926	Lyons, Chi. (A)	Bost.	6–0
Sept. 13, 1925	Vance, B'klyn. (N)	Phila.	10–1
July 17, 1924	Haines, S.L. (N)	Bost.	5–0
Sept. 7, 1923	Ehmke, Bost. (A)	Phila.	4–0
Sept. 4, 1923	Jones, N.Y. (A)	Phila.	2–0
May 7, 1922	Barnes, N.Y. (N)	Phila.	6–0
†Apr. 30, 1922	Robertson, Chi. (A)	Det.	2–0
July 1, 1920	Johnson, Wash. (A)	Bost.	1–0
Sept. 10, 1919	Caldwell, Cleve. (A)	N.Y.	3–0
May 11, 1919	Eller, Cin. (N)	S.L.	6–0
June 3, 1918	Leonard, Bost. (A)	Det.	5–0
‡June 23, 1917	Shore, Bost. (A)	Wash.	4–0
May 6, 1917	Groom, S.L. (A)	Chi.	3–0
May 5, 1917	Koob, S.L. (A)	Chi.	1–0

Date	Pitcher, Club	Against	Score
May 2, 1917	Vaughn, Chi. (N)	Cin.	0–1
May 2, 1917	Toney, Cin. (N)	Chi.	1–0
Apr. 24, 1917	Mogridge, N.Y. (A)	Bost.	2–1
Apr. 14, 1917	Cicotte, Chi. (A)	S.L.	11–0
Aug. 30, 1916	Leonard, Bost. (A)	S.L.	4–0
Aug. 26, 1916	Bush, Phila. (A)	Cleve.	5–0
June 21, 1916	Foster, Bost. (A)	N.Y.	2–0
June 16, 1916	Hughes, Bost. (N)	Pitt.	2–0
Aug. 31, 1915	Lavender, Chi. (N)	N.Y.	2–0
Apr. 15, 1915	Marquard, N.Y. (N)	B'klyn.	2–0
Sept. 9, 1914	Davis, Bost. (N)	Phila.	7–0
May 31, 1914	Benz, Chi. (A)	Cleve.	6–1
May 14, 1914	Scott, Chi. (A)	Wash.	0–1
Sept. 6, 1912	Tesreau, N.Y. (N)	Phila.	3–0
Aug. 30, 1912	Hamilton, S.L. (A)	Det.	5–1
July 4, 1912	Mullin, Det. (A)	S.L.	7–0
Aug. 27, 1911	Walsh, Chi. (A)	Bost.	5–0
July 29, 1911	Wood, Bost. (A)	S.L.	5–0
Aug. 30, 1910	Hughes, N.Y. (A)	Cleve.	0–5
May 12, 1910	Bender, Phila. (A)	Cleve.	4–0
Apr. 20, 1910	Joss, Cleve. (A)	Chi.	1–0
Apr. 15, 1909	Ames, N.Y. (N)	B'klyn.	0–3
†Oct. 2, 1908	Joss, Cleve. (A)	Chi.	1–0
Sept. 20, 1908	Smith, Chi. (A)	Phila.	1–0
Sept. 18, 1908	Rhoades, Cleve. (A)	Bost.	2–1
Sept. 5, 1908	Rucker, B'klyn. (N)	Bost.	6–0
July 4, 1908	Wiltse, N.Y. (N)	Phila.	1–0
June 30, 1908	Young, Bost. (A)	N.Y.	8–0
Sept. 20, 1907	Maddox, Pitt. (N)	B'klyn.	2–1
May 8, 1907	Pfeffer, Bost. (N)	Cin.	6–0
Aug. 1, 1906	McIntire, B'klyn. (N)	Pitt.	0–1
July 20, 1906	Eason, B'klyn. (N)	S.L.	2–0
May 1, 1906	Lush, Phila. (N)	B'klyn.	1–0
Sept. 27, 1905	Dinneen, Bost. (A)	Chi.	2–0
Sept. 6, 1905	Smith, Chi. (A)	Det.	15–0
July 22, 1905	Henley, Phila. (A)	S.L.	6–0
June 13, 1905	Mathewson, N.Y. (N)	Chi.	1–0
Aug. 17, 1904	Tannehill, Bost. (A)	Chi.	6–0
June 11, 1904	Wicker, Chi. (N)	N.Y.	1–0
†May 5, 1904	Young, Bost. (A)	Phila.	3–0
Sept. 18, 1903	Fraser, Phila. (N)	Chi.	10–0
Sept. 20, 1902	Callahan, Chi. (A)	Det.	3–0
July 15, 1901	Mathewson, N.Y. (N)	S.L.	5–0
May 9, 1901	Moore, Cleve. (A)	Chi.	2–4
July 12, 1900	Hahn, Cin. (N)	Phila.	4–0

† Perfect Game
* World Series
‡ 12 innings, perfect game, lost in 13th.
** Lost game on 2 errors in 9th.
*** 10 hitless innings. Allowed 2 hits in 11th.

130

Pitchers with 300 Victories

Three hundred victories for a career—this represents the charmed circle for major league pitchers. Only fourteen men have ever attained that mark, the most recent having been Warren Spahn.

Won	Pitcher	Years	Games	Won	Pitcher	Years	Games
511	Cy Young	22	906	346	Tim Keefe	14	587
416	Walter Johnson	21	802	328	John Clarkson	12	529
373	Grover Alexander	20	696	325	Eddie Plank	17	620
373	Christy Mathewson	17	634	316	Mike Welch	13	540
365	Jim Galvin	15	684	308	Hoss Radbourne	11	517
363	Warren Spahn	21	750	300	Lefty Grove	17	616
360	Kid Nichols	15	586	300	Early Wynn	23	691

Most Valuable Players

Most valuable players were designated as far back as 1911, but the award did not become officially recognized until the Baseball Writers Association of America took over the voting in 1931.

NATIONAL LEAGUE

Year	Player, Position, Club	Batting or Pitching Record	Year	Player, Position, Club	Batting or Pitching Record
1969	Willie McCovey, 1B, S. F.	.320	1949	Jackie Robinson, 2B, B'klyn.	.342
1968	Bob Gibson, P, St. Louis	22–9	1948	Stan Musial, 1B, St. Louis	.376
1967	Orlando Cepeda, 1B, St. L.	.325	1947	Bob Elliott, 3B, Boston	.317
1966	Rob. Clemente, OF, Pitt.	.317	1946	Stan Musial, 1B, St. Louis	.365
1965	Willie Mays, OF, S.F.	.317	1945	Phil Cavarretta, 1B, Chi.	.355
1964	Ken Boyer, 3B, St. Louis	.295	1944	Marty Marion, SS, St. Louis	.267
1963	Sandy Koufax, P, L.A.	25–5	1943	Stan Musial, OF, St. Louis	.357
1962	Maury Wills, SS, L.A.	.299	1942	Mort Cooper, P, St. Louis	22–7
1961	Frank Robinson, OF, Cin.	.323	1941	Dolph Camilli, 1B, B'klyn.	.285
1960	Dick Groat, SS, Pitt.	.325	1940	Frank McCormick, 1B, Cin.	.309
1959	Ernie Banks, SS, Chi.	.304	1939	Bucky Walters, P, Cin.	27–11
1958	Ernie Banks, SS, Chi.	.313	1938	Ernie Lombardi, C, Cin.	.342
1957	Hank Aaron, OF, Mil.	.322	1937	Joe Medwick, OF, St. Louis	.374
1956	Don Newcombe, P, B'klyn.	27–7	1936	Carl Hubbell, P, N.Y.	26–6
1955	Roy Campanella, C, B'klyn.	.318	1935	Gabby Hartnett, C, Chi.	.344
1954	Willie Mays, OF, N.Y.	.345	1934	Dizzy Dean, P, St. Louis	30–7
1953	Roy Campanella, C, B'klyn.	.312	1933	Carl Hubbell, P, N.Y.	23–12
1952	Hank Sauer, OF, Chi.	.270	1932	Chuck Klein, OF, Phila.	.348
1951	Roy Campanella, C, B'klyn.	.325	1931	Frank Frisch, 2B, St. Louis	.311
1950	Jim Konstanty, P, Phila.	16–7			

132

AMERICAN LEAGUE

Year	Player, Position, Club	Batting or Pitching Record	Year	Player, Position, Club	Batting or Pitching Record
1969	H. Killebrew, 1B, Minn.	.276	1949	Ted Williams, OF, Boston	.343
1968	Dennis McLain, P, Detroit	31–6	1948	Lou Boudreau, SS, Cleve.	.355
1967	C.Yastrzemski, OF, Bost.	.326	1947	Joe DiMaggio, OF, N.Y.	.315
1966	F. Robinson, OF, Baltimore	.316	1946	Ted Williams, OF, Boston	.342
1965	Zoilo Versalles, OF, Minn.	.273	1945	Hal Newhouser, P, Det.	25–9
1964	Brooks Robinson, 3B, Balt.	.317	1944	Hal Newhouser, P, Det.	29–9
1963	Elston Howard, C, N.Y.	.287	1943	Spud Chandler, P, N.Y.	20–4
1962	Mickey Mantle, OF, N.Y.	.321	1942	Joe Gordon, 2B, N.Y.	.322
1961	Roger Maris, OF, N.Y.	.269	1941	Joe DiMaggio, OF, N.Y.	.357
1960	Roger Maris, OF, N.Y.	.283	1940	Hank Greenberg, OF, Det.	.340
1959	Nelson Fox, 2B, Chi.	.306	1939	Joe DiMaggio, OF, N.Y.	.381
1958	Jackie Jensen, OF, Bost.	.286	1938	Jimmy Foxx, 1B, Boston	.349
1957	Mickey Mantle, OF, N.Y.	.365	1937	Charley Gehringer, 2B, Det.	.371
1956	Mickey Mantle, OF, N.Y.	.353	1936	Lou Gehrig, 1B, N.Y.	.354
1955	Yogi Berra, C, N.Y.	.272	1935	Hank Greenberg, 1B, Det.	.328
1954	Yogi Berra, C, N.Y.	.307	1934	Mickey Cochran, C, Det.	.320
1953	Al Rosen, 3B, Cleve.	.336	1933	Jimmy Foxx, 1B, Phila.	.356
1952	Bobby Shantz, P, Phila.	24–7	1932	Jimmy Foxx, 1B, Phila.	.364
1951	Yogi Berra, C, N.Y.	.294	1931	Lefty Grove, P, Phila.	31–4
1950	Phil Rizzuto, SS, N.Y.	.324			

League-Leading Pitchers

In recent years, much attention has been paid to earned-run averages in pitching. However, interest still centers on a pitcher's quest for victory by any score, and the won-lost record usually is the one by which he is best remembered.

NATIONAL LEAGUE

Year	Player	Won-Lost	Year	Player	Won-Lost
1969	Seaver, New York	25–7	1965	Koufax, Los Angeles	26–8
1968	Blass, Pittsburgh	18–6	1964	Jackson, Chicago	24–11
1967	Hughes, St. Louis	16–6	1963	Koufax, Los Angeles	25–5
1966	Marichal, San Francisco	25–6	1962	Purkey, Cincinnati	23–5

133

Year	Player	Won-Lost	Year	Player	Won-Lost
1961	Podres, Los Angeles	18–5	1929	Root, Chicago	19–6
1960	Broglio, St. Louis	21–9	1928	Benton, New York	25–9
1959	Face, Pittsburgh	18–1	1927	Benton, New York	13–5
1958	Spahn, Milwaukee	22–11	1926	Kremer, Pittsburgh	20–6
1957	Buhl, Milwaukee	18–7	1925	Sherdel, St. Louis	15–6
1956	Newcombe, Brooklyn	27–7	1924	Yde, Pittsburgh	16–3
1955	Newcombe, Brooklyn	20–5	1923	Luque, Cincinnati	27–8
1954	Antonelli, New York	21–7	1922	Douglas, New York	11–4
1953	Erskine, Brooklyn	20–6	1921	Adams, Pittsburgh/	
1952	Wilhelm, New York	15–3		Glazner, Pittsburgh	14–5
1951	Roe, Brooklyn	22–3	1920	Grimes, Brooklyn	23–11
1950	Maglie, New York	18–4	1919	Reuther, Cincinnati	19–6
1949	Roe, Brooklyn	15–6	1918	Hendrix, Chicago	20–7
1948	Sewell, Pittsburgh	13–3	1917	Schupp, New York	21–7
1947	Jansen, New York	21–5	1916	Hughes, Boston	16–3
1946	Rowe, Philadelphia	11–4	1915	Alexander, Philadelphia	31–10
1945	Brecheen, St. Louis	15–4	1914	James, Boston	26–7
1944	Wilks, St. Louis	17–4	1913	Humphries, Chicago	16–4
1943	Shoun, Cincinnati/		1912	Hendrix, Pittsburgh	24–9
	Wyatt, Brooklyn	14–5	1911	Marquard, New York	24–7
1942	Krist, St. Louis	13–3	1910	Phillippe, Pittsburgh	14–2
1941	Riddle, E., Cincinnati	19–4	1909	Mathewson, New York/	
1940	Fitzsimmons, Brooklyn	16–2		Cannitz, Pittsburgh	25–6
1939	Derringer, Cincinnati	25–7	1908	Reulbach, Chicago	24–7
1938	Lee, Chicago	22–9	1907	Reulbach, Chicago	17–4
1937	Hubbell, New York	22–8	1906	Reulbach, Chicago	19–4
1936	Hubbell, New York	26–6	1905	Leever, Pittsburgh	20–5
1935	Lee, Chicago	20–6	1904	McGinnity, New York	35–8
1934	Dean, J., St. Louis	30–7	1903	Leever, Pittsburgh	25–7
1933	Tinning, Chicago	13–6	1902	Chesbro, Pittsburgh	28–6
1932	Warneke, Chicago	22–6	1901	Leever, Pittsburgh	14–5
1931	Haines, St. Louis	12–3	1900	McGinnity, Brooklyn	27–8
1930	Teachout, Chicago	11–4			

AMERICAN LEAGUE

Year	Player	Won-Lost	Year	Player	Won-Lost
1969	Palmer, Baltimore	16–4	1959	Shaw, Chicago	18–6
1968	McLain, Detroit	31–6	1958	Turley, New York	21–7
1967	Horlen, Chicago	19–7	1957	Donovan, Chicago/	
1966	Siebert, Cleveland	16–8		Sturdivant, New York	16–6
1965	Grant, Minnesota	21–7	1956	Ford, New York	19–6
1964	Bunker, Baltimore	19–5	1955	Byrne, New York	16–5
1963	Ford, New York	24–7	1954	Consuegra, Chicago	16–3
1962	Herbert, Chicago	20–9	1953	Lopat, New York	16–4
1961	Ford, New York	25–4	1952	Shantz, Philadelphia	24–7
1960	Coates, New York	13–3	1951	Feller, Cleveland	22–8

134

Year	Player	Won-Lost	Year	Player	Won-Lost
1950	Raschi, New York	21–8	1924	Johnson, Washington	23–7
1949	Kinder, Boston	23–6	1923	Pennock, New York	19–6
1948	Kramer, Boston	18–5	1922	Bush, New York	26–7
1947	Shea, New York	14–5	1921	Mays, New York	27–9
1946	Ferriss, Boston	25–6	1920	Bagby, Cleveland	31–12
1945	Muncrief, St. Louis	13–4	1919	Cicotte, Chicago	29–7
1944	Hughson, Boston	18–5	1918	Jones, Boston	16–5
1943	Chandler, New York	20–4	1917	Klepher, Cleveland	13–4
1942	Bonham, New York	21–5	1916	Coveleskie, Detroit	23–10
1941	Gomez, New York	15–5	1915	Ruth, Boston	18–6
1940	Rowe, Detroit	16–3	1914	Bender, Philadelphia	17–3
1939	Donald, New York	13–3	1913	Johnson, Washington	36–7
1938	Grove, Boston	14–4	1912	Wood, Boston	34–5
1937	Allen, Cleveland	15–1	1911	Bender, Philadelphia	17–5
1936	Hadley, New York	14–4	1910	Bender, Philadelphia	23–5
1935	Auker, Detroit	18–7	1909	Mullin, Detroit	29–8
1934	Gomez, New York	26–5	1908	Walsh, Chicago	40–15
1933	Grove, Philadelphia	24–8	1907	Donovan, Detroit	25–4
1932	Allen, New York	17–4	1906	Plank, Philadelphia	19–6
1931	Grove, Philadelphia	31–4	1905	Coakley, Philadelphia	20–8
1930	Grove, Philadelphia	28–5	1904	Chesbro, New York	41–12
1929	Grove, Philadelphia	20–6	1903	Moore, Cleveland	22–7
1928	Crowder, St. Louis	21–5	1902	Hughes, Boston	12–3
1927	Hoyt, New York	22–7	1901	Young, Boston	31–10
1926	Ehmke, Philadelphia	12–4	1900	(AL not organized)	
1925	Coveleskie, Washington	20–5			

Basketball

The History of Basketball

If we ask ten youngsters what major sport they have seen or played most, nine will undoubtedly answer "basketball."

There is no other team activity in the United States played so frequently and by so many as this sport of strictly American origin invented by a Canadian. So quickly has it grown and so widely has it spread that it is impossible to imagine a boy or girl of grade-school age who has never passed, dribbled, or shot a basketball.

Our country seems to be a land of supermarkets, highways—and basketball courts, hoops, and nets. Just take a short walk around your city and you'll quickly notice the outdoor basketball court, busy just about every pleasant day of the year. Drive in the suburbs and you will see hoops and nets attached to the rear of many houses and garages. Basketball is all around us, and every town and village has at least one basketball court—indoor or outdoor—placed somewhere for its younger residents.

Who plays the game? Just about everybody—from January through December. In gymnasiums and on outdoor courts the game is on a year-round basis, although the regular school basketball season starts in December and ends in March. Summer recreational leagues make the game a midyear activity, especially in those areas where the high school or college player wants to stay in shape during the off season.

Boys and girls are introduced to the game while still in grade school. Basketball becomes part of their church recreational program; it follows them as they attend high school and college and enter industry. Many businesses consider basketball a great morale builder for their employees, and industrial leagues are spread throughout the land.

It all started with a pair of peach baskets hung in the gymnasium of the Springfield, Massachusetts, Young Men's Christian Association. Dr. James Naismith, who had been an all-round athlete at McGill University in Montreal, Canada, was an instructor at this YMCA in 1891 when he noticed that his students found their physical exercise program boring.

Lifting weights and jumping over parallel bars throughout the long winter months, reasoned young Naismith, would bore anyone. So he thought of something else to put some spark and interest in his students.

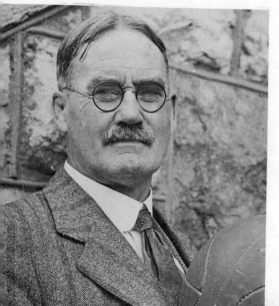

Noticing an abandoned pair of peach baskets lying in the alley outside his gymnasium hall, Naismith was inspired. Why not a game in which the boys can throw a ball into these baskets? The baskets were hung from each end of the gymnasium's balcony—and the game of basketball was born.

Dr. James Naismith

Associated Press

The original game permitted no running with the ball, no pushing, shoving, tripping, or striking of an opponent; and a goal was made when the ball was thrown or batted into the basket. Although many of the rules of basketball have changed through the years, the basic regulations as set by Naismith are still in effect.

So quickly did this new game catch on that many teams were started before a set of rules was introduced and approved. It made little difference how many players constituted a team. Some had seven on a side, others nine, and still others eight. It was soon discovered that the bottoms of the peach baskets slowed up play. They were taken out to enable the ball to drop through and down to the playing area.

YMCA's throughout the East soon cleared their gymnasiums of weights, Indian clubs, parallel and chinning bars. Basketball was the new activity to make a long winter seem shorter, and more athletes started to flock to the gyms to take advantage of this new action-packed sport.

At first the rules of the game and conduct of play were governed by the YMCA and the Amateur Athletic Union (AAU). These two sports groups formed leagues and had a schedule of games. A game consisted of three 20-minute periods, and play was hectic.

The game started to gain popularity in secondary schools and colleges, but it wasn't until 1902 that the first college league—the Eastern Intercollegiate League—was formed. In fact, the game was popularized by the professionals before the colleges decided to make it part of their athletic program. Basketball's first pro circuit, the National Basketball League, began in 1898, with teams located in New Jersey, New York, Brooklyn, and Philadelphia.

141

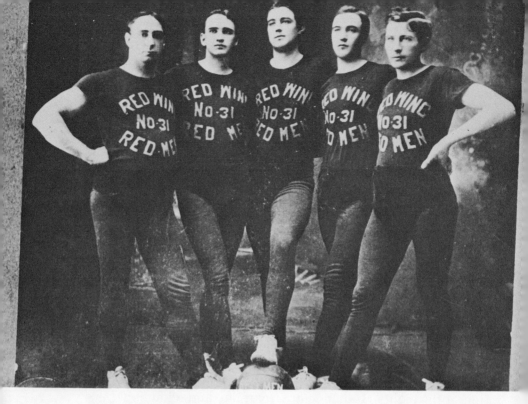

Bill Mokray

One of the first professional teams—
the Red Wings of Minnesota, 1905–06.

Once the Eastern Intercollegiate League was formed, the sport soon spread to other areas. From the Eastern seaboard the game went to the Midwest where the Western Conference was organized. Then the Southern, Southwestern, and Far Western colleges started play and formed their own conferences, or leagues.

The early coaches continually experimented with playing techniques and strategies. Unlike today's version, the ball did not pass to the opponents as soon as a goal was scored. Play began—as today—with a jump between two opponents at center court. Once a goal was scored, from field or the foul line, the two centers faced each other again at midcourt.

142

The 1959 pro champions—the Boston Celtics.
Number 14 is captain Bob Cousy.

The center jump after each score was an important part of the game. The team that had the best jumper and the tallest player could then control the ball for as long as it wanted. Yet tall players did not dominate the game in its early history. The players were of average size, and the usual center was about 6 feet 2 inches tall.

Low-scoring games were in style, and scores of 13–10 and 15–8 were normal. Shooting was done strictly with two hands, and no long shots were attempted. There was much emphasis on dribbling and passing. Shots were attempted from an 8- to 10-foot radius around the basket. There were five positions—center, left and right forwards, left and right guards. And the positions, unlike today's, meant exactly what they said.

The center was the jumper at midcourt and the main rebounder. The forwards were used to work the ball in close to the basket; they also fired the greatest percentage of shots. The guards seldom moved beyond midcourt into their front court. They were used as dogged defenders and stayed with the opposing forwards wherever they went. Defense was the order of the day, and the guards took great pride in holding the opposing forwards to the fewest points possible.

The pivot play, the zone defense, the switching man-to-man, the hook, and the jump shot were still many years away.

The peach baskets soon gave way to metal baskets. In 1906 hoops, such as are in use today, were introduced. When spectators interfered with shots that went beyond the hoop, wire-mesh backboards were placed behind the hoops. These were soon replaced by backboards of wood, which in turn gave way to the glass backboard of today.

As the years passed, basketball began to take on different characteristics in different parts of the country. The East concentrated on speed and dribbling in an effort to work the ball into the basket. The Midwest used a "blocker" around whom they worked a deliberate offense. The blocker, or blockers, would be stationed in front of the defensive player whose job was to guard the ball-handler. Once this defensive man was blocked out of play, the ball-handler then swept by his guard and set up the play.

Teams in the Rocky Mountain area and on the Pacific Coast began experimenting with the one-hand shot. Their players

144

started to fire at the basket after transferring the ball to the shooting hand.

During the early 1920's the game grew far beyond anyone's expectations. High schools began to hold state tournaments which drew capacity crowds. College gymnasiums were far too small to accommodate the fans who wanted to see their favorites play. The sports pages of the newspapers began to give more space to the game, and some of the names became as familiar to the sports fan as his favorite baseball and football players.

Howard Cann of New York University and Paul Hinkle of the University of Chicago were the best forward and guard of 1920. Forrest Di Bernardi of Westminster, Ray Miller of Purdue, Charlie Black of Kansas, Vic Hanson of Syracuse, Abb Curtis of Texas, Noble Kizer of Notre Dame, Bennie Oosterbaan of Michigan, Charlie Murphy of Purdue, and Chuck Hyatt of Pittsburgh were other famous players during the 1920's.

The 1930's marked the most radical changes in the game. Many of the coaches and spectators thought the game moved too slowly. Too much time was wasted after each score by walking back to center court for a jump ball, they agreed. The jump following a goal was eliminated, and play was continued, with the scored-on team taking possession under its opponent's basket.

The scoring pace quickened and the coaches were forced to revise their strategies and techniques of play. The fans took to this new style of fast play, so much so that the college sport actually grew out of its own gymnasium.

145

A New York sports writer, entering a college gymnasium one night, saw disappointed fans being turned away at the entrances. "All sold out," was the cry. Inside the arena all seats were filled, and there was not even space in which to stand. But he noticed that more people were on the outside of the building than had been admitted.

Ned Irish was the writer, and he decided to do something about it. He convinced the Madison Square Garden officials that the game was now popular enough to play in New York's largest arena. So persuasive was he that a double-header was scheduled in 1934. The response was overwhelming, and the Garden soon became the basketball capital of the country.

Hank Luisetti

United Press International

Soon other cities began to use large indoor arenas to take care of the fans who wanted to see the top games. Philadelphia, Boston, Buffalo, Chicago, Kansas City (Missouri), and San Francisco were some of the cities that put on doubleheaders on off-campus courts. Those schools which did not play on noncollege courts were forced to rebuild their own gymnasiums or break ground for more spacious college arenas.

The style of play—clever passing, quick dribbling, two-handed set shot—suddenly gave way to the one-hand jump shot, made on the run or from the set position. The change came about when a fine Stanford University team visited the East in 1936. Hank Luisetti was the star of this fast-moving team, and the accuracy of his one-hand shots and those of his teammates amazed the Easterners. This marked a new style in shooting technique, one which is now in wide use from grade school through the professional level.

Basketball is universal. It is a part of the Olympic Games program, and world tournaments among nations have been held. It is conceivable that the spread of the game to just about every corner of the globe has been made possible by a touring professional squad known as the Harlem Globetrotters. This team of Negro players was organized in Chicago in 1927 by the late Abe Saperstein. It first traveled throughout the United States, playing in towns that were small specks on the map. As the fame of the Globetrotters grew, they began to appear in major cities. So popular and unusual was their style of play that foreign countries were anxious to see this amazing group of Americans who could do just about everything with a basketball but make it talk.

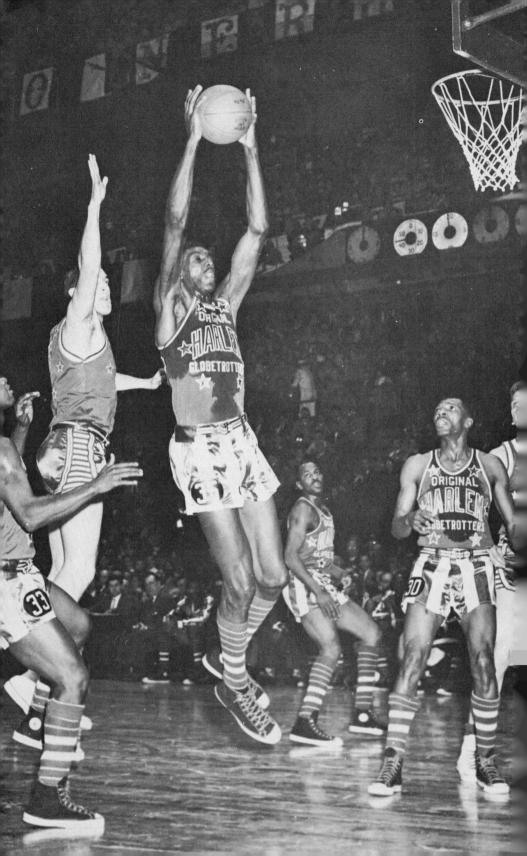

The Globetrotters have since touched almost every foreign country in the world, finally appearing in the Soviet Union in 1959. They travel with their own opposing team, and their play is merely for exhibition, not competition. Each year, however, the Globetrotters and a team of outstanding college stars play a series of games at the conclusion of the college season in different cities. These one-night stands usually find the collegians on the short end of the score.

The professional game has grown to major status since 1946. In that year the Basketball Association of America, a new league that included teams from St. Louis to Toronto, Canada, was competing with the older National Basketball League. The two leagues merged for the start of the 1949 season, and the National Basketball Association has been active since.

With the start of the 1969–70 season, the NBA had expanded to fourteen teams. The Eastern Division consisted of Baltimore, Boston, Cincinnati, Detroit, Milwaukee, New York and Philadelphia. In the Western Division were Atlanta, Chicago, Los Angeles, Phoenix, San Diego, San Francisco and Seattle.

Three additional teams were granted NBA franchises for the 1970–71 season: Buffalo, Cleveland and Portland, Oregon.

Also in 1969–70, a second pro circuit, the American Basketball Association, embarked on its third season with eleven teams—Carolina, Indiana, Kentucky, Miami, New York and Pittsburgh in the East and Dallas, Denver, Los Angeles, New Orleans and Washington, D.C., in the West.

The Lakers of Minneapolis, led by George Mikan, monopolized championship play during the early 1950's. But Bos-

The Harlem Globetrotters

ton, led by Bob Cousy and Bill Russell and with Red Auerbach as its coach, has been the professionals' most consistent winner since then.

In fact, the Celtics failed to win the NBA title only twice between 1956–57 and 1969–70. Between 1958–59 and 1965–66 they captured a record seven championships in a row.

Cousy retired as a player in 1963 but returned to the NBA in 1969 as coach of the Cincinnati Royals. Russell ended his career after the 1968–69 season and after his sweetest victory. The Celtics barely made it into the playoffs, but with Russell functioning brilliantly as player and coach, Boston fought its way to its 11th crown in 13 seasons.

On the college scene, the powerhouse team of the 1960's was the University of California at Los Angeles, winner of the National Collegiate Athletic Association championship six times in seven years from 1964 to 1970.

There are three major rule differences between professional and school play: (1) The pros play 12-minute quarters; the colleges play two 20-minute halves. (2) Six personal fouls disqualify a professional player; five personals is the school rule. (3) In the pros, the offensive team must shoot within 24 seconds of possessing the ball; there is no time limit on possession in school play. This rule on possession among the pros makes for very high scoring games, and each team averages better than 100 points a game over a season's play.

Great Names in Basketball

LEW ALCINDOR

Even before he joined the professional ranks in the 1969–70 season, Lew Alcindor was conceded by basketball experts across the land a place among the game's super players.

UCLA center Lew Alcindor walks off the court holding up one finger as the team and cheering section chant, "We're number one!" UCLA had just beat Houston 101-69 in the NCAA semi-finals, March 22, 1968.

United Press International

In fact, the 7-foot 1⅜-inch Alcindor started to become the talk of the basketball world while he was still in high school. At the University of California at Los Angeles, he dominated the college ranks for three seasons, and then the professionals welcomed him not only as a tremendous box office attraction but as a player marked for greatness.

Born in New York City on April 16, 1947, Ferdinand Lewis Alcindor Jr. was 22½ inches long and weighed 12 pounds 11 ounces at birth. His parents could be sure he was not going to be a little fellow.

At the age of fourteen, Alcindor already was 6 feet 8 inches tall and could dunk a basketball—that is, reach high enough to stuff the ball through the hoop. He remembers scoring as many as 33 points in one grade school game.

It was while attending Power Memorial High School in New York that big Lew began to attract national attention. In three seasons, he amassed 2,067 points and led Power Memorial to three successive New York City Catholic school championships—with a 71-game winning streak en route.

Apart from his height and his well distributed 235 pounds, Alcindor was a polished player. This was not mainly a case of a big man having the edge on the rest of the fellows. Lew demonstrated he was a slick ball handler and a fine playmaker.

So his record at UCLA surprised no one. In three varsity seasons, during which UCLA won an unprecedented three national collegiate championships and lost but two games, Lew was three times voted an All-American and three times named the outstanding player in the National Collegiate Athletic Association tournament. He also was chosen Collegiate Player of the Year for 1966–67 and again for 1968–69.

152

During those three varsity years, he recorded 2,325 points, for an average of 26.4 per game; was credited with 1,367 rebounds, and set an all-time field goal percentage of .641.

The Milwaukee Bucks, a new team in the National Basketball Association, were the lucky pro outfit to acquire him. In his first pro game—at Milwaukee on October 18, 1969—Alcindor scored 29 points on 12 field goals and 5 fouls.

Despite all of the pressure that came from being the most publicized player in many years, Alcindor was terrific in his debut. And it was only the beginning. . . .

ELGIN BAYLOR

No other rookie ever had such a sensational first-year NBA season as Elgin Baylor of the Minneapolis Lakers.

Minneapolis had decided to make the 1958–59 season its test year. If the club drew, the franchise would remain. If uninspired performance and box-office nonappeal continued, the team would have to move to another city.

Baylor saved the Lakers temporarily for Minneapolis, and was personally responsible for leading what was considered an average team into the championship playoffs. But after the 1959–60 season, the Lakers transferred their franchise to Los Angeles and thus brought pro basketball to the West Coast.

Baylor—an All-American at Seattle University and the nation's top college scorer in the 1957–58 season, averaging 32.5 points per game—became the NBA's finest rookie, with his wide assortment of shots, his keen passing and speed afoot, and his leadership qualities.

153

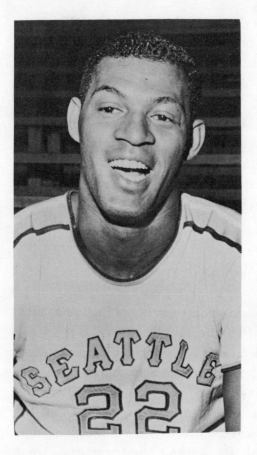

Elgin Baylor

This native of Washington, D. C., still had another year of college eligibility when he decided to try his lot with the pros in 1958. He was unanimously voted Rookie of the Year, and by 1969 had become the second highest scorer in NBA history with a total of 21,725 points in 11 seasons.

Baylor, an all-pro selection ever since he entered the NBA, had his finest hour at New York on November 15, 1960, when he threw in 71 points (28 field goals and 15 fouls) against the Knickerbockers for what was then a one-game record.

WILT CHAMBERLAIN

The most phenomenal of all the professional stars is Wilt the Stilt Chamberlain, all 7 feet 1 inch and 250 pounds of him.

United Press International

Wilt Chamberlain

Wilt broke the one-season pro scoring record before he had completed his first year with the Philadelphia Warriors in 1959–60. He closed out the season with a total of 2,707 points for a per-game average of 37.6, another NBA record.

But it was only the beginning. Chamberlain exceeded both records the following year, scoring 3,033 points for an average of 38.4 per game. Never before had a player hit for 3,000 points in a season.

The 1961–62 season was even more astounding. The campaign was hardly under way when Chamberlain started cracking records. On December 8, 1961, Wilt ran up 78 points against the Los Angeles Lakers. The tally was not recognized as a record because the game was a triple overtime. But the one-game mark did fall to him on January 13, 1962, when he poured in 73 points on 29 field goals and 15 fouls in four regulation periods against the Chicago Packers.

155

Then came the "impossible." On March 2, 1962, against the New York Knicks, the unstoppable Wilt blasted three records in one performance. He hit for a high of 36 field goals and a record 28 out of 32 foul shots—the first time in pro history an individual had scored 100 points in a single game. When the season ended, he had amassed 4,031 points, an average of better than 50 per game!

Chamberlain closed the 1964–65 season with 18,837 points and passed Bob Pettit of the St. Louis Hawks as the game's all-time scoring champion in the 1965–66 season. He went into the 1969–70 season with a career total of 27,098 points for an average of 34.4 per game—both all-time highs.

It was while he was a schoolboy at Overbrook High in Philadelphia that the sports world first began to read stories of this "gigantic steeple" who could simply turn around, take a little jump in the air, and throw the ball *down* through the basket. The stories were true.

Wilt was the "Big Dipper" then, and so well did he "dip" that just about every college in the country wanted him to play for them. He finally chose the University of Kansas. Chamberlain played for the Jayhawks for two years (1956–1958), and was twice named All-American. He left in his senior year to play with the Harlem Globetrotters in 1958–59, and joined the Warriors of the NBA the next season.

BOB COUSY

Wilt Chamberlain may score the most points, Elgin Baylor may have the finest shot, and Adolph Schayes may have been the most durable, but none was more spectacular than the magician himself, Bob Cousy.

156

This sleight-of-hand artist, who could confuse the opponents, the spectators, and his own teammates with his tricks, was All-American at Holy Cross and went to the local Boston Celtics only because his name was pulled out of a hat.

Cousy was the game's greatest passer, dribbler, and ball-handler. Old-time fans and players who saw the original Celtics and the first of the many greats were convinced that none could match Cousy in the art of handling a ball. Bob could send a pass through the eye of a needle, and he broke up more enemy passing attacks and stole more opponents' dribbles than any two players in the game.

Bob Cousy

Associated Press

Bob also piled up more assists—passes that lead to goals—than any other player in the game. Beginning in 1951 he made the Celtics the best gate attraction in the league, and was one of the highest salaried stars in the NBA. His point-scored total was the fourth highest among all players when he retired.

Cousy, who is 6 feet 1 inch tall, was born August 9, 1928. He was twice voted the league's Most Valuable Player and was an all-pro selection for eleven seasons.

Bob retired after the Celtics won the 1962–63 championship and became head coach at Boston College the next year. In 1969 he returned to the pro ranks as coach of the Cincinnati Royals.

HANK LUISETTI

In the 1930's the game of basketball had a uniform offense —the deliberate pass and the two-hand set shot. There were some teams that used the fast break and the one-hand shot while on the run, but they were too few and not too successful. Most of the teams adopted the "New York style"—ball control and a two-hand set when within reasonable shooting distance.

Long Island University had a great team in this period. It stressed possession play and the "good" shot, and this type of offense was sound enough to beat all its opponents. But on the West Coast a Stanford University team was whipping everyone with a breakneck type of attack and a player who could shoot with one hand while running at full speed. He was Angelo (Hank) Luisetti, a 6-foot-2-inch wizard who could score from just about any point on the floor.

Stanford came East to play LIU, and now the test of Western style versus Eastern style was about to be settled. LIU was not expected to have too much trouble. Surely its fine players would have control of the ball during most of the game, thus permitting Stanford and Luisetti only a minimum number of shots.

The game was played on December 30, 1936, at New York's Madison Square Garden. After eleven minutes of even play, Luisetti started to outrace, outpass, and outshoot every LIU opponent assigned to him. His speed, his rapid method of dribbling, and his one-hand passes and shots while on the run ripped LIU to shreds. Stanford went on to a 45–31 victory, pinning LIU with its first loss in three years. New York had never seen anything like it. This black-haired dynamo with the number 7 on his jersey was unstoppable.

Many colleges soon abandoned their former offensive style and began to concentrate on teaching their players the lessons Luisetti and his Stanford mates had taught LIU. Although not a high scorer by today's standards, Luisetti, in this one contest, revolutionized the style of the game.

Hank was an All-American for four years and was twice named Player of the Year. He won more honors than any other collegian until Oscar Robertson came along, more than twenty years later.

GEORGE MIKAN

The best player in the first fifty years of the 20th century? That would be George Mikan, who was voted this high honor by the nation's sports writers.

Mikan, a 6-foot-9-inch, 240-pound, weak-eyed giant of a man, was one of the strongest of all pivot players. He used his height and weight to set single game, season, and lifetime scoring records (which have since been bettered).

Mikan, who played his college ball at De Paul University in Chicago, was the pro game's first major star in modern times. He was an All-American for three years at De Paul, and in two of these seasons was named Player of the Year. He has since been placed on the all-time All-American team, the first of the modern era to be so honored.

George, born July 18, 1924, came into the pro ranks with the Chicago team of the National League. He went into the NBA with the Minneapolis Lakers in 1948. In seven seasons, George led the Lakers to six championships and became the game's first performer to score more than 10,000 points. For six straight seasons he averaged better than 20 points a game, going as high as 28.4 in the 1950–51 season.

Mikan, a full-time lawyer and all-pro center during his playing career, helped the NBA attain major status. His presence on the court brought out fans in every city in the league, and he was the NBA's top money-maker and its highest salaried star at the time.

George Mikan
Minneapolis Lakers

Bob Pettit

BOB PETTIT

Ask the pro players and coaches to select one of the best who ever played in the NBA and there's little doubt that the biggest Hawk of them all, St. Louis' Bob Pettit, would win a large share of the votes.

Petitt, the 6-foot-9-inch sharpshooter who was an All-American at Louisiana State, had been an all-pro selection for the first team in ten of his eleven years in the league before he retired after the 1964–65 season. He was named to the second team in his last year as a competitor.

Bob was regarded as the league's best scorer from the pivot position. He was about the strongest man to guard, and was often two-teamed in the closing stages of a game.

Pettit murdered the opposition from beneath the boards. On offense he was difficult to control, and was especially good at tapping in rebounds. On defense, only Boston's Bill Russell was tougher at grabbing rebounds. Bob could also shoot while moving away from the basket. He had an almost unstoppable hook shot, one which started with his back to the basket while his opponent waited for him to turn around and jump shoot.

Bob averaged better than 25 points a game in seven of his years as a pro. At the close of his career he was the all-time point-maker with 20,880 and an over-all career average of 26.4 points per game. Wilt Chamberlain passed Pettit's total the next season—1965–66.

OSCAR ROBERTSON

It has been said that there is no standard with which to judge the greatness of a basketball player. But, until Lew Alcindor came along, there was no doubt about selecting Oscar Robertson as the greatest college performer of all time.

The "Big O" played for the University of Cincinnati from

162

Oscar Robertson

University of Cincinnati

1958 to 1960. During his three years on the varsity he re-wrote all the record books. He was an All-American for three seasons. He was voted the college Player of the Year for three seasons. He scored more points than any other college player in history.

Why was the Big O the wonder college star? Simply because he did just about everything better than any other player of his period. Not a skyscraper, Oscar used every inch of his 6 feet 4 and every ounce of his 200 pounds to deceive and out-maneuver his opposition.

He had "savvy"—a knowledge that told him exactly what to do at any time on the court. He had amazing control of his body while it was in the air, could turn and twist it in any direction while off the floor. Oscar also was smart enough to realize that he couldn't be the high scorer in every game.

After nine seasons as a pro, Robertson had risen to fourth place among the all-time high scorers with a total of 20,261, and his per game average of 29.7 points was second only to that of Wilt Chamberlain. He also had been named to the all-pro team in each of his nine seasons.

Every outstanding player needs confidence in his ability. Oscar has it in great quantities. It is his opinion that he can always come through with the key play—pass, shot, or defensive maneuver. And he rarely fails.

Robertson was born November 26, 1938. He was a star at Crispus Attucks High School, in Indianapolis, Indiana, before entering college.

BILL RUSSELL

Today's emphasis is on the scorers and the shooters. But Bill Russell was a fellow who made the fans wonder if perhaps the defense wasn't finally catching up with the offense.

A former U. S. Olympic cage star, Bill played at San Francisco University, where he led his team to two national titles. His amazing leg spring and extra long arm reach made him about the toughest of all defenders.

It was only natural that he would carry that style of play into pro basketball with the Boston Celtics. But defense was only part of the Bill Russell story.

He called it a career in 1969 in fifteenth place on the all-time scoring list (14,522 points for an average of 15.1) and with the distinction of having made every all-star team except the one in his rookie year. He was voted Most Valuable Player in 1961, 1962, 1963, and 1965.

Bill Russell

Boston Celtics

The lean 6-foot-10-inch Russell had an uncanny ability to leap and block a shot at the last moment, and his speed and spring also made him a dangerous threat on the offense. His method of "stuffing" the ball in the basket—jumping just above the hoop and shoving the ball downward—was one of the most colorful of all NBA offensive tactics.

Russell, who was born February 12, 1934, was especially clever at converting passes from teammate Bob Cousy into key goals. Cousy would start the play by tossing a pass high in the air toward Russell's area. Just as the ball started its downward arc, Russell would leap and tip, aiming the ball toward the hoop with his long, strong fingers.

At the close of the 1965–66 season Bill was named coach of the Celtics when Red Auerbach decided to devote all of his time to being general manager and president of the team. Bill became the first Negro coach in the history of the National Basketball Association. He led the Celtics to titles in 1968 and 1969 and then retired.

ADOLPH SCHAYES

Until his retirement at the end of the 1963–64 season after sixteen years as an active player, nobody could argue about Dolph Schayes' being nominated as the most consistent of all players in the professional ranks.

The 6-foot-8-inch, 220-pound hustler seemed never to have a bad night, and his durability and desire were unlimited. He was barely out of his teens when he started his brilliant career playing for New York University. As a professional with the Syracuse Nationals, he scored 19,249 points in 1,059 games for an average of 18.2 per game. In that span he also collared 11,256 rebounds.

Dolph had an amazing assortment of shots. When he was hot, those old-fashioned two-handed set shots rarely missed. His long set shot was a thing of beauty. From near midcourt or the corners, he'd let go with a long, high arch, and the ball would sink through the basket, barely brushing the net.

Schayes was an unstoppable driver. He worked from the pivot, and using his weight and quick speed to good advantage, drove on his man and the basket. Those drives enabled him to draw a great number of fouls, and his accuracy from the free-throw line was matched only by Boston's Bill Sharman.

Dolph was named to the all-pro six times, and as of 1969 he ranked fifth in all-time scoring.

Adolph Schayes

Leslie H. Swenson

All-Time Records

COLLEGE SCORING CHAMPIONS

Year		Team	Games	Points	Avg.
1969	Maravich, Pete	Louisiana State	26	1,148	44.2
1968	Maravich, Pete	Louisiana State	26	1,138	43.8
1967	Walker, Jim	Providence	28	851	30.4
1966	Schellhase, Dave	Purdue	24	781	32.5
1965	Barry, Rick	Miami (Fla.)	26	973	37.4
1964	Komives, Harold	Bowling Green (O.)	23	844	36.7
1963	Werkman, Nick	Seton Hall	22	650	29.5
1962	McGill, Billy	Utah	26	1,009	38.8
1961	Burgess, Frank	Gonzaga	26	842	32.4
1960	Robertson, Oscar	Cincinnati	30	1,011	33.7
1959	Robertson, Oscar	Cincinnati	30	978	32.6
1958	Robertson, Oscar	Cincinnati	28	984	35.1
1957	Wallace, Grady	South Carolina	29	906	31.2
1956	Floyd, Darrell	Furman	28	946	33.8
1955	Floyd, Darrell	Furman	25	897	35.9
1954	Selvy, Frank	Furman	29	1,209	41.7
1953	Selvy, Frank	Furman	25	738	29.5
1952	Lovellette, Clyde	Kansas	28	795	28.4
1951	Mlkvy, Bill	Temple	25	731	29.2
1950	Arizin, Paul	Villanova	28	714	25.5
1949	Lavelli, Tony	Yale	30	671	22.4
1948	Haskins, Hal	Lawrence Tech.	28	630	22.5
1947	Lacy, Bob	Loyola (Balt.)	31	645	20.8
1946	Mikan, George	De Paul	21	485	23.1
1945	Mikan, George	De Paul	19	454	23.9
1944	Calverley, Ernie	Rhode Island	20	534	26.7
1943	Senesky, George	St. Joseph's (Phila.)	20	466	23.3

168

Tournament Champions

NATIONAL INVITATION

Year	Winner	Year	Winner
1970	Marquette	1953	Seton Hall
1969	Temple	1952	La Salle
1968	Dayton	1951	Brigham Young
1967	Southern Illinois	1950	CCNY
1966	Brigham Young	1949	San Francisco
1965	St. John's (N.Y.)	1948	St. Louis
1964	Bradley	1947	Utah
1963	Providence	1946	Kentucky
1962	Dayton	1945	De Paul
1961	Providence	1944	St. John's (N.Y.)
1960	Bradley	1943	St. John's (N.Y.)
1959	St. John's (N.Y.)	1942	West Virginia
1958	Xavier	1941	Long Island U.
1957	Bradley	1940	Colorado
1956	Louisville	1939	Long Island U.
1955	Duquesne	1938	Temple
1954	Holy Cross		

NATIONAL COLLEGIATE

Year	Winner	Year	Winner
1970	UCLA	1954	La Salle
1969	UCLA	1953	Indiana
1968	UCLA	1952	Kansas
1967	UCLA	1951	Kentucky
1966	Texas Western	1950	CCNY
1965	UCLA	1949	Kentucky
1964	UCLA	1948	Kentucky
1963	Loyola (Chicago)	1947	Holy Cross
1962	Cincinnati	1946	Oklahoma A&M
1961	Cincinnati	1945	Oklahoma A&M
1960	Ohio State	1944	Utah
1959	California	1943	Wyoming
1958	Kentucky	1942	Stanford
1957	North Carolina	1941	Wisconsin
1956	San Francisco	1940	Indiana
1955	San Francisco	1939	Oregon

169

Conference Champions

EASTERN INTERCOLLEGIATE

Year		Won	Lost	Pct.	Year		Won	Lost	Pct.
1970	Pennsylvania	14	0	1.000	1934	Pennsylvania	10	2	.833
1969	Princeton	14	0	1.000	1933	Yale	8	2	.800
1968	Columbia°	12	2	.857	1932	Princeton°	9	2	.818
1967	Princeton	13	1	.929	1931	Columbia	10	0	1.000
1966	Pennsylvania	12	2	.857	1930	Columbia	9	1	.900
1965	Princeton	13	1	.929	1929	Pennsylvania	8	2	.800
1964	Princeton	12	2	.857	1928	Pennsylvania°	8	3	.727
1963	Princeton	12	3	.800	1927	Dartmouth°	8	3	.727
1962	Yale	13	1	.929	1926	Columbia	9	1	.900
1961	Princeton	11	3	.786	1925	Princeton	9	1	.900
1960	Princeton	11	3	.786	1924	Cornell	8	2	.800
1959	Dartmouth	13	1	.929	1923	Yale	7	3	.700
1958	Dartmouth	11	3	.786	1922	Princeton°	9	2	.818
1957	Yale	12	2	.857	1921	Pennsylvania	9	1	.900
1956	Dartmouth	10	4	.714	1920	Pennsylvania	10	0	1.000
1955	Princeton°	11	4	.733	1919	No competition			
1954	Cornell°	12	3	.800	1918	Pennsylvania	9	1	.900
1953	Pennsylvania	10	2	.833	1917	Yale	9	1	.900
1952	Princeton	10	2	.833	1916	Pennsylvania°	9	2	.818
1951	Columbia	12	0	1.000	1915	Yale	8	2	.800
1950	Princeton	11	1	.917	1914	Cornell/			
1949	Yale	9	3	.750		Columbia	8	2	.800
1948	Columbia	11	1	.917	1913	Cornell	7	1	.875
1947	Columbia	11	1	.917	1912	Columbia	8	2	.800
1946	Dartmouth	7	1	.875	1911	Columbia	7	1	.875
1945	Pennsylvania	5	1	.833	1910	No competition			
1944	Dartmouth	8	0	1.000	1909	No competition			
1943	Dartmouth	11	1	.917	1908	Pennsylvania	8	0	1.000
1942	Dartmouth°	11	2	.846	1907	Yale	9	1	.900
1941	Dartmouth	10	2	.833	1906	Pennsylvania	9	1	.900
1940	Dartmouth	11	1	.917	1905	Columbia	8	0	1.000
1939	Dartmouth	10	2	.833	1904	Columbia	10	0	1.000
1938	Dartmouth	8	4	.667	1903	Yale	7	3	.700
1937	Pennsylvania	12	0	1.000	1902	Yale	5	3	.675
1936	Columbia	12	0	1.000					
1935	Pennsylvania°	11	2	.846	° Won playoff.				

170

WESTERN (BIG TEN)

Year		Won	Lost	Pct.	Year		Won	Lost	Pct.
1970	Iowa	14	0	1.000	1937	Ill./Minn.	10	2	.833
1969	Purdue	13	1	.929	1936	Ind./Purdue	11	1	.917
1968	Ohio State/				1935	Ill./Wis./			
	Iowa	10	4	.714		Purdue	9	3	.750
1967	Ind./Mich.				1934	Purdue	10	2	.833
	State	10	4	.714	1933	Ohio State/			
1966	Michigan	11	3	.786		Northwestern	10	2	.833
1965	Michigan	13	1	.929	1932	Purdue	11	1	.917
1964	Michigan/				1931	Northwestern	11	1	.917
	Ohio State	11	3	.786	1930	Purdue	10	0	1.000
1963	Illinois/				1929	Mich./Wis.	10	2	.833
	Ohio State	11	3	.786	1928	Ind./Purdue	10	2	.833
1962	Ohio State	13	1	.929	1927	Michigan	10	2	.833
1961	Ohio State	14	0	1.000	1926	Ind./Ia./			
1960	Ohio State	13	1	.929		Mich./Purdue	8	4	.667
1959	Michigan State	12	2	.857	1925	Ohio State	11	1	.917
1958	Indiana	10	4	.714	1924	Wis./Ill./Chi.	8	4	.667
1957	Ind./Mich. St.	10	4	.714	1923	Iowa/Wis.	11	1	.917
1956	Iowa	13	1	.929	1922	Purdue	8	1	.888
1955	Iowa	11	3	.786	1921	Mich./Wis./			
1954	Indiana	12	2	.857		Purdue	8	4	.667
1953	Indiana	17	1	.944	1920	Chicago	11	2	.846
1952	Illinois	12	2	.857	1919	Minnesota	10	2	.833
1951	Illinois	13	1	.929	1918	Wisconsin	9	3	.750
1950	Ohio State	11	1	.917	1917	Ill./Minn.	10	2	.833
1949	Illinois	10	2	.833	1916	Wisconsin	11	0	1.000
1948	Michigan	10	2	.833	1915	Illinois	12	0	1.000
1947	Wisconsin	9	3	.750	1914	Wisconsin	12	0	1.000
1946	Ohio State	10	2	.833	1913	Wisconsin	12	0	1.000
1945	Iowa	11	1	.917	1912	Wis./Purdue	12	0	1.000
1944	Ohio State	10	2	.833	1911	Purdue/Minn.	8	4	.667
1943	Illinois	12	0	1.000	1910	Chicago	9	3	.750
1942	Illinois	13	2	.867	1909	Chicago	12	0	1.000
1941	Wisconsin	11	1	.917	1908	Chicago	8	1	.888
1940	Purdue	10	2	.833	1907	Chi./Wis./			
1939	Ohio State	10	2	.833		Minn.	6	2	.750
1938	Purdue	10	2	.833	1906	Minnesota	7	1	.875

SOUTHEASTERN

Champion	Year	Runner-up
Kentucky	1970	LSU
Kentucky	1969	Tennessee
Kentucky	1968	Tennessee
Tennessee	1967	Florida

171

Champion	Year	Runner-up
Kentucky	1966	Vanderbilt
Vanderbilt	1965	Tennessee
Kentucky	1964	Georgia Tech/Tennessee
Mississippi State	1963	Georgia Tech
Miss. State/Kentucky	1962	Auburn
Mississippi State	1961	Vanderbilt
Auburn	1960	Georgia Tech
Mississippi State	1959	Auburn
Kentucky	1958	Auburn
Kentucky	1957	Vanderbilt
Alabama	1956	Kentucky
Kentucky	1955	Alabama
Kentucky	1954	LSU
LSU	1953	Tulane
Kentucky	1952	LSU/Vanderbilt/Alabama
Kentucky	1951	Vanderbilt/Alabama
Kentucky	1950	Tennessee
Kentucky	1949	Tulane
Kentucky	1948	Georgia Tech
Kentucky	1947	Tulane
Kentucky	1946	LSU
Kentucky	1945	Tennessee
Kentucky	1944	Tulane
Tennessee	1943	Kentucky
Kentucky	1942	Alabama
Tennessee	1941	Kentucky
Kentucky	1940	Georgia
Kentucky	1939	Tennessee
Georgia Tech	1938	Mississippi
Kentucky	1937	Tennessee
Tennessee	1936	Alabama
LSU	1935	Kentucky
Alabama	1934	Florida
Kentucky	1933	Mississippi

BIG EIGHT

Year		Won	Lost	Pct.	Year		Won	Lost	Pct.
1970	Kansas State	10	4	.714	1964	Kansas State	12	2	.857
1969	Colorado	10	4	.714	1963	Colorado/			
1968	Kansas State	11	3	.786		Kansas State	11	3	.786
1967	Kansas	13	1	.929	1962	Colorado	13	1	.929
1966	Kansas	13	1	.929	1961	Kansas State	12	2	.857
1965	Oklahoma St.	12	2	.857	1960	Kansas*	11	4	.733
* Won playoff.					1959	Kansas State	14	0	1.000

172

Year		Won	Lost	Pct.	Year		Won	Lost	Pct.
1958	Kansas State	10	2	.833	1943	Kansas	10	0	1.000
1957	Kansas	11	1	.917	1942	Kan./Okla.	8	2	.800
1956	Kansas State	9	3	.750	1941	Kan./Ia. St.	7	3	.700
1955	Colorado	11	1	.917	1940	Kan./Okla./			
1954	Kan./Colo.	10	2	.833		Mo.	8	2	.800
1953	Kansas	10	2	.833	1939	Mo./Okla.	7	3	.700
1952	Kansas	11	1	.917	1938	Kansas	9	1	.900
1951	Kansas State	11	1	.917	1937	Kan./Nebr.	8	2	.800
1950	Kan./Nebr./				1936	Kansas	10	0	1.000
	Kan. St.	8	4	.667	1935	Iowa State	8	2	.800
1949	Okla./Nebr.	9	3	.750	1934	Kansas	9	1	.900
1948	Kansas State	9	3	.750	1933	Kansas	8	2	.800
1947	Oklahoma	8	2	.800	1932	Kansas	7	3	.700
1946	Kansas	10	0	1.000	1931	Kansas	7	3	.700
1945	Iowa State	8	2	.800	1930	Missouri	8	2	.800
1944	Iowa St./Okla.	9	1	.900	1929	Oklahoma	10	0	1.000

MISSOURI VALLEY

Year		Won	Lost	Pct.	Year		Won	Lost	Pct.
1970	Drake	14	2	.875	1944	Okla. A&M†	—	—	—
1969	Drake°	13	3	.813	1943	Creighton	10	0	1.000
1968	Louisville	14	2	.875	1942	Creighton/			
1967	Louisville	12	2	.857		Okla. A&M	9	1	.900
1966	Cincinnati	10	4	.714	1941	Creighton	9	3	.750
1965	Wichita	11	3	.786	1940	Okla. A&M	12	0	1.000
1964	Wichita°	11	2	.846	1939	Okla. A&M/			
1963	Cincinnati	11	1	.917		Drake	11	3	.786
1962	Cincinnati°	11	2	.846	1938	Okla. A&M	13	1	.929
1961	Cincinnati	10	2	.833	1937	Okla. A&M	11	1	.917
1960	Cincinnati	13	1	.929	1936	Drake/			
1959	Cincinnati	13	1	.929		Okla. A&M/			
1958	Cincinnati	13	1	.929		Creighton	8	4	.667
1957	St. Louis	12	2	.857	1935	Drake/			
1956	Houston	9	3	.750		Creighton	8	4	.667
1955	Tulsa/St. Louis	8	2	.800	1934	Butler	9	1	.900
1954	Okla. A&M	9	1	.900	1933	Butler	9	1	.900
1953	Okla. A&M	8	2	.800	1932	Creighton	8	0	1.000
1952	St. Louis	9	1	.900	1931	Creighton/			
1951	Okla. A&M	12	2	.857		Wash./			
1950	Bradley	11	1	.917		Okla. A&M	5	3	.600
1949	Okla. A&M	9	1	.900	1930	Wash./			
1948	Okla. A&M	10	0	1.000		Creighton	6	2	.750
1947	St. Louis	11	1	.917	° Won playoff.				
1946	Okla. A&M	12	0	1.000	† No conference competition held;				
1945	Okla. A&M†	—	—	—	Oklahoma A&M voted title.				

Year		Won	Lost	Pct.	Year		Won	Lost	Pct.
1929	Washington	7	0	1.000	1918	Missouri	15	1	.937
1928	Oklahoma	18	0	1.000	1917	Kansas State	10	2	.833
1927	Kansas	10	2	.833	1916	Nebraska	8	0	1.000
1926	Kansas	16	2	.889	1915	Kansas	13	1	.929
1925	Kansas	15	1	.937	1914	Kansas	13	1	.929
1924	Kansas	15	1	.937	1913	Nebraska	10	5	.667
1923	Kansas	16	0	1.000	1912	Kan./Nebr.	10	2	.833
1922	Mo./Kan.	15	1	.937	1911	Kansas	10	2	.833
1921	Missouri	17	1	.944	1910	Kansas	13	1	.929
1920	Missouri	17	1	.944	1909	Kansas	10	2	.833
1919	Kansas State	10	0	1.000	1908	Kansas	7	2	.778

SOUTHWEST

Year		Won	Lost	Pct.	Year		Won	Lost	Pct.
1970	Rice	10	4	.714	1943	Texas/Rice	9	3	.750
1969	Texas A&M	12	2	.857	1942	Rice/Arkansas	10	2	.833
1968	Texas Christian	9	5	.643	1941	Arkansas	12	0	1.000
1967	SMU	12	2	.857	1940	Rice	10	2	.833
1966	SMU	11	3	.786	1939	Texas	10	2	.833
1965	Texas Tech*	12	2	.857	1938	Arkansas	11	1	.917
1964	Texas A&M	13	1	.929	1937	SMU	10	2	.833
1963	Texas	13	1	.929	1936	Arkansas	11	1	.917
1962	Texas Tech/ SMU	11	3	.786	1935	SMU/Rice/ Arkansas	9	3	.750
1961	Texas Tech	11	3	.786	1934	Texas Christian	10	2	.833
1960	Texas	11	3	.786	1933	Texas	11	1	.917
1959	Texas Christian	12	2	.857	1932	Baylor	10	2	.833
1958	Arkansas/ SMU	9	5	.643	1931	Texas Christian	9	3	.750
1957	SMU	11	1	.917	1930	Arkansas	10	2	.833
1956	SMU	12	0	1.000	1929	Arkansas	11	1	.917
1955	SMU	9	3	.750	1928	Arkansas	12	0	1.000
1954	Rice/Texas	9	3	.750	1927	Arkansas	8	2	.800
1953	Texas Christian	9	3	.750	1926	Arkansas	11	1	.917
1952	Texas Christian	11	1	.917	1925	Okla. A&M	12	2	.857
1951	Texas A&M/ Texas/TCU	8	4	.667	1924	Texas	20	0	1.000
					1923	Texas A&M	15	3	.833
1950	Arkansas/ Baylor	8	4	.667	1922	Texas A&M	13	3	.812
					1921	Texas A&M	10	2	.833
1949	Rice/Baylor/ Arkansas	9	3	.750	1920	Texas A&M	16	0	1.000
					1919	Texas	11	2	.846
1948	Baylor	11	1	.917	1918	Rice	7	3	.700
1947	Texas	12	0	1.000	1917	Texas	7	1	.875
1946	Baylor	11	1	.917	1916	Texas	6	0	1.000
1945	Rice	12	0	1.000	1915	Texas	5	0	1.000
1944	Arkansas/Rice	11	1	.917					

* Forfeited championship for having ineligible player.

PACIFIC EIGHT

Year		Won	Lost	Pct.	Year		Won	Lost	Pct.
1970	UCLA	12	2	.857	1942	Stanford	13	2	.867
1969	UCLA	13	1	.929	1941	Wash. State	15	3	.833
1968	UCLA	14	0	1.000	1940	So. California	12	2	.857
1967	UCLA	14	0	1.000	1939	Oregon	16	2	.889
1966	Oregon State	12	2	.857	1938	Stanford	12	2	.857
1965	UCLA	14	0	1.000	1937	Stanford	12	2	.857
1964	UCLA	13	0	1.000	1936	Stanford	11	4	.733
1963	UCLA†	8	5	.615	1935	So. California	13	2	.867
1961	So. California	11	3	.786	1934	Washington	16	3	.842
1960	California	11	1	.917	1933	Oregon State	14	5	.737
1959	California	14	2	.875	1932	California	11	3	.786
1958	California	13	4	.765	1931	Washington	16	3	.842
1957	California	14	2	.875	1930	So. California	9	3	.750
1956	UCLA	16	0	1.000	1929	California	11	0	1.000
1955	Oregon State	17	1	.944	1928	So. California	8	3	.727
1954	So. California	10	5	.667	1927	California	7	0	1.000
1953	Washington	17	1	.944	1926	California	7	0	1.000
1952	UCLA	10	4	.714	1925	California	5	2	.734
1951	Washington	13	5	.722	1924	California	7	3	.700
1950	UCLA	12	2	.857	1923	Idaho	8	3	.727
1949	Oregon State	14	5	.737	1922	Idaho	7	0	1.000
1948	Washington	13	7	.650	1921	Calif./Stanford	8	3	.727
1947	Oregon State	15	3	.833	1920	Stanford	9	1	.900
1946	California	13	2	.867	1919	Oregon	10	4	.714
1945	Oregon°	13	6	.684	1918	No competition			
	UCLA°	4	2	.667	1917	Wash. State	8	1	.889
1944	California°	4	0	1.000	1916	Calif./			
	Washington°	15	1	.937		Ore. State	5	3	.625
1943	Washington°	14	4	.777					

° No inter-division playoff held; division winners named co-champions.
† Won playoff.

175

Professional Records

DIVISION CHAMPIONS

Eastern Division				Western Division		
Team	Won	Lost	Season	Team	Won	Lost
New York	60	22	1969–70	Atlanta	48	34
Baltimore	57	25	1968–69	Los Angeles	56	27
Philadelphia	62	20	1967–68	St. Louis	55	26
Philadelphia	68	13	1966–67	San Francisco	44	37
Philadelphia	55	25	1965–66	Los Angeles	45	35
Boston	62	18	1964–65	Los Angeles	49	31
Boston	59	21	1963–64	San Francisco	48	32
Boston	58	22	1962–63	Los Angeles	53	27
Boston	60	20	1961–62	Los Angeles	54	26
Boston	57	22	1960–61	St. Louis	51	28
Boston	59	16	1959–60	St. Louis	46	29
Boston	52	20	1958–59	St. Louis	49	23
Boston	49	23	1957–58	St. Louis	41	31
Boston	44	28	1956–57	°St. Louis	34	38
Philadelphia	45	27	1955–56	Fort Wayne	37	35
Syracuse	43	29	1954–55	Fort Wayne	43	29
New York	72	28	1953–54	Minneapolis	46	26
New York	47	23	1952–53	Minneapolis	48	22
Syracuse	40	26	1951–52	Rochester	41	25
Philadelphia	40	26	1950–51	Minneapolis	44	24
Syracuse	51	13	1949–50°°	Indianapolis	39	25
Washington	38	22	1948–49	Rochester	45	15
Philadelphia	27	21	1947–48	St. Louis	29	19
Washington	49	11	1946–47	Chicago	39	22

° St. Louis beat Minneapolis and Fort Wayne in special playoff games.
°° During this year there were three professional divisions—Central being the third division with Minneapolis winning 51 games and losing 17.

PLAYOFF CHAMPIONS

Winner	Year	Runner-up
Boston (4)	1969	Los Angeles (3)
Boston (4)	1968	Los Angeles (2)
Philadelphia (4)	1967	San Francisco (2)
Boston (4)	1966	Los Angeles (3)
Los Angeles (4)	1965	Boston (1)
San Francisco (4)	1964	Boston (1)
Boston (4)	1963	Los Angeles (2)
Boston (4)	1962	Los Angeles (3)
Boston (4)	1961	St. Louis (1)
Boston (4)	1960	St. Louis (3)
Boston (4)	1959	Minneapolis (0)
St. Louis (4)	1958	Boston (2)
Boston (4)	1957	St. Louis (3)
Philadelphia (4)	1956	Fort Wayne (1)
Syracuse (4)	1955	Fort Wayne (3)
Minneapolis (4)	1954	Syracuse (3)
Minneapolis (4)	1953	New York (1)
Minneapolis (4)	1952	New York (3)
Rochester (4)	1951	New York (3)
Minneapolis (4)	1950	Syracuse (2)

(Note: Numbers in parentheses indicate games won in best-of-seven series.)

LEADING SCORERS

Players	Team	Games	Goals	Fouls	Pts.	Avg.
1968-69						
Hayes, Elvin	San Diego	82	930	467	2,327	28.4
Monroe, Earl	Baltimore	80	809	447	2,065	25.8
1967-68						
Bing, Dave	Detroit	79	835	472	2,142	27.1
Baylor, Elgin	Los Angeles	77	757	488	2,002	26.0
1966-67						
Barry, Rick	San Francisco	78	1,011	753	2,775	35.6
Robertson, Oscar	Cincinnati	79	838	736	2,412	30.5
1965–66						
Chamberlain, Wilt	Philadelphia	79	1,074	501	2,649	33.5
West, Jerry	Los Angeles	79	818	840	2,476	31.4
1964–65						
Chamberlain, Wilt	San Francisco	73	1,063	408	2,534	34.7
West, Jerry	Los Angeles	74	822	648	2,292	31.0

Players	Team	Games	Goals	Fouls	Pts.	Avg.
1963–64						
Chamberlain, Wilt	San Francisco	80	1,204	540	2,948	36.9
Robertson, Oscar	Cincinnati	79	840	800	2,480	31.4
1962–63						
Chamberlain, Wilt	San Francisco	80	1,463	660	3,586	44.8
Baylor, Elgin	Los Angeles	80	1,029	661	2,719	34.0
1961–62						
Chamberlain, Wilt	Philadelphia	80	1,597	835	4,029	50.4
Bellamy, Walt	Chicago	79	973	549	2,495	31.6
1960–61						
Chamberlain, Wilt	Philadelphia	79	1,251	531	3,033	38.4
Baylor, Elgin	Los Angeles	73	931	676	2,538	34.8
1959–60						
Chamberlain, Wilt	Philadelphia	72	1,065	577	2,707	37.6
Twyman, Jack	Cincinnati	75	870	598	2,338	32.2
1958–59						
Pettit, Bob	St. Louis	72	719	667	2,105	29.2
Twyman, Jack	Cincinnati	72	710	437	1,857	25.8
1957–58						
Yardley, George	Detroit	72	673	655	2,001	27.8
Schayes, Dolph	Syracuse	72	581	629	1,791	24.9
1956–57						
Arizin, Paul	Philadelphia	71	613	591	1,817	25.6
Pettit, Bob	St. Louis	71	613	529	1,755	24.7
1955–56						
Pettit, Bob	St. Louis	72	646	557	1,849	25.7
Arizin, Paul	Philadelphia	72	617	507	1,741	24.2
1954–55						
Johnston, Neil	Philadelphia	72	521	589	1,631	22.7
Arizin, Paul	Philadelphia	72	529	454	1,512	21.0
1953–54						
Johnston, Neil	Philadelphia	72	591	577	1,759	24.4
Cousy, Bob	Boston	72	486	411	1,383	19.2
1952–53						
Johnston, Neil	Philadelphia	70	504	556	1,564	22.3
Mikan, George	Minneapolis	70	500	442	1,442	20.6
1951–52						
Arizin, Paul	Philadelphia	66	548	578	1,674	25.4
Mikan, George	Minneapolis	64	545	433	1,523	23.8
1950–51						
Mikan, George	Minneapolis	68	678	576	1,932	28.4
Groza, Alex	Indianapolis	66	492	445	1,429	21.7
1949–50						
Mikan, George	Minneapolis	68	649	567	1,865	27.4
Groza, Alex	Indianapolis	64	521	454	1,496	23.4

TOP TWENTY ALL-TIME SCORERS

(At Close of 1968–69 Season)

Years	Player	Team	Games	Goals	Fouls	Pts.	Avg.
10	Chamberlain, Wilt	Los Angeles	787	10,962	5,174	27,098	34.4
11	Baylor, Elgin	Los Angeles	781	8,132	5,461	21,725	27.8
11	Pettit, Bob	St. Louis	792	7,349	6,182	20,880	26.4
9	Robertson, Oscar	Cincinnati	683	7,066	6,129	20,261	29.7
16	Schayes, Dolph	Philadelphia	1,059	6,135	6,979	19,249	18.2
11	Greer, Hal	Philadelphia	842	6,728	3,684	17,140	20.4
13	Cousy, Bob	Boston	917	6,167	4,621	16,955	18.5
9	West, Jerry	Los Angeles	613	5,933	4,969	16,835	27.5
12	Arizin, Paul	Philadelphia	713	5,628	5,010	16,266	22.8
10	Howell, Bailey	Boston	787	5,792	4,275	15,859	20.2
11	Twyman, Jack	Cincinnati	823	6,237	3,366	15,840	19.2
12	Jones, Sam	Boston	872	6,258	2,864	15,380	17.6
8	Bellamy, Walt	Detroit	648	5,691	3,704	15,086	23.3
12	Guerin, Richie	Atlanta	830	5,171	4,327	14,669	17.7
13	Russell, Bill	Boston	963	5,687	3,148	14,522	15.1
10	Hagan, Cliff	St. Louis	746	5,239	2,969	13,447	18.0
11	Sharman, Bill	Boston	710	4,761	3,143	12,665	17.8
12	Kerr, John	Baltimore	995	4,909	2,662	12,480	13.8
9	Heinsohn, Tom	Boston	654	4,773	2,648	12,194	18.6
11	Lovellette, Clyde	Boston	704	4,784	2,379	11,947	17.0

MOST VALUABLE PLAYER AWARD

Season	Player	Team
1968–69	Unseld, Wes	Baltimore
1967–68	Chamberlain, Wilt	Philadelphia
1966–67	Chamberlain, Wilt	Philadelphia
1965–66	Chamberlain, Wilt	Philadelphia
1964–65	Russell, Bill	Boston
1963–64	Robertson, Oscar	Cincinnati
1962–63	Russell, Bill	Boston
1961–62	Russell, Bill	Boston
1960–61	Russell, Bill	Boston
1959–60	Chamberlain, Wilt	Philadelphia
1958–59	Pettit, Bob	St. Louis
1957–58	Russell, Bill	Boston
1956–57	Cousy, Bob	Boston
1955–56	Pettit, Bob	St. Louis

179

ALL-TIME RECORDS

Most Games Played	Dolph Schayes	1,059
Most Field Goals	Wilt Chamberlain	10,962
Best Field Goal Average	Wilt Chamberlain	.529
Most Foul Goals	Dolph Schayes	6,979
Best Foul Goal Average	Bill Sharman	.883
*Best Scoring Average	Wilt Chamberlain	34.4
Most Rebounds	Bill Russell	21,721
Most Assists	Oscar Robertson	7,173

*—Points per game, including field goals and foul goals.

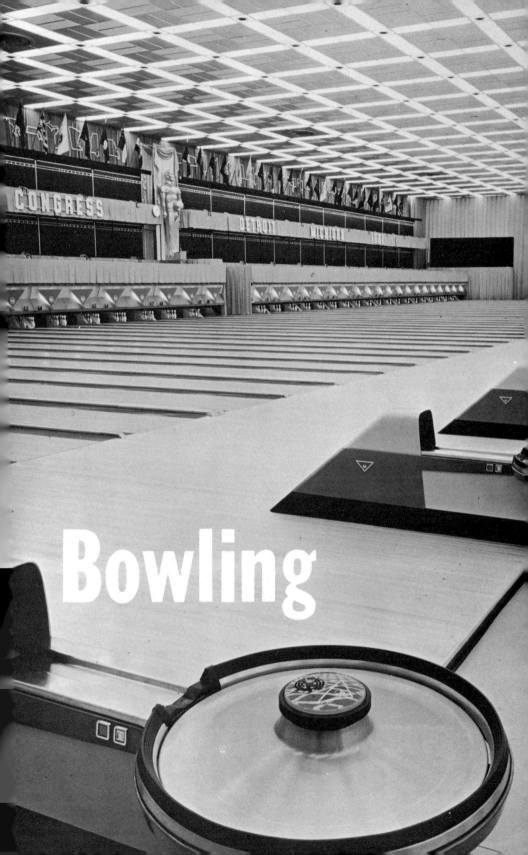

Bowling

The History of Bowling

Every schoolboy who has read Washington Irving's story of Rip Van Winkle is familiar with the author's reference to the "thunder" created by mountain folk rolling wooden balls against wooden pins.

If it was thunder back in those days—the early 1800's—one would be hard put to describe the din that echoes and reechoes across our land today as millions participate in the modern version of the game Washington Irving wrote about.

The game is, of course, bowling. Like so many of our popular games, this one had its origin in distant times and in distant lands. But nowhere has it boomed as in the United States, ranking only behind swimming and fishing as the greatest participant sport.

No other sport anywhere has had the phenomenal growth of bowling, with the greatest strides taking place since World War II. Through every season of the year men and women and youngsters of all ages can be found having healthy fun at the art of knocking down pins with bowling balls.

Their number defies accurate estimate. Some put it at

more than 30,000,000. Even if we limit ourselves to organized bowlers, the figures are quite amazing.

The American Bowling Congress, grandfather of all bowling organizations, has more than 4,500,000 members; the Woman's International Bowling Congress claims more than 2,000,000 and the American Junior Bowling Congress, serving youngsters ranging in age from eight to eighteen, has 480,000.

In the ABC tournament, the "world series" of bowling, winners have ranged from Pat Romano of Toledo, Ohio, who was fifteen years old when he rolled a three-game series of 702 in 1953, to E. D. (Sarge) Easter, who was sixty-seven when he helped his Detroit, Michigan, team win a prize in 1950.

Just about every town in the country has at least one league, and it is not uncommon to find bowling centers with sixty or more lanes, all of them going full blast, with whole families taking part. In 1968 the largest center in the country was at Willow Grove, Pennsylvania, with 116 alleys.

By 1968 bowling had taken on an international flavor. Through formation of the Fédération Internationale des Quilleurs (FIQ), American teams were sent to Mexico, Guatemala, Venezuela, Sweden, Canada and Puerto Rico. Europe was to be the next stop on a regular yearly basis with formation of teams in Warsaw, Romania and Rome.

Tournaments with huge prize lists attract participants by the thousands and spectators by the millions, if you include those who watch via television. In 1953, when it set records for prizes and contestants, the ABC tournament drew 8,180 five-man teams, 14,862 doubles combinations, and 29,817 singles participants shooting for prizes totaling $577,283. Compare this with the first ABC tournament in 1901, when 41 teams, 78 doubles, and 115 singles competed for $1,592.

184

Some of our top professional bowlers have been known to earn more than $100,000 a year through special matches and tournaments. To bowling devotees, these stars belong on the same pedestal with baseball and football greats.

The history of bowling can be traced back to the Egypt of seven thousand years ago, but its formal origin belongs to Germany and neighboring countries around A.D. 300, when the practice of rolling a large stone or ball at an array of pins was part of a religious ceremony.

England caught the craze in the 1300's. In fact, so many of the folk were so busy bowling at one point that the king had a law passed against it. He felt the people were neglecting their archery practice, and good archers were essential to defend the country against military attack.

Through the years various forms of bowling sprang up in European countries. The number of pins ranged from nine to fifteen, the balls differed in size and weight, and there was no uniform distance for the balls to be rolled. But the basic principle was always the same: knock down as many pins as possible with each roll of the ball.

The most popular game, especially among the Germans and the Dutch, was ninepins. First bowled on an alley bed of clay, the game later employed a single board, about a foot in width, the forerunner of the highly polished surface now in use.

The early Dutch settlers of New York brought the game of ninepins with them to America in the early 1700's. The most famous site of the contests was a patch of land at the lower end of Manhattan that is still known as Bowling Green.

As the contests grew more popular, so did the practice of betting on them, and gamblers soon captured control of the

185

sport. As a result, first Connecticut and then New York passed laws making ninepins illegal. But bowling lovers were not to be denied. By adding another pin, they stayed strictly within the law and had their game too. Thus, around 1845, the first form of tenpins was born.

Organizations to govern the sport were established in 1875 and 1890, but it was not until September 9, 1895, when the American Bowling Congress was created by a small group of dedicated bowling enthusiasts, that a durable organization came into being.

The ABC has since become the largest sports organization in the world. It not only set up uniform rules, but it also standardized all of the equipment. No matter where one may bowl today, he will find that the alley is the same size—60 feet long from the foul line to the center of the head pin, and between 41 and 42 inches wide. He will find, too, that the pins are of standard dimension and that the bowling ball cannot be more than 27 inches in circumference and must weigh between 10 and 16 pounds (most bowlers use a 16-pound ball).

By 1916 a sufficient number of women were participating in bowling to warrant the formation of the Woman's International Bowling Congress. Other groups that have contributed to the healthy growth of the game are the Bowling Proprietors' Association of America, founded in 1932; the American Junior Bowling Congress, established in 1935; and the National Bowling Council, active since 1943.

Although the popularity of bowling has been growing since the turn of the century, the game got a tremendous boost during the years of World War II. Factory workers seeking exercise and recreation found bowling a natural outlet. To bowl

186

58th annual American Bowling Congress.

does not require great skill or physical stamina (literally anyone can play), and it is relatively inexpensive.

Once introduced to the sport, these hundreds of thousands of wartime workers went at it with even greater fervor when the war ended, and brought their families and friends along. New bowling centers, offering a variety of comforts (baby sitters, soda fountains) and modern equipment (automatic pin-setting machines), sprang up all over the country, and thousands of new leagues were organized.

Today there are leagues for children as well as for men and women. High schools have taken up the game competitively, and tournaments are staged by a number of college organizations.

The "thunder" Washington Irving wrote about is now heard in bowling alleys throughout the land in the zoom and clatter of rolling balls and spilled pins.

Great Names in Bowling

It would be no exaggeration to say that bowling has produced more stars than any other sport, more participants who have performed feats of scoring that must be considered outstanding. As a result, even the most expert and veteran observers of the game find it difficult to agree on a list of all-time greats.

There is, however, almost unanimous agreement that two names belong on the list—Don Carter and Marion Ladewig.

Carter, who hails from St. Louis, Missouri, has been described as "the Babe Ruth of bowling." He has an unusual style in which he seems to push the ball on the alley with a crooked elbow. But, classic form or not, he has been a kingpin since 1951—against the strongest competition in the history of the game.

He is the only man to have won four All-Star tournament titles and the only man to have been voted Bowler of the Year six times. In the first six World's Invitational Match Game Championships (1957–1962), he was the winner five times and runner-up once.

Perhaps the greatest mark of his ability is that, in May 1956, under the pressure of competing before millions of viewers watching the live telecast, he won seven matches in a row.

Mrs. Ladewig, up to 1969, had been elected woman Bowler of the Year nine times. This stylish pin queen from Grand Rapids, Michigan, was the first winner of the women's match game crown, in 1957, repeated the victory in 1960, was runner-up in 1961, and took top laurels again in 1962. Match game bowling differs from tournament bowling. In match game play, a bowler meets one person at a time, the one with the best score moving on to another opponent. In tourney bowl-

Don Carter

ing, a man rolls anywhere from three to 16 games against any number of opponents and the highest score wins.

Other male stars who qualify for consideration as all-time greats include Jimmy Smith, who was a standout match game and exhibition performer for thirty years (1906–1936); Hank Marino, who bowled eleven sanctioned 300 games; Andy Varipapa, a two-time individual cham-

Marion Ladewig

pion; Ned Day, top man in the ABC tournament in 1940 and 1941 and one of the game's finest instructors; Junie McMahon, who ruled the pins in the late 1940's and early 1950's; Jimmy Blouin, who gave Jimmy Smith his toughest competition; Joe Falcaro, one of the sport's most colorful men; Joe Norris, who piled up a long list of accomplishments over twenty-five years, and Dick Weber, Bowler of the Year in 1961 and 1963 and All-Star champion of 1962.

Still others generally accorded all-time rank are Joe Wilman, who was at his best in the 1940's; George Young, who had the top average four times in the ABC tournament; Billy Knox; Steve Nagy; and Ed Lubanski, the only man between 1957 and 1961 to beat Don Carter for the match game championship.

Among the women who share honors with Mrs. Ladewig

190

are Mrs. Floretta McCutcheon, who was outstanding in the 1930's; Marie Warmbier, another star of a generation ago; Sylvia Wene, only woman to roll three perfect games in competition and twice elected Bowler of the Year, and four other national title winners, Marge Merrick, Phyllis Notaro, Shirley Garms and Laverne Carter.

On July 1, 1945, there were only six television stations operating in the United States, and as they grew in number so did bowling money prizes. With the growth came Dick Weber, and by 1968 he was the leading money winner in the United States with $363,235, surpassing Don Carter's $237,950.

Thus, Weber, in the late 1960's, was the hottest bowler in the U.S. The muscular competitor from Indianapolis compiled a 211.01 lifetime average; Carter had a 210.95 average. As the 1950's belonged to Don Carter, the 1960's belonged to Dick Weber. Other stars were Jim Stefanich, Dave Davis and Wayne Zahn.

As the 1960's drew to a close, more and more women became prominent in the game. While Marion Ladewig was the particular star of the 1950's, there were too many standout women bowlers in the '60's to single one out for an individual star role.

For example, there was the Queens Tournament champion of 1969, Ann Feigel of Tucson. Before her there were Mildred Martorella of Rochester, who won the title in 1968, and Irene Monterosso of New York City, another Queens Tournament winner. Other newcomers to make some important strides were Jane Leszczynski of Milwaukee, the American Indian from San Francisco, Neva Running Wolf, and '68 Bowler of the Year Dotty Fothergill.

191

Bowling Hall of Fame

The American Bowling Congress Hall of Fame was established in 1941. Selections are made by members of the Bowling Writers Association of America who have covered the game for at least ten years.

Member	Year Elected
°BAUMGARTEN, Elmer, Milwaukee, Wis.	1951
BENKOVIC, Frank, Milwaukee, Wis.	1958
BLOUIN, Jimmy, Blue Island, Ill.	1953
BODIS, Joe, Cleveland, Ohio	1941
BOMAR, Herbert (Buddy), Chicago, Ill.	1966
BRANDT, Allie, Lockport, N.Y.	1960
BUJACK, Fred, Sacramento, Calif.	1967
BUNETTA, William, Fresno, Calif.	1968
BURTON, Nelson, St. Louis, Mo.	1964
CAMPI, Louis, Dumont, N.J.	1968
CARLSON, Adolph, Chicago, Ill.	1941
CRIMMINS, Johnny, Milwaukee, Wis.	1962
DAW, Charley, Milwaukee, Wis.	1941
DAY, Ned, Milwaukee, Wis.	1952
EASTER, Ebber, Winston-Salem, N.C.	1963
FARAGALLI, Alfred, Wayne, N.J.	1968
FAZIO, Basil, Detroit, Mich.	1963
GERSONDE, Russell, Milwaukee, Wis.	1968
GIBSON, Therman, Detroit, Mich.	1965
°HOWLEY, Peter, Chicago, Ill.	1941
JOSEPH, Joe, Lansing, Mich.	1969
°°KARTHEISER, Frank, Chicago, Ill.	1967
KNOX, Bill, Philadelphia, Pa.	1954
KRISTOF, Joseph, Columbus, Ohio	1968
KRUMSKE, Paul, Chicago, Ill.	1968
LANGE, Herb, Watertown, Wis.	1941
LINDSEY, Mort, Stamford, Conn.	1941
MARINO, Hank, Milwaukee, Wis.	1941
MARTINO, John, Syracuse, N.Y.	1969
McMAHON, Junie, River Edge, N.J.	1955
MERCURIO, Walter (Skang), Cleveland, Ohio	1967
NAGY, Steve, Los Angeles, Calif.	1963
NORRIS, Joe, Chicago, Ill.	1954
O'DONNELL, Charles, St. Louis, Mo.	1968
SCHWOEGLER, Conrad, Madison, Wis.	1968
SIELAFF, Louis, Detroit, Mich.	1968
SIXTY, Billy, Milwaukee, Wis.	1961

Member	Year Elected
SMITH, Jimmy, Brooklyn, N.Y.	1957
SPINELLA, Barney, Los Angeles, Calif.	1968
STEERS, Harry, Phoenix, Ariz.	1941
VARIPAPA, Andy, Hempstead, N.Y.	1957
WARD, Walter, Cleveland, Ohio	1959
WHITNEY, Eli, Milwaukee, Wis.	1956
WILMAN, Joe, Chicago, Ill.	1951
WOLF, Phil, Chicago, Ill.	1941
YOUNG, George, Detroit, Mich.	1959
ZUNKER, Gil, Milwaukee, Wis.	1941

*For distinguished service.
**Veterans Commitee selection.

Bowler of the Year

The Bowler of the Year award is voted by members of the Bowling Writers Association of America.

	MEN	WOMEN
1969	Billy Hardwick, Louisville, Ky.	Dotty Fothergill, N. Attleboro, Mass.
1968	Jim Stefanich, Joliet, Ill.	Dotty Fothergill, N. Attleboro, Mass.
1967	Dave Davis, Phoenix, Ariz.	Mildred Martorella, Rochester, N.Y.
1966	Wayne Zahn, Atlanta, Ga.	Joy Abel, Chicago
1965	Dick Weber, St. Louis	Betty Kuczynski, Chicago
1964	Billy Hardwick, San Mateo, Calif.	Laverne Carter, St. Louis
1963	Dick Weber, St. Louis	Laverne Carter, St. Louis
1962	Don Carter, St. Louis	Shirley Garms, Palatine, Ill.
1961	Dick Weber, St. Louis	Shirley Garms, Palatine, Ill.
1960	Don Carter, St. Louis	Sylvia Wene, Philadelphia
1959	Ed Lubanski, Detroit	Marion Ladewig, Grand Rapids
1958	Don Carter, St. Louis	Marion Ladewig, Grand Rapids
1957	Don Carter, St. Louis	Marion Ladewig, Grand Rapids
1956	Bill Lillard, Chicago	Marion Ladewig, Grand Rapids
1955	Steve Nagy, Detroit	Sylvia Wene, Philadelphia
1954	Don Carter, St. Louis	Marion Ladewig, Grand Rapids
1953	Don Carter, St. Louis	Marion Ladewig, Grand Rapids
1952	Steve Nagy, Cleveland	Marion Ladewig, Grand Rapids
1951	Lee Jouglard, Detroit	Marion Ladewig, Grand Rapids
1950	Junie McMahon, Chicago	Marion Ladewig, Grand Rapids
1949	Connie Schwoegler, Madison, Wis.	Val Mikiel, Detroit
1948	Andy Varipapa, Brooklyn	Val Mikiel, Detroit
1947	Buddy Bomar, Chicago	
1946	Joe Wilman, Chicago	
1945	Buddy Bomar, Chicago	
1944	Ned Day, West Allis, Wis.	
1943	Ned Day, West Allis, Wis.	
1942	Johnny Crimmins, Detroit	

American Bowling Congress Tournament

Except for the World War II years of 1943, 1944, and 1945, the American Bowling Congress' annual tournament has been held without interruption since it was started in 1901. It is the world's largest participation sports event, and the entry list has grown so large that the tournament now takes more than three months to complete.

TOURNAMENT RECORDS

	Year	Pins
Team (All Events)		
Falstaff Beer, St. Louis, Mo.	1958	9,608
Team (3 Games)		
Ace Mitchell Shur-Hooks, Akron, Ohio	1966	3,357
Team (1 Game)		
Falstaff Beer, San Antonio, Tex.	1958	1,226
Doubles (3 Games)		
John Klares (755)–Steve Nagy (698), Cleveland, Ohio	1952	1,453
Doubles (1 Game)		
John Gworek (279)–Henry Kmidowski (265), Buffalo, N.Y.	1946	544
Singles (3 Games)		
Lee Jouglard, Detroit, Mich. (242–255–278)	1951	775
Individual All Events		
Jack Winters, Philadelphia, Pa.	1962	2,147
Highest Series, Any Event		
Jack Winters, Philadelphia, Pa.	1962	792

194

TOURNAMENT CHAMPIONS

TEAM

Year		Score	Year		Score
1969	PAC Adv. Co., Lansing, Mich.	3,165	1933	Flaig's Opticians, Covington, Ky.	3,021
1968	Dave's Auto Sup. Philadelphia	3,084	1932	Jefferson Clothiers, Dayton, O.	3,108
1967	Pinky's Bowl, Milwaukee	3,327	1931	S. & L. Motors, Chicago	3,013
1966	Plaza Lanes,		1930	D. Graff & Sons, Kalamazoo, Mich.	3,100
	Sault Ste. Marie, Canada	3,066	1929	Hub Recreation, Joliet, Ill.	3,063
1965	G & C McDermitt, Inc., Pittsb'gh	3,074	1928	Oh Henry Candy, Chicago	3,057
1964	300 Bowl, Pontiac, Mich.	3,117	1927	Tea Shops, Milwaukee	3,199
1963	Old Fitzgerald, Chicago	3,180	1926	Castany, Chicago	3,063
1962	Strike'n Spare, Chicago	3,128	1925	Weisser Blue Ribbons, Buffalo	3,230
1961	Meyerland Builders, Houston	3,134	1924	Herb's Indians, Cleveland	3,044
1960	A & A Asphalt, Detroit	3,096	1923	Nelson Mitchells, Milwaukee	3,139
1959	Pfeiffer Beer, Detroit	3,243	1922	Lincoln Life Ins. Co., Ft. Wayne	2,998
1958	Falstaff Beer, St. Louis	3,210	1921	Saunders, Toronto, Ont., Canada	3,066
1957	Peter Hand Reserve Beer, Chicago	3,126	1920	Brucks No. 1, Chicago	3,096
1956	Falstaff Beer, Chicago	3,092	1919	Athern Hotel, Oshkosh, Wis.	2,992
1955	Pfeiffer Beer, Detroit	3,136	1918	Aquilas Cigars, St. Paul	3,022
1954	Tri-Par Radio, Chicago	3,226	1917	Birk Bros. (Windy City), Chicago	3,061
1953	Pfeiffer Beer, Detroit	3,181	1916	Commodore Barry, Chicago	2,905
1952	E&B Beer, Detroit	3,115	1915	Barry-Ketteler, Chicago	2,907
1951	O'Malley Oldsmobile, Chicago	3,070	1914	New Haven, New Haven, Conn.	2,944
1950	Pepsi-Cola, Detroit	2,952	1913	Flor De Knispel, St. Paul	3,006
1949	Jimmie Smith's, South Bend, Ind.	3,027	1912	Brunswick All-Stars, New York	2,904
1948	Washington Shirts, Chicago	3,007	1911	Flenners, Chicago	2,924
1947	Eddie and Earl Linsz, Cleveland	3,032	1910	Cosmos, Chicago	2,880
1946	Llo-Da-Mar Bowl, Santa Monica	3,023	1909	Lipman, Chicago	2,962
1942	Budweiser, Chicago	3,131	1908	Bond, Columbus, Ohio	2,927
1941	Vogel Brothers, Forest Park, Ill.	3,065	1907	Furniture City, Grand Rapids	2,775
1940	Monarch Beer, Chicago	3,047	1906	Century, Chicago	2,794
1939	Fife Electric Supply Co., Detroit	3,151	1905	Gunther No. 2, Chicago	2,795
1938	Birk Bros. Brewing Co., Chicago	3,234	1904	Anson's, Chicago	2,737
1937	Krakow Furniture Co., Detroit	3,118	1903	O'Leary, Chicago	2,819
1936	Falls City Hi-Bru, Indianapolis	3,089	1902	Fidelia, New York	2,792
1935	Wolfe Tire Service, Niagara Falls	3,029	1901	Standard, Chicago	2,720
1934	Stroh's Bohemian Beer, Detroit	3,089			

DOUBLES

Year		Score
1969	Robert Maschmeyer—Charles Guedel, Indianapolis, Ind.	1,379
1968	Rich Stark—Walt Roy, Glenwood Springs, Colo.	1,325
1967	Mark Kuglitsch—Ron Wheeler, Milwaukee	1,357
1966	Tony Loiacano—Bob Kwiecien, Detroit	1,351
1965	Buzz Bosler—Dan Slak, Milwaukee	1,300
1964	Pat Russo—Tony Russo, Teaneck, N. J.	1,343
1963	Bus Oswalt—Gerry Schmidt, Ft. Wayne, Ind.	1,337
1962	John Gribin—Gary Madison, Riverside, Calif.	1,376
1961	Joe Macaluso—Eugene Hering, Irvington, N. J.	1,342
1960	Andy Marzich—Dick Jensen, Los Angeles	1,369
1959	Barney Vehige—Gib Fischbach, St. Louis	1,372
1958	John (Bill) Tucker—Jim Vrenick, St. Louis	1,414
1957	Ronnie Jones—Joe Meszaros, Sterling, Ohio	1,369
1956	Bill Lillard—Stan Gifford, Chicago	1,331
1955	George Pacropis—Harry Zoeller, Wilkes-Barre, Pa.	1,565
1954	Don McClaren, St. Louis—Billy Welu, Houston	1,335
1953	Ed Koepp—Joe Kissoff, Cleveland	1,339

Year		Score
1952	John Klares–Steve Nagy, Cleveland	1,453
1951	Bob Benson–Ed Marshall, Lansing, Mich.	1,334
1950	Willis Ebosh–Earl Linsz, Cleveland	1,325
1949	D. VonBoxel, G. Bay–G. Bernhardt, Stgn. Bay, Wis.	1,332
1948	James Towns–William Sweeney, Chicago	1,361
1947	Edward Doerr–Leonard Springmeyer, St. Louis	1,356
1946	John Gworek–Hank Kmidowski, Buffalo	1,360
1942	Edward Nowicki–George Baier, Milwaukee	1,377
1941	Wm. Lee–Ray Farness, Madison	1,346
1940	Herbert Freitag–Joe Sinke, Chicago	1,346
1939	Philip Icuss–Murray Fowler, Steubenville, Ohio	1,405
1938	Don Johnson–Fonnie Snyder, Indianapolis	1,337
1937	V. Gibbs, K. City, Mo.–N. Burton, Dallas	1,359
1936	Anthony Slanina–Mike Straka, Chicago	1,347
1935	Clyde Sumerix–Harry Souers, Akron, Ohio	1,348
1934	George Rudolph–John Ryan, Waukegan, Ill.	1,321
1933	Gilbert Zunker–Frank Benkovic, Milwaukee	1,415
1932	Frank Benkovic–Charles Daw, Milwaukee	1,358
1931	Edw. Rafferty–Chas. Reilly, Philadelphia	1,316
1930	James Divine–Geo. Heup, Beloit, Wis.	1,339
1929	Walter Klecz–Peter Butler, Chicago	1,353
1928	Henry Will–Joe Hradek, Cicero, Ill.	1,363
1927	Michael Flick–Frank Snyder, Erie, Pa.	1,317
1926	°Chas. Aston–Phil. Young, Akron, Ohio	1,355
1925	Ed Schupp–Ed Karich, Chicago	1,318
1924	Harry Thoma–Clarence Thoma, Chicago	1,380
1923	Chas. Daw–Finnis Wilson, Milwaukee	1,358
1922	Chris Spinella–Barney Spinella, New York	1,336
1921	Otto Kallusch–Art Schieman, Rochester, N. Y.	1,314
1920	Marvin Erickson–Edw. Krems, Chicago	1,301
1919	Otto Kallusch–Ernie Barnes, Rochester, N. Y.	1,305
1918	Harry Steers–Fred Thoma, Chicago	1,335
1917	G. Satorius–Wm. Holzschuh, Peoria, Ill.	1,346
1916	Frank Thoma–Henry Marino, Chicago	1,279
1915	Harold Allen–Ray Allen, Detroit	1,297
1914	John Negley–D. Van Ness, Newark, N. J.	1,245
1913	Peter Schultz–John Koster, Newark, N. J.	1,291
1912	N. P. Owen–Phil Sutton, Louisville, Ky.	1,259
1911	W. Hartley–L. Seiler, East Liverpool, Ohio	1,246
1910	Al Daiker–Ed Wetterman, Cincinnati	1,231
1909	A. Schwoegler–Tony Schwoegler, Madison	1,304
1908	James Chalmers–Henry Kiene, Chicago	1,254
1907	E. G. Richter–E. Bigley, Louisville, Ky.	1,164
1906	J. N. Reed–Earl Dresbach, Columbus, Ohio	1,247
1905	Ed Stretch–Robert Rolfe, Chicago	1,213
1904	H. H. Krause–C. H. Spies, Washington, D. C.	1,184
1903	Harry Collin–A. Selbach, Columbus, Ohio	1,227
1902	J. McClean–Harry Steers, Chicago	1,237
1901	J. Voorhies–C. K. Starr, New York	1,203

° Won rolloff.

SINGLES

Year		Score	Year		Score
1969	Greg Campbell, St. Louis, Mo.	751	1962	Andrew Renaldy, Youngstown, O.	720
1968	Wayne Kowalski, Revere, Mass.	778	1961	Lyle Spooner, St. Cloud, Minn.	726
1967	Frank Perry, Lorain, Ohio	723	1960	Paul Kulbaga, Cleveland	726
1966	Don Chapman, Scranton, Pa.	761	1959	Ed Lubanski, Detroit	764
1965	Kenneth Roeth, Dubuque, Iowa	700	1958	Ed Shay, Chester, Pa.	733
1964	Jim Stefanich, Chicago	726	1957	Bob Allen, Yonkers, N. Y.	729
1963	Fred Delello, Oneonta, N. Y.	744	1956	Geo. Wade, Steubenville, Ohio	744

Year		Score	Year		Score
1955	Eddie Gerzine, Milwaukee	738	1925	Al Green, Chicago	706
1954	Tony Sparando, Rego Park, N. Y.	723	1924	Harry E. Snyers, Pittsburgh	749
1953	Frank Santore, L. I. City, N. Y.	749	1923	Carl A. Baumgartner, Cincinnati	724
1952	Al Sharkey, Chicago	758	1922	Walter Lundgren, Chicago	729
1951	Lee Jouglard, Detroit	775	1921	F. Smith, Detroit	702
1950	Everett Leins, Aurora, Ill	757	1920	Joe Shaw, Chicago	713
1949	Bernard Rusche, St. Bernard, O.	716	1919	Harry Cavan, Pittsburgh	718
1948	Lincoln Protich, Akron, Ohio	721	1918	C. Styles, Detroit	702
1947	Junie McMahon, Chicago	740	1917	Otto Kallusch, Rochester, N. Y.	698
1946	Leo Rollick, Santa Monica, Calif.	737	1916	°Sam Schliman, Toronto, Canada	685
1942	John Stanley, Cleveland	756	1915	Wallace H. Pierce, Pueblo, Colo.	711
1941	Fred Ruff, Jr., Belleville, Ill.	745	1914	Wm. Miller, Detroit	675
1940	Ray Brown, Terre Haute, Ind.	742	1913	F. Peterson, Columbus, Ohio	693
1939	James Danek, Forest Park, Ill.	730	1912	Larry Sutton, Rochester	679
1938	Knute Anderson, Moline, Ill.	746	1911	James Blouin, Chicago	681
1937	Gene Gagliardi, Mt. Vernon, N. Y.	749	1910	Thos. Haley, Detroit	705
1936	Chas. Warren, Springfield, Ill.	735	1909	°Larry Sutton, Rochester, N. Y.	691
1935	Don Brokaw, Canton, Ohio	733	1908	Archie Wengler, Chicago	699
1934	Jerry Vidro, Grand Rapids, Mich.	721	1907	°M. T. Levey, Indianapolis	624
1933	Earl Hewitt, Erie, Pa.	724	1906	Frank J. Favour, Oshkosh, Wis.	669
1932	Otto Nitschke, Cleveland	731	1905	C. M. Anderson, St. Paul	651
1931	Walter Lachowski, Erie, Pa.	712	1904	Martin Kern, St. Louis	647
1930	Larry Shotwell, Covington, Ky.	774	1903	Dan A. Jones, Milwaukee	683
1929	Adolph Unke, Milwaukee	728	1902	Fred Strong, Chicago	649
1928	Henry Summers, St. Louis	705	1901	Frank Briell, Chicago	648
1927	Wm. Eggars, Chicago	706			
1926	Ed Votel, Braddock, Pa.	731		° Won rolloff.	

ALL EVENTS

Year		Score	Year		Score
1969	Eddie Jackson, Cincinnati, O.	1,988	1933	Gilbert Zunker, Milwaukee	2,060
1968	Vince Mazzanti, Philadelphia	1,971	1932	Hugh Stewart, Cincinnati	1,980
1967	Gary Lewis, Chicago	2,010	1931	Michael Mauser, Youngstown, O.	1,966
1966	John Wilcox, Jr., Will'm'spt, Pa.	2,004	1930	George Morrison, Chicago	1,985
1965	Tom Hathaway, Los Angeles	1,922	1929	Otto Stein, Jr., St. Louis	1,974
1964	Les Zikes, Jr., Chicago	2,001	1928	Phil Wolf, Chicago	1,937
1963	Bus Oswalt, Ft. Wayne, Ind.	2,055	1927	Barney Spinella, Brooklyn	2,014
1962	Billy Young, Tulsa, Okla.	2,015	1926	Harry Gerloski, Detroit	1,981
1961	Luke Karan, Detroit	1,960	1925	Clarence Long, Buffalo, N. Y.	1,9/7
1960	Vince Lucci, Trenton, N. J.	1,985	1924	A. F. Weber, Elizabeth, N. J.	1,975
1959	Ed Lubanski, Detroit	2,116	1923	Wm. J. Knox, Philadelphia	2,019
1958	Al Faragalli, Paterson, N. J.	2,043	1922	Barney Spinella, Brooklyn	1,999
1957	Jim Spalding, Louisville, Ky.	2,088	1921	Art Schieman, Rochester, N. Y.	1,909
1956	Bill Lillard, Chicago	2,018	1920	Jimmy Smith, Milwaukee	1,915
1955	Fred Bujack, Detroit	1,993	1919	Mort Lindsey, New Haven, Conn.	1,933
1954	Brad Lewis, Ashland, Ohio	1,985	1918	Harry Steers, Chicago	1,959
1953	Frank Santore, L. I. City, N. Y.	1,994	1917	H. Miller, Detroit	1,945
1952	Steve Nagy, Cleveland	2,065	1916	Frank Thoma, Chicago	1,919
1951	Tony Lindemann, Detroit	2,005	1915	Matty E. Faetz, Chicago	1,876
1950	Frank Santore, L. I. City	1,981	1914	Wm. Miller, Detroit	1,897
1949	Johnny Small, Chicago	1,941	1913	Ed. Hermann, Cleveland	1,972
1948	Ned Day, West Allis, Wis.	1,979	1912	Phil Sutton, Louisville, Ky.	1,843
1947	Junie McMahon, Chicago	1,965	1911	Jimmy Smith, Buffalo	1,919
1946	Joseph Wilman, Chicago	2,054	1910	Thos. Haley, Detroit	1,961
1942	Stanley Moskal, Saginaw, Mich.	1,973	1909	James Blouin, Chicago	1,885
1941	Harold Kelly, South Bend, Ind.	2,013	1908	Russell Crable, E. Liverpool, O.	1,924
1940	Fred Fischer, Buffalo, N. Y.	2,001	1907	H. C. Ellis, Grand Rapids, Mich.	1,775
1939	Joseph Wilman, Chicago	2,028	1906	J. T. Peacock, Indianapolis	1,794
1938	Don L. Beatty, Jackson, Mich.	1,978	1905	Jack G. Reilly, Chicago	1,791
1937	Max Stein, Belleville, Ill.	2,070	1904	Martin Kern, St. Louis	1,804
1936	John Murphy, Indianapolis	2,006	1903	Fred Strong, Chicago	1,896
1935	Ora Mayer, San Francisco	2,022	1902	John Koster, New York	1,841
1934	Walter Reppenhagen, Detroit	1,972	1901	Frank Briell, Chicago	1,736

197

TOURNAMENT AVERAGE LEADERS

Year	Bowler	Average
1969	Bob Strampe, Detroit, Mich.	209–52
1968	Billy Hardwick, Louisville, Ky.	225–35
1967	Jim Stefanich, Joliet, Ill.	219–30
1966	Les Schissler, Denver, Colo.	215–44
1965	Dick Weber, St. Louis, Mo.	206–53
1964	Dick Weber, St. Louis, Mo.	206–62
1963	Ed Lubanski, Detroit, Mich.	207–6
1962	Ed Lubanski, Detroit, Mich.	205–56
1961	Ed Lubanski, Detroit, Mich.	205–40
1960	Steve Nagy, St. Louis, Mo.	208–22
1959	Steve Nagy, St. Louis, Mo.	206–88
1958	George Young, Detroit, Mich.	206–75
1957	George Young, Detroit, Mich.	205–60
1956	George Young, Detroit, Mich.	204–73
1955	Junie McMahon, Fair Lawn, N.J.	204–69
1954	George Young, Detroit, Mich.	205–52
1953	Junie McMahon, Fair Lawn, N.J.	205–38
1952	Junie McMahon, Fair Lawn, N.J.	206–76
1951	Junie McMahon, Chicago, Ill.	207–1
1950	Joe Wilman, Chicago, Ill.	206–62
1949	Junie McMahon, Chicago, Ill.	206–69
1948	Joe Wilman, Chicago, Ill.	205–27
1947	Andy Varipapa, Hempstead, N.Y.	204–65
1946	Marty Cassio, Rahway, N.J.	203–67
1945–1943	No tournament.	
1942	Johnny Crimmins, Detroit, Mich.	203–38
1941	Ned Day, Milwaukee, Wis.	204–23
1940	Ned Day, Milwaukee, Wis.	202–85
1939	Hank Marino, Milwaukee, Wis.	201–72
1938	Gil Zunker, Milwaukee, Wis.	201–85
1937	Joe Bodis, Cleveland, Ohio	204–2
1936	Joe Bodis, Cleveland, Ohio	204–85
1935	Joe Bodis, Cleveland, Ohio	205–76
1934	Joe Bodis, Cleveland, Ohio	205–20

300 GAMES IN ABC TOURNAMENT

Bowler	Year
Bob Poole, Denver	1969
Robert DeGraff, Grand Rapids, Mich.	1961
Louis Facsko, Lorain, Ohio	1960

Bowler	Year
Edward Shay, Chester, Pa.	1958
Myron Ericksen, Racine, Wis.	1955
Tony Sparando, New York, N.Y.	1954
Ray Mihm, Green Bay, Wis.	1953
Vince Lucci, Trenton, N.J.	1951
Leo Rollick, Los Angeles, Calif.	1946
William Hoar, Cicero, Ill.	1941
Michael Domenico, Canton, Ohio	1940
George Pallage, Akron, Ohio	1940
William McGeorge, Kent, Ohio	1939
Michael Blazek, Conneaut, Ohio	1938
Carl Mensenberg, Scranton, Pa.	1935
Jack Karstens, Fort Sheridan, Ill.	1933
Charles Reinlie, Racine, Wis.	1926
William J. Knox, Philadelphia, Pa.	1913

Masters Tournament Champions

Started in 1951, the ABC Masters Tournament has been noted for producing some of bowling's greatest moments. More than 400 bowlers annually seek the coveted match game crown. Bob Poole of Denver rolled a 300 game in the 1969 finals.

Year	Winner	Runner-up	Won	Lost	Avg.
1969	Jim Chestney, Denver	Barry Asher, Costa Mesa, Calif.	10	1	223–2
1968	Pete Tountas, Tucson	Buzz Fazio, Detroit	9	1	220–15
1967	Lou Scalia, Miami	Bill Johnson, New Orleans	7	0	216–9
1966	Bob Strampe, Detroit	Al Thompson, Cleveland	7	0	219–8
1965	Billy Welu, St. Louis	Don Ellis, Houston	9	1	202–12
1964	Billy Welu, St. Louis	Harry Smith, Baltimore	7	0	227
1963	Harry Smith, St. Louis	Bobby Meadows, Dallas	7	0	219–3
1962	Billy Golembiewski, Detroit	Ron Winger, Los Angeles	7	0	223–12
1961	Don Carter, St. Louis	Dick Hoover, St. Louis	8	1	211–18
1960	Billy Golembiewski, Detroit	Steve Nagy, St. Louis	7	0	206–13

199

1959 Ray Bluth, St. Louis	B. Golembiewski, Detroit	7	0	214–26
1958 Tom Hennessey, St. Louis	Lou Frantz, Louisville	7	0	209–15
1957 Dick Hoover, Akron	Bill Lillard, Chicago	9	1	216–39
1956 Dick Hoover, Akron	Ray Bluth, St. Louis	7	1	209–9
1955 Buzz Fazio, Detroit	Joe Kristof, Chicago	7	0	204–13
1954 Eugene Elkins, San Carlos, Calif.	Willard Taylor, Charleston, W. Va.	7	0	205–19
1953 Rudy Habetler, Chicago	Ed Brosius, Chicago	10	1	200–13
1952 Willard Taylor, Charleston, W. Va.	Andy Varipapa, New York	8	1	200–32
1951 Lee Jouglard, Detroit	Joe Wilman, Chicago	6	1	201–8

MASTERS TOURNAMENT RECORDS

HIGH SERIES

Don Carter, St. Louis (1962)	1,084
Ray Bluth, St. Louis (1962)	1,051
Wayne Zahn, Atlanta (1966)	1,038
Tony Lindemann, Detroit (1958)	1,021
Don Johnson, Kokomo, Ind. (1967)	1,019

HIGH GAME

Bob Poole, Denver (1969)	300
Bob Hart, Erie, Pa. (1967)	300
Ray Bluth, St. Louis (1962)	300
Don Carter, St. Louis (1962)	300
Al Horn, Jr., Los Angeles (1961)	300

All-Star Tournament

The Bowling Proprietors Association of America inaugurated the All-Star championships in 1941 and opened the tournament to women in 1949. Since 1942 the winners have been recognized as national individual match game champions.

MEN	WOMEN
1969 Billy Hardwick, Louisville, Ky.	Dotty Fothergill, N. Attleboro, Mass.
1968 Jim Stefanich, Joliet, Ill.	Dotty Fothergill, N. Attleboro, Mass.
1967 Les Schissler, Denver	Gloria Bouvia, Portland
1966 Dick Weber, St. Louis	Jay Abel, Chicago
1965 Dick Weber, St. Louis	Ann Slattery, Salt Lake City

	MEN	WOMEN
1964	Bob Strampe, Detroit	Laverne Carter, St. Louis
1963	Dick Weber, St. Louis	Marion Ladewig, Grand Rapids
1962	Dick Weber, St. Louis	Shirley Garms, Chicago
1961	Bill Tucker, Rock Hill, Mo.	Phyllis Notaro, Brant, N.Y.
1960	Harry Smith, St. Louis	Sylvia Wene, Philadelphia
1959	Billy Welu, St. Louis	Marion Ladewig, Grand Rapids
1958	Don Carter, St. Louis	Merle Matthews, Long Beach, Calif.
1956	Don Carter, St. Louis	Marion Ladewig, Grand Rapids
1955	Bill Lillard, Chicago	Anita Cantaline, Detroit
1954	Steve Nagy, St. Louis	Sylvia Wene, Philadelphia
1953	Don Carter, Detroit	Marion Ladewig, Grand Rapids
1952	Don Carter, Detroit	Marion Ladewig, Grand Rapids
1951	Junie McMahon, Chicago	Marion Ladewig, Grand Rapids
1950	Dick Hoover, Akron, Ohio	Marion Ladewig, Grand Rapids
1949	Junie McMahon, Chicago	Marion Ladewig, Grand Rapids
1948	Connie Schwoegler, Madison, Wis.	
1947	Andy Varipapa, West Hempstead, N.Y.	
1946	Andy Varipapa, West Hempstead, N.Y.	
1945	Joe Wilman, Chicago	
1944	Buddy Bomar, Chicago	
1943	Ned Day, West Allis, Wis.	
1942	Connie Schwoegler, Madison	
1941	Johnny Crimmins, Detroit	

Professional Bowlers Association

One of the newest of the bowling organizations, quick to gain national attention, is the Professional Bowlers Association. Its membership of about a thousand is limited to bowlers with long-time high averages who depend almost entirely on the game for their income.

Events are held in cities around the country and occasionally outside of the United States. A major new attraction, begun in 1965 as part of the PBA series, is the $100,000 Firestone Tournament of Champions, held annually in Akron, Ohio. It carries a top prize of $25,000.

1970 FIRST PRIZE WINNERS

City	Name	Prize
Wichita, Kan.	Ski Foremsky	$ 6,000
Los Angeles, Calif.	Ed Bourdase	6,000
Las Vegas, Nev.	Dave Soutar	11,111
San Jose, Calif.	Dave Davis	10,000
Denver, Colo.	Nelson Burton	6,000
Kansas City, Mo.	Jim Stefanich	8,000
Milwaukee, Wis.	George Pappas	10,000
Toledo, Ohio	Nelson Burton	6,000
Buffalo, N.Y.	George Pappas	6,000
New York, N.Y.	Mike Limongello	7,500
Miami, Fla.	Mike McGrath	10,000
New Orleans, La.	Don Johnson	6,000
Akron, Ohio	Don Johnson	25,000

1969 FIRST PRIZE WINNERS

City	Name	Prize
Los Angeles, Calif.	Wayne Zahn	$ 6,000
Phoenix, Ariz.	Don Glover	6,000
Las Vegas, Nev.	Ski Foremsky	10,000
San Jose, Calif.	Johnny Guenther	9,000
Denver, Colo.	Billy Hardwick	6,000
Kansas City, Mo.	Don Glover	8,000
Paramus, N.J.	Ralph Engan	10,000
Buffalo, N.Y.	Dick Ritger	6,000
Milwaukee, Wis.	Billy Hardwick	10,000
Toledo, Ohio	Ray Bluth	6,000
Portsmouth, Va.	Tommy Tuttle	6,000
New Orleans, La.	Dick Weber	6,000
Akron, Ohio	Jim Godman	25,000

1968 FIRST PRIZE WINNERS

Akron, Ohio	Dave Davis	$25,000
Las Vegas, Nev.	Bill Allen	10,000
Milwaukee, Wis.	Johnny Guenther	10,000
Mountainside, N.J.	Teata Semiz	8,000
San Jose, Calif.	Bill Allen	7,000
Denver, Colo.	Dave Soutar	6,000
Tampa, Fla.	Jim Stefanich	6,000
Buffalo, N.Y.	Bob Strampe	6,000
New Orleans	Dick Ritger	6,000
Mobile, Ala.	Jim Stefanich	6,000

1967 FIRST PRIZE WINNERS

Akron, Ohio	Jim Stefanich	$25,000
Las Vegas, Nev.	Dave Davis	10,000
St. Paul, Minn.	Carmen Salvino	10,000
Kansas City, Mo.	Tim Harahan	10,000
Milwaukee, Wis.	Dave Davis	10,000
Edison, N.J.	Sam Baca	10,000
Tucson, Ariz.	John Juni	5,000
San Jose, Calif.	Jim St. John	5,000
Buffalo, N.Y.	Nelson Burton, Jr.	5,000
Denver, Colo.	Dave Davis	5,000

1966 FIRST PRIZE WINNERS

City	Name	Prize
Akron, Ohio	Wayne Zahn	$25,000
Dallas, Tex.	Bill Lillard	10,000
Las Vegas, Nev.	Skee Foremsky	7,500
Edison, N.J.	Dennis Chapis	5,000
Charlotte, N.C.	Gene Rhoda	5,000
San Jose, Calif.	Jim Goodman	5,000
Denver, Colo.	Dick Weber	5,000
Hialeah, Fla.	Les Schissler	5,000
Mobile, Ala.	Mike Limongello	5,000
Fresno, Calif.	Dick Weber	5,000

1965 FIRST PRIZE WINNERS

Akron, Ohio	Billy Hardwick	$25,000
Sacramento, Calif.	Buzz Fazio	5,000
Hialeah, Fla.	Billy Golembiewski	5,000
Wichita, Kan.	Dick Weber	5,000
Oklahoma City, Okla.	Mike Limongello	5,000
Detroit, Mich.	Bob Strampe	5,000
Buffalo, N.Y.	Bill Allen	5,000
Hartford, Conn.	Bill Allen	5,000
Caracas, Venezuela	Harry Smith	2,000
San Jose, Calif.	Bill Tucker	4,000

1964 FIRST PRIZE WINNERS

Jacksonville, Fla.	Carmen Salvino	$4,000
Hialeah, Fla.	Johnny King	4,000
St. Louis, Mo.	Andy Marzich	4,000
Mobile, Ala.	Bill Allen	4,000
Birmingham, Ala.	Billy Hardwick	4,000
Princeton, N.J.	Buzz Fazio	4,000
Pontiac, Mich.	Billy Hardwick	4,000
Spokane, Wash.	Ray Bluth	3,000
Rockford, Ill.	Carmen Salvino	3,000
Mesa, Ariz.	Billy Welu	3,000

1963 FIRST PRIZE WINNERS

City	Name	Prize
Atlanta, Ga.	Dennis Chapis	$5,000
Charlotte, N.C.	Billy Golembiewski	4,000
Denver, Colo.	Andy Marzich	5,050
Louisville, Ky.	Earl Johnson	5,000
Dallas, Tex.	Bill Johnson	5,000
Mobile, Ala.	Billy Hardwick	5,000
Indianapolis, Ind.	Les Schissler	5,000
Akron, Ohio	Harry Smith	5,000
North Brunswick, N.J.	Dick Weber	5,000
Baltimore, Md.	Lewis Ray	3,000

1962 FIRST PRIZE WINNERS

Chicago, Ill.	Dick Weber	$4,000
San Juan, Puerto Rico	Dick Weber	4,000
Albany, N.Y.	Fred Lening	5,000
Philadelphia, Pa.	Harry Smith	5,000
Baltimore, Md.	Dick Hoover	5,000
Akron, Ohio	Glen Blakesley	5,000
Cleveland, Ohio	Skip Vigars	5,000
Winston-Salem, N.C.	Al Savas	5,000
Birmingham, Ala.	Andy Rogoznica	5,000

1961 FIRST PRIZE WINNERS

Albany, N.Y.	Carmen Salvino	$ 3,000
Paramus, N.J.	Roy Lown	15,000
Dallas, Tex.	Dick Weber	3,000
Shreveport, La.	Dick Weber	1,500
Houston, Tex.	Dick Weber	3,000
El Paso, Tex.	Harry Smith	2,500
Redondo Beach, Calif.	Dick Weber	3,000
San Jose, Calif.	Dick Weber	3,000
San Francisco, Calif.	Vern Downing	2,500
Las Vegas, Nev.	George Howard	4,000
Cleveland, Ohio	Dave Soutar	6,000

Bowling Proprietors Association of America

1969 CHAMPIONS

Men's Singles (All-Star)—Billy Hardwick, Louisville, Ky.
Women's Singles (All-Star)—Dotty Fothergill, N. Attleboro, Mass.
Men's Duckpin (All-Star)—Charles Evans, Rockville, Md.
Women's Duckpin (All-Star)—Frances Wilson, Washington, D.C.
Men's Team Handicap—Discontinued
Boys' Junior Scratch—Larry Johnson, San Francisco, Calif.
Boys' Junior Handicap—Rick Healy, Stockton, Calif.
Girls' Junior Handicap—Deborah Ann Stewart, Lakewood, Calif.

1968 CHAMPIONS

Men's Singles (All-Star)—Jim Stefanich, Joliet, Ill.
Women's Singles (All-Star)—Dotty Fothergill, N. Attleboro, Mass.
Men's Duckpin (All-Star)—Andy Constantinople, New Haven, Conn.
Women's Duckpin (All-Star)—Mary Ann Mitchell, Avon, Conn.
Men's Team Handicap—Pterodactyls, Seattle
Boys' Junior Scratch—David Pearson, Thousand Oaks, Calif.
Boys' Junior Handicap—Mike Goings, Seward, Neb.
Girls' Junior Handicap—Pearl Bakken, Eugene, Ore.

1967 CHAMPIONS

Men's Singles (All-Stars)—Les Schissler, Denver
Women's Singles (All-Star)—Gloria Bouvia, Portland, Ore.
Men's Doubles—Discontinued
Men's Duckpin (All-Star)—Charles Guess, Richmond, Va.
Men's Team Handicap—North American Van Lines, Anniston, Ala.
Boys' Junior Scratch—Les Richmond, Elmira, N.Y.
Boys' Junior Handicap—George Senopole, Jr., Warren, Mich.
Girls' Junior Handicap—Virginia Simmons, Excelsior, Minn.

1966 CHAMPIONS

Men's Singles (All-Star)—Dick Weber, St. Louis
Women's Singles (All-Star)—Jay Abel, Chicago
Men's Team—Discontinued
Women's Team—Discontinued
Men's Doubles—Jack Biondolillo (Houston) and Fred Foremsky (El Paso)
Women's Doubles—Discontinued
Men's Duckpin (All-Star)—Leon Stetson, Winsted, Conn.
Women's Duckpin (All-Star)—Cecelia Rohlfing, Baltimore
Men's Team Handicap—Lakepoint Chrysler, Detroit
Boys' Junior Scratch—Gary Lechuga, Denver
Boys' Junior Handicap—Rick Healy, Stockton, Calif.
Girls' Junior Handicap—Deborah Ann Stewart, Lakewood, Calif.

1965 CHAMPIONS

Men's Singles (All-Star)—Dick Weber, St. Louis
Women's Singles (All-Star)—Doris Rudell, Whittier, Calif.
Men's Team—G & C McDermitt, Inc., Pittsburgh
Women's Team—Belmont Bowl Pro Shop, Chicago
Men's Doubles—Dave Soutar and Tom Harnisch
Women's Doubles—Betty Remmick and Mary Ann White, Denver
Men's Duckpin (All-Star)—Norwood Heselbach, Baltimore
Women's Duckpin (All-Star)—Ruth King, Washington, D.C.
Men's Team Handicap—Bowl American, Baltimore
Boys' Junior Scratch—Peter Norn, Ridgewood, N.J.
Boys' Junior Handicap—None held
Girls' Junior Handicap—Marion Brisk, New Hyde Park, N.Y.

1964 CHAMPIONS

Men's Singles (All-Star)—Bob Strampe, Detroit
Women's Singles (All-Star)—Laverne Carter, St. Louis
Men's Team—Lakepointe Chrysler, Detroit
Women's Team—Pitch's Lounge & Restaurant, Milwaukee
Men's Doubles—Ray Bluth and Dick Weber, St. Louis
Women's Doubles—Jean Abet and Betty Kuczynski, Chicago
Men's Duckpin (All-Star)—Jack Barkley, Rockville, Md.
Women's Duckpin (All-Star)—Jean Morris, Chesapeake, Va.
Men's Team Handicap—Caithness Buick, Bethesda, Md.
Boys' Junior Scratch—Ed Rymer, Deland, Fla.
Boys' Junior Handicap—Michael Whittaker, Anaheim, Calif.
Girls' Junior Handicap—Margaret Anderson, La Marque, Tex.

1963 CHAMPIONS

Men's Singles (All-Star)—Dick Weber, St. Louis
Women's Singles (All-Star)—Dorothy Wilkinson, Phoenix, Ariz.
Men's Team—Falstaff Beer, St. Louis
Women's Team—Linbrook Bowl, Anaheim, Calif.
Men's Doubles—Jack Biondolillo and Don Ellis, Houston
Women's Doubles—Ruth Redfox and Ann Heyman, Toledo, Ohio
Men's Duckpin (All-Star)—Earl Hartman, Baltimore
Women's Duckpin (All-Star)—Donna Moissonnier, Danbury, Conn.
Men's Team Handicap—Brogialio's Sausage, Stamford, Conn.
Boys' Junior Scratch—Dick Ernst, Indianapolis
Boys' Junior Handicap—Lloyd Kaneshiro, Los Angeles
Girls' Junior Handicap—Paula Weise, Detroit

1962 CHAMPIONS

Men's Singles (All-Star)—Dick Weber, St. Louis
Women's Singles (All-Star)—Shirley Garms, Chicago
Men's Team—Don Carter Bowling Glove, St. Louis
Women's Team—Falstaff Beer, Chicago
Men's Doubles—Ray Bluth and Dick Weber, St. Louis
Women's Doubles—Helen Duval and Nobu Asami, Richmond, Calif.
Men's Duckpin (All-Star)—Dave Volk, Baltimore
Women's Duckpin (All-Star)—Frances Wilson, Washington, D.C.
Men's Team Handicap—Machinist 830, Western Lanes, Louisville, Ky.
Boys' Junior Scratch—Dick Ernst, Indianapolis
Boys' Junior Handicap—Dennis Jennison, Boise, Idaho
Girls' Junior Handicap—Kit Konkle, Grand Rapids, Mich.

Woman's International Bowling Congress

The Woman's International Bowling Congress dates back to 1916 and has conducted an annual tournament since 1918. It represents more than two million women and is the country's largest and most influential organization among feminine devotees of the sport.

TOURNAMENT RECORDS

Record-Holder	Year	Score
TEAM (3 Games)		
Linbrook Bowl, Los Angeles, Calif.	1962	3,061
TEAM (1 Game)		
Sims, Chicago, Ill.	1956	1,109
DOUBLES (3 Games)		
Gloria Bouvia, Portland, Ore.–Judy Cook, Grandview, Mo.	1969	1,315
DOUBLES (1 Game)		
Marge Merrick–Lib Miller, Columbus, Ohio	1962	504
SINGLES (3 Games)		
Marie Clemensen, Chicago, Ill.	1934	712
SINGLES (1 Game)		
Martha Hoffman, Madison, Wis.	1962	296
ALL EVENTS		
Jean Havlish, St. Paul, Minn.	1964	1,980

ALL-TIME RECORDS

Record-Holder	Season	Score
TEAM (3 Games)		
Freeway Washer & Stamping, Cleveland, Ohio	1959–60	3,379
TEAM (1 Game)		
Pitch's Lounge, Milwaukee, Wis.	1964–65	1,193
INDIVIDUAL (3 Games)		
Beverly Ortner, Galva, Iowa	1968–69	818
LEAGUE AVERAGE		
Mildred Martorella, Rochester, N.Y.	1967–68	219
DOUBLES (3 Games)		
Carol Shevlin–Rose Coletti, Buffalo, N.Y.	1960–61	1,401
DOUBLES (1 Game)		
Gladys Gay –Janet Hoodenpyl	1965–66	533

American Junior Bowling Congress

The American Junior Bowling Congress was founded in 1935, and it now boasts a membership of half a million boys and girls.

Two tournaments, on a handicap basis, are conducted each year by mail. One is a local tournament, with the winning scores in each local competition mailed to the AJBC's national offices in Milwaukee, Wisconsin, for comparison. The events are singles, doubles, and mixed doubles. The other is the national "mailographic." Teams in three age divisions compete in tenpins, duckpins, rubberband duckpins, and candlepins.

Because competition and good spirit, rather than individual achievement, are stressed, the AJBC does not keep a list of winners in the various age divisions. But its compilation of over-all records shows how skilled boys and girls have become at the game.

Division	High Team Series	High Team Game	High Individual Series	High Individual Game
Senior Boys	3,430	1,273	804	300
Junior Boys	3,292	1,187	847	299
Bantam Boys	2,055 (2 games)	1,139	531 (2 games)	299
Senior Girls	3,208	1,191	735	289
Junior Girls	3,167	1,078	727	287
Bantam Girls	1,772 (2 games)	949	485 (2 games)	267

United Press International

Boxing

The History of Boxing

Few contests are as exciting to watch as a good, hard-fought boxing match. The millions of fight fans all over the world are proof of the popularity of this ancient sport. And ancient is the word for it too, since boxing is one of the oldest forms of competition known to man.

The Greeks first included boxing in their Olympic games of 688 B.C. Boxing was popular among the Romans, a rough lot who wrapped a leather cestus (often weighted with lead) around each fist to cause more damage. When Rome fell, boxing apparently fell with it.

The next word we find of boxing appears centuries later, from England, where the forerunner of modern prizefighting originated. British royalty and noblemen, by betting on the matches and offering prizes to contestants, helped to revive the sport. From here on, the story of boxing falls into two main chapters: the early one of bare knuckles and the later one of boxing gloves.

The man generally acknowledged as the first of the great fighters was James Figg. Not only did he become the first

British heavyweight champion (in 1719), but he was the first real teacher of the "manly art of self-defense."

He established a school in London called Figg's Amphitheatre. It attracted scores of young men eager to learn how to box, and a number of the "graduates" opened schools of their own. As a result, the sport gained great popularity in England.

Figg died in 1734, four years after his retirement without ever having lost a fight. While he lived, boxing had one basic rule: the contestants were to keep pounding each other with bare fists until one of them was unable to continue. No rest periods were allowed, either.

Then in 1743, Jack Broughton, another great fighter and student of the sport, drew up a set of regulations that became famous as the London Prize Ring Rules. One, for example, stated that "no person is to hit his adversary when he is down or seize him by the hair, the breeches or any part below the waist."

But even the Broughton rules failed to eliminate much of the brutality and confusion in boxing. Nevertheless, they remained in effect for more than 120 years. In 1865 John Sholto Douglas, 8th Marquess of Queensberry, with the help of John G. Chambers, drafted the code of rules that eventually put an end to bare-knuckle fighting. Although they were drawn up a century ago, and standardized in 1889, the Queensberry rules remain in effect today essentially as first written.

Boxing got its start in the United States many years before the Queensberry rules, but it remained for the famed John L. Sullivan to whip up public interest in the sport.

The first American champion of any sort was Jacob Hyer,

who claimed the honor purely on the basis of beating a man in a grudge fight in 1816. So small was interest in boxing in the United States at that time that no one challenged the claim.

Twenty-four years later, Tom Hyer, Jacob's son, claimed the American title. He didn't create much more excitement than his father, but he did score one victory of note—over a Britisher by the name of Yankee Sullivan, on February 7, 1849.

The turning point for boxing in America came on May 30, 1880, when a young giant named Paddy Ryan did what no other fighter in American ring history has done: He won a world championship in his first professional fight.

On that date Ryan, whose experience had been limited to barroom brawls, accepted a match with the British heavy-weight ruler, Joe Goss, at Colliers Station, West Virginia. They went at it for eighty-six rounds, with the title going to Ryan when Goss was unable to come out for the eighty-seventh.

Ryan held the title less than two years, for on February 7, 1882, John L. Sullivan reduced him to ruin in nine rounds.

Sullivan went on to become our first great and popular champion. The Boston Strong Boy realized that boxing had to earn the affection of the "nice people" of the country if it was to become a successful attraction. So he joined a theatrical troupe and staged exhibitions in many places where fights had never before been seen publicly.

He offered $100 to any man he could not knock out in four rounds, and later increased the amount to $500. The effect of all this was to give boxing a tremendous boost in public interest and to encourage the establishment of boxing schools.

An artist's impression of the last bare-knuckle fight—between John L. Sullivan (right) and Jake Kilrain, at Richburg, Mississippi, 1889.

As Sullivan knocked out challenger after challenger in less than four rounds, he became a national hero.

The last bare-knuckle battle took place at Richburg, Mississippi, on July 8, 1889, when Sullivan and Jake Kilrain hammered each other for seventy-five rounds, with Kilrain unable to come out for the seventy-sixth.

The first championship fight under Queensberry rules—with gloves, three-minute rounds, one-minute rest periods, and so forth—was fought on September 7, 1892, at New Orleans between Sullivan and James J. Corbett. Corbett won in twenty-one rounds, though he weighed only 178 to Sullivan's 212.

The United States was now the center of boxing interest, having taken the play away from England.

Gentleman Jim Corbett drops Bob Fitzsimmons in the sixth round at Carson City, March 17, 1897. But Fitzsimmons recovered and won the heavyweight title.

Corbett, known as Gentleman Jim, added further luster to the sport with his classy, clever style of fighting. In the almost five years that he held the title, Corbett proved that prizefighting was a matter of brains as well as brawn, and even women became avid followers of the matches.

Competition in weight divisions below the heavyweight class started in the middle to late 1800's. Maximum weights were established for several divisions. Bantamweights (118 pounds), featherweights (126 pounds), lightweights (135 pounds), welterweights (147 pounds), and middleweights (160 pounds) were tossing punches at each other before the turn of the 20th century; the light-heavyweight division (175 pounds) was begun in 1903, and the flyweight, lightest of all at 112 pounds, in 1910.

217

But it was the heavyweights who provided most of the drama and glamour, even as they do today. Behind Corbett came such great champions as Bob Fitzsimmons, James J. Jeffries, Tommy Burns, Jack Johnson, and Jess Willard.

And then came Jack Dempsey.

With Dempsey, who won the heavyweight crown on July 4, 1919, by knocking out Willard in three rounds, boxing moved into an era that surpassed anything the sport had ever known. Thousands upon thousands of fans turned out to see the slashing, smashing Dempsey in action, and with such frenzy came the million-dollar gate.

Top promoter at the time was Tex Rickard, who formed the corporation that built the Eighth Avenue Madison Square Garden in New York. With Rickard promoting, Dempsey fought in bouts that drew both record crowds and record sums of money. This was before television and the fights of that day far outdrew today's fights.

A throng of 120,757 saw Gene Tunney dethrone Dempsey in ten rounds on September 23, 1926, in Philadelphia, and 104,943 witnessed the famous "long count" battle between them in Chicago on September 22, 1927.

The second Dempsey–Tunney fight is still the most talked-about in the history of the sport. Behind on points going into the seventh round, Dempsey suddenly caught up with Tunney and floored him with two right-hand smashes to the head.

But referee Dave Barry refused to start the count until Dempsey went to a neutral corner. The precious seconds of delay enabled Tunney to clear his head and rise at the count of nine. He weathered Dempsey's rushes for the rest of the round and went on to retain the title.

Max Schmeling faces the Brown Bomber, June 22, 1938.

Estimates are that the count was fourteen when Tunney lifted himself off the canvas. But there was no denying that Dempsey had only himself to blame by failing to go to a neutral corner immediately.

Tunney retired as undefeated champion after knocking out Tom Heeney in eleven rounds on July 26, 1928. The heavyweight division went through a somewhat erratic period until Joe Louis, the Brown Bomber from Detroit, came along to rewrite the record books and scale new heights of popularity.

Louis became world champion by knocking out James J. Braddock in eight rounds on June 22, 1937, and defended his honors an unprecedented twenty-five times before retiring as undefeated king of the ring on March 1, 1949.

Ezzard Charles succeeded Louis as champion on June 22, 1949, by defeating Jersey Joe Walcott in fifteen rounds. Louis, coming out of retirement, tried to unseat Charles on September 27, 1950, but lost the fifteen-round decision.

Jersey Joe Walcott, thirty-seven years old at the time, startled the boxing world on July 18, 1951, by knocking out Charles in the seventh round. On September 23, 1952, rough-and-ready Rocky Marciano took the title away from Joe by knocking him out in the thirteenth round in Philadelphia.

Marciano, who had little finesse but was as tough as they come, defended the title six times and announced his own retirement on April 27, 1956, without ever having lost a pro fight.

The following November 30, Floyd Patterson became champ by knocking out Archie Moore in five rounds. Patterson lost the title in a third-round knockout to Ingemar Johansson on June 26, 1959. Then on June 20, 1960, Patterson flattened Johansson in the fifth and became the first man in ring history to regain the heavyweight crown. Floyd's second reign ended on September 25, 1962, when Sonny Liston knocked him out in 2:06 of the first round.

Liston had a short reign. Cassius Clay won the title when Sonny failed to answer the bell for the seventh round in Miami Beach, Florida, on February 25, 1964.

220

Clay lost his title in 1967 when he refused to take the traditional one step forward at the Army induction center in Houston on April 28. He drew a five-year prison sentence and $10,000 fine, but in 1970 he was still free fighting the conviction through many court battles.

The day Cassius defied the induction center, his title was vacated by the New York State Athletic Commission and the World Boxing Association.

The heavyweight crown remained in dispute until the night of February 16, 1970, when Joe Frazier knocked out Jimmy Ellis after four rounds to win recognition as Clay's successor.

Boxing has produced great gladiators in the other weight divisions, too. Some of these names may be familiar to young fight fans of today—Tommy Loughran, in the light-heavyweight class; Mickey Walker and Ray Robinson among the middleweights; Henry Armstrong, Barney Ross, and Jimmy McLarnin, welterweights; Benny Leonard and Tony Canzoneri, lightweights; Willie Pep, featherweight; Kid Williams, bantamweight; and Frankie Genaro and Fidel La Barba, flyweights.

Without doubt, the most famous boxer outside the heavyweight class has been Ray Robinson. Many consider him the greatest fighter, pound for pound, in modern ring history. Certainly his record is unique. Sugar Ray won the middleweight championship no fewer than five times, the welterweight title once, and made an unsuccessful bid for still a third crown, the light-heavyweight.

One of boxing's many problems is the rivalry between New York State and the World Boxing Association, formerly the

National Boxing Association. As a result, it is not unusual to find two champions in one division—one recognized by New York, the other by the WBA.

Another, and more serious, problem is the question of safety. Boxing can be a brutal sport. Several hundred fighters have died as a result of injuries in the recorded history of boxing.

Not until the Benny (Kid) Paret–Emile Griffith fight, however, had a champion ever been fatally injured in defense of his title. Paret was battered unconscious on March 24, 1962, in his third meeting with Griffith for the welterweight crown. The courageous little Cuban died ten days later.

Floyd Patterson vs. Sonny Liston, Chicago, September 25, 1962.

World Champions

JOE FRAZIER

Heavyweight Champion

A shade under 6 feet (5 feet 11½ inches), Joe Frazier does not resemble the accepted version of a heavyweight champion. The picture-book champ is usually over 6 feet and weighs at least 210 pounds. However, Frazier can't be faulted on his punching ability.

Frazier was born January 12, 1944, the youngest of seven sons in a family of thirteen children. He was born in Beauford, South Carolina, but moved to Philadelphia at an early age and started his boxing career there. As an amateur he won 38 of 40, including six straight KOs in the 1964 Olympic trials. He lost in the finals to Buster Mathis but won the Olympic crown in Tokyo when Mathis could not represent the U.S. because of a broken finger.

Frazier won a piece of Cassius Clay's vacated title on March 4, 1968, with an eleventh-round knockout of Mathis. He was recognized as champion in five states, including New York, as well as Mexico and part of the Orient.

Meanwhile, the World Boxing Association conducted a series of elimination bouts that resulted in Jimmy Ellis of Louisville, Kentucky, once a sparring partner of Clay, being crowned as champion.

It was only natural that the two claimants should meet, and when they did—on February 16, 1970, in the new Madison Square Garden in New York—Frazier put aside all doubt as to who should be undisputed champ.

In the fourth round, Frazier hammered Ellis to the canvas twice, the bell saving Ellis after the second knockdown. When the bell rang for the start of the fifth round, Ellis was unable to respond, and so the title victory for Frazier went into the record books as a technical knockout in the fifth round.

With that triumph, Frazier, undefeated as a professional, boasted a record of 22 knockouts in 25 fights.

224

Ducking, Buster Mathis gets a pounding from Joe Frazier (right) during their world heavyweight championship fight at Madison Square Garden, March 4, 1968. Frazier won by a TKO in the 11th round.

BOB FOSTER

Light Heavyweight Champion

At 6 feet 3½ inches, Bob Foster is the tallest man ever to hold the light heavyweight title. He won it from Dick Tiger on May 24, 1968, with a fourth-round knockout. Tiger had never been knocked out before.

Foster was born December 15, 1938, in Lubbock, Texas, but moved to Albuquerque, New Mexico, at a very early age. Tall and skinny, he had to learn how to use his fists quite young because the heavier kids were always picking on him.

Bob's career is very similar to those of James J. Braddock and Jersey Joe Walcott in that he was not going anywhere early in the game and came out of retirement to win a championship. Because of his height, Foster was fed a steady diet of heavyweights and was beaten quite often. And he never made any big money against the bigger men.

Foster turned pro in 1961 and by December of '65 decided to quit fighting because he was making no money. He changed his mind in 1966 and started to click. By the end of May he was champion.

Bob is an authoritative puncher and could possibly be a big threat as a heavyweight.

NINO BENVENUTI

Middleweight Champion

For awhile, Nino Benvenuti and Emile Griffith appeared to be lending the middleweight title to each other. The Italian from Trieste came to the United States to beat Griffith and take the title back to Italy. This happened on April 17, 1967, in Madison Square Garden.

Griffith had a return-bout contract and in September of the same year regained the title at Shea Stadium in New York. The following year, on March 4, again in the Garden, Benvenuti defeated Griffith to become champion again.

The popular Italian was born in Trieste on April 26, 1938, the son of a fisherman. He started boxing at an early age and in 1960 won the Olympic welterweight title in Rome. He turned pro the next year.

Benvenuti is handsome, with long sandy hair and a profile good enough to get him an acting job. He loves mod clothes and sports cars. He is also interested in fine literature, politics and fine food.

Nino has a fair punch, is very quick, and is an exceptionally fine boxer. He is also an elegant dresser, leaning to the latest jet-set styles.

JOSE NAPOLES

Welterweight Champion

Jose Napoles was an heir to poverty when he was born on April 14, 1940, in Cuba. As most children of poverty, Napoles turned to boxing as an escape from the filthy slum where he lived. He made it.

He drifted to the amateurs and won the Cuban Gloves lightweight championship. After that came a spectacular switch to professional boxing. He ran up a string of nineteen straight before he was beaten and then ran up another string of fifteen straight.

Jose did most of his early boxing in Castro Cuba. He won many fights but was making no money at all. In 1961 he decided to apply for a visa to Mexico, where he was to join with an old friend who had fled pro-Communist Cuba. After

227

eight months, Napoles was finally given his freedom and he flew to Mexico City.

Napoles began his boxing career all over and had good and bad years. But he was learning all the time: Mexican and American fighters had styles different from the Cubans. By the time he got his chance at the welter title, on April 19, 1968, he took out all his frustrations on the champion, Curtis Cokes, and was the new welterweight champion when Cokes could not answer the bell for the fourteenth round. Tears streamed down the side of Napoles' battered face that glorious night in Los Angeles.

ISMAEL LAGUNA

Lightweight Champion

Ismael Laguna of Panama hasn't always been a champion, but ever since he turned professional in 1961, he has never stopped trying to be one. And when he regained the world lightweight crown on March 4, 1970, it was his second visit to the top of that division.

Laguna first won the lightweight title on April 10, 1965, with a fifteen-round decision over Carlos Ortiz of Panama City. But he lost it back to Ortiz on November 13 of that same year.

On August 16, 1967, Laguna was hammering at the championship again, but again he lost to Ortiz in fifteen rounds.

And so it remained for his 1970 battle with Mexican-born Mando Ramos of Los Angeles to return him to supremacy. Ramos, the defending champion, was so battered after nine rounds that his manager signaled the referee to stop the bout.

Laguna, born June 28, 1943, first tasted championship combat in 1962 when he captured the Panama featherweight title.

JOHNNY FAMECHON

Featherweight Champion

Johnny Famechon—his real name is Jean Pierre—was born in France in 1948. He was born into a family of fighters, his father, Andre, having had mild success as a welter and his uncle, Ray, having had a bit more success as a featherweight.

When Johnny was five years old, his father decided to move to Melbourne, Australia, hoping for a better life. By the time Johnny was fifteen he had made up his mind: he wanted to be the third fighting Famechon. Though his father didn't approve, Johnny went into the amateurs. By the time he was seventeen he was fighting professional. He won the Australian feather title when he was only nineteen and a half years old.

Outside of Australia, people doubted his ability so he went to France to prove himself against the top contender in France. Johnny returned to Australia with a draw.

During Johnny's absence Vincente Saldivar, the world's champion retired and his title was put up for grabs. On May 20, 1968, Johnny met Californian Bobby Valdez in Sydney for the championship. Valdez was disqualified in the thirteenth round for butting, and Famechon was declared king of the featherweights.

He defended against Fighting Harada on July 28, 1968, and at first, the referee, former world featherweight champion

Willie Pep, called the fight a draw but upon a careful check of the scorecards, Famechon was declared the winner.

RUBEN OLIVARES

Bantamweight Champion

Ruben Olivares was another Mexican champion, but one who really didn't have to fight to eat. His father was a successful businessman in Mexico City and deplored Ruben's interest in boxing. But Ruben had a mind of his own.

He was a high school dropout at fifteen, running with hooligans around the pool rooms in Mexico City. To help work off his excess energy, he spent some time in gymnasiums and started boxing.

By the time he was sixteen he could handle himself against any Mexican amateur and won the Mexican Golden Gloves title despite a broken jaw. He turned pro in February of 1965 and won the world bantamweight championship from Lionel Rose, the Australian, on Aug. 22, 1969, in Los Angeles. Rose was knocked out in the eighth round.

Olivares, only twenty-three, had a fantastic KO record of 51 knockouts in 53 fights going into 1970.

FLYWEIGHT DIVISION

There was no clear-cut champion as 1969 drew to a close. The world Boxing Association declared the title vacant but *Ring* Magazine carried Thailand's Chartchai Chionoi as king of the flyweights. However, Japan disputed both agencies by declaring Hiroyuki Ebihara as world champion.

All-Time Records

NAT FLEISCHER'S ALL-TIME
RANKING OF WORLD BOXERS*

Heavyweights (Weight Unlimited)

1. Jack Johnson
2. James J. Jeffries
3. Bob Fitzsimmons
4. Jack Dempsey
5. James J. Corbett
6. Joe Louis
7. Sam Langford
8. Gene Tunney
9. Max Schmeling
10. Rocky Marciano

Light Heavyweights (Weight Limit: 175 Pounds)

1. Kid McCoy
2. Philadelphia Jack O'Brien
3. Jack Dillon
4. Tommy Loughran
5. Jack Root
6. Battling Levinsky
7. Georges Carpentier
8. Tom Gibbons
9. Jack Delaney
10. Paul Berlenbach

Middleweights (Weight Limit: 160 Pounds)

1. Stanley Ketchel
2. Tommy Ryan
3. Harry Greb
4. Mickey Walker
5. Ray Robinson
6. Frank Klaus
7. Billy Papke
8. Les Darcy
9. Mike Gibbons
10. Jeff Smith

* Nat Fleischer for years has been recognized as boxing's expert historian. He is editor and publisher of *The Ring Magazine*, compiler of *Nat Fleischer's Ring Record Book and Encyclopedia of Boxing*, and founder of The Ring Museum and The Boxing Hall of Fame, both located in New York.

Welterweights (Weight Limit: 147 Pounds)

1. Joe Walcott
2. Mysterious Billy Smith
3. Jack Britton
4. Ted Kid Lewis
5. Dixie Kid
6. Harry Lewis
7. Willie Lewis
8. Henry Armstrong
9. Barney Ross
10. Jimmy McLarnin

Lightweights (Weight Limit: 135 Pounds)

1. Joe Gans
2. Benny Leonard
3. Owen Moran
4. Freddy Welsh
5. Battling Nelson
6. George Kid Lavigne
7. Tony Canzoneri
8. Willie Ritchie
9. Lew Tendler
10. Ad Wolgast

Featherweights (Weight Limit: 126 Pounds)

1. Terry McGovern
2. Jem Driscoll
3. Abe Attell
4. Willie Pep
5. Johnny Dundee
6. Young Griffo
7. Johnny Kilbane
8. Kid Chocolate
9. George K.O. Chaney
10. Louis Kid Kaplan

Bantamweights (Weight Limit: 118 Pounds)

1. George Dixon
2. Pete Herman
3. Kid Williams
4. Eder Jofre
5. Joe Lynch
6. Bud Taylor
7. Johnny Coulon
8. Frankie Burns
9. Eddie Campi
10. Panama Al Brown

Flyweights (Weight Limit: 112 Pounds)

1. Jimmy Wilde
2. Pancho Villa
3. Frankie Genaro
4. Fidel La Barba
5. Benny Lynch
6. Elky Clark
7. Johnny Buff
8. Midget Wolgast
9. Peter Kane
10. Pascual Perez

BOXING HALL OF FAME

The Boxing Hall of Fame was established in 1954 by *The Ring Magazine*. The list is made up of three groups—the Pioneer, for fighters who were active in the days when they fought with bare knuckles; the Old Timers, who were active before 1919; and the Modern Group, who fought after 1919 and have been retired at least two years.

Plaques honoring all these men, together with countless relics of boxing, are on view at the headquarters of the Hall of Fame in New York.

Elected in 1969

MODERN GROUP—Jersey Joe Walcott, heavyweight; Carmen Basilio, welterweight and middleweight.
OLD TIMERS GROUP—Leo Houck, middleweight; Jeff Smith, middleweight.
PIONEER GROUP—Joe Goss, heavyweight.

Elected in 1968

MODERN GROUP—Max Baer, heavyweight.
OLD TIMERS GROUP—Philadelphia Jack O'Brien, light heavyweight.
PIONEER GROUP—Jacob Hyer, heavyweight.

Elected in 1967

MODERN GROUP—Ray Robinson, middleweight.
OLD TIMERS GROUP—Joe Jeannette, heavyweight.
PIONEER GROUP—Barney (Young) Aaron, lightweight and welterweight.

Elected in 1966

MODERN GROUP—Kid Gavilan, welterweight; Archie Moore, light heavyweight.
OLD TIMERS GROUP—Battling Levinsky, light heavyweight.
PIONEER GROUP—James (Deaf) Burke, heavyweight.

Elected in 1965

MODERN GROUP—Billy Conn, light heavyweight.
OLD TIMERS GROUP—Johnny Coulon, bantamweight; Owen Moran, featherweight; Young Corbett II, featherweight.
PIONEER GROUP—Jake Kilrain, heavyweight.

Elected in 1964

MODERN GROUP—Lou Ambers, lightweight; James J. Braddock, heavyweight.
OLD TIMERS GROUP—Georges Carpentier, light heavyweight; Ted (Kid) Lewis, welterweight.
PIONEER GROUP—Sam Collyer, lightweight.

Elected in 1963

MODERN GROUP—Willie Pep, featherweight.
OLD TIMERS GROUP—Tom Gibbons, light heavyweight.
PIONEER GROUP—Jem Ward, heavyweight.

Elected in 1962

MODERN GROUP—Billy Petrolle, lightweight and welterweight; Marcel Cerdan, middleweight.
OLD TIMERS GROUP—Willie Ritchie, lightweight.
PIONEER GROUP—Ned Price, heavyweight.

Elected in 1961

MODERN GROUP—Lew Tendler, lightweight; Pancho Villa, flyweight.
OLD TIMERS GROUP—Jack Root, light heavyweight.
PIONEER GROUP—Tom Spring, heavyweight.

Elected in 1960

MODERN GROUP—Jack Britton, welterweight.
OLD TIMERS GROUP—Tommy Burns, heavyweight; Joe Choynski, heavyweight; Freddie Welsh, lightweight; Johnny Kilbane, featherweight.
PIONEER GROUP—Dan Donnelly, heavyweight.

Elected in 1959

MODERN GROUP—Rocky Marciano, heavyweight; Kid Chocolate, featherweight.
OLD TIMERS GROUP—Pete Herman, bantamweight; Jimmy Wilde, flyweight; Tom Sharkey, heavyweight; George Kid Lavigne, lightweight; Jack Dillon, light heavyweight; John Gully, heavyweight.

Elected in 1958

MODERN GROUP—Tony Zale, middleweight.
OLD TIMERS GROUP—Mike Gibbons, welterweight; Tommy Ryan, middleweight; Ad Wolgast, lightweight.
PIONEER GROUP—Tom Molineaux, heavyweight.

Elected in 1957

MODERN GROUP—Johnny Dundee, featherweight.
OLD TIMERS GROUP—Les Darcy, middleweight; Packey McFarland, lightweight; Kid McCoy, welterweight; Battling Nelson, lightweight.
PIONEER GROUP—Charley Mitchell, heavyweight.

Elected in 1956

MODERN GROUP—Tony Canzoneri, lightweight; Jimmy McLarnin, welterweight; Barney Ross, welterweight; Tommy Loughran, light heavyweight.
OLD TIMERS GROUP—Jem Driscoll, featherweight; George Dixon, bantamweight and featherweight.
PIONEER GROUP—Peter Jackson, heavyweight.

234

Elected in 1955

MODERN GROUP—Harry Greb, middleweight; Gene Tunney, heavyweight; Benny Leonard, lightweight; Mickey Walker, welterweight and middleweight.

OLD TIMERS GROUP—Terry McGovern, featherweight; Abe Attell, featherweight; Sam Langford, middleweight; Joe Walcott, welterweight.

PIONEER GROUP—William Richmond, heavyweight; William Thompson (Bendigo), heavyweight.

Elected in 1954

MODERN GROUP—Jack Dempsey, heavyweight; Joe Louis, heavyweight; Henry Armstrong, featherweight, lightweight, and welterweight.

OLD TIMERS GROUP—Stanley Ketchel, middleweight; Jack Johnson, heavyweight; James J. Jeffries, heavyweight; Bob Fitzsimmons, heavyweight; Joe Gans, lightweight; James J. Corbett, heavyweight.

PIONEER GROUP—James Figg, heavyweight; John Jackson, heavyweight; Daniel Mendoza, heavyweight; John Morrissey, heavyweight; Tom Hyer, heavyweight; Arthur Chambers, lightweight; Jack McAuliffe, lightweight; Tom Cribb, heavyweight; Jem Mace, heavyweight; John C. Heenan, heavyweight; Jack Broughton, heavyweight; Tom Sayers, heavyweight; Young Griffo, featherweight; John L. Sullivan, heavyweight; Nonpareil Jack Dempsey, middleweight.

CHAMPIONS WHO HELD TITLE LONGEST

HEAVYWEIGHT: Joe Louis, 11 years 8 months. (Won title June 22, 1937, retired undefeated March 1, 1949.)

LIGHT HEAVYWEIGHT: Archie Moore, 9 years 2 months. (Won title December 17, 1952, lost recognition as champion February 9, 1962.)

MIDDLEWEIGHT: Tony Zale, 5 years 7½ months. (Won title November 28, 1941, lost July 16, 1947.)

WELTERWEIGHT: Freddie (Red) Cochrane, 4 years 6 months. (Won title July 29, 1941, lost February 1, 1946.)

LIGHTWEIGHT: Benny Leonard, 7 years 7½ months. (Won title May 28, 1917, retired undefeated January 15, 1925.)

FEATHERWEIGHT: Johnny Kilbane, 11 years 3½ months. (Won title February 22, 1912, lost June 2, 1923.)

BANTAMWEIGHT: Panama Al Brown, 5 years 11½ months. (Won title June 18, 1929, lost June 1, 1935.)

FLYWEIGHT: Jimmy Wilde, 6 years 6 months. (Won title December 18, 1916, lost June 18, 1923.)

JOE LOUIS' TITLE FIGHTS

Joe Louis set a record of twenty-five successful title defenses during his reign as world heavyweight champion. No other champion in any class ever held a title as long as Louis— eleven years eight months seven days.

Date	Opponent	Result	Time of KO
June 22, 1937	James J. Braddock	KO–8	1:10
Aug. 30, 1937	Tommy Farr	D–15	—
Feb. 23, 1938	Nathan Mann	KO–3	1:56
April 1, 1938	Harry Thomas	KO–5	2:50
June 22, 1938	Max Schmeling	KO–1	2:04
Jan. 25, 1939	John Henry Lewis	KO–1	2:29
April 17, 1939	Jack Roper	KO–1	2:20
June 28, 1939	Tony Galento	KO–4	2:29
Sept. 20, 1939	Bob Pastor	KO–11	:38
Feb. 9, 1940	Arturo Godoy	D–15	—
March 29, 1940	Johnny Paychek	KO–2	:44
June 20, 1940	Arturo Godoy	KO–8	1:24
Dec. 16, 1940	Al McCoy	KO–6	°
Jan. 31, 1941	Red Burman	KO–5	2:49
Feb. 17, 1941	Gus Dorazio	KO–2	1:30
March 21, 1941	Abe Simon	KO–13	1:20
April 8, 1941	Tony Musto	KO–9	1:36
May 23, 1941	Buddy Baer	D–7	°°
June 18, 1941	Billy Conn	KO–13	2:58
Sept. 29, 1941	Lou Nova	KO–6	2:59
Jan. 9, 1942	Buddy Baer	KO–1	2:56
March 27, 1942	Abe Simon	KO–6	:16
June 19, 1946	Billy Conn	KO–8	2:19
Sept. 18, 1946	Tami Mauriello	KO–1	2:09
Dec. 5, 1947	Jersey Joe Walcott	D–15	—
June 25, 1948	Jersey Joe Walcott	KO–11	2:56
†Sept. 27, 1950	Ezzard Charles	L–15	—

° McCoy unable to answer bell for sixth round.
°° Baer disqualified in seventh round.
† Comeback bout after retirement.

THE EDWARD J. NEIL TROPHY

The Edward J. Neil Trophy is voted annually by the Boxing Writers Association of New York to the person who has done most for boxing during the preceding year. It honors the memory of a former Associated Press sports writer who was killed January 3, 1938, while serving as a war correspondent in the Spanish civil war.

Year	Winner
1969	Joe Frazier
1968	Bob Foster
1967	Carlos Ortiz
1966	Dick Tiger
1965	Cassius Clay
1964	Willie Pastrano
1963	Emile Griffith
1962	Dick Tiger
1961	Gene Fullmer
1960	Floyd Patterson
1959	Ingemar Johansson
1958	Archie Moore
1957	Carmen Basilio
1956	Floyd Patterson
1955	Carmen Basilio
1954	Carl (Bobo) Olson
1953	Kid Gavilan
1952	Rocky Marciano
1951	Jersey Joe Walcott
1950	Ray Robinson
1949	Ezzard Charles
1948	Ike Williams
1947	Gus Lesnevich
1946	Tony Zale
1945	James J. Walker
1944	Benny Leonard
1943	The Boxers in All Branches of the Armed Forces of Our Country
1942	Barney Ross
1941	Joe Louis
1940	Henry Armstrong
1939	Billy Conn
1938	Jack Dempsey

Football

The History of Football

In the East, the West, the North, and the South, from the middle of September through much of January, football is king. To the true fan, football is also a disease to which he succumbs every year.

The main symptom is a feverish excitement that is particularly severe on weekends. Then the suffering fan seeks relief by going to football games, watching football on TV, listening to football on radio. During the week he reads the sports pages at breakfast, thinks of touchdown plays at school or work, kicks field goals in his dreams at night.

The disease lasts roughly four months and is not fatal; the fan always survives. But he is never cured. Come September, he and millions like him will gladly succumb to virus football once again.

How did football get so popular? How did it start?

For years record books have stated that the first intercollegiate football game in this country was played between Rutgers and Princeton on November 6, 1869. The game, however, was not football. They played a soccer game with twenty-five

241

How Rutgers and Princeton looked when they started it all in 1869.

players to a team. Running with the ball or touching it with the hands was not permitted.

In America the first recorded version of any game played only with the feet has been traced to 1609, the year the colonists settled here. The early sport consisted of kicking a round ball from one end of a field to another. Hands were not used and the ball was not carried.

Going way back in history, there is evidence that some form of football was played by the ancient Greeks. Just what kind of ball they used is not clear. But it is a matter of record that the Greeks played a game known as *harpaston*, in which a ball

Yale's football team of 1879, which played in the first 11-man game.

was kicked from one participant to another. It's reasonable to
assume that the Greeks passed the ball game on to the ancient
Romans, who played a game they called *harpastum.*

The game of football—but not as we know it—received its
official name in the British Isles. The game actually was soccer, a sport in which only the feet are used to kick the ball
into a net-enclosure. The British, however, call it football.

For many centuries soccer was the only major sport in the
British Isles. Then in the 19th century an event took place
which eventually led to the game of football as we know it
today. At Rugby School in England, a soccer player named

243

William Webb Ellis suddenly decided to pick up the ball from the ground and run with it. This violated all the rules, and Ellis' fellow students were shocked.

The mad run by Ellis, however, convinced his fellow players that running with the ball gave the ancient game of football some variety. Thus was born the game of Rugby, a rugged combination of kicking and running with a ball.

Although Rugby—in which the ball is carried—originated in the early 1820's, it was not until 1871 that a sport that combined kicking and carrying the ball was played in the United States. Before that year schools and informal teams stuck quite closely to the ancient version of football (the same game as our soccer).

In 1876, the first Intercollegiate Football Association was formed. Columbia, Harvard, and Princeton established the first uniform rules in the United States: fifteen players per team, two 45-minute halves. Yale refused to join, holding out for an eleven-man team.

The eleven-man team finally was approved by the association in 1880. The playing area was reduced to 110 yards by

The straight-arm, tackling above the knees, and the dropkick in the early days.

Yesterday in Sports

The wedge formation of blocking meant moving the ball by brute force.

53 yards. The kickoff was made from midfield, and a scrimmage line was established.

Yale and Harvard played the first game with eleven-man teams in 1879. Since it established a definite number of players, this may have done more to develop the future growth of American football than any other contest. The period from 1880 to 1890 produced many more changes in the conduct of play.

A system of downs was established in 1882. It required the offensive team to gain at least 5 yards in three downs or surrender possession of the ball. Starting with the 1885 season a touchdown carried a value of 4 points; goal from field, 5; goal after touchdown, 2; safety, 2. The scoring system was changed again in 1897. The value of a touchdown was increased to 5 points, and a goal after touchdown was reduced to 1 point.

The wedge formation of blocking meant moving the ball

by brute force. In this offense, the blockers formed a V-shaped mass of humanity for their ball carrier by linking their arms together. This mass blocking led to brutality, severe injuries, and in some cases, death.

The Big Three—Yale, Harvard, and Princeton—were the leaders of the sport as the 19th century came to a close. In fact, the greatest players of this period were from Yale—Pudge Heffelfinger, an almost immovable guard who had strength enough to penetrate the firmest of wedges, and Frank Hinkey, a fiery competitor who was the first of the rushing ends.

Walter Camp, the Yale coach, originated the idea of choosing football's best players at the close of the season. In 1889 his outstanding choices were called All-Americans. The practice of naming an annual All-America squad has continued since.

Because of the alarming growth of injuries resulting from power blocking and mass tackling the game became more difficult to control, and the newspapers started to campaign for a modification of some of the rules.

Some schools decided to drop the game because too many students were being injured. President Theodore Roosevelt, anxious to see the sport continue, requested a meeting with representatives from Yale, Harvard, and Princeton.

"Clean up your game," demanded Rough-Rider Teddy in 1905, "or I'll see that it's abolished."

The representatives took the President's advice seriously, called a conference of some sixty schools and formed the American Intercollegiate Football Rules Committee.

New rules designed to eliminate some of the bone-crushing tactics were placed into effect immediately. The forward pass was made legal, the two 45-minute halves were reduced to 30

Pictorial History of American Sports

Things sometimes got out of hand in the 1880's, and many injuries resulted.

minutes each, and a neutral zone, the distance of the length of the ball between the two scrimmage lines, was abolished. The distance to be gained on downs was increased to 10 yards.

The forward pass became a favorite offensive play of the Midwestern teams around 1908. The Eastern squads, using players of huge physique and great power, stayed with their fierce ground attack, which remained successful.

In 1910 the rules required seven men to stay on the line of scrimmage. No longer could the offensive linemen drop to the rear to protect the ball carrier. Forbidden were the flying tackle, crawling, pulling the runner, and interlocked interference. And the two 30-minute halves now became four 15-minute periods.

More rules changed in 1912. The length of the field was made 100 yards, the value of the touchdown was increased to 6 points, and the offensive team was now allowed four downs to move the ball the required 10 yards.

The early teachers of these pioneer football teams introduced certain offensive and defensive methods that have been improved over the years.

Fielding (Hurry-Up) Yost of Michigan, Amos Alonzo Stagg of Chicago, Walter Camp of Yale, Percy Haughton of Harvard, Glenn (Pop) Warner of Carlisle, John Heisman of Clemson, Eddie Cochems of St. Louis (who made extensive use of the forward pass), and Harry Williams of Minnesota were some of the first coaches whose ideas have been carried on through the years.

Football gained major status from 1913 to 1917. This was the period that produced Jim

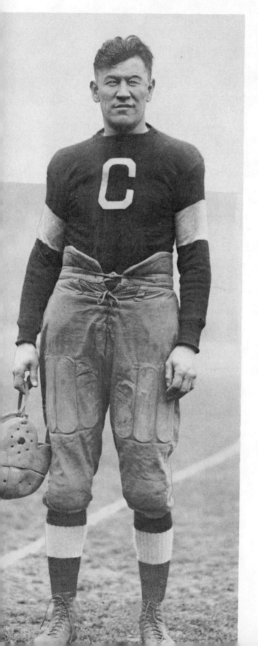

Jim Thorpe

Thorpe, perhaps the greatest of all-round athletes. Thorpe played for a tiny Indian school at Carlisle, Pennsylvania, and was virtually unstoppable.

No team record during the first twenty years of the new century could compare with the amazing mark compiled by the University of Washington. Consider this startling statistic: For nine straight seasons (1908 through 1916) the team did not lose a game. Gil Dobie was the coach during this period who saw his team play 61 games, win 58 and tie 3.

The Golden Twenties were indeed a historic era. It was the glory of Rockne and powerful Notre Dame teams; the emergence of Illinois' Red Grange as the game's most publicized player; Warner's effective double wing coaching system at Stanford; the brute strength of Bronko Nagurski of Minnesota, and an honor roll of famous coaches, including Bill Roper, Princeton; Tad Jones, Yale; Gil Dobie, Cornell; Biff Jones, Army; Jock Sutherland, Pittsburgh; Wallace Wade, Alabama; Bob Neyland, Tennessee; Bill Alexander, Georgia Tech; Andy Smith, California; and Howard Jones, Southern California.

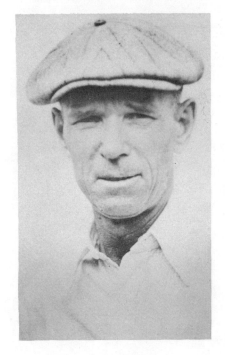

Gil Dobie

University of Washington

Some of the players in this decade were public idols.

Football was now an accepted way of athletic life. Despite an economic depression in the 1930's, crowds of fifty thousand, especially at some of the Midwestern fields, were no longer considered unusually large. The Sunday newspapers devoted more space to sports as readers' interest in football news increased.

Notre Dame, despite the tragic death of the beloved Rockne in an airplane crash, remained among the best. The Four Horsemen of the Twenties were now replaced by the famous Frank Carideo-quarter-backed teams. Michigan and Minnesota, coached by Harry Kipke and Bernie Bierman, respectively, continued to dominate the Big Ten.

In the South the famed Frank Thomas was developing championship teams at Alabama. The feared Crimson Tide won the Rose Bowl in 1935 with three All-Americans in its lineup—

Knute Rockne

Christy Walsh Management

William C. Greene

Don Hutson

Don Hutson, a fabulous pass-catcher, passer Dixie Howell, and Bill Lee, a granitelike tackle.

Tennessee, too, was strong under Neyland. It had one of the finest of all-time guards, Herman Hickman, who later became coach of Yale. In this period Wallace Wade also led a Duke squad to the Rose Bowl.

But for long gains, spectacular play, and high-scoring fireworks the fans looked to the Southwest. Texas Christian and Southern Methodist were the particular crowd-pleasing teams. Sammy Baugh, and later Davey O'Brien, showed the rest of the country just how to pass the ball as the Horned Frogs of TCU, under Coach Dutch Meyer, were among the national leaders.

On the West Coast, Stanford, with Coach Tiny Thornhill, and Southern California, under Howard Jones, were Rose Bowl representatives. The Trojans of Southern California, paced by tackle Aaron Rosenberg and halfback Ernie Pinckert, went undefeated in 32 straight games (1931–1933). They also won three Rose Bowl games (1930, 1932, 1933). The Stanford Indians, with a great backfield featuring Bobby Grayson, Frank Alustiza, and Bones Hamilton, played in the Rose Bowl three straight seasons (1934–1936).

The Panthers of Pitt were supreme in 1937. Coach Jock Sutherland had the perfect eleven and a marvelous backfield made up of Marshall Goldberg, John Michelosen, Curley Stebbins, and Frank Patrick.

Surprise teams in the East were Yale and Columbia. Yale had tiny Albie Booth, a whirling dervish of a quarterback who was one of the smallest and lightest ever to play for a major college. Later the Blues were blessed with end Larry Kelley,

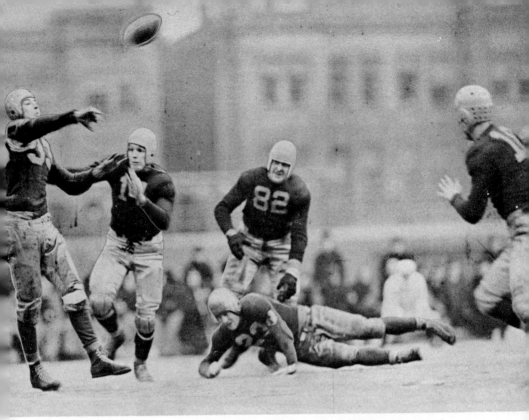

Sammy Baugh, one of football's greatest passers, tosses one against the Chicago Bears in the 1937 pro title game, won by his Washington Redskins, 28 to 21.

who made almost impossible pass catches, and Clint Frank, just about the best halfback in Eli's football history.

Lou Little, who was to coach Columbia for twenty-six years, was surprised when his team received an invitation to play in the Rose Bowl in 1934. The light Lions, rated as a good little team, were to meet the feared Stanford club. The result was an astonishing 7–0 victory for the Easterners, the greatest of all upsets in Rose Bowl history.

Fordham, too, with Jim Crowley at the helm, was particularly powerful in 1937. The Rams line, bolstered by Alex

253

Precision blocking paves the way for an Ohio State ball carrier against Notre Dame in the memorable 1935 battle before a throng of 81,000 spectators.

Wojciechowicz, will always be considered one of the strongest to play. So unyielding were they that they earned the name "Seven Blocks of Granite."

The Rocky Mountain region produced one of the sport's most publicized players of the decade, Byron (Whizzer) White, a genuine triple-threat star and Phi Beta Kappa student, who paced the University of Colorado to the Cotton Bowl in 1938.

The University of Chicago, one of the football's early lead-

Ohio State's Dick Heekin sidesteps a Notre Dame tackler. The Buckeyes were in command in the first half, but the Irish roared back to win, 18 to 13.

ers, came upon dull days. The Maroons produced undistinguished teams and were soon to discontinue the game. But in 1935 they had the greatest back in the country in Jay Berwanger. He was the first winner of the Heisman Trophy, the annual award given to the best college player in the land.

Without doubt the most thrilling college game of all time took place between Notre Dame and Ohio State on November 2, 1935. Ohio State's stadium held a whopping 81,000, and none of them could believe their eyes.

Ohio State led 13 to 0 at the start of the fourth quarter. Striking quickly, Notre Dame, with Andy Pilney running and passing, scored two touchdowns. But they missed both conversion attempts and the Buckeyes clung to a 13–12 lead as the game entered its last ninety seconds.

Pilney, hemmed in while trying to pass on Ohio State's 41-yard line, broke loose through the middle and dashed to the 19. But Pilney was not able to continue. He was carried off the field, and it seemed that the last Irish spark had burned out. Then thirty seconds later Bill Shakespeare threw a pass over the goal line. Notre Dame end Wayne Milner appeared from a group of Ohio State defenders, caught the ball, and made a touchdown for football's most dramatic victory.

In 1940 a radical new attacking formation, which only a few teams had used, came from the Pacific Coast. Clark Shaughnessy, coach at Stanford, began to run all his offensive plays from the T-formation. Basically this formation was the same as the single wing, in that one flanking back was stationed directly behind his left or right end. The main difference, however, was the position of the quarterback. He was moved directly to the rear of the center and received the ball by merely placing his hands between the center's legs.

Fans were enthusiastic about the tricky ball-handling of the quarterback and the suspense of watching a play develop into an end run or a pass-off to the side. T-formation football started a new change in coaching procedures, one which alerted the defense as well.

With the T-formation firmly established in the early forties, the defense had to shift its tactics to meet this fast-striking attack. So this early period was marked by another shift in both offensive and defensive play.

The Midwest was perhaps the strongest football area during this time. Minnesota, Northwestern, with passer-quarterback Otto Graham, and Michigan, helped by the spectacular running of Tom Harmon and the strong blocking of quarterback Forest Evashevski, monopolized play.

Stanford, with Frankie Albert as the first recognized T-quarterback of top ability, was supreme on the West Coast. Tennessee and Texas were standouts in the South and the Southwest. But the military services were soon to have the best players, and college football was below par from 1941 through 1944.

In 1944 the cadets of West Point began a reign of supremacy which lasted until the 1950's. Earl Blaik, the coach of the Army team, was blessed with perhaps the two most talented backs ever to play in one unit at the same time. Glenn Davis was the halfback and Felix (Doc) Blanchard the fullback. Together they carried Army to national honors for three seasons. Both were named All-Americans in 1944, 1945, and 1946.

Army compiled two magnificent winning streaks in this ten-year period, not losing a game from 1944 until Columbia upset it in 1947. Then they started a new streak which lasted until Navy beat them in 1950.

After World War II, Notre Dame, coached by Frank Leahy and sparked by quarterback Johnny Lujack, shared national laurels with Army and two undefeated Michigan teams. Notre Dame won 37 games and tied 2 from 1946 to 1949 as it put together four undefeated seasons.

This was also the period when free substitutions were permitted. The Rules Committee, recognizing that the tricky T-attack was getting more difficult to halt, agreed to permit free substitutions in 1941. Thus was started wholesale substitu-

Army's Glenn Davis eludes a Navy tackler and romps for a TD in the 1944 contest. This was the season the cadets began a three-year winning streak.

tions. Michigan first took advantage of this rule by inserting a complete team of eleven players skilled in offensive maneuvers. Upon surrendering the ball, it substituted a full team of eleven players equally skilled in defensive maneuvers. This was known as the two-platoon system and was in effect from 1945 through 1952.

The late forties witnessed the emergence of California, under Coach Lynn Waldorf, as a leading force on the Coast. But perhaps the most significant year in this period was 1948. This was the season that Bud Wilkinson, a onetime Minnesota

University of Oklahoma

Leon Heath, one of Oklahoma's running stars during its 31-game winning streak, on his way for an 81-yard touchdown gallop against Santa Clara.

lineman and quarterback, became head coach at Oklahoma. He was to start a dynasty without equal in modern football history.

The 1950's had their share of superlative teams, coaches, and players. But no record of this era can approach the high standards achieved by Wilkinson and his Sooners of Oklahoma.

Here's what Oklahoma accomplished from 1948—Wilkinson's first year—through the close of the 1958 season, eleven years later: The Sooners were undefeated from 1948 until 1951, winning 31 straight games before being upset by Notre

Dame. Another streak began in 1952 and went for 45 games—until Notre Dame again smashed it in 1957. Thus, in eleven years Oklahoma won 99 games, lost 7, and tied 2.

The 1950's were also distinguished for the continuing emphasis on the T-formation and the various defenses that were designed to halt it. The standard T gave birth to such formations as the winged-T and the split-T attacks, which are merely trickier and more complicated variations of the standard T.

When the two-platoon system was ruled out in 1953 coaches were no longer able to meet the T attack with a fresh wave of eleven defensive specialists. The result was a sharpening of defensive teaching and tactics and an emphasis on defensive drills.

With television converting more and more people to football mania, attendance at college games soared to new highs in the 1960's. Attendance for the 1969 season was placed at more than 27 million, compared with some 20 million in 1960, despite the fact that the number of teams during that period had declined from 620 to 615, according to the National Collegiate Athletic Association.

Many colleges belong to athletic conferences, which are actually leagues. In many cases conference champions qualify to play in a bowl game, usually at the completion of the regular season. The major bowls, which attempt to pit one conference champion against another, are the Rose Bowl, the Sugar Bowl, the Orange Bowl, the Cotton Bowl, and the Gator Bowl.

The first professional game was played in 1895 between teams from the towns of Latrobe and Jeannette, Pennsylvania. Many professional teams were soon formed, mostly in an effort to make a profit on the reputation that the college players had acquired. Schedules, however, were loosely organized. Crowds were small, and the professional game was slow in gaining respect and prestige.

The first attempt to organize a pro league of high quality was in 1920 when the American Professional Football Association was formed. Jim Thorpe was named its first president. But this league, consisting mainly of teams in the Midwest, was loosely governed and was forced to regroup in 1922 as the National Football League.

The NFL worked long and hard to create interest and increase attendance. There was a pickup in both when Red Grange joined the league in 1926; but after the Illinois star was no longer a novelty, both attendance and interest dropped again.

At the start of the 1930's the NFL slowly began to gain the recognition it had sought for so long. Crowds began to appreciate the hard-hitting brand of ball, and interest was revived with the formation of two divisions, East and West. The first playoff game in 1933 between the Chicago Bears and New York Giants also proved to the public that the NFL would produce an annual champion.

Bronko Nagurski and Ken Strong were among the early stars who carried their clubs (the Bears and the Giants) to division crowns.

Two of the greatest players in the NFL were also All-Americans. Sammy Baugh played sixteen years with the Boston and Washington Redskins and at one time held all the passing records. Don Hutson, with the Green Bay Packers for eleven years, scored more points than any other pro player with his

261

pass receptions, setting a record that stood until the 1960's.

A rival league, the All-American Conference, was organized in 1946. The NFL refused to recognize this new professional group, and the battle to secure college players was fierce and highly competitive. Both leagues suffered loss in attendance, but the NFL, under the guidance of commissioner Bert Bell, had established a firmer foundation. It survived this war when the All-American Conference was discontinued after the 1949 season. Many of the best players came over to the NFL. The standout team, the Cleveland Browns, which had won every All-American Conference championship, came into the NFL as a unit. Under coach Paul Brown they quickly established themselves as an NFL power, with field-kicker Lou Groza, passer Otto Graham, and line-plunger Marion Motley. The Browns compiled the best record in the NFL in the 1950's.

In 1960 the American Football League was organized. Its eight teams were Boston, Buffalo, Dallas (transferred to Kansas City in 1963), Los Angeles (transferred to San Diego in 1961), Oakland, Denver, Houston, and New York.

The league chose as its commissioner Joe Foss, former governor of South Dakota and World War II hero, and

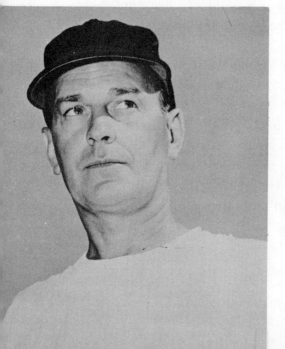

Paul Brown

Cleveland Browns

negotiated a television contract with the National Broadcasting Company that helped cover its early expenses and kept many teams from going bankrupt.

In 1962 the Dallas Texans and Houston Oilers played an exciting double overtime game to decide the league championship, the first time a professional team had played that long in a title contest. Dallas won 20–17, then moved to Kansas City in 1963 and was renamed the Chiefs.

In 1965 the league added a ninth team, the Dolphins, in Miami. It also negotiated a five-year television contract with NBC for more than $35,000,000.

With the beginning of a new decade, the 1970's, pro football set out upon a new era of its own with a merger of the National and American Leagues.

Two conferences of three divisions each were set up as follows:

National Conference

Eastern Division: Dallas, New York Giants, Philadelphia, St. Louis, Washington.

Central Division: Chicago, Detroit, Green Bay, Minnesota.

Western Division: Atlanta, Los Angeles, New Orleans, San Francisco.

American Conference

Eastern Division: Baltimore, Boston, Buffalo, Miami, New York Jets.

Central Division: Cincinnati, Cleveland, Houston, Pittsburgh.

Western Division: Oakland, Kansas City, San Diego, Denver.

The growth pattern seemed certain to continue into the '70's, so popular had the pro game become—huge crowds, higher salaries for more and flashier players, fabulous television audiences, new stadiums. No one was prepared to say what the limit would be.

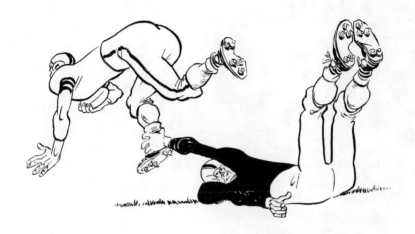

Great Names in Football

SAMMY BAUGH

The finest of all forward passers, this slim, whipcord Texan starred at Texas Christian University in 1935 and 1936. His amazing skill made the coaches in the rest of the nation pass-conscious. Baugh, who played in the National Football League, continued to be the best of them all at throwing a football for accuracy and distance.

Pictorial History of American Sports

Sammy Baugh

Sammy was more than just a passer. During his college days and his early professional career he was outstanding as a punter and runner. He was also one of the most effective tacklers when used as a defensive halfback.

Up until 1963 Baugh held almost every pro passing record. Briefly, here's the statistical breakdown of Sammy's phenomenal sixteen-year NFL record (1937–1952) with the Boston and Washington Redskins:

Passes completed: 1,709 —over 50 percent, or slightly better than one out of two.

Yards gained passing: 22,085. Touchdown passes: 187.

Imagine, if you can, a pro passer connecting safely on 7 of every 10 passes attempted. That's what Baugh did in 1945, the year he completed 128 in 182 attempts.

Baugh returned to the pro ranks in 1960, serving for two seasons as head coach of the New York Titans.

JIMMY BROWN

When one considers the weight of the linemen in pro football (most of them have been compared with steel tanks), the ball-carrying record of Jimmy Brown is truly remarkable.

Running through them, around them and over them, the indestructible Brown spent nine seasons in the service of the NFL's Cleveland Browns and after the 1965 season retired in possession of every career ball-toting mark in the books.

Here are his prizes:

Most seasons leading the league—8 (1957–61, 1963–65).

Most attempts, lifetime—2,359.

Most yards gained, lifetime—12,312.

William C. Greene

Jimmy Brown

Highest average gain, lifetime—5.22 yards per carry.

Most touchdowns rushing, lifetime—106.

And that's not all. The powerfully constructed Syracuse University graduate set records for consecutive seasons as league rushing leader (5, including his rookie year); most yards gained in a season (1,863 in 1963); most yards gained in game (237 in 1957 and again in 1961). He gained more than 1,000 yards seven different seasons, and he registered more than 100 yards in no fewer than 58 games.

There is not a major rushing category in which Brown did not lead the NFL at least once, including the most touchdowns in five different seasons.

Brown was no slouch at catching a pass, either. Apart from the yardage he piled up on the ground, he caught 262 passes in his career for an additional 2,499 yards and 20 touchdowns.

A natural athlete, Jimmy won schoolboy letters in football, basketball, lacrosse and track and field at Manhasset, Long Island, and was an All-American choice in lacrosse as well as football at Syracuse.

His career at Syracuse was capped in the 1957 Cotton Bowl game against Texas Christian, when he scored 21 points as Syracuse was nosed out, 28–27.

As headstrong as he was muscular, Brown retired from football just before the start of the 1966 training season and became a screen actor. Even with nine seasons behind him, he was only thirty years old and as strong as ever. In fact, he had led the league during the previous season in attempts, yards and touchdowns and gave promise of going on indefinitely.

But, like many another champion athlete, Brown wanted to go out while he was still riding high. And that's what he did.

GLENN DAVIS AND DOC BLANCHARD

The most power-packed pair to play in one backfield at the same time were Glenn Davis and Felix (Doc) Blanchard.

They were the twin scoring threats who played on three un-defeated Army teams from 1944 to 1946.

Davis, the speedy halfback from California, was known as "Mr. Outside" because he could run around the ends better than any other back in the country. Blanchard, the smashing fullback from South Carolina, was tagged "Mr. Inside" because he could rip through the middle of a line better than anyone else.

Both led Army to its greatest victories. Both were voted the Heisman Trophy, awarded to college football's best player. Both were named twice to All-America teams.

Davis spread terror in the opposition every time he started to take off around one of his flanks. So spectacular was he in 1944 that he scored 20 touchdowns in nine games and averaged a gain of 11 yards every time he carried the ball.

"Twin engines of destruction" they were called, and Blanchard was the motor that made them go. It was Doc who shattered the line and caused the opponents to pull in tight in an effort to halt him before he got too far. This left the outside open for Davis and he made the most of it.

Both had exceptional speed and there was very little their opponents could do when either shifted into high gear. Both could do everything expected of the complete player. They could run in and out, pass and kick, tackle and block. And both could reverse their favorite individual style of running, with Blanchard occasionally streaking to the outside and Davis hitting between tackle and guard.

Defensively they were just as remarkable. Seldom was a pass completed in their territory. Very few ball carriers advanced past their sure tackling hands.

Davis played pro ball with the Los Angeles Rams for a few

seasons but never attained his college greatness. Blanchard made the Air Force his career. Although both went their separate ways after West Point, their feats will always be remembered as joint efforts.

THE FOUR HORSEMEN

The Golden Twenties had Red Grange, the most famous back of all. The same period also produced the Four Horsemen, the most famous backfield of all time.

The Four Horsemen rode to glory for Notre Dame from 1922 through the Rose Bowl game of 1925. They were quarterback Harry Stuhldreher, halfbacks Don Miller and Jim Crowley, and fullback Elmer Layden. No other team has ever had a backfield to compare with this famous quartet of Notre Dame.

It is hard to believe, but the heaviest of the Horsemen was Crowley, at 164 pounds. Miller and Layden each weighed 162, and Stuhldreher was all of 154. Together they were the most explosive 642 pounds ever to play football as a unit.

Stuhldreher, later to coach at Wisconsin, was the supreme leader. He was a fearless blocker and the shrewdest of strategists. He was best at reading the opponent's strategy and organizing his own in an attempt to master it. He was the passer—not particularly brilliant—who made use of the aerial attack only when he was certain the other team's defense was not prepared for it.

Layden was the fastest of the four. He could run 100 yards in less than 10 seconds, which made him a star on pass defense. Layden was also the punter and a hard-charging line plunger who made the most of his blazing speed when shooting off from his mark at fullback. Elmer later was coach at his alma mater.

270

The Four Horsemen. From left to right—Don Miller, Elmer Layden, Jimmy Crowley, and Harry Stuhldreher.

Crowley, who was to coach at Michigan State and Fordham, seemed the most unconcerned of his backfield mates, who called him "Sleepy Jim." But he was far from sleepy when called on to block or carry the ball on a critical play. Crowley was the man Stuhldreher would call on when it was necessary to gain the yardage required in order to keep possession of the ball.

Miller was perhaps the most dangerous runner of the four once past the line of scrimmage. Shifty and elusive, Miller was the one who came up with the long, spectacular dash. He was the best pass-receiver and kept many a scoring drive rolling with fine catches of Stuhldreher's passes. Miller went into law practice and later became a judge.

The Four Horsemen reserved their finest performance for 1924, their last time together. By crushing Army in their traditional clash, Notre Dame again was named national college champion. Stanford, with its famed fullback Ernie Nevers, hurled the Rose Bowl challenge at Notre Dame, which accepted.

This time Layden was the pacemaker. He outplayed Nevers and scored 3 touchdowns, 2 on intercepted passes, as the Irish whipped Stanford, 27–10.

Light, speedy, spectacular, and versatile, the Four Horsemen were the greatest backfield in football.

CLINT FRANK

Twelve players from Yale University are in Football's Hall of Fame. Eleven are from the era of the noseguard and the flying wedge. Only Clinton Frank, twice an All-American halfback, can be termed a "modern."

Frank was outstanding for three seasons, 1935–1937. He was an offensive mechanic who refused to permit injury or overwhelming odds to upset him. He could run, pass, kick, tackle, and block. He was a 60-minute player who was, game after game, the finest ever to play in a Yale backfield.

Clint's dramatic deeds made him the idol of young fans throughout the nation. He always seemed to throw the winning touchdown pass, run for the critical first down, tackle the ball carrier at the crucial moment. He was steady, solid, and reliable.

Playing with Frank in two of his three years was another

All-American, end Larry Kelley. Kelley's brilliant pass catches made Yale a dangerous opponent. But it was Frank who inspired the cocky and colorful Kelley to his outstanding achievements.

Yale was no mighty power when Clint Frank was its captain in 1937. It wasn't even rated among the first ten teams in the country. In fact, the last game of Clint's career was a 13–6 loss to arch enemy Harvard. But even Harvard supporters rose to give the gallant Frank a standing ovation when he limped off the field moments before the game ended.

Frank was supreme in his senior season. His play earned him the Heisman Trophy as football's best player of the year.

RED GRANGE

Never was a football figure so fabulously publicized as Harold (Red) Grange. Grange played in the early twenties, when the word *television* was not to be found in a standard dictionary, when radio was full of static, and when the chief medium of communication was the daily newspaper. Yet Red Grange, with his long sweeping runs, his bursts of speed around enemy lines, his ability to score a touchdown just about any time it was needed and from any place on the field, captured the imagination of a football-mad country.

Red Grange was born in Wheaton, Illinois, on November 21, 1903, and began his climb to fame at the University of Illinois. He reported for the college football squad as an end, but coach Bob Zuppke recognized his great ability as a broken-field runner and switched him to halfback in 1923. Red made the most of it, and thus was started the career of the player acclaimed "the greatest runner in all of football."

Grange's elusiveness and his ability to change direction while in full speed earned him the colorful name "The Galloping Ghost." He would slip and slide through the grasps of enemy tacklers with uncanny ease and take off down the field, the number 77 on the back of his uniform seen by the thousands who filled any stadium in which he played.

The Midwest was proud of Red Grange, but his reputation was somewhat doubted in the eastern part of the country. It didn't take him long to convince the Easterners that he was indeed all that people had said he was.

His team came East to play a heavier and stronger University of Pennsylvania team on November 15, 1924. Despite a steady downpour and a field of mud, Grange scored 3 touchdowns the first four times he handled the ball. Number 77's per-

Red Grange
United Press International

formance was proof positive that he merited selection as an All-American from 1923 to 1925, one of the few players to be chosen three times.

Red's College football career ended in November, 1925, and he turned professional the week after his final collegiate game. He headed one of two all-star pro teams that went on tour, playing sometimes as many as three games a week. In five weeks Grange made about $45,000.

Red became a member of the Chicago Bears of the NFL, playing until 1935, and has been honored as an all-time all-league halfback. In recent years, he has been a television sportscaster.

PAUL HORNUNG

The football hero in the movies is usually a handsome, wisecracking, personable giant. On the screen he does anything and everything. He runs, blocks, throws and catches passes, kicks field goals, scores touchdowns, and sometimes gets into trouble.

Real-life football produced such a hero in the person of Paul Hornung, the Golden Boy of the Green Bay Packers in the National Football League. Golden Boy was undoubtedly the best all-round offensive machine of the 1960's. He holds the NFL scoring mark for a single season (176 points) and was the first player since 1949 to lead the league in scoring three years in a row.

Paul was the toast of Green Bay, Wisconsin, until he was forced to sit out the 1963 season because he bet on his own team. The news hit pro football hard, especially since Commissioner Pete Rozelle also suspended Alex Karas of the

Detroit Lions for the same reason. Technically, both were under indefinite suspension, but Rozelle lifted the ban in time for the 1964 season.

With Hornung, the Packers won championships in 1960, 1961, and 1962. They finished second in 1963, and in 1964 were second again as the reinstated Hornung had, for him, a poor year. He finished eighteenth among the rushers, scoring only 107 points. The opposition held him to 415 yards in 103 carries. They were calling him the Tarnished Golden Boy.

The Packers won the championship and playoff in 1965, but Hornung wasn't much better. He was, however, his best in one of the most crucial games of the season. Against the Colts in Memorial Stadium, Baltimore, Hornung scored five touchdowns to put the Packers on top in the standings.

A week before the big game, martinet coach Vince Lombardi had benched Hornung, but he had enough faith in his coming alive for the big one to start him against the Colts. He was Mr. Everything as the Packers ran up a 42–27 victory.

In the playoff against the Browns, Hornung became a Golden Boy once more when he gained 105 yards in 18 carries and scored a touchdown. The Packers won 23–12, and Hornung was back in the limelight again, the darling of Green Bay and the pro football world.

It was a rocky climb to pro fame for Hornung. Twice an All-American at Notre Dame (1955–1956), Paul was voted the nation's outstanding college player in his senior year. Drafted by the Packers, he was expected to set the pro league on fire immediately.

No such thing happened. Hornung was unable to make the grade at quarterback, his college position. He was shifted to fullback and again proved inadequate. Given a last try at halfback, he became a sensation.

Hornung won his first league scoring title in 1959 with 94 points. In 1960, sparking the Packers to their first Western Division championship in sixteen years, he ran up 176 points to shatter Don Hutson's eighteen-year-old record.

In 1961, even though Army service kept him out of two games, Paul scored 145 points as the Packers retained their division title. He was the big gun in their 37–0 rout of the New York Giants for the league championship.

DON HUTSON

Don Hutson was pro football's human adding machine. This soft-spoken end from Alabama was without doubt the greatest one-man scoring unit in the National Football League.

Slim Don, who could stop his sprinter's stride in a split second, first made the headlines at the University of Alabama. He showed the country that any football thrown reasonably close to him would be caught. After pacing his school to a Rose Bowl triumph in 1935, Don went to the Green Bay Packers in the NFL. He was to begin a career that would not end until he held every all-time pro scoring record.

From 1935 through 1945 Don was the most elusive of all the Packers. He was almost impossible to guard when he raced downfield to get under a pass. Many teams would put two or three defenders on Dangerous Don. Green Bay would then use Hutson as a decoy, passing to the unguarded receivers, so Don could help his team score even when he wasn't catching passes.

What else could Hutson do? He could run once he caught the ball, so well in fact that he was often used as a flanking back. He could place-kick so well that only one other player in history has kicked more points after touchdown. He could play defensive halfback so outstandingly that he was among the finest in the league protecting against passes and spilling ambitious runners.

Here are some of the records he held: most seasons leading league in pass receptions (8); most consecutive seasons leading league (5); most consecutive games, pass receptions (95); most touchdown passes lifetime (100); most touchdown passes season (17, tied by Elroy Hirsch in 1951).

In nine of his eleven seasons Hutson was named an all-league end. Small wonder that he must be recognized as the most offensive-minded player ever to catch a falling football.

BRONKO NAGURSKI

The best tackle football ever had was Bronko Nagurski, say those who saw him in action. The best fullback football ever knew was Bronko Nagurski, say those who played against him.

Tackle or fullback, the Bronk was all ballplayer. A 230-pound mass of muscle who kept moving forward all the time, he has been named the all-time best at both positions.

Bronko began his college career at the University of Minnesota. He played three years (1927–1929) at the two positions he knew best—tackle on the defense, fullback on the offense. So well did he perform at both spots that the All-America selectors didn't know at what position to place him.

The professionals knew where Bronk could do the most damage. Joining the Chicago Bears, he was a star fullback in his very first game. He played in the NFL for eight years before retiring in 1937. But Bronko and football were not ready to call it quits. In 1943 the Bears asked him to come back for one last fling. When the Bronk agreed, the only people who were unhappy were those who had to play against him.

"He's impossible," said one coach. "You stop him only one way—with a pistol."

"Tackling Nagurski is like getting electrocuted," said a battered lineman after a particularly rough season with Nagurski. "I wish someone would pay him enough *not* to show up when he plays us."

Nagurski is a member of both the college football Hall of Fame and the NFL Hall of Fame.

P. and A. Photos

Bronko Nagurski

JOE NAMATH

If Joe Namath had done nothing else to win fame, he assured himself of a special place on pro football's honor roll by his deeds before and during the 1969 Super Bowl game.

279

Joe Namath

With the skill and daring so typical of his manner, Namath had guided the New York Jets to their first American Football League championship during the 1968 season. And so they came into the Super Bowl against the powerful and haughty Baltimore Colts, kingpins of the NFL.

Few gave the Jets much of a chance. Even Namath's persistent predictions that the Jets would win were brushed off. Most people thought Namath's confidence was just typical pregame talk designed to heighten interest in the playoff and lift the spirits of his teammates.

Truth is that Broadway Joe, as good as he was cocky, meant every word. He never doubted his team would win. By game time, every member of the Jets believed as Joe did.

And win they did, 16–7, in a game of high drama and rich with rewards, for it proved to one and all that the AFL, in action only since 1960, had reached a par with the NFL, whose roots went back to 1933.

It was the AFL's first Super Bowl victory after two humbling defeats.

Namath set no colossal records that afternoon, but the deft style in which he handled the Jets will long be remembered. The classic of the day was the 12-play, 80-yard drive Namath engineered for the Jets' only touchdown. That was in the second quarter.

Three more times Namath brought his team into scoring position, and each time Jim Turner kicked a field goal. In fact, the New Yorkers ran up a 16-point lead before the Colts were able to score, in the final quarter. If ever there was a time when team play and inspiration worked magic, this was it—and Namath was the architect.

Namath was superb throughout the 1968 season and walked off with just about every individual honor. It was a year in which he could hardly do wrong. In the playoff for the AFL championship, for example, the Jets trailed the Western Division champions, the Oakland Raiders, by 23–20, with eight minutes to play.

In thirty-one seconds, Namath rang up the winning touchdown, passing first for 10 yards, then for 52 yards and finally for 6 yards.

Born on May 31, 1943, in Beaver Falls, Pa., Joe Willie Namath was a standout quarterback for three seasons at the University of Alabama, graduating in 1964. Most of the All-America selectors passed him over, but the New York Jets made him their number one draft choice in 1965, at a reported record cost of $400,000, and he was good enough in his first pro season to be chosen AFL Rookie of the Year.

In 1966, he led the league in passes attempted (471), passes completed (232) and yards gained (3,379). His best year was 1967, when he passed for a record 4,007 yards.

Actually, however, you'll find Namath's name pops up infrequently as you thumb through AFL records. But for color, courage (bad knees have hampered him throughout his career), take-charge qualities and a penchant for heroics, he has been one of a kind.

O. J. Simpson eyes running room.

O. J. SIMPSON

In a mere two seasons of college football, O. J. Simpson ran right into the record books and earned a place among the best men ever to appear on a collegiate gridiron.

To quote the All-Time Record Book of the National Collegiate Athletic Association, "No rusher in college football's first 100 years worked harder or produced more on a career per-game basis than did Simpson."

O. J.—he was born Orenthal James—was able to play only two seasons for the University of Southern California because he was a junior college transfer student. But in those two seasons (19 regular-season games), he carried the ball 621 times for 3,124 yards, or eighth place on the all-time list. He was the only college back ever to reach the 3,000 mark in but two seasons.

His per-game average of 164.4 yards rushing is by far the best ever for a college career.

Simpson won the Heisman Trophy as the outstanding college player of 1968 after leading the nation in rushing with 1,079 yards on 355 carries and scoring 22 touchdowns. Few players in college sports annals had been hailed as much as O. J. when he signed a pro contract with the Buffalo Bills of the American Football League for 1969.

But all this didn't come easily to O. J. Born in San Francisco on July 9, 1947, he lacked calcium in his bones as a child and had to have leg braces to walk. One of his early nicknames was "Pencil Legs."

He developed into a 6-foot-2-inch, 207-pound athlete who could run the 100-yard dash in 9.3 seconds, who had the strength of a workhorse on his smashes into the line and who had great balance and a fine pair of hands.

Ironically, although Simpson led the USC Trojans through two championship seasons, his team was beaten in the 1969 Rose Bowl game. Nor was his pro debut with Buffalo auspicious. But O. J. already had left a record that was sure to be spoken of in awe for a long time to come.

JIM THORPE

Jim Thorpe was an Indian of the Sac and Fox Tribe who was born on an Oklahoma reservation. He came East to attend the small Indian school at Carlisle, Pennsylvania, and began making sports history.

Jim made the Carlisle Indians, coached by Pop Warner, one of the most feared football teams in the early 1900's. Jim, a powerfully built halfback who never seemed to tire, played at Carlisle five years (1907–1909, 1911–1912). He was at his best against the most formidable competition. He could run through tackle or speed around the ends. He could kick a ball about 65 yards every time he went back to punt and was deadly as a field-goal kicker. In 1911 and 1912 his spectacular play accounted for two or three touchdowns a game. He raced for long scoring dashes against mighty Harvard and a superior-manned Army team.

Thorpe excelled as a pro. He played for Canton, Cleveland, Oorang, Rock Island, and New York from 1920 to 1926 and was the most powerful line-smasher of his time. Opposing lines were often torn apart by his bull-like rushes.

A versatile and superior athlete, Jim was also a big-league

outfielder with the Giants, Braves, and Reds from 1913 to 1919. But Thorpe's greatest and most famous exploits were reserved for track and field. In the 1912 Olympic Games in Stockholm he won the two most difficult events, the pentathlon and decathlon.

Unfortunately, all the medals presented to Jim later had to be returned. It was learned that he had accepted money for playing baseball with a town team, thus qualifying as a professional.

Jim Thorpe lived to be sixty-four. He died in 1953, broken in health and spirit, in a town now named Jim Thorpe, Pennsylvania. Football, too, remembered Jim by electing him to its Hall of Fame.

Y. A. TITTLE

On a hot August afternoon in 1961 the New York Giants climbed the bleachers at their Fairfield (Conn.) University training camp to have their team picture taken. Standing at the end of the last row was a slightly built, bald man wearing a blue jersey with a large 14 on the front. He wore no shoulder pads and casual observers ignored him as they sought to identify members of the team.

True, he could have been one of the equipment men, looking older than his years because of the scarcity of hair and the lines that ran from his beetle brows. Two months later Y. A. Tittle looked young again, a rejuvenation brought about by his expert passing and his exciting quarterbacking, and the Giants began to move toward the NFL's Eastern Conference title.

For seven Sundays that season, and for the next three seasons, more than 60,000 persons jammed New York's Yankee Stadium, and thousands more poured into stadiums in other NFL cities, to watch this wonderful quarterback. He would astound them with his passing to Del Shofner, Joe Walton, Frank Gifford, and Alex Webster. His play calling would defy reason as he confused opposing defenses by running when they expected passing, by carrying the ball himself when they expected him to hand it to bigger, stronger, faster backs; and by berating himself in front of thousands for missing a pass or flubbing a play.

Though he was 35 years old when he took over as quarterback with the Giants, Tittle was as keen a competitor as any boy out of college. He would drive his teammates to do the impossible, and he was dedicated to one thing only: winning.

The records of the National Football League attest to his aggressive hustle. When he retired after the 1964 season, Tittle had completed 2,118 passes in 3,817 attempts, better than 55 percent and more than any quarterback in history. His passing gained 28,339 yards, or nearly 19 miles, since he started playing in the NFL in 1950. He completed 212 of his passes for touchdowns and set a season record of 36 when he helped the Giants win the 1963 Eastern Conference title, breaking his own record of 33 set in 1962.

Y. A. Tittle played college football at Louisiana State University in Baton Rouge, and when he graduated he joined the Baltimore Colts (in 1949) of the old All-American Conference. When the All-American Conference disbanded after the 1949 season, the team joined the National Football League. The team folded after the 1950 season and Tittle went to the San Francisco 49ers, where he backed up Frank

Y. A. Tittle

Albert, one of pro football's all-time players. When Albert retired a couple of years later, Y. A. became the team's top quarterback.

San Francisco did not get a team of top quality until 1957, and Tittle helped them to a tie for first place in the Western Conference. In a playoff with Detroit for the right to meet Cleveland in the title game, San Francisco lost; Detroit went on to win the NFL championship.

Y. A. continued as first-string quarterback until the middle of the 1960 season when San Francisco coach Red Hickey devised the "shotgun" offense. This called for a quarterback who could run as well as pass, and Y. A. was not a fast runner. He played little during the "shotgun" days, and before the 1961 season San Francisco traded him to the Giants for tackle Lou Cordileone.

Tittle took over as number one quarterback midway through the 1961 season and, teaming with veteran quarterback Chuck Conerly, led the Giants to the conference title. Conerly retired after the season, and Tittle helped the Giants to titles the next two years; but they lost the NFL championship all three years.

JOHNNY UNITAS

The story of Johnny Unitas is one of inspiration and perspiration. This sharp-shooting quarterback, who led the Baltimore Colts to the 1958 and 1959 championships, got a second chance after every team had given up on him.

He came to the NFL as a T quarterback with the Pittsburgh Steelers. For some reason he failed to impress the coaches and tried to hook on with another team. Nobody needed Unitas at the time, and Johnny decided to take a job in order to support his family.

In 1956 he got in some practice licks quarterbacking a semipro team in Pittsburgh. Johnny's pay was six dollars a game, but he was happy to stay close to the game he loved.

Suddenly the Colts' regular quarterback was injured and someone remembered "that kid who was cut loose by the Steelers." Johnny answered the Baltimore call for help and went on to become the Colts' number one player of all time.

Johnny played his college ball at the University of Louisville, where he showed average skill as a quarterback and passer. None of the scouts saw in the 6-foot-1-inch 190-pounder the brilliance he has since displayed. Unitas became the most daring of gamblers and a brilliant field general as well as a passer with deadly accuracy on both long and short throws.

Despite an ailment in his throwing elbow that kept him on the sidelines most of the 1968 season, Unitas began his fourteenth season with the Colts in 1969 with a total of more than 33,000 yards and 250 touchdowns to his credit.

Johnny Unitas

In 1958, he established one of his proudest records. In his third season with Baltimore, he had led the Colts to the Western Division title. In a game memorable for many things —including the fact that it was the first sudden-death overtime playoff in pro history—Unitas set a championship game passing record with 349 yards as the Colts conquered the New York Giants, 23–17.

In the 1959 title playoff, Unitas brought his team into the fourth quarter trailing the same Giants, 9–7. The Unitas passing wizardry helped produce 24 points in the final period as the Colts retained their crown with a 31–16 triumph.

WHIZZER WHITE

Football has developed many All-Americans, players whose deeds will forever be recalled when old grads get together at reunions. Football, however, has produced only one "perfect" All-American in everything: athletic ability plus scholastic achievement—Byron (Whizzer) White.

Whizzer White of the University of Colorado was named to every All-American team in 1937. He drove his school to its first bowl game by scoring more points than any other player in the country—16 touchdowns and 23 extra points, for a total of 119 points.

The Whizzer, according to his coach Bernie Oakes, was "a great triple threat, fast and shifty in the open with his powerful 190 pounds. He was a fine passer, capable of throwing accurately at any distance. He was also an excellent long-distance punter who could place his kicks."

White played almost sixty minutes of every game from 1935 through 1937. He was also an all-Rocky Mountain Conference selection in basketball and baseball. Playing for the Pittsburgh Steelers of the NFL, in 1938 and 1939, he was the league's number one ball carrier.

In the legal profession White reached the heights. In 1961 he was made Deputy Attorney General of the United States, and in 1962 he was appointed an Associate Justice of the United States Supreme Court.

THE GREAT COACHES

Walter Camp, known as the Father of American Football, must be the first name in any roster of football's best coaches. Camp, who was a halfback at Yale, became his school's first coach in 1888. He had a creative and imaginative mind and was the first to draw up a complete set of playing rules and establish the number of players at eleven to a side. Camp also was the first to have the guards pull out of the line and run interference.

Camp's most famous contribution to football is the All-America team. In 1889 he selected those eleven players he considered the best in the country and called them "All-Americans." Thus it is to Camp that we owe our present system of selecting college football's best players of the year.

A player under Camp and a member of his first All-America team was Amos Alonzo Stagg, who was a head coach for fifty-seven consecutive years—1889–1946.

He started his career at Springfield (Mass.) College, 1889–1891. Stagg had his heart set on entering the ministry. But when the president of the University of Chicago offered him a combined post as physical education teacher and football coach, he accepted.

Under Stagg, Chicago soon became one of the most power-ful of the Midwest teams. His style of play was revolutionary and imaginative. Chicago and Stagg had a happy friendship that lasted forty-one years, from 1892 to 1933.

At seventy-one Stagg started a new coaching career at the College of the Pacific. He stayed there thirteen years (1933–1946) and in 1943 was voted college football Coach of the Year. Disdaining retirement, Stagg next served as assistant coach to his son at Susquehanna University (1947–1952). The "grand old man of football" died in 1965 at the age of 103.

John Heisman, who played at Brown and Pennsylvania, coached for thirty-six years. He started at Oberlin College in 1892, then coached at Akron, Auburn, Clemson, Georgia Tech, Pennsylvania, Washington and Jefferson, and Rice Institute. During this period he introduced the shift, fought for the legislation of the forward pass, was the first to use his quarter-back as a safety man, and was constantly tinkering with the offense and experimenting with the defense.

Heisman is still honored for his keen vision and devotion to the game: The trophy awarded annually to college foot-ball's top player bears his name.

In the twenties a small school in Indiana, virtually unknown outside the state during its seventy-five years of existence, became famous throughout the land. It was the energetic, flat-nosed Knute Rockne, with his daring style of play, his endless spirit, and his colorful innovations who made Notre Dame a household name and the football giant of the country.

An immigrant from Norway, Rockne soon mastered the English language and went to Notre Dame to study chemistry. There he played halfback and end under coach Jesse Harper in 1913 and 1914.

It was Rockne and his roommate, quarterback Gus Dorias, who proved to the football world that the forward pass was a tremendous offensive weapon. In 1913 Notre Dame overwhelmed mighty Army with its aerial attack. With Dorias throwing to Rockne, Notre Dame scored a stunning 35–13 upset. Notre Dame was now on the football map. In the years that followed Rockne made it the football capital of the nation.

Rockne, who was killed in an airplane crash in 1931, was Notre Dame's coach for thirteen years. From 1918 to 1930 he lost only 12 games. Against Army (1919–1930) he won 9, lost 2, and tied 1.

Glenn Scobey (Pop) Warner was a football coach for forty-four years, a record for longevity second only to Alonzo Stagg's. During this time, from 1895 to 1938, Warner coached at Georgia, Cornell, Carlisle, Pittsburgh, Stanford, and Temple.

The famed Jim Thorpe played for Pop when he was at Carlisle, and the equally famed Ernie Nevers was the thundering fullback at Stanford when Warner led the California Indians to the 1925 Rose Bowl.

A fellow like Frank Leahy—who predicted the worst for any team he coached—couldn't have been born in any other place but Winner, South Dakota. This intense, jutting-jawed Irishman, who learned the theory and fundamentals of the game at the shrine of his hero, Knute Rockne, coached at Boston College (1939–1940) and at Notre Dame (1941–1953).

Upon becoming Notre Dame coach, Leahy scrapped the famed Notre Dame system of attack and installed the quick-striking T. Old Notre Damers were shocked, but Frank believed in keeping up with the offensive times. His record speaks for itself at South Bend: 107 victories, 13 defeats and 9 ties.

Perhaps no other coach in the history of the sport has been so successful as Paul Brown, founder and for seventeen years mentor of the NFL Cleveland Browns. Brown, the only man ever to have a football team named after him, had his first major coaching assignment at Ohio State, from 1941 through 1943. He was appointed coach at Great Lakes Naval Station during World War II, then went to Cleveland when that city entered the pro ranks in 1946.

Through the 1962 season, his last with the Browns, Paul led his team to seven division titles and three league championships.

After Brown's departure from Cleveland, the mantle of greatness fell on Vince Lombardi. He piloted the Green Bay Packers to six division championships, five league crowns (including a never-before-attained three in a row) and two triumphs in the Super Bowl.

All-Time Records

COLLEGE SCORING CHAMPIONS

Year	Player	Points
1969	Owens, Steve (Oklahoma)	138
1968	Stevens, Howard (Randolph-Macon)	142
	O'Brien, Jim (Cincinnati)	142
1967	Nye, Bert (West Chester)	127
1966	Garrett, Carl (New Mexico Highlands)	158
1965	Smith, Allen (Findlay)	146
1964	Piccolo, Brian (Wake Forest)	111
1963	Switzer, Jim (Emporia, Kansas)	168
1962	Logan, Jerry (West Texas State)	110
1961	Murio, John (Whitworth)	129
1960	Cooper, Bill (Muskingum)	152
1959	Henley, Garney (Huron)	141
1958	Herakovich, Carl (Rose Poly, Ind.)	168
1957	Lyles, Len (Louisville)	132
1956	Houdek, Larry (Kansas West)	114
1955	Clark, Nate (Hillsdale)	144
1954	Luppino, Art (Arizona)	166
1953	Lewis, Leo (Lincoln, Mo.)	132

Year	Player	Points
1952	Conway, Al (William Jewell)	133
1951	Yackley, Paul (Heidelberg)	132
1950	Reynolds, Bob (Nebraska)	157
1949	Polk, Sylvester (Maryland State)	129
1948	Scown, Ted (Sul Ross State)	168
1947	Horn, Darwin (Pepperdine)	115
	Schoenherr (Wheaton)	115
1946	Carter, Joe (Florida A&I)	152
1945	Trojanowski, Walt (Connecticut)	132
1944	Davis, Glenn (Army)	120
1943	Steuber, Bob (DePauw)	129
1942	McGovern, Ed (Rose Poly, Ind.)	165
1941	Dudley, Bill (Virginia)	134
1940	Hunt, John (Marshall, W. Va.)	162
1939	Madden, Lloyd (Colorado Mines)	141
1938	Smith, Edward (Rust, Miss.)	122
1937	Locke, Douglas (St. Mary's, Texas)	160

Year	Player	Points	Year	Player	Points
1936	Thomas, Charles (Delta Teachers)	119	1924	Levi, John (Haskell)	112
1935	Zeh, Ray (Western Reserve)	112	1923	Levi, John (Haskell)	149
1934	Shepherd, Bill (Western Maryland)	133	1922	Kingsley, Bob (Franklin and Marshall)	120
1933	Young, Pete (Bluefield Inst.)	108	1921	Bowser, Al (Bucknell)	91
1932	Bush, Louis (Mass. State)	114	1920	Leech, Jim (Virginia Military)	210
1931	Campiglio, Bob (West Liberty Teachers)	145	1919	Rodgers, Ira (West Virginia)	147
1930	Macaluso, Len (Colgate)	145	1918	(No Record)	
1929	McEver, Gene (Tennessee)	130	1917	Ingram, Bill (Navy)	162
1928	Strong, Ken (New York U.)	153	1916	Grove, Ivan (Henry-Kendall)	196
1927	Lane, Myles (Dartmouth)	125	1915	DePrato, John (Michigan State)	188
1926	McClain, Mayes (Haskell)	253	1914	Imlay, John (Missouri Mines)	180
1925	Flournoy, Charles (Tulane)	128	1913	Spiegel, Al (Washington and Jefferson)	127
			1912	Thorpe, Jim (Carlisle)	198

Bowl Games

Most widely publicized and well attended of all the post-season bowl contests is the Rose Bowl in Pasadena, California. It was first played in 1902 but the second game in this long series was not played until 1916.

Other major bowl games are the Orange Bowl in Miami, Florida, the Sugar Bowl in New Orleans, Louisiana, the Cotton Bowl in Dallas, Texas.

ROSE BOWL

Year	Teams	
1970	Southern California	10
	Michigan	3
1969	Ohio State	27
	Southern California	16
1968	Southern California	14
	Indiana	3
1967	Purdue	14
	Southern California	13
1966	UCLA	14
	Michigan State	12
1965	Michigan	34
	Oregon State	7
1964	Illinois	17
	Washington	7
1963	Southern California	42
	Wisconsin	37
1962	Minnesota	21
	UCLA	3
1961	Washington	17
	Minnesota	7
1960	Washington	44
	Wisconsin	8
1959	Iowa	38
	California	12
1958	Ohio State	10
	Oregon	7
1957	Iowa	35
	Oregon State	19
1956	Michigan State	17
	UCLA	14
1955	Ohio State	20
	Southern California	0
1954	Michigan State	28
	UCLA	20
1953	Southern California	7
	Wisconsin	0
1952	Illinois	40
	Stanford	7
1951	Michigan	14
	California	6

Year	Teams	
1950	Ohio State	17
	California	14
1949	Northwestern	20
	California	14
1948	Michigan	49
	Southern California	0
1947	Illinois	45
	UCLA	14
1946	Alabama	34
	Southern California	14
1945	Southern California	25
	Tennessee	0
1944	Southern California	29
	Washington	0
1943	Georgia	9
	UCLA	0
1942*	Oregon State	20
	Duke	16
1941	Stanford	21
	Nebraska	13
1940	Southern California	14
	Tennessee	0
1939	Southern California	7
	Duke	3
1938	California	13
	Alabama	0
1937	Pittsburgh	21
	Washington	0
1936	Stanford	7
	Southern Methodist	0
1935	Alabama	29
	Stanford	13
1934	Columbia	7
	Stanford	0
1933	Southern California	35
	Pittsburgh	0
1932	Southern California	21
	Tulane	12
1931	Alabama	24
	Washington State	0

* Played in Durham, N.C.

Year	Teams		Year	Teams	
1930	Southern California	47	1922	California	0
	Pittsburgh	14		Washington & Jefferson	0
1929	Georgia Tech	8	1921	California	28
	California	7		Ohio State	0
1928	Stanford	7	1920	Harvard	7
	Pittsburgh	6		Oregon	6
1927	Stanford	7	1919	Great Lakes (Navy)	17
	Alabama	7		Mare Island (Marines)	0
1926	Alabama	20	1918	Mare Island (Marines)	19
	Washington	19		Camp Lewis (Army)	7
1925	Notre Dame	27	1917	Oregon	14
	Stanford	10		Pennsylvania	0
1924	Washington	14	1916	Washington State	14
	Navy	14		Brown	0
1923	Southern California	14	1902	Michigan	49
	Penn State	3		Stanford	0

COTTON BOWL

Year	Teams		Year	Teams	
1970	Texas	21	1959	Air Force Academy	0
	Notre Dame	17		Texas Christian	0
1969	Texas	36	1958	Navy	20
	Tennessee	13		Rice	7
1968	Texas A&M	20	1957	Texas Christian	28
	Alabama	16		Syracuse	27
1967	Georgia	23	1956	Mississippi	14
	Southern Methodist	9		Texas Christian	13
1966	Louisiana State	14	1955	Georgia Tech	14
	Arkansas	7		Arkansas	6
1965	Arkansas	10	1954	Rice	28
	Nebraska	7		Alabama	6
1964	Texas	28	1953	Texas	16
	Navy	6		Tennessee	0
1963	Louisiana State	13	1952	Kentucky	20
	Texas	0		Texas Christian	7
1962	Texas	12	1951	Tennessee	20
	Mississippi	7		Texas	14
1961	Duke	7	1950	Rice	27
	Arkansas	6		North Carolina	13
1960	Syracuse	23	1949	Southern Methodist	21
	Texas	14		Oregon	13

Year	Teams	Year	Teams
1948	Southern Methodist 13	1942	Alabama 29
	Penn State 13		Texas A&M 21
1947	Arkansas 0	1941	Texas A&M 13
	Louisiana State 0		Fordham 12
1946	Texas 40	1940	Clemson 6
	Missouri 27		Boston College 3
1945	Oklahoma A&M 34	1939	St. Mary's 20
	Texas Christian 0		Texas Tech 13
1944	Texas 7	1938	Rice 28
	Randolph Field 7		Colorado 14
1943	Texas 14	1937	Texas Christian 16
	Georgia Tech 7		Marquette 6

SUGAR BOWL

Year	Teams	Year	Teams
1970	Mississippi 27	1957	Baylor 13
	Arkansas 22		Tennessee 7
1969	Arkansas 16	1956	Georgia Tech 7
	Georgia 2		Pittsburgh 0
1968	Louisiana State 20	1955	Navy 21
	Wyoming 13		Mississippi 0
1967	Alabama 34	1954	Georgia Tech 42
	Nebraska 7		West Virginia 19
1966	Missouri 20	1953	Georgia Tech 24
	Florida 18		Mississippi 7
1965	Louisiana State 13	1952	Maryland 28
	Syracuse 10		Tennessee 13
1964	Alabama 12	1951	Kentucky 13
	Mississippi 7		Oklahoma 7
1963	Mississippi 17	1950	Oklahoma 35
	Arkansas 13		Louisiana State 0
1962	Alabama 10	1949	Oklahoma 14
	Arkansas 3		North Carolina 6
1961	Mississippi 14	1948	Texas 27
	Rice 6		Alabama 7
1960	Mississippi 21	1947	Georgia 20
	Louisiana State 0		North Carolina 10
1959	Louisiana State 7	1946	Oklahoma A&M 33
	Clemson 0		St. Mary's 13
1958	Mississippi 39	1945	Duke 29
	Texas 7		Alabama 26

Year	Teams		Year	Teams	
1944	Georgia Tech	20	1939	Texas Christian	15
	Tulsa	18		Carnegie Tech	7
1943	Tennessee	17	1938	Santa Clara	0
	Tulsa	7		Louisiana State	0
1942	Fordham	2	1937	Santa Clara	21
	Missouri	0		Louisiana State	14
1941	Boston College	19	1936	Texas Christian	3
	Tennessee	13		Louisiana State	2
1940	Texas A&M	14	1935	Tulane	20
	Tulane	13		Temple	14

ORANGE BOWL

Year	Teams		Year	Teams	
1970	Penn State	10	1956	Oklahoma	20
	Missouri	3		Maryland	6
1969	Penn State	15	1955	Duke	34
	Kansas	14		Nebraska	7
1968	Oklahoma	26	1954	Oklahoma	7
	Tennessee	24		Maryland	0
1967	Florida	27	1953	Alabama	61
	Georgia Tech	12		Syracuse	6
1966	Alabama	39	1952	Georgia Tech	17
	Nebraska	28		Baylor	14
1965	Texas	21	1951	Clemson	15
	Alabama	17		Miami	14
1964	Nebraska	13	1950	Santa Clara	21
	Auburn	7		Kentucky	13
1963	Alabama	17	1949	Texas	41
	Oklahoma	0		Georgia	28
1962	Louisiana State	25	1948	Georgia Tech	20
	Colorado	7		Kansas	14
1961	Missouri	21	1947	Rice	8
	Navy	14		Tennessee	0
1960	Georgia	14	1946	Miami	13
	Missouri	0		Holy Cross	6
1959	Oklahoma	21	1945	Tulsa	26
	Syracuse	6		Georgia Tech	12
1958	Oklahoma	48	1944	Louisiana State	19
	Duke	21		Texas A&M	14
1957	Colorado	27	1943	Alabama	37
	Clemson	21		Boston College	21

300

Year	Teams		Year	Teams
1942	Georgia 40		1937	Duquesne 13
	Texas Christian 26			Mississippi State 12
1941	Mississippi State 14		1936	Catholic University 20
	Georgetown 7			Mississippi 19
1940	Georgia Tech 21		1935	Bucknell 26
	Missouri 7			Miami 0
1939	Tennessee 17		1934	Duquesne 33
	Oklahoma 0			Miami 7
1938	Auburn 6		1933	Miami 7
	Michigan State 0			Manhattan 0

Hall of Fame

College football's highest honor—election to the Hall of Fame—is conferred on those individuals who have proved themselves worthy on the field and in later life. Candidates are picked by a panel of sports writers and college athletic directors, many of whom are coaches. Players and coaches deemed worthy of election are inducted annually in December. National headquarters of the Hall of Fame are at Rutgers University in New Brunswick, New Jersey.

PLAYERS

Name	School (Position)	Years Played
Agase, Alex	Purdue (guard)	1943–46
Albert, Frank	Stanford (quarterback)	1939–41
Aldrich, Charles "Ki"	Texas Christian (center)	1936–38
Alexander, Joseph	Syracuse (guard)	1918–20
Ames, Knowlton	Princeton (fullback)	1886–89
Bacon, Clarence E.	Wesleyan (quarterback)	1909–12
Barnes, Stanley N.	California (end)	1918–21
Barrett, Charles	Cornell (quarterback)	1913–15
Baston, Bert	Minnesota (end)	1914–16
Battles, Clifford F.	W. Va. Wesleyan (halfback)	1929–31
Baugh, Samuel	Texas Christian (halfback)	1934–36
Bausch, James	Kansas (halfback)	1929–30

301

Name	School (Position)	Years Played
Bednarik, Charles	Pennsylvania (center)	1945–48
Berwanger, John J.	Chicago (quarterback)	1933–35
Blanchard, Felix "Doc"	Army (fullback)	1944–46
Bomar, Lynn	Vanderbilt (end)	1921–24
Booth, Francis "Albie"	Yale (halfback)	1929–31
Borries, Fred "Buzz" Jr.	Navy (halfback)	1932–34
Boynton, Benny Lee	Williams (quarterback)	1917–19
Brooke, George	Pennsylvania (halfback)	1894–95
Brown, Gordon F.	Yale (guard)	1897–1900
Brown, John H. "Babe" Jr.	Navy (guard)	1910–13
Brown, John Mack	Alabama (halfback)	1923–25
Bunker, Paul	Army (tackle, fullback)	1901–02
Cafego, George	Tennessee (halfback)	1937–39
Cagle, Christian K.	Army (halfback)	1926–29
Campbell, David C.	Harvard (end)	1899–1901
Cannon, John	Notre Dame (guard)	1927–29
Carideo, Frank	Notre Dame (quarterback)	1928–30
Carney, Charles R.	Mississippi (end)	1918–21
Carpenter, C. Hunter	VPI (halfback)	1900–03, 1905
Carroll, Charles	Washington (halfback)	1926–28
Casey, Edward L.	Harvard (halfback)	1916, 1919
Chamberlin, Guy	Nebraska (halfback, end)	1913–15
Christman, Paul	Missouri (halfback)	1938–40
Clark, Earl "Dutch"	Colorado Col. (quarterback)	1927–29
Clevenger, Zora	Indiana (halfback)	1900–03
Conerly, Charles A. "Chuck"	Mississippi (tailback)	1942, 1946–47
Connor, George	Holy Cross (tackle)	1942–43
Corbin, William	Yale (center)	1886–88
Corbus, William	Stanford (guard)	1931–33
Cowan, Hector W.	Princeton (tackle)	1885–89
Coy, Edward H. "Ted"	Yale (fullback)	1907–09
Crowley, James	Notre Dame (halfback)	1922–24
Cutter, Slade	Navy (tackle)	1932–34
Dalrymple, Gerald	Tulane (end)	1929–31
Daly, Charles D.	Harvard (quarterback)	1898–1900
	Army (quarterback)	1901–02
Davis, Glenn	Army (halfback)	1943–46
DesJardien, Paul R.	Chicago (center)	1912–14
DeWitt, John	Princeton (guard)	1901–03
Dodd, Robert Lee "Bobby"	Tennessee (quarterback)	1928–30
Dougherty, Nathan	Tennessee (guard)	1907–09
Drury, Morley	Southern California (quarterback)	1925–27
Dudley, William M.	Virginia (halfback)	1939–41
Eckersall, Walter H.	Chicago (quarterback)	1904–06
Evans, Ray	Kansas (halfback)	1941–42, 46–47
Feathers, William Beattie	Tennessee (halfback)	1931–33

302

Name	School (Position)	Years Played
Fesler, Wesley E.	Ohio State (end)	1928–30
Fish, Hamilton	Harvard (tackle)	1907–09
Flowers, A. R. "Buck"	Georgia Tech (halfback)	1918–20
Frank, Clinton E.	Yale (halfback)	1935–37
Friedman, Benjamin	Michigan (quarterback)	1924–26
Garbisch, Edgar W.	Wash. & Jefferson (guard)	1917–20
	Army (center)	1921–24
Gelbert, Charles	Pennsylvania (end)	1894–96
Gilbert, Walter	Auburn (center)	1934–36
Gipp, George	Notre Dame (fullback)	1917–20
Goldberg, Marshall	Pittsburgh (halfback)	1936–38
Graham, Otto	Northwestern (halfback)	1941–43
Grange, Harold E. "Red"	Illinois (halfback)	1923–25
Grayson, Robert H.	Stanford (fullback)	1933–35
Gulick, Merle	Toledo (quarterback)	1925
	Hobart (quarterback)	1927–29
Hale, Edwin	Mississippi Coll. (halfback)	1915–16, 20–21
Hamilton, Thomas	Navy (halfback)	1924–26
Hardwick, H. R. "Tack"	Harvard (end)	1912–14
Hare, T. Truxton	Pennsylvania (guard)	1897–1900
Harley, Charles W. "Chick"	Ohio State (fullback)	1916–19
Harmon, Thomas D.	Michigan (halfback)	1938–40
Harpster, Howard	Carnegie Tech (quarterback)	1926–28
Hart, Edward J.	Princeton (tackle)	1909–11
Hazel, Homer H.	Rutgers (fullback)	1922–24
Heffelfinger, W. W. "Pudge"	Yale (guard)	1888–91
Hein, Melvin J.	Washington State (center)	1928–30
Henry, William F. "Fats"	Wash. & Jefferson (tackle)	1917–19
Herwig, Robert J.	California (center)	1935–37
Heston, William M.	Michigan (halfback)	1901–04
Hickman, Herman Michael	Tennessee (guard)	1929–31
Hill, Dan	Duke (center)	1936–38
Hinkey, Frank A.	Yale (end)	1891–94
Hinkle, Carl	Vanderbilt (center)	1935–37
Hitchcock, James	Auburn (halfback)	1930–32
Hogan, James J.	Yale (tackle)	1902–04
Holland, Jerome "Brud"	Cornell (end)	1936–38
Hollenback, William M.	Pennsylvania (halfback)	1906–08
Horrell, Edwin "Babe"	California (center)	1922–24
Horvath, Les	Ohio State (halfback, quarterback)	1940–42, 44
Hubbard, Robert "Cal"	Centenary (end, tackle, fullback)	1922–24
	Geneva (end, tackle)	1925–26
Hubbard, John Houghton	Amherst (halfback)	1903–06
Humble, Weldon G.	Rice (guard)	1941–42, 1946
Hunt, Joel	Texas A&M (halfback)	1925
Hutson, Donald	Alabama (end)	1932–34
Ingram, Adm. Jonas H.	Navy (fullback)	1904–06

303

Name	School (Position)	Years Played
Isbell, Cecil	Purdue (back)	1935–37
Joesting, Herbert	Minnesota (fullback)	1925–27
Johnson, Jimmie	Carlisle (quarterback)	1899–1903
Justice, Charles "Choo Choo"	North Carolina (halfback)	1946–49
Juhan, Frank Alexander Bishop	U. of South (center)	1908–10
Kavanaugh, Ken	Louisiana State (end)	1937–39
Kaw, Edgar L.	Cornell (halfback)	1920–22
Kazmaier, Richard W.	Princeton (halfback)	1949–51
Keck, James Stanton	Princeton (tackle)	1920–21
Kelley, Lawrence M.	Yale (end)	1934–36
Kelly, William	Montana (quarterback)	1924–26
Ketcham, Henry	Yale (center, guard)	1911–13
Kilpatrick, John Reed	Yale (end)	1908–10
Kimbrough, John C.	Texas A&M (fullback)	1938–40
Kinard, Frank "Bruiser"	Mississippi (tackle)	1935–37
King, Philip	Princeton (quarterback)	1890–93
Kinnick, Nile	Iowa (halfback)	1937–39
Kipke, Harry	Michigan (halfback)	1921–23
Kitzmiller, Johnny	Oregon (halfback)	1927–29
Layden, Elmer F.	Notre Dame (halfback)	1922–24
Layne, Robert	Texas (back)	1944, 46–47
Lea, Langdon	Princeton (tackle, end)	1892–95
Leech, James	VMI (halfback)	1919–20
Locke, Gordon C.	Iowa (fullback)	1920–22
Luckman, Sid	Columbia (quarterback)	1936–38
Lujack, John	Notre Dame (quarterback)	1943, 1946–47
Lund, Francis L. "Pug"	Minnesota (halfback)	1932–34
Mahan, Edward W.	Harvard (fullback)	1913–15
Mallory, William	Yale (fullback)	1921–23
Mann, Gerald	Southern Methodist (quarterback)	1925–27
Mauthe, J. L. "Pete"	Penn State (halfback)	1910–12
McAfee, George A.	Duke (halfback)	1937–39
McCormick, James B.	Princeton (fullback)	1905–07
McEver, Eugene T.	Tennessee (halfback)	1928–29, 1931
McEwan, John	Army (center)	1914–16
McFadden, James Banks	Clemson (halfback)	1937–39
McGovern, John F.	Minnesota (quarterback)	1908–10
McLaren, George	Pittsburgh (fullback)	1915–18
McMillin, Alvin "Bo"	Centre (quarterback)	1919–21
McWhorter, Robert	Georgia (halfback)	1910–13
Mercer, E. LeRoy	Pennsylvania (fullback)	1910–12
Mickal, Abe	Louisiana State (halfback)	1933–35
Miller, Edgar E.	Notre Dame (tackle)	1922–24
Minds, John	Pennsylvania (fullback, tackle)	1894–97
Montgomery, Cliff	Columbia (quarterback)	1931–33
Muller, Harold "Brick"	California (end)	1920–22
Nagurski, Bronko	Minnesota (tackle)	1927–29

Name	School (Position)	Years Played
Nevers, Ernest A.	Stanford (fullback)	1923–25
Newell, Marshall	Harvard (tackle)	1890–93
Oberlander, Andrew J.	Dartmouth (halfback)	1923–25
O'Brien, Robert David	Texas Christian (halfback)	1936–38
O'Dea, Pat	Wisconsin (halfback, fullback)	1896–99
Oliphant, Elmer	Purdue (halfback)	1911–13
	Army (halfback)	1915–17
Oosterbaan, Benjamin G.	Michigan (end)	1925–27
Parker, Clarence "Ace"	Duke (halfback)	1934–36
Pazzetti, Vincent "Pat"	Wesleyan (quarterback)	1908–09
	Lehigh (quarterback)	1910–12
Peck, Robert	Pittsburgh (center)	1914–16
Pennock, Stanley B.	Harvard (guard)	1912–14
Pfann, George R.	Cornell (quarterback)	1921–23
Phillips, Henry Disbrow	U. of South (guard)	1901–04
Pihos, Peter Louis	Indiana (end, fullback)	1942–46
Pingel, John	Michigan State (halfback)	1936–38
Pinckert, Ernie	Southern California (halfback)	1929–31
Poe, Arthur	Princeton (end)	1898–99
Pollard, Frederick "Fritz"	Brown (halfback)	1914–16
Pund, Henry R.	Georgia Tech (center)	1926–28
Reeds, Claude	Oklahoma (fullback)	1910–13
Reynolds, Robert "Horse"	Stanford (tackle)	1933–35
Rinehart, Charles "Babe"	Lafayette (guard)	1894–97
Rodgers, Ira E.	West Virginia (fullback)	1917–19
Rogers, Edward L.	Carlisle (end)	1896–1900
	Minnesota (end)	1901–03
Rosenberg, Aaron David	Southern California (guard)	1931–33
Rote, Kyle	Southern Methodist (halfback)	1948–50
Routt, John	Texas A&M (guard)	1935–37
Sauer, George H.	Nebraska (fullback)	1931–33
Schoonover, Wear K.	Arkansas (end)	1927–29
Schreiner, David N.	Wisconsin (end)	1940–42
Schwegler, Paul	Washington (tackle)	1929–31
Schulz, Adolph "Germany"	Michigan (center)	1905–08
Schwab, Frank J.	Lafayette (guard)	1919–22
Shevlin, Thomas L.	Yale (end)	1903–05
Simons, Claude "Monk"	Tulane (halfback)	1932–34
Sington, Frederick W.	Alabama (tackle)	1928–30
Sinkwich, Frank	Georgia (halfback)	1940–42
Slater, F. F. "Duke"	Iowa (tackle)	1918–21
Smith, Harry	Southern California (guard)	1937–39
Snow, Neil	Michigan (halfback)	1898–1901
Spears, Clarence W.	Dartmouth (guard)	1914–15
Spears, W. E.	Vanderbilt (quarterback)	1925–27
Sprackling, William E.	Brown (quarterback)	1908–11
Stagg, Amos Alonzo	Yale (end)	1885–89
Steffen, Wally	Chicago (quarterback)	1907–08

Name	School (Position)	Years Played
Stein, Herb	Pittsburgh (center)	1918–21
Stevenson, Vincent M.	Pennsylvania (quarterback)	1903–05
Strong, Kenneth	NYU (fullback)	1926–28
Stuhldreher, Harry	Notre Dame (quarterback)	1922–24
Suffridge, Robert L.	Tennessee (guard)	1938–40
Thorpe, James	Carlisle (halfback)	1908, 1911–12
Ticknor, Benjamin H.	Harvard (center)	1928–30
Tinsley, Gaynell	Louisiana State (end)	1934–36
Trippi, Charles	Georgia (halfback)	1945–46
Turner, Clyde "Bulldog"	Hardin-Simmons (center)	1937–39
VanBrocklin, Norman	Oregon (quarterback)	1947–48
Walker, Ewell Doak	SMU (quarterback)	1946–49
Walsh, Adam	Notre Dame (center)	1922–24
Washington, Kenneth	UCLA (halfback)	1937–39
Weekes, Harold H.	Columbia (halfback)	1900–02
Weir, Ed	Nebraska (tackle)	1923–25
Weller, John A. C.	Princeton (guard)	1933–35
West, D. Belford	Colgate (tackle)	1915–16, 1919
Wharton, Charles "Buck"	Pennsylvania (guard)	1893–96
Wheeler, Arthur	Princeton (guard)	1892–94
White, Byron "Whizzer"	Colorado (halfback)	1936–38
Whitmire, Donald	Alabama (tackle)	1941–42
	Navy (tackle)	1943–44
Widseth, Edwin	Minnesota (tackle)	1934–36
Wildung, Richard	Minnesota (tackle)	1940–42
Williams, James "Froggy"	Rice (end)	1947–49
Wilson, George	Washington (halfback)	1923–25
Wistert, Francis "Whitey"	Michigan (tackle)	1931–33
Wojciechowicz, Alexander	Fordham (center)	1934–36
Wyant, Andrew	Bucknell (center, guard)	1887–91
	Chicago (center, guard)	1892–95
Young, Claude "Buddy"	Illinois (halfback)	1944–46
Young, H. K. "Cy"	Washington & Lee (halfback)	1913–16

COACHES

Name	Coached at	Years
Alexander, William A.	Georgia Tech	1921–44
Armstrong, Ike	Utah	1925–49
Bell, Madison "Matty"	Haskell Institute	1920–21
	Carroll College	1922
	Texas Christian	1923–28
	Texas A&M	1929–33
	Southern Methodist	1935–41, 1945–49
Bezdek, Hugo	Arkansas	1908–12
	Oregon	1913–17
	Penn State	1918–29

306

Name	Coached at	Years
Bible, Dana X.	Louisiana State	1916
	Texas A&M	1917, 1919, 1928
	Nebraska	1929–36
	Texas	1937–45
Bierman, Bernard W.	Mississippi A&M	1925–26
	Tulane	1927–32
	Minnesota	1932–41, 1945–50
Blaik, Earl H. "Red"	Dartmouth	1934–40
	Army	1941–58
Caldwell, Charles W., Jr.	Williams	1928–42
	Princeton	1945–56
Camp, Walter	Yale	1888–92
	Stanford	1893–95
	Yale (Advisory)	1882–1910
Cavanaugh, Frank W.	Holy Cross	1903–05
	Dartmouth	1911–16
	Boston College	1919–26
	Fordham	1927–32
Crisler, Herbert O. "Fritz"	Minnesota	1930–31
	Princeton	1932–37
	Michigan	1938–47
Dobie, Gilmour	Washington	1908–16
	Navy	1917–19
	Cornell	1920–35
	Boston College	1936–38
Donohue, Michael J.	Auburn	1904–22
	Louisiana State	1923–27
Dorais, Charles E. "Gus"	Detroit	1925–44
Faurot, Donald B.	Missouri	1925, 1935–56
	Kirksville	1926–34
Hall, Edward K.	Illinois	1892–93
Harlow, Richard C.	Penn State	1914–17
	Colgate	1922–25
	Western Md.	1926–34
	Harvard	1935–42, 1945–47
Haughton, Percy P.	Cornell	1899–1900
	Harvard	1908–16
	Columbia	1923–24
Heisman, John W.	Oberlin	1892–94
	Akron	1893
	Auburn	1895–99
	Clemson	1900–03
	Georgia Tech	1904–19
	Pennsylvania	1920–22
	Wash. & Jefferson	1923
	Rice	1924–27
Higgins, Robert A.	W. Va. Wesleyan	1920–24
	Wash. (St. Louis)	1925–27
	Penn State	1930–48

Name	Coached at	Years
Jones, Howard H.	Syracuse	1908
	Yale	1909, 1913
	Ohio State	1910
	Iowa	1916–23
	Duke	1924
	Southern California	1925–40
Jones, Thomas A. D. "Tad"	Syracuse	1909–10
	Yale	1916, 1920–27
Jones, L. McC. "Biff"	Army	1926–29
	Louisiana State	1932–34
	Oklahoma	1935–36
	Nebraska	1937–42
Kerr, Andrew	Stanford	1922–23
	Wash. & Jefferson	1926–28
	Colgate	1929–46
Little, George E.	Miami (Ohio)	1916–17, 1919–22
	Wisconsin	1925–27
	Cincinnati	1914–16
Little, Lou	Georgetown	1924–29
	Columbia	1930–56
McGugin, Daniel	Vanderbilt	1904–34
McLaughry, DeOrmond (Tuss)	Westminster	1916, 1918, 1921
	Amherst	1922–25
	Brown	1926–40
	Dartmouth	1941–42, 1945–54
Meyer, L. R. "Dutch"	Texas Christian	1934–52
Moore, Bernie H.	Louisiana State	1935–47
Morrison, Ray.	Southern Methodist	1915–16, 1922–34
	Vanderbilt.	1935–39
	Temple	1940–48
	Austin	1949–52
Munn, Clarence "Biggie"	Albright	1935–36
	Syracuse	1946
	Michigan State	1947–53
Neale, Earle "Greasy"	Muskingum	1915
	West Virginia Wesleyan	1916–17
	Marietta	1919–20
	Washington & Jefferson	1921–22
	Virginia	1923–28
	West Virginia	1931–33
Neyland, Robert R.	Tennessee	1926–34, 1936–40
		1946–52
O'Neill, Frank J. "Buck"	Colgate	1902
	Syracuse	1906–07
	Columbia	1920–22
Owen, Bennie	Oklahoma	1905–26
Robinson, E. N.	Nebraska	1896–97
	Brown	1898–01, 1904–07
		1910–25

Name	Coached at	Years
Rockne, Knute K.	Notre Dame	1918–31
Romney, E. L. "Dick"	Utah State	1919–48
Roper, William W.	Princeton	1906–08
	Missouri	1909
	Princeton	1910–11, 1919–30
Shaughnessy, Clark D.	Tulane	1915–20, 22–26
	Loyola (Louisiana)	1927–32
	Chicago	1933–39
	Stanford	1940–41
	Maryland	1942–46
	Pittsburgh	1943–45
	Hawaii	1965
Snavely, Carl G.	Bucknell	1927–33
	North Carolina	1933–35, 45–52
	Cornell	1936–44
	Washington (Missouri)	1953–58
Smith, Andrew L.	Pennsylvania	1909–12
	Purdue	1913–15
	California	1916–25
Stagg, Amos Alonzo	Springfield	1890–91
	Chicago	1892–1932
	Col. of Pacific	1933–46
Sutherland, John B. "Jock"	Lafayette	1919–23
	Pittsburgh	1924–38
Thomas, Frank W.	Chattanooga	1925–28
	Alabama	1931–46
Wade, W. Wallace	Alabama	1922–30
	Duke	1931–41
Waldorf, Lynn "Pappy"	California	1947–56
	Northwestern	1935–46
	Kansas State	1934
	Oklahoma A&M	1929–33
Warner, Glenn S. "Pop"	Georgia	1895–96
	Cornell	1897–98
	Carlisle	1899–1914
	Pittsburgh	1915–24
	Stanford	1925–32
	Temple	1933–38
Wieman, E. E. "Ted"	Michigan	1927–28
	Princeton	1938–42
Wilce, John W.	Ohio State	1913–28
Williams, Henry L.	Minnesota	1900–21
Yost, Fielding H.	Michigan	1900–28
Zuppke, Robert	Illinois	1913–41

Player of the Year

The sports writers vote annually on college football's outstanding players and present an award to the player judged the best in the country. One of the most coveted of these awards is the John W. Heisman Memorial Trophy.

Year	Player (School)	Position
1969	Owens, Steve (Oklahoma)	Halfback
1968	Simpson, O. J. (Southern California)	Halfback
1967	Beban, Gary (UCLA)	Quarterback
1966	Spurrier, Steve (Florida)	Quarterback
1965	Garrett, Mike (USC)	Halfback
1964	Huarte, John (Notre Dame)	Quarterback
1963	Staubach, Roger (Navy)	Quarterback
1962	Baker, Terry (Oregon State)	Quarterback
1961	Davis, Ernie (Syracuse)	Back
1960	Bellino, Joe (Navy)	Back
1959	Cannon, Billy (Louisiana State)	Back
1958	Dawkins, Pete (Army)	Back
1957	Crow, John (Texas A&M)	Back
1956	Hornung, Paul (Notre Dame)	Quarterback
1955	Cassady, Howard (Ohio State)	Back
1954	Ameche, Alan (Wisconsin)	Back
1953	Lattner, John (Notre Dame)	Back
1952	Vessels, Billy (Oklahoma)	Back
1951	Kazmaier, Dick (Princeton)	Back
1950	Janowicz, Vic (Ohio State)	Back
1949	Hart, Leon (Notre Dame)	End
1948	Walker, Doak (Southern Methodist)	Back
1947	Lujack, John (Notre Dame)	Quarterback
1946	Davis, Glenn (Army)	Back
1945	Blanchard, Felix (Army)	Back
1944	Horvath, Les (Ohio State)	Quarterback
1943	Bertelli, Angelo (Notre Dame)	Quarterback
1942	Sinkwich, Frank (Georgia)	Back

Year	Player (School)	Position
1941	Smith, Bruce (Minnesota)	Back
1940	Harmon, Tom (Michigan)	Back
1939	Kinnick, Nile (Iowa)	Back
1938	O'Brien, Davey (Texas Christian)	Quarterback
1937	Frank, Clint (Yale)	Back
1936	Kelley, Larry (Yale)	End
1935	Berwanger, Jay (University of Chicago)	Back

Coach of the Year

Members of the American Football Coaches Association vote annually for the outstanding college coach of the year. The winner's record for the season is a major factor, but all that goes into the word "character" also has a great deal to do with the selection.

Year	Coach (School)	Record
1969	Schembechler, Bo (Michigan)	8–2–0
1968	Paterno, Joe (Penn State)	10–0–0
1967	Pont, John (Indiana)	9–1–0
1966	Cahill, Tom (Army)	8–2–0
1965	Prothro, Tommy (UCLA)	7–2–1
1964	Parseghian, Ara (Notre Dame)	9–1–0
	Broyles, Frank (Arkansas)	10–0–0
1963	Royal, Darrell (Texas)	10–0–0
1962	McKay, John (Southern California)	10–0–0
1961	Bryant, Paul (Alabama)	10–0–0
1960	Warmath, Murray (Minnesota)	8–1–0
1959	Schwartzwalder, Ben (Syracuse)	10–0–0
1958	Dietzel, Paul (Louisiana State)	10–0–0
1957	Hayes, Woody (Ohio State)	8–1–0
1956	Wyatt, Bowden (Tennessee)	10–0–0
1955	Daugherty, Duffy (Michigan State)	8–1–0
1954	Sanders, Henry (UCLA)	9–0–0

311

Year	Coach (School)	Record
1953	Tatum, Jim (Maryland)	10–0–0
1952	Munn, Briggie (Michigan State)	9–0–0
1951	Taylor, Chuck (Stanford)	9–1–0
1950	Caldwell, Charlie (Princeton)	9–0–0
1949	Wilkinson, Bud (Oklahoma)	10–0–0
1948	Oosterbaan, Benny (Michigan)	9–0–0
1947	Crisler, Fritz (Michigan)	9–0–0
1946	Blaik, Earl (Army)	9–0–1
1945	McMillin, Bo (Indiana)	9–0–1
1944	Widdoes, Carroll (Ohio State)	9–0–0
1943	Stagg, Amos Alonzo (College of Pacific)	7–2–0
1942	Alexander, Bill (Georgia Tech)	9–1–0
1941	Leahy, Frank (Notre Dame)	8–0–1
1940	Shaughnessy, Clark (Stanford)	9–0–0
1939	Anderson, Eddie (Iowa)	6–1–1
1938	Kern, Bill (Carnegie Tech)	7–2–0
1937	Mylin, Edward (Lafayette)	8–0–0
1936	Harlow, Dick (Harvard)	3–4–1
1935	Waldorf, Lynn (Northwestern)	4–3–1

Conference Champions

The major college conferences in football are the Western (Big Ten), Pacific Eight, Southwest, Big Eight, Atlantic Coast, Southeastern, and Eastern Intercollegiate (Ivy League). Each season a conference champion is recognized, and must go on to compete in bowl games.

EASTERN INTERCOLLEGIATE (IVY LEAGUE)

1969	Dartmouth	1968	Yale
	Princeton		Harvard
	Yale	1967	Yale

312

1966	Dartmouth	1934	Navy
	Harvard	1933	Princeton
	Princeton	1932	Army
1965	Dartmouth		Brown
1964	Princeton	1931	Cornell
1963	Princeton	1930	Army
1962	Dartmouth	1929	Dartmouth
1961	Columbia	1928	Army
	Harvard		Navy
1960	Yale	1927	Yale
1959	Pennsylvania	1926	Brown
1958	Dartmouth	1925	Dartmouth
1957	Princeton		Pennsylvania
1956	Yale	1924	Pennsylvania
1955	Princeton	1923	Yale
1954	Yale		Cornell
	Cornell	1922	Cornell
1953	Cornell		Princeton
1952	Pennsylvania	1921	Cornell
1951	Princeton		Navy
1950	Princeton	1920	Dartmouth
1949	Cornell	1919	Navy
1948	Cornell	1918	Pennsylvania
1947	Pennsylvania	1917	Pennsylvania
1946	Yale	1916	Brown
	Harvard	1915.	Cornell
	Pennsylvania	1914	Cornell
1945	Army	1913	Harvard
1944	Army		Dartmouth
1943	Navy	1912	Harvard
1942	Navy	1911	Princeton
1941	Pennsylvania	1910	Pennsylvania
1940	Pennsylvania	1909	Yale
1939	Cornell		Pennsylvania
1938	Cornell	1908	Harvard
1937	Dartmouth	1907	Pennsylvania
1936	Dartmouth		Dartmouth
1935	Princeton	1906	Princeton

1905	Yale	1902	Yale
	Pennsylvania	1901	Harvard
1904	Pennsylvania	1900	Yale
1903	Princeton		

WESTERN (BIG TEN)

1969	Michigan	1945	Indiana
	Ohio State	1944	Ohio State
1968	Ohio State	1943	Michigan
1967	Indiana		Purdue
	Purdue	1942	Ohio State
1966	Michigan State	1941	Minnesota
1965	Michigan State	1940	Minnesota
1964	Michigan	1939	Ohio State
1963	Illinois	1938	Minnesota
1962	Wisconsin	1937	Minnesota
1961	Ohio State	1936	Northwestern
1960	Iowa	1935	Minnesota
	Minnesota		Ohio State
1959	Wisconsin	1934	Minnesota
1958	Iowa	1933	Michigan
1957	Ohio State	1932	Michigan
1956	Iowa	1931	Michigan
1955	Ohio State		Northwestern
1954	Ohio State		Purdue
1953	Michigan State	1930	Michigan
	Illinois		Northwestern
1952	Wisconsin	1929	Purdue
	Purdue	1928	Illinois
1951	Illinois	1927	Illinois
1950	Michigan	1926	Michigan
1949	Ohio State		Northwestern
	Michigan	1925	Michigan
1948	Michigan	1924	Chicago
1947	Michigan	1923	Illinois
1946	Illinois		Michigan

314

1922	Iowa	1908	Chicago
	Michigan	1907	Chicago
	Chicago	1906	Minnesota
1921	Iowa		Wisconsin
1920	Ohio State	1905	Chicago
1919	Illinois	1904	Michigan
1918	Illinois		Minnesota
1917	Ohio State	1903	Michigan
1916	Ohio State		Minnesota
1915	Illinois	1902	Michigan
	Minnesota	1901	Michigan
1914	Illinois		Wisconsin
1913	Chicago	1900	Minnesota
1912	Wisconsin		Iowa
1911	Minnesota	1899	Chicago
1910	Illinois	1898	Michigan
	Minnesota	1897	Wisconsin
1909	Minnesota	1896	Wisconsin

BIG EIGHT

1969	Missouri	1953	Oklahoma
	Nebraska	1952	Oklahoma
1968	Kansas	1951	Oklahoma
1967	Oklahoma	1950	Oklahoma
1966	Nebraska	1949	Oklahoma
1965	Nebraska	1948	Oklahoma
1964	Nebraska	1947	Oklahoma
1963	Nebraska		Kansas
1962	Oklahoma	1946	Oklahoma
1961	Colorado		Kansas
1960	Missouri	1945	Missouri
1959	Oklahoma	1944	Oklahoma
1958	Oklahoma	1943	Oklahoma
1957	Oklahoma	1942	Missouri
1956	Oklahoma	1941	Missouri
1955	Oklahoma	1940	Nebraska
1954	Oklahoma	1939	Missouri

1938	Oklahoma	1932	Nebraska
1937	Nebraska	1931	Nebraska
1936	Nebraska	1930	Kansas
1935	Nebraska	1929	Nebraska
1934	Kansas State	1928	Nebraska
1933	Nebraska		

SOUTHEASTERN

1969	Tennessee	1950	Kentucky
1968	Georgia	1949	Tulane
1967	Tennessee	1948	Georgia
1966	Alabama	1947	Mississippi
	Georgia	1946	Georgia
1965	Alabama		Tennessee
1964	Alabama	1945	Alabama
1963	Mississippi	1944	Georgia Tech
1962	Mississippi	1943	Georgia Tech
1961	Alabama	1942	Georgia
	Louisiana State	1941	Mississippi State
1960	Mississippi	1940	Tennessee
1959	Louisiana State	1939	Tennessee
1958	Louisiana State		Georgia Tech
1957	Auburn		Tulane
1956	Tennessee	1938	Tennessee
1955	Mississippi	1937	Alabama
1954	Mississippi	1936	Louisiana State
1953	Alabama	1935	Louisiana State
1952	Georgia Tech	1934	Tulane
1951	Georgia Tech		Alabama
	Tennessee	1933	Alabama

ATLANTIC COAST

1969	South Carolina	1967	Clemson
1968	North Carolina State	1966	Clemson

316

1965	South Carolina	1944	Duke
	Duke	1943	Duke
1964	North Carolina State	1942	William and Mary
1963	North Carolina State	1941	Duke
	North Carolina	1940	Clemson
1962	Duke	1939	Duke
1961	Duke	1938	Duke
1960	Duke	1937	North Carolina
1959	Clemson	1936	Duke
1958	Clemson	1935	Duke
1957	North Carolina State	1934	Washington and Lee
1956	Clemson	1933	Duke
1955	Maryland	1932	Tennessee
	Duke		Auburn
1954	Duke	1931	Tulane
1953	Duke	1930	Alabama
1952	Duke		Tulane
1951	Maryland	1929	Tulane
	Virginia Military Inst.	1928	Georgia Tech
1950	Washington and Lee	1927	Georgia Tech
1949	North Carolina	1926	Alabama
1948	Clemson	1925	Alabama
1947	William and Mary	1924	Alabama
1946	North Carolina	1923	Vanderbilt
1945	Duke	1922	Georgia Tech

SOUTHWEST

1969	Texas	1960	Arkansas
1968	Arkansas	1959	Texas
1967	Texas A&M	1958	Texas Christian
1966	Southern Methodist	1957	Rice
1965	Arkansas	1956	Texas A&M
1964	Arkansas	1955	Texas Christian
1963	Texas	1954	Arkansas
1962	Texas	1953	Rice
1961	Arkansas		Texas
	Texas	1952	Texas

317

1951	Texas Christian	1933	(None)
1950	Texas	1932	Texas Christian
1949	Rice	1931	Southern Methodist
1948	Southern Methodist	1930	Texas
1947	Southern Methodist	1929	Texas Christian
1946	Arkansas	1928	Texas
	Rice	1927	Texas A&M
1945	Texas	1926	Southern Methodist
1944	Texas Christian	1925	Texas
1943	Texas	1924	Baylor
1942	Texas	1923	Southern Methodist
1941	Texas A&M	1922	Baylor
1940	Texas A&M	1921	Texas A&M
	Southern Methodist	1920	Texas
1939	Texas A&M	1919	Texas A&M
1938	Texas Christian	1918	(None)
1937	Rice	1917	Texas A&M
1936	Arkansas	1916	(None)
1935	Southern Methodist	1915	Baylor
1934	Rice		

PACIFIC EIGHT

1969	Southern California	1956	Oregon
1968	Southern California	1955	UCLA
1967	Southern California	1954	UCLA
1966	Southern California	1953	UCLA
1965	UCLA	1952	Southern California
1964	Oregon State	1951	Stanford
	Southern California	1950	Southern California
1963	Washington	1949	Southern California
1962	Southern California	1948	California
1961	UCLA		Oregon
1960	Washington	1947	Southern California
1959	Washington	1946	UCLA
1958	California	1945	Southern California
1957	Oregon State	1944	Southern California
	Oregon	1943	Southern California

318

1942	UCLA	1929	Southern California
1941	Oregon State	1928	Southern California
1940	Stanford	1927	Southern California
1939	Southern California		Stanford
1938	California	1926	Stanford
1937	California	1925	Washington
1936	Washington	1924	Stanford
	Southern California	1923	California
1935	California	1922	California
	UCLA	1921	California
	Stanford	1920	California
1934	Stanford	1919	Oregon
1933	Oregon		Washington
	Stanford	1918	(None)
1932	Southern California	1917	Washington State
1931	Southern California	1916	Washington
1930	Washington State		

Professional Football

SUPER BOWL

The Super Bowl, bringing together the champions of the National and American Leagues, is the newest "dream game." But even though it was begun as recently as 1967, the contest already ranks as one of the great annual spectacles in all the world of sports.

Year	Winner	Loser	Score
1970	Kansas City Chiefs (AFL)	Minnesota Vikings (NFL)	23–7
1969	New York Jets (AFL)	Baltimore Colts (NFL)	16–7
1968	Green Bay Packers (NFL)	Oakland Raiders (AFL)	33–14
1967	Green Bay Packers (NFL)	Kansas City Chiefs (AFL)	35–10

319

National Football League Champions

	EASTERN DIVISION	WESTERN DIVISION
1969	Cleveland Browns (7)	*Minnesota Vikings (27)
1968	Cleveland Browns (10)	*Baltimore Colts (34)
1967	Dallas Cowboys (17)	*Green Bay Packers (21)
1966	Dallas Cowboys (27)	*Green Bay Packers (34)
1965	Cleveland Browns (12)	*Green Bay Packers (23)
1964	*Cleveland Browns (27)	Baltimore Colts (0)
1963	New York Giants (10)	*Chicago Bears (14)
1962	New York Giants (7)	*Green Bay Packers (16)
1961	New York Giants (0)	*Green Bay Packers (37)
1960	*Philadelphia Eagles (17)	Green Bay Packers (13)
1959	New York Giants (16)	*Baltimore Colts (31)
1958	New York Giants (17)	*Baltimore Colts (23)
1957	Cleveland Browns (14)	*Detroit Lions (59)
1956	*New York Giants (47)	Chicago Bears (7)
1955	*Cleveland Browns (38)	Los Angeles Rams (14)
1954	*Cleveland Browns (56)	Detroit Lions (10)
1953	Cleveland Browns (16)	*Detroit Lions (17)
1952	Cleveland Browns (7)	*Detroit Lions (17)
1951	Cleveland Browns (17)	*Los Angeles Rams (24)
1950	*Cleveland Browns (30)	Los Angeles Rams (28)
1949	*Philadelphia Eagles (14)	Los Angeles Rams (0)
1948	*Philadelphia Eagles (7)	Chicago Cardinals (0)
1947	Philadelphia Eagles (21)	*Chicago Cardinals (28)
1946	New York Giants (14)	*Chicago Bears (24)
1945	Washington Redskins (14)	*Cleveland Rams (15)
1944	New York Giants (7)	*Green Bay Packers (14)
1943	Washington Redskins (21)	*Chicago Bears (41)
1942	*Washington Redskins (14)	Chicago Bears (6)
1941	New York Giants (9)	*Chicago Bears (37)
1940	Washington Redskins (0)	*Chicago Bears (73)
1939	New York Giants (0)	*Green Bay Packers (27)

* Playoff winner.
(Playoff scores in parentheses.)

1938	*New York Giants (23)	Green Bay Packers (17)
1937	*Washington Redskins (28)	Chicago Bears (21)
1936	Boston Redskins (6)	*Green Bay Packers (21)
1935	New York Giants (7)	*Detroit Lions (26)
1934	*New York Giants (30)	Chicago Bears (13)
1933	New York Giants (21)	*Chicago Bears (23)

National Football League

SCORING CHAMPIONS

TD: touchdown; EP: extra points (points after touchdown); FG: field goals; TP: total points.

Year	Player	Club	TD	EP	FG	TP
1969	Cox, Fred	Minnesota Vikings	0	43	26	121
1968	Kelly, Leroy	Cleveland Browns	20	0	0	120
1967	Gossett, Bruce	Los Angeles Rams	0	29	28	113
1966	Bakken, Jim	St. Louis Cardinals	0	36	27	117
1965	Sayers, Gale	Chicago Bears	22	0	0	132
1964	Moore, Lenny	Baltimore Colts	20	0	0	120
1963	Chandler, Don	New York Giants	0	52	18	106
1962	Taylor, Jim	Green Bay Packers	19	0	0	114
1961	Hornung, Paul	Green Bay Packers	10	41	15	146
1960	Hornung, Paul	Green Bay Packers	15	41	15	176
1959	Hornung, Paul	Green Bay Packers	7	31	7	94
1958	Brown, Jimmy	Cleveland Browns	18	0	0	108
1957	Baker, Sam	Washington Redskins	1	29	14	77
	Groza, Lou	Cleveland Browns	0	32	15	77
1956	Layne, Bobby	Detroit Lions	5	33	12	99
1955	Walker, Doak	Detroit Lions	7	27	9	96
1954	Walston, Bobby	Philadelphia Eagles	11	36	4	114
1953	Soltau, Gordy	San Francisco 49ers	6	48	10	114
1952	Soltau, Gordy	San Francisco 49ers	7	34	6	94
1951	Hirsch, Elroy	Los Angeles Rams	17	0	0	102
1950	Walker, Doak	Detroit Lions	11	38	8	128
1949	Harder, Pat	Chicago Cardinals	8	45	3	102
	Roberts, Gene	New York Giants	17	0	0	102
1948	Harder, Pat	Chicago Cardinals	6	53	7	110
1947	Harder, Pat	Chicago Cardinals	7	39	7	102
1946	Fritsch, Ted	Green Bay Packers	10	13	9	100
1945	Van Buren, Steve	Philadelphia Eagles	18	2	0	110
1944	Hutson, Don	Green Bay Packers	9	31	0	85
1943	Hutson, Don	Green Bay Packers	12	36	3	117

Year	Player	Club	TD	EP	FG	TP
1942	Hutson, Don	Green Bay Packers	17	33	1	138
1941	Hutson, Don	Green Bay Packers	12	20	0	95
1940	Hutson, Don	Green Bay Packers	7	15	0	57
1939	Farkas, Andy	Washington Redskins	11	2	0	68
1938	Hinkle, Clarke	Green Bay Packers	7	7	3	58
1937	Manders, Jack	Chicago Bears	5	15	8	69
1936	Clark, Dutch	Detroit Lions	7	19	4	73
1935	Clark, Dutch	Detroit Lions	6	16	1	55
1934	Manders, Jack	Chicago Bears	3	31	10	79
1933	Strong, Ken	New York Giants	6	13	5	64
	Presnell, Glenn	Portsmouth Spartans	6	10	6	64
1932	Clark, Dutch	Portsmouth Spartans	4	6	3	39

American Football League Champions

	EASTERN DIVISION	WESTERN DIVISION
1969	*Kansas City Chiefs (17)	Oakland Raiders (7)
1968	*New York Jets (27)	Oakland Raiders (23)
1967	Houston Oilers (7)	*Oakland Raiders (40)
1966	Buffalo Bills (7)	*Kansas City Chiefs (31)
1965	*Buffalo Bills (23)	San Diego Chargers (0)
1964	*Buffalo Bills (20)	San Diego Chargers (7)
1963	Boston Patriots (10)	*San Diego Chargers (51)
1962	Houston Oilers (17)	*Dallas Texans (20)
1961	*Houston Oilers (10)	San Diego Chargers (3)
1960	*Houston Oilers (24)	Los Angeles Chargers (16)

* Indicates playoff winner.
(Playoff scores in parentheses.)

American Football League

SCORING CHAMPIONS

Year	Player	Club	TD	EP	FG	TP
1969	Turner, Jim	New York Jets	0	33	32	129
1968	Turner, Jim	New York Jets	0	43	34	145
1967	Blanda, George	Oakland Raiders	0	56	20	116
1966	Cappelletti, Gino	Boston Patriots	6	35	16	119
1965	Cappelletti, Gino	Boston Patriots	9	27	17	132
1964	Cappelletti, Gino	Boston Patriots	7	38	25	155
1963	Cappelletti, Gino	Boston Patriots	0	35	22	113
1962	Mingo, Gene	Denver Broncos	4	32	27	137
1961	Cappelletti, Gino	Boston Patriots	8	48	17	147
1960	Mingo, Gene	Denver Broncos	6	33	18	123

Pro Football Hall of Fame

Established in 1963, the Pro Football Hall of Fame is situated at Canton, Ohio, and as of 1969 contained fifty-nine members. Closed only on Christmas, it can be visited from 9 A.M. to 8 P.M., Memorial Day through Labor Day, and from 9 A.M. to 5 P.M., at other times. Admission is a dollar and a half for adults and fifty cents for children under fourteen.

PLAYERS

Member	Position	Year Inducted
Battles, Cliff	Back	1968
Baugh, Sammy	Back	1963
Bednarik, Chuck	Center	1967
Chamberlin, Guy	End	1965
Christiansen, Jack	Back	1970
Clark, Dutch	Back	1963
Donovan, Art	Tackle	1968

Member	Position	Year Inducted
Driscoll, Paddy	Back	1965
Dudley, Bill	Back	1966
Edwards, Turk	Tackle	1969
Fears, Tom	End	1970
Fortmann, Danny	Guard	1965
Graham, Otto	Back	1965
Grange, Harold (Red)	Back	1963
Guyon, Joe	Back	1966
Healey, Ed	Tackle	1964
Hein, Mel	Center	1963
Henry, Wilbur	Tackle	1963
Herber, Arnie	Back	1966
Hinkle, Clarke	Back	1964
Hirsch, Elroy	Back	1968
Hubbard, Robert (Cal)	Tackle	1963
Hutson, Don	End	1963
Kiesling, Walt	Guard	1966
Layne, Bobby	Back	1967
Luckman, Sid	Back	1965
Lyman, Link	Tackle	1964
McAfee, George	Back	1966
McElhenny, Hugh	Back	1970
McNally, John (Blood)	Back	1963
Michalske, Mike	Guard	1964
Millner, Wayne	End	1968
Motley, Marion	Back	1968
Nagurski, Bronko	Back	1963
Nevers, Ernie	Back	1963
Nomellini, Leo	Tackle	1969
Perry, Fletcher (Joe)	Back	1969
Pihos, Pete	End	1970
Stautner, Ernie	Tackle	1969
Strong, Ken	Back	1967
Stydahar, Joe	Tackle	1967
Thorpe, Jim	Back	1963
Trafton, George	Center	1964
Trippi, Charley	Back	1968
Tunnell, Emlen	Back	1967
Turner, Clyde (Bulldog)	Center	1966
Van Buren, Steve	Back	1965
Waterfield, Bob	Back	1965
Wojciechowicz, Alex	Center	1968

OTHERS

Member	Title	Year Inducted
Bell, Bert	Commissioner	1963
Bidwell, Charles	Owner	1967
Brown, Paul	Coach	1967
Carr, Joe	NFL President	1963
Conzelman, Jimmy	Coach	1964
Halas, George	Coach	1963
Lambeau, Earl (Curly)	Coach	1963
Mara, Tim	Owner	1963
Marshall, George Preston	Owner	1963
Neale, Earle (Greasy)	Coach	1969
Owen, Steve	Coach	1966
Ray, Hugh	Advisor	1966
Reeves, Dan	Owner	1967
Rooney, Art	Owner	1964

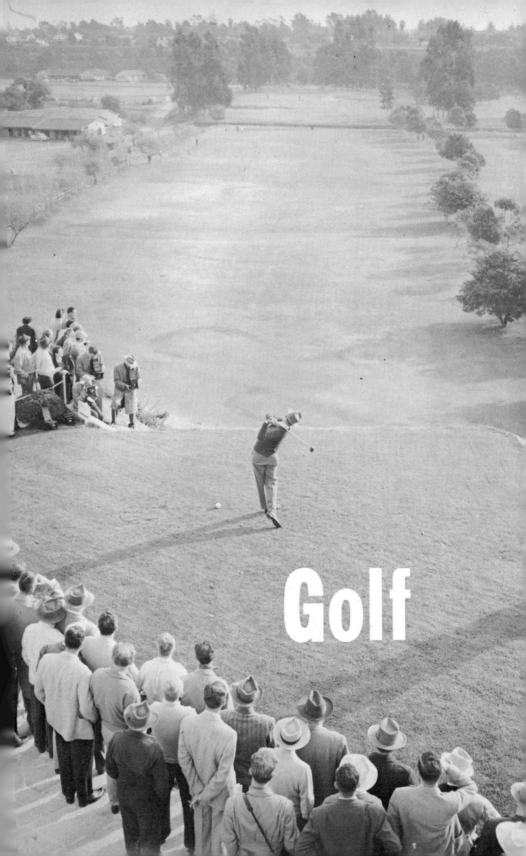

Golf

The History of Golf

It has been estimated that 5,000,000 Americans play golf fairly regularly every year. They play on the country's more than 5,000 courses, and spend more than $30,000,000 a year on golf balls alone.

These are whopping figures for a sport that is comparatively new in our land. The game got its first foothold in the United States in the 1880's, but not until 1913 did it really capture the public's imagination.

Today golf, with all its frustrations and its joys, is as much a part of the American scene as Sunday picnics. It may have been born in the British Isles, but Americans have taken it to their hearts as though it were their own child.

The game originated in Scotland around 1440, and by 1457 so many Scots were playing golf that the government outlawed the game. Scotsmen were told they would do better to practice archery, since men skilled with bow and arrow would always be needed to defend the country.

But when King James IV himself took up the game in the

early 1550's, the objections subsided. Later in the same century Mary Queen of Scots became attracted to golf. She was probably the first woman golfer of note.

Not until more than three hundred years after the game's earliest beginnings was the first golfing society organized. This was the Honorable Company of Edinburgh Golfers, founded in 1744. Ten years later the most famous club in the world, the Royal and Ancient Golf Club of St. Andrews, came into being. It has been in continuous operation ever since and has been the scene of much golf drama.

An early photograph taken at St. Andrews in Scotland.

U. S. Golf Association

Clubs continued to spring up around Scotland, but golf balls, golf sticks and the courses themselves were a far cry from those of today.

The courses consisted of anywhere from five to eighteen holes. St. Andrews had eighteen, but even there the same greens were used for the outgoing and incoming nine holes. The greens, or putting surfaces, were very rough, and there were no teeing areas.

The first balls were called featheries. They were made by stuffing a small bag of very thin leather as tightly as possible

with feathers. When the packing was completed, the small opening that had been made for the feathers was sewn together.

The clubs that were used to hit the ball generally had wooden shafts and wooden heads. A player could use as many clubs as he wished or could carry by hand, and he wore whatever clothing seemed to suit him. Usually the clothing was so bulky that it interfered with his swing.

Refinements in the game took place over the span of many years. For instance, the featheries didn't go out of use until 1848, when the gutta-percha ball, made of resin or gum, was adopted.

The forerunner of today's rubber golf ball was introduced in 1899. It was invented in the United States and it went through many changes in size and weight before it was made universally standard.

The first tournament considered an official championship contest was played in 1860 on Scotland's Prestwick course. In 1861 the tournament became known as the British Open, which meant it was open to anyone, amateur or professional, club member or not. The 1860 tournament drew only eight

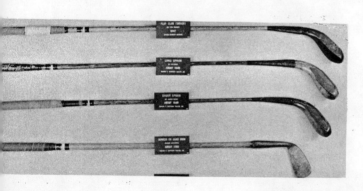

Early golf clubs.

A feather ball, made prior to 1850.

contestants. They played three rounds of twelve holes each, and the title went to Willie Park.

Park and Tom Morris were the stars of those early days, each of them winning the title four times. Starting in 1868, Morris' son, Tom, Jr., captured the title four times in succession—a feat that has yet to be equaled.

During the 1870's golf spread to England and other countries, including Ireland, Canada, and some of the British colonies, and it was only natural that it should reach the United States.

Actually, historical references to golf in this country can be found as early as the 1700's, but the story of the game in the United States really begins in the 1880's. Joseph Mickle Fox of Philadelphia was exposed to the sport on a trip to Scotland in 1884, and in 1887 he was instrumental in the founding of the Foxburg (Pennsylvania) Golf Club, believed to be the oldest in the United States.

Others say the oldest American club was, and is, the St. Andrews Golf Club of Yonkers, New York, and that the principal founding father was John Reid, a Scotsman living in Yonkers.

A star of the early days—Willie Park— winner of the first British Open.

Courtesy Nevin H. Gibson

In any case, St. Andrews of Yonkers, named in honor of the original St. Andrews in Scotland, had the greater influence on the growth of golf in this country.

Its first course was a three-hole affair in a cow pasture owned by Reid. It was to move to several more sites—including an apple orchard, where the players became famous as the Apple Tree Gang—before establishing its permanent home at Mt. Hope, New York, in 1897.

So rapid was the growth of golfing groups that by 1894 a golfer could find a course in almost every section of the country, including the West Coast. Most were located in the East, however, and the same year saw the St. Andrews

This rare photograph, taken in 1888, is believed to be the first picture of golf in America. It shows the first green of the original St. Andrews Golf course at Yonkers, New York.

H. B. Martin and
U. S. Golf Association

Club of Yonkers sponsor the first American open tournament. The winner was Willie Dunn.

Since the game had developed so quickly it seemed time to establish a governing body for it, and in December of 1894 the United States Golf Association was founded. Golf was now firmly rooted in America.

The first official U. S. Open, the first U. S. Amateur, and the first U. S. Women's Amateur were all played in 1895, with the titles going to Horace Rawlins, C. B. Macdonald, and Mrs. C. S. Brown.

But even with all this, golf still had very little public appeal. Most of the players were amateurs who preferred the privacy of their own clubs. There were few professionals, and most of them were instructors. Tournaments drew comparatively few players, and the number of spectators was limited.

By 1900 more than a thousand golf courses, at least one in every state, were sprinkled over the country. This was the year, too, that Harry Vardon, greatest of all British golfers, paid his first visit to America—and went home with the U. S. Open crown.

America by now had produced at least two golfers good enough to rank with the British. One was Walter J. Travis, who won the U. S. Amateur three times and the British Amateur in his only attempt in 1904. The other was Willie Anderson, our first great professional, who won the U. S. Open in 1901 and set a record that still stands, by taking the title three years in a row—1903, 1904, and 1905.

Other fine American players of this time were John J. McDermott and Jerome D. Travers, but the sport was dominated by three Britons—Vardon, John H. Taylor, and James Braid, who became famous as "the great triumvirate."

Still another British standout was Edward (Ted) Ray. He, Vardon, and an unknown American amateur, Francis Ouimet, were the central figures in a 1913 drama that was to give golf in the United States a tremendous shot in the arm.

The two Englishmen arrived confident of romping off with the U. S. Open crown, but Ouimet tied them in the 72 holes of regular play, then beat them in the playoff.

The surprise victory of Ouimet put golf on the front pages and probably won more followers for the game in this country than any other single event in its history.

Golf World Magazine

The famous British trio of the early 1900's.
From left to right: John H. Taylor, James Braid, and Harry Vardon.

In this rare photograph Francis Ouimet is seen at upper left, crouching behind his ball on the 18th green during a playoff for the 1913 U. S. Open. Ouimet won a surprise victory from Harry Vardon and Ted Ray (leaning on putters).

Walter Hagen, who still ranks as the greatest American professional ever to step out on the links, began his reign in 1914 by winning the Open. Two years later the game had another important development in the formation of the Professional Golfers Association (PGA) of America, whose first title went to James M. Barnes.

After World War I came the "golden decade" of sports—the 1920's—and though golf like other sports had heroes in bunches, one man led the parade—Bobby Jones, Jr.

Hagen and Gene Sarazen were the top professionals, giants of the game by every standard, but young Bobby, the Atlanta

338

Walter Hagen defeats English golf pro Henry Cotton in their challenge match on July 29, 1933.

Lawson Little clears the rough in finals match with Jimmy Wallace of Scotland for 1934 British Amateur title.

amateur, held the golfing world in the palm of his hand.

The climax to Bobby's career came when he scored his grand slam in 1930, winning the Amateur and Open championships of both the United States and Great Britain.

It was during the golden decade that the first professional (Ryder Cup) and amateur (Walker Cup) matches between this country and England were played, and that rules and tools on both sides of the Atlantic were made generally uniform.

Top events of the 1930's included the first women's amateur matches between the United States and England (1932), the beginning of the now-famed Masters tournament (1934), and Lawson Little's double "little slam," in which he won both the U. S. and British Amateur titles in 1934 and 1935.

The 1930–1940 period saw pro golf become big business. And such new stars as Byron Nelson, Sam Snead, Ben Hogan, Ralph Guldahl, Denny Shute, Craig Wood, Jimmy Thomson, and Jimmy Demaret joined the quest for the large sums of money at stake in tournaments all over the country.

Byron Nelson stood head and shoulders above the rest during the years of World War II. He captured thirty tour-

Ben Hogan blasts out of the sand in the second round of the $5,000 San Francisco golf tournament on January 25, 1942.

Associated Press

naments in 1944 and 1945 and collected more than $100,000 in War Bonds as prizes.

With the return to peace, the PGA set a minimum purse of $10,000 for each tournament, and record fields and record spectator galleries became an ordinary thing at golf events all over the country. More and more people took up the game. The youngsters caught the craze, too. The Junior Amateur for boys was started in 1948 and the Junior Amateur for girls the following year.

A small group of women professionals held their first Open championship in 1946, with Patty Berg the winner. Patty

Byron Nelson getting out of the rough on the 16th hole as he continues to lead the field in the $5,000 Oakland Open, January 16, 1942.

Associated Press

was easily the outstanding woman professional in this country until Babe Didrikson Zaharias, former Olympic track star, came along to seize the honors. Louise Suggs and Mickey Wright also have been standouts.

Among the men, the story of golf through much of the 1950's featured two all-time greats—Hogan and Snead. Hogan has won every major professional title in the world. Snead has taken them all except the U. S. Open, a tournament that has been a jinx to him throughout his career.

The 1960's found Hogan and Snead yielding the limelight to such stars as Arnold Palmer, Gene Littler, Bill Casper, Jack Nicklaus, Ken Venturi, and South Africa's Gary Player.

Ben Hogan playing in the Los Angeles Open at Riviera, January 10, 1950.

The records set by yesterday's stars may be difficult to break, but there will always be challengers . . . today and tomorrow.

Great Names in Golf

TOMMY ARMOUR

One of the game's great teachers as well as one of its great players—that's the honor Tommy Armour has earned for himself after more than forty years on the golf links.

Armour, known as the Silver Scot because of his white hair, now devotes most of his time to teaching the fine points of the game he mastered as a young man in his native Scotland.

Thomas Dickson Armour writes and speaks from experience gained on the links of both Europe and America. In fact, he is the only golfer to have represented both Great Britain and the United States in international matches.

Tommy was a member of the 1921 British team that played in the first international amateur matches. He came over again the following year, decided to stay, then turned professional.

In the next seven years he won every major pro championship for which he was eligible—the U. S. Open in 1927, the PGA in 1930, and the British Open in 1931. In 1926 he was

344

Tommy Armour

Associated Press

a member of the American team that played Great Britain in the first international pro matches.

Armour still considers the Open victory of 1927 his greatest, not only because it was his first major triumph in his newly adopted country, but because it was his toughest test. He had to sink a 10-foot birdie putt to tie Harry Cooper in the regular 72 holes, and then won the playoff with a 76 to Cooper's 79.

Billy Casper displays the first-place $20,000 check he received as winner of the 42nd Annual Los Angeles Open Golf Tournament, January 28, 1968.

BILL CASPER

In 1965 and 1966, Bill Casper was the talk of the golf world not only because of his performances on the links but because of a victory over himself.

Early in 1965, Casper, already a pretty hefty individual, began to put on more weight. If you watched golf tournaments on television—as millions did and do—you could always pick out Casper coming up the fairway. He was the fat one.

Doctors determined that Bill was allergic to a number of foods, many of them everyday items. The only way he could trim his weight, he was told, was to go on an extremely strict diet—of such foods as buffalo meat, swordfish and avocado pears.

With the same determination he has displayed as a golfer, Casper put himself to the test, and before 1965 was over he had the figure of a movie star. Victory in four major tournaments also came to him that year as Casper, already a fine golfer, moved up among the game's real greats.

In 1966, he won the United States Open for the second time, and so thoroughly did he dominate the scene in 1968, despite the fact he did not win any of the classic tournaments, that he set a money-winning record of $205,168—the first player in the history of the game to top the $200,000 mark.

Casper won his first tournament in 1956, and between that year and 1970, when he won the Masters, there was never a year in which he failed to capture at least one tourney.

Consistency has been his hallmark. The Vardon Trophy, truest yardstick of how well a golfer plays over the course of a year, went to Casper a record five times—in 1960, '63, '65, '66 and '68. He was runner-up for the PGA championship in 1958 and 1965. His first United States Open Victory came in 1959. When he won the event again in '66, he beat the toughest man in the game one of the toughest ways. He overcame a seven-stroke deficit on the final round to tie Arnold Palmer and then defeated Palmer by four strokes in an eighteen-hole playoff.

WALTER HAGEN

The only golfer who came close to challenging Bobby Jones as the greatest of them all was Walter Hagen, undisputed king of the professionals. Like Jones, he made links history on both sides of the Atlantic.

From 1914, when he was twenty-two years old, to 1929 the Haig won eleven major titles. No other professional has approached that record, even though there are more major tournaments now than when Hagen was active.

Hagen won enough honors in the PGA championship alone to earn immortality. He captured the title a record five times—in 1921, 1924, 1925, 1926, and 1927—and the string of four straight, from 1924 through 1927, is another record that has never been threatened.

No other American has ever done so well in the British Open as Sir Walter. He took that title four times—1922, 1924, 1928, and 1929—during an era when English golfers were among the world's best.

In the U. S. Open he was the victor in 1914 and 1919 and finished second in 1921.

Hagen and Jones crossed clubs only once, and those who argue that Walter was the all-time best can point to the outcome as evidence. The Haig and Bobby played a 72-hole challenge match in Florida in 1926, with Hagen the winner, 11 up and 10 to play.

The stocky, slick-haired Hagen is credited with doing more for pro golfers than any other man in the history of the game. He broke down social barriers at a time when the pros were snubbed in many amateur circles. To him the pro golfer was the royal man of the links, and he lived up to his conception in both manner and dress—and in the magic of his clubs.

He died in 1969 at the age of seventy-seven.

BEN HOGAN

No golfer has won more respect for personal courage than bantam Ben Hogan. His feats on the links are more than enough to place him among the all-time greats, but his dramatic comeback after a brush with death put him in a class by himself.

The little Texan was at the top of his game in 1949, when he was critically injured in an auto accident. There was doubt he would ever play again. But when the final stroke of the 1950 U. S. Open was recorded, the name of William Benjamin Hogan led all the rest.

Weak and limping, Ben played the 72 holes in 287 strokes to tie Lloyd Mangrum and George Fazio for the title. In the playoff it was all Hogan, with a brilliant 69 to Mangrum's 73 and Fazio's 75.

Yet, as remarkable as the victory was, it was only the first chapter of Hogan's unforgettable comeback story. He won the Open again in 1951 and 1953, the third player in golf history to capture the coveted crown four times. (His first Open victory was in 1948 with a record score of 276.)

He was first in the Masters in 1951, and won again in 1953 with another record total—274. But perhaps Hogan's finest hour came when, competing in the event for the first time, he captured the 1953 British Open with still another record—284.

Like a number of other golf masters, Hogan learned the game as a caddie. His first big year was 1940, when he was the nation's leading money winner and won the Vardon Trophy, awarded annually to the best shotmaker in the game. For the next two decades Hogan made headlines and history, winning every major title at least once.

BOBBY JONES

The greatest of the greats in golf was Bobby Jones. In fact, no other sport has produced a champion so supreme. Many years have passed since his reign, but even today his name is to golf what the name of Babe Ruth is to baseball.

Robert Tyre Jones, Jr., was a pink-cheeked boy in knee pants when he played in his first national championship in 1916 at the age of fourteen. It was nine years before he won his first major title, but he so completely swept the field once he took command that he retired at twenty-eight with no worlds left to conquer.

Popularly known as the Boy Wonder and the Emperor Jones, smooth-swinging Bobby stroked his way to a record thirteen American and British national championships be-

350

Bobby Jones

tween 1923 and 1930. His grand slam of 1930—winning the U. S. Amateur, the U. S. Open, the British Amateur, and the British Open—is the greatest feat in the game.

It is important to remember that Bobby was an amateur all through his career. There is no telling how many more titles he could have won had he turned professional.

Jones started his march through golfing ranks by winning the 1923 U. S. Open in an 18-hole playoff with Bobby Cruickshank after the two had tied at 296 in the regulation 72 holes. Here is his record of major victories:

U. S. Amateur Open: 1924, 1925, 1927, 1928, and 1930. (Runner-up in 1919 and 1926.)

U. S. Open Champion: 1923, 1926, 1929, and 1930. (Tied in 1925 and 1928 but lost in playoffs; runner-up four times in all.)

British Open Champion: 1926, 1927, and 1930.

British Amateur Champion: 1930.

In Walker Cup competition, pitting the best American amateurs against the best British, Jones won six individual matches without a defeat.

Since his retirement Bobby has maintained an active interest in the game, although illness has forced him to stay close to home in Atlanta, Georgia. He has helped make the Masters tournament—begun in 1934 and played annually in Augusta, Georgia—one of the top golf events in the world.

LAWSON LITTLE

The finest amateur golfer after the era of Bobby Jones was Lawson Little, Jr. He could never hope to equal Bobby's grand slam. But what he did accomplish is also a record, and it may stand as long as Jones'.

When handsome, husky Lawson won the U. S. Amateur and the British Amateur championships in the same year (1934), he joined a select few who had scored a little slam. But when he swept both titles again the very next year, he achieved a real distinction. It had never been done before. It hasn't been since. What's more, his victory in the final round of the 1935 British Amateur was by a record margin of 14 up and 13 to play.

Little also went after the British Open crown in 1935. He had to be satisfied with a tie for fourth place, but even at that his total was the best score posted by an American.

Little turned professional in 1936 and four years later won the big prize, the U. S. Open. A powerful long-distance hitter, he played 72 holes in 287 to tie the veteran Gene Sarazen. Then he shot a 70, despite rain and soggy turf, to win the playoff by three strokes.

The judgment of many golf experts is that for match play Little was the best amateur golfer the United States ever produced. In one stretch he won thirty-one consecutive matches in major competition, not counting those he added as a member of the Walker Cup team.

In medal play, the U. S. Open gave him his only major victory, but he won many semimajor events.

BYRON NELSON

The year 1945 saw Byron Nelson set a record that has since stood up under every assault and may never be surpassed.

Lord Byron captured eleven consecutive professional tournaments in that one year. Considering that a golf ball, like a football, can take some funny bounces at times, it was an achievement that defied the law of averages.

But that isn't the whole story. Of the thirty-eight pro tournaments played in 1945, Nelson competed in thirty-one, won seventeen, including the PGA title, and was runner-up in seven. His average round for the year was a record 68.33, and his total money winnings for the year ($63,355.66) established still another high.

A boyhood buddy of Ben Hogan, with whom he caddied at Fort Worth, Texas, John Byron Nelson, Jr., turned professional in 1933 and hit the big time in 1937, when he led the field in the Masters. He snared the U. S. Open crown in 1939, won the PGA championship for the first time in 1940, and repeated in the Masters in 1942.

If 1945 was his greatest year, 1944 set the stage for it. Lord Byron won thirteen of the twenty-three events he entered and earned almost $38,000—a record until he almost doubled it the next year.

Nelson dropped out of regular tournament play after the 1946 season but was runner-up in the Masters in 1947. He won the French Open as recently as 1955.

JACK NICKLAUS

No other player in professional golf has made such a tremendous impression so quickly as has Jack Nicklaus. In four seasons on the PGA tour, the bulky, powerful Nicklaus attained rank as one of the half-dozen or so great players in the modern era of golf.

Nicklaus was born on January 21, 1940, and turned professional after 1961. In his first four years as a pro, he won seventeen official PGA tour tournaments and collected $415,-945.59 in prize money.

Nicklaus is the youngest of the five players who have won the PGA championship, the USGA Open, and the Masters.

And yet this only begins to describe the record compiled by the rust-blond bomber who said, after winning his second USGA Amateur championship in 1961, that he had no intention of turning professional. He changed his mind the next year in the Los Angeles Open and finished in a tie for last-place money, earning $33.33.

He won his first big tournament when he beat Arnold Palmer by three strokes in a playoff for the USGA Open championship in 1962. He won two more big ones that year, the Greater Seattle Open and the Portland Open.

In 1963 Nicklaus won the PGA and Masters. In 1964, he picked up four more titles, among them his second Tournament of Champions. The highlight of Jack's 1965 campaign was a record 271 to win his second Masters championship by nine strokes. He broke Ben Hogan's 1953 Masters record by three strokes, and was fifth or better in fourteen of twenty official starts.

In 1966, the long-hitting Ohioan, by this time affectionately known as the Golden Bear, added the British Open to his collection of championships. but even more dramatic was his victory the same year in the Masters. Nicklaus thus became the first golfer to capture the Masters in successive years.

High point of the 1967 season for Nicklaus was his triumph in the United States Open with a record score of 275. Purses in golf tournaments had grown so large and so consistent a winner was Nicklaus during 1967 that he was able to amass official earnings of $188,998, topping his own record of the previous year by almost $50,000.

Nicklaus was born to golf. He was encouraged and helped greatly by his father and shot a 51 for 9 holes when he was only ten years old. At sixteen he won his first important title —the Ohio Open; and he took the NCAA Golf Championship while a student at Ohio State University.

FRANCIS OUIMET

If one man could be said to have given golf its biggest boost in America, that man would be Francis D. Ouimet.

The game was still in the toddling stage here in 1913. Most of the great players were British; Americans were looked upon as poor cousins. Spectator interest in the sport was negligible, and little space was devoted to it in the newspapers.

Things were running true to form when two of Britain's greats, Harry Vardon and Edward (Ted) Ray, finished in what seemed an all-British tie for the 1913 U. S. Open championship at the Brookline Country Club in Massachusetts.

But still out on the course was twenty-year-old Francis Ouimet, a little-known American amateur. Six holes remained for him to play on the wet and soggy course. He would have to shoot them in two under par to tie Vardon and Ray at 304.

Ouimet, a Massachusetts product, was equal to the challenge. Aided by a 30-foot chip shot, a 9-foot putt, and a 15-footer, he scored 3, 5, 4, 3, 3, and 4 to tie the Britishers. Even then Ouimet was given little chance in the playoff. But he took the lead on the 10th hole and won the title with a round of 72 to Vardon's 77 and Ray's 78.

The victory thrilled the country, won countless fans for golf, and assured Ouimet of his ranking as an immortal.

Was the victory a fluke? It was not. The slim, quiet Ouimet never won the U. S. Open again, but he captured the U. S. Amateur in 1914, was runner-up in 1920, and won the Amateur again in 1931, when he was thirty-eight years old.

His record doesn't compare with those of golf stars the United States has produced since 1913. But he was the man who waved the magic putter that turned golf into a major American sport.

ARNOLD PALMER

Professional golf has soared to tremendous popularity since the mid-1950's, and if any one player deserves credit for this, it has to be Arnold Palmer. The Pennsylvanian won forty-eight championships around the world, forty-three of them on the PGA tour, in a ten-year sweep following his first victory in the 1955 Canadian Open.

In the process, Palmer ran his official winnings to $643,-982.17, an all-time high in the game. His magnetic personality earned him, and golf, millions of fans throughout the world.

As great as he is, 1965 and 1964 were not very good years for Palmer. In 1965 his only victory was the Tournament of

Arnold Palmer

Champions, and he won a mere $57,770.71, finishing tenth on the money list, his lowest in ten years. In 1964 he won $113,203.37 while winning only two titles—his fourth Masters and the Oklahoma City Open.

With his 1964 Masters victory Palmer became the first golfer ever to win that tournament four times; he also won at Augusta in 1958, 1960 and 1962.

Among the world's recognized major titles, only the PGA championship has eluded him. He landed the U. S. Open in 1960 and twice won the British Open—1960 and 1961.

The early sixties were great years for Palmer and his followers, known as Arnie's Army. In 1960 he won eight tournaments; in 1962 he won seven. In 1963 he was the tour's leading money winner for a fourth time with $128,230, then a record. He also captained the Ryder Cup team to victory over the British at Atlanta that year.

In 1962 his victories came in spurts. He won his third Masters and the American Golf Classic. He was voted PGA Player of the Year for the second time, having also won that honor in 1960.

His record prize money year was 1963, when he picked up three of the biggest prizes offered—$26,000 in the Whitemarsh Open, $25,000 in the Thunderbird Classic, and $22,000 in the Cleveland Open. He finished the year with $130,835.18.

Palmer received his first set of cut-down clubs from his father when he was only three years old. His father, Milfred, a pro since 1921 at the Latrobe Country Club, was responsible for Arnold's development. As a youngster Arnold dominated the golf scene in western Pennsylvania and played as number one man on the Wake Forest College team for four years. The 5-foot-10, 180-pounder was born September 10, 1929.

GENE SARAZEN

It sometimes takes but a single shot to give a golfer a special place in the record books. Such is the case with Gene Sarazen. By any standard, the muscular ex-caddie ranks with the great. But he'll always be remembered best for his famous double eagle in the 1935 Masters, the second year the tournament was played.

It was the final round of the 72-hole tournament. Sarazen trailed by three strokes with four holes to play—a deficit that seemed impossible to overcome. It was then that Gene made the shot that thrilled the world of golf. He sank a 230-yard spoon shot for a 2 on the par-5, 485-yard 15th hole.

He finished the last three holes in even par to tie Craig Wood for the title at 272, and then won the 36-hole playoff by a smashing five-stroke margin.

Sarazen joined the giants of golf in 1922, when he was twenty years old, by winning both the U. S. Open and the PGA title. Only he and Ben Hogan have ever taken these two championships in the same year. With Bobby Jones and Ben Hogan he shares the honor of having won the U. S. and British Opens in the same year. Sarazen did it in 1932, the greatest year of his career.

Still another distinction held by Sarazen is that he is one of only three golfers in the game's history (Ben Hogan and Jack Nicklaus are the others) to have won the U. S. Open, the

360

Gene Sarazen

British Open, the Masters, and the PGA. It is worth noting that he was in his prime at the same time as Walter Hagen and Jones. There were no soft touches for him.

One of golf's most durable players, Sarazen won the PGA Seniors title in 1954 at the age of fifty-two.

SAM SNEAD

Samuel Jackson Snead has been one of the world's most famous golfers since 1937, and followers of the game never think of him without recalling the crushing disappointments he has had in the U. S. Open, a tournament he has never won.

The jinx started in 1937, the very first year Slammin' Sam competed in the Open. He came in with an apparent winning score of 283, only to see Craig Wood top him with a late finish of 281.

In 1939 he needed only a five on the last hole to win, but blew it with an 8 and finished fifth.

In 1947 he missed a 30-inch putt on the last hole of a playoff and lost to Lew Worsham.

In 1949 he used a putter instead of a chipping iron on the 71st hole and tied for second.

In 1953 he was runner-up again.

But every other major title has fallen to the long-hitting West Virginian. Further, he has won the Vardon Trophy four times as the golfer with the year's lowest 18-hole average in tournament play.

Snead, owner of one of the most natural swings in the game, has won the Masters three times, in 1949, 1952, and

Sam Snead

Associated Press

1954—and was runner-up in 1939. He also is a three-time winner of the PGA championship—1941, 1949, and 1951; was PGA runner-up in 1938 and 1940, and added the British Open to his collection in 1946.

The Slammer's greatest year was 1949: He blazed his way to victory in the PGA, the Masters, and six other tournaments, was the leading money winner, and won the Vardon Trophy.

All-Time Records

LEADING MONEY WINNERS

Golf fans follow with interest the winnings piled up each year by the leading pros. The figures vary as tournaments are discontinued, new ones are added, or there is a change in the amount of money offered. One thing is clear: pro golf pays well, especially if you win often. Official records, incidentally, have been kept only since 1934.

Year	Winner	Amount	Year	Winner	Amount
1969	Frank Beard	$175,223	1951	Lloyd Mangrum	$26,088
1968	Bill Casper	205,168	1950	Sam Snead	35,758
1967	Jack Nicklaus	188,998	1949	Sam Snead	31,593
1966	Bill Casper	121,944	1948	Ben Hogan	36,812
1965	Jack Nicklaus	140,752	1947	Jimmy Demaret	27,936
1964	Jack Nicklaus	113,284	1946	Ben Hogan	42,556
1963	Arnold Palmer	130,835	1945	Byron Nelson	63,335
1962	Arnold Palmer	81,448	1944	Byron Nelson	37,967
1961	Gary Player	64,540	1943	(No official compila-	
1960	Arnold Palmer	75,262		tion—World War II.)	
1959	Art Wall, Jr.	53,167	1942	Ben Hogan	13,143
1958	Arnold Palmer	42,607	1941	Ben Hogan	18,358
1957	Dick Mayer	65,835	1940	Ben Hogan	10,655
1956	Ted Kroll	72,835	1939	Henry Picard	10,303
1955	Julius Boros	65,121	1938	Sam Snead	19,543
1954	Bob Toski	65,819	1937	Harry Cooper	14,138
1953	Lew Worsham	34,002	1936	Horton Smith	7,682
1952	Julius Boros	37,032	1935	Johnny Revolta	9,543
			1934	Paul Runyan	6,767

THE VARDON TROPHY

The Vardon Trophy goes to the pro golfer with the best 18-hole average for the year in tournaments sanctioned by the Professional Golfers Association. The trophy honors Harry Vardon, greatest of all British pros.

Year	Winner	Average	Year	Winner	Average
1969	Dave Hill	70.34	1954	E. J. (Dutch) Harrison	70.41
1968	Bill Casper	69.82	1953	Lloyd Mangrum	70.22
1967	Arnold Palmer	70.18	1952	Jack Burke, Jr.	70.54
1966	Bill Casper	70.16	1951	Lloyd Mangrum	70.05
1965	Bill Casper	70.59	1950	Sam Snead	69.23
1964	Arnold Palmer	70.01	1949	Sam Snead	69.37
1963	Bill Casper	70.58	1948	Ben Hogan	69.30
1962	Arnold Palmer	70.27	1947	Jimmy Demaret	69.90
1961	Arnold Palmer	69.86	1946–42—(World War II)		
1960	Bill Casper	69.95	1941	Ben Hogan	°494
1959	Art Wall, Jr.	70.35	1940	Ben Hogan	423
1958	Bob Rosburg	70.11	1939	Byron Nelson	473
1957	Dow Finsterwald	70.30	1938	Sam Snead	520
1956	Cary Middlecoff	70.35	1937	Harry Cooper	500
1955	Sam Snead	69.86			

° Special point system used until 1941.

THE VARE TROPHY

The Glenna Vare Trophy, named in honor of one of America's finest women golfers, is awarded annually (since 1953) to the woman professional who has averaged the lowest number of strokes per 18-hole round in tournaments endorsed by the Ladies Professional Golfers Association.

Year	Winner	Average	Year	Winner	Average
1969	Kathy Whitworth	72.38	1960	Mickey Wright	73.25
1968	Carol Mann	72.04	1959	Louise Suggs	73.58
1967	Kathy Whitworth	72.74	1958	Beverly Hanson	74.92
1966	Kathy Whitworth	72.60	1957	Louise Suggs	74.64
1965	Kathy Whitworth	72.61	1956	Patty Berg	74.57
1964	Mickey Wright	72.46	1955	Patty Berg	74.47
1963	Mickey Wright	72.81	1954	Babe Zaharias	75.48
1962	Mickey Wright	73.67	1953	Patty Berg	75.00
1961	Mickey Wright	73.55			

The United States Open

The United States Open championship is the most prized in all golf. Started in 1895 with a field of eleven contestants, it now attracts more than two thousand players—the best from countries all over the world. The first winner, nineteen-year-old Horace Rawlins, a British pro who had been in the United States only nine months, is still the youngest ever to have captured the title. Only three golfers—Willie Anderson, Bobby Jones, and Ben Hogan—have won the Open four times.

367

Year	Winner	Score	Runner-up
1969	Orville Moody	281	Al Geiberger
			Deane Beman
			Bob Rosburg
1968	Lee Trevino	275	Jack Nicklaus
1967	Jack Nicklaus	275	Arnold Palmer
1966	°Bill Casper (69)	286	Arnold Palmer (72)
1965	°Gary Player (71)	282	Kel Nagle (73)
1964	Ken Venturi	278	Tommy Jacobs
1963	°Julius Boros (70)	293	Jacky Cupit (73)
1962	°Jack Nicklaus (71)	283	Arnold Palmer (74)
1961	Gene Littler	281	Bob Goalby
			Doug Sanders
1960	Arnold Palmer	280	Jack Nicklaus
1959	Bill Casper	282	Bob Rosburg
1958	Tommy Bolt	283	Gary Player
1957	°Dick Mayer (72)	282	Cary Middlecoff (79)
1956	Cary Middlecoff	281	Ben Hogan
			Julius Boros
1955	°Jack Fleck (69)	287	Ben Hogan (72)
1954	Ed Furgol	284	Gene Littler
1953	Ben Hogan	283	Sam Snead
1952	Julius Boros	281	Ed Oliver
1951	Ben Hogan	287	Clayton Heafner
1950	°Ben Hogan (69)	287	Lloyd Mangrum (73)
			George Fazio (75)
1949	Cary Middlecoff	286	Sam Snead
			Clayton Heafner
1948	Ben Hogan	276	Jimmy Demaret
1947	°Lew Worsham (69)	282	Sam Snead (70)
1946	°Lloyd Mangrum (72–72)	284	Vic Ghezzi (72–73)
			Byron Nelson (72–73)
1945–42	(No championship—World War II.)		
1941	Craig Wood	284	Denny Shute
1940	°Lawson Little (70)	287	Gene Sarazen (73)
1939	°Byron Nelson (68–70)	284	Craig Wood (68–73)
			Denny Shute (76–elim.)
1938	Ralph Guldahl	284	Dick Metz
1937	Ralph Guldahl	281	Sam Snead
1936	Tony Manero	282	Harry Cooper
1935	Sam Parks, Jr.	299	Jimmy Thomson
1934	Olin Dutra	293	Gene Sarazen
1933	John G. Goodman	287	Ralph Guldahl
1932	Gene Sarazen	286	Robert A. Cruickshank
			T. Philip Perkins
1931	°Billy Burke (149–148)	292	George Von Elm (149–149)

368

Year	Winner	Score	Runner-up
1930	Robert T. Jones, Jr.	287	Macdonald Smith
1929	°Robert T. Jones, Jr. (141)	294	Al Espinosa (164)
1928	°Johnny Farrell (143)	294	Robert T. Jones, Jr. (144)
1927	°Tommy Armour (76)	301	Harry Cooper (79)
1926	Robert T. Jones, Jr.	293	Joe Turnesa
1925	°Willie Macfarlane (75–72)	291	Robert T. Jones, Jr. (75–73)
1924	Cyril Walker	297	Robert T. Jones, Jr.
1923	°Robert T. Jones, Jr. (76)	296	Robert A. Cruickshank (78)
1922	Gene Sarazen	288	Robert T. Jones, Jr.
			John L. Black
1921	James M. Barnes	289	Walter Hagen
			Fred McLeod
1920	Edward Ray	295	Harry Vardon
			Jack Burke
			Leo Diegel
			Jock Hutchison
1919	°Walter Hagen (77)	301	Michael J. Brady (78)
1918–17	(No championship—World War I.)		
1916	Charles Evans, Jr.	286	Jock Hutchison
1915	Jerome D. Travers	297	Tom McNamara
1914	Walter Hagen	290	Charles Evans, Jr.
1913	°Francis Ouimet (72)	304	Harry Vardon (77)
			Edward Ray (78)
1912	John J. McDermott	294	Tom McNamara
1911	°John J. McDermott (80)	307	Michael J. Brady (82)
			George O. Simpson (85)
1910	°Alex Smith (71)	298	John J. McDermott (75)
			Macdonald Smith (77)
1909	George Sargent	290	Tom McNamara
1908	°Fred McLeod (77)	322	Willie Smith (83)
1907	Alex Ross	302	Gil Nicholls
1906	Alex Smith	295	Willie Smith
1905	Willie Anderson	314	Alex Smith
1904	Willie Anderson	303	Gil Nicholls
1903	°Willie Anderson (82)	307	David Brown (84)
1902	Lawrence Auchterlonie	307	Stewart Gardner
			W. J. Travis
1901	°Willie Anderson (85)	331	Alex Smith (86)
1900	Harry Vardon	313	J. H. Taylor
1899	Willie Smith	315	G. Low
1898	Fred Herd	328	Alex Smith
1897	Joe Lloyd	† 162	Willie Anderson
1896	James Foulis	† 152	Horace Rawlins
1895	Horace Rawlins	† 173	Willie Dunn

° Playoff winner. † 36 holes. (Playoff scores in parentheses.)

369

The United States Amateur

Like the United States Open, the United States Amateur was begun in 1895. No other amateur golf event tops it in importance, and it was in this tournament that Bobby Jones set one of his many records, winning the title five times. Only two foreigners have ever taken the crown out of the United States—Harold Hilton of England in 1911 and Ross Somerville of Canada in 1932.

In 1965 the tournament scoring was changed from match play to stroke competition. Figures in parentheses indicate number of holes played. All finals are at 36 holes.

Year	Winner	Runner-up	Score
1969	Steve Melnyk	Vinnie Giles	286
1968	Bruce Fleisher	Vinnie Giles	284
1967	Bob Dickson	Vinnie Giles	285
1966	*Gary Cowan (75)	Deane Beman (76)	285
1965	Bob Murphy	Bob Dickson	291
1964	Bill Campbell	Ed Tutwiler	1 up
1963	Deane Beman	Dick Sikes	2 and 1
1962	Labron Harris, Jr.	Downing Gray	1 up
1961	Jack Nicklaus	Dudley Wysong	8 and 6
1960	Deane Beman	Bob Gardner	6 and 4
1959	Jack Nicklaus	Charles Coe	1 up
1958	Charles Coe	Tommy Aaron	5 and 4
1957	Hillman Robbins	Dr. Frank Taylor	5 and 4
1956	Harvie Ward	Chuck Kocsis	5 and 4
1955	Harvie Ward	William Hyndman	9 and 8
1954	Arnold Palmer	Robert Sweeney	1 up
1953	Gene Littler	Dale Morey	1 up
1952	Jack Westland	Al Mengert	3 and 2
1951	Billy Maxwell	Joe Gagliardi	4 and 3
1950	Sam Urzetta	Frank Stranahan	1 up (39)
1949	Charles Coe	Rufus King	11 and 10
1948	Willie Turnesa	Ray Billows	2 and 1
1947	Skee Riegel	John Dawson	2 and 1
1946	Ted Bishop	Smiley Quick	1 up (37)

1945–42 (No championship—World War II.)

* Winner of playoff.

Year	Winner	Runner-up	Score
1941	Marvin H. Ward	B. Patrick Abbott	4 and 3
1940	Richard D. Chapman	W. B. McCullough, Jr.	11 and 9
1939	Marvin H. Ward	Raymond E. Billows	7 and 5
1938	Willie Turnesa	B. Patrick Abbott	8 and 7
1937	John Goodman	Raymond E. Billows	2 up
1936	John W. Fischer	Jack McLean	1 up (37)
1935	W. Lawson Little, Jr.	Walter Emery	4 and 2
1934	W. Lawson Little, Jr.	David Goldman	8 and 7
1933	George T. Dunlap, Jr.	Max R. Marston	6 and 5
1932	C. Ross Somerville	John Goodman	2 and 1
1931	Francis Ouimet	Jack Westland	6 and 5
1930	Robert T. Jones, Jr.	Eugene V. Homans	8 and 7
1929	Harrison R. Johnston	Dr. O. F. Willing	4 and 3
1928	Robert T. Jones, Jr.	T. Philip Perkins	10 and 9
1927	Robert T. Jones, Jr.	Charles Evans, Jr.	8 and 7
1926	George Von Elm	Robert T. Jones, Jr.	2 and 1
1925	Robert T. Jones, Jr.	Watts Gunn	8 and 7
1924	Robert T. Jones, Jr.	George Von Elm	9 and 8
1923	Max R. Marston	Jess W. Sweetser	1 up (38)
1922	Jess W. Sweetser	Charles Evans, Jr.	3 and 2
1921	Jesse P. Guilford	Robert A. Gardner	7 and 6
1920	Charles Evans, Jr.	Francis Ouimet	7 and 6
1919	S. Davidson Herron	Robert T. Jones, Jr.	5 and 4
1918–17	(No championship—World War I.)		
1916	Charles Evans, Jr.	Robert A. Gardner	4 and 3
1915	Robert A. Gardner	John G. Anderson	5 and 4
1914	Francis Ouimet	Jerome D. Travers	6 and 5
1913	Jerome D. Travers	John G. Anderson	5 and 4
1912	Jerome D. Travers	Charles Evans, Jr.	7 and 6
1911	Harold H. Hilton	Fred Herreshoff	1 up (37)
1910	William C. Fownes, Jr.	Warren K. Wood	4 and 3
1909	Robert A. Gardner	H. Chandler Egan	4 and 3
1908	Jerome D. Travers	Max Behr	8 and 7
1907	Jerome D. Travers	Archibald Graham	6 and 5
1906	Elben M. Byers	G. S. Lyon	2 up
1905	H. Chandler Egan	D. E. Sawyer	6 and 5
1904	H. Chandler Egan	Fred Herreshoff	8 and 6
1903	Walter J. Travis	Eben M. Byers	5 and 4
1902	Louis N. James	Eben M. Byers	4 and 2
1901	Walter J. Travis	Walter E. Egan	5 and 4
1900	Walter J. Travis	Findley S. Douglas	2 up
1899	H. M. Harriman	Findley S. Douglas	3 and 2
1898	Findley S. Douglas	W. B. Smith	5 and 3
1897	H. J. Whigham	W. R. Betts	8 and 6
1896	H. J. Whigham	J. G. Thorp	3 and 2
1895	Charles B. Macdonald	Charles E. Sands	12 and 11

The PGA

One name stands out in the history of the annual tournament of the Professional Golfers Association of America—Walter Hagen. He is the only man to have won the title five times, four of them in a row. The PGA, whose membership includes more than four thousand pros, supervises tournaments that offer over $1,000,000 a year in prizes. Except for the United States Golf Association, no organization has had greater influence on golf in this country than the PGA.

The PGA changed from match play to stroke competition in 1958. Numbers in parentheses indicate winning playoff score.

Year	Winner	Runner-up	Score
1969	Ray Floyd	Gary Player	276
1968	Julius Boros	Arnold Palmer	281
1967	°Don January (69)	Don Massengale (71)	281
1966	Al Geiberger	Dudley Wysong	280
1965	Dave Marr	Bill Casper (282)	280
		Jack Nicklaus (282)	
1964	Bobby Nichols	Jack Nicklaus (274)	271
		Arnold Palmer (274)	
1963	Jack Nicklaus	Dave Ragan	279
1962	Gary Player	Bob Goalby	278
1961	°Jerry Barber (67)	Don January (68)	277
1960	Jay Hebert	Jim Ferrier	281
1959	Bob Rosburg	Doug Sanders	277

Year	Winner	Runner-up	Score
1958	Dow Finsterwald	Bill Casper	276
1957	Lionel Hebert	Dow Finsterwald	2 and 1
1956	Jack Burke, Jr.	Ted Kroll	3 and 2
1955	Doug Ford	Cary Middlecoff	4 and 3
1954	Chick Harbert	Walter Burkemo	4 and 3
1953	Walter Burkemo	Felice Torza	2 and 1
1952	Jim Turnesa	Chick Harbert	1 up
1951	Sam Snead	Walter Burkemo	7 and 6
1950	Chandler Harper	Henry Williams, Jr.	4 and 3
1949	Sam Snead	Johnny Palmer	3 and 2
1948	Ben Hogan	Mike Turnesa	7 and 6
1947	Jim Ferrier	Chick Harbert	2 and 1
1946	Ben Hogan	Ed Oliver	6 and 4
1945	Byron Nelson	Sam Byrd	4 and 3
1944	Bob Hamilton	Byron Nelson	1 up
1943	(No championship—World War II.)		
1942	Sam Snead	Jim Turnesa	2 and 1
1941	Vic Ghezzi	Byron Nelson	1 up (38)
1940	Byron Nelson	Sam Snead	1 up
1939	Henry Picard	Byron Nelson	1 up (37)
1938	Paul Runyan	Sam Snead	8 and 7
1937	Denny Shute	Harold McSpaden	1 up (37)
1936	Denny Shute	Jimmy Thomson	3 and 2
1935	Johnny Revolta	Tommy Armour	5 and 4
1934	Paul Runyan	Craig Wood	1 up (38)
1933	Gene Sarazen	Willie Goggin	5 and 4
1932	Olin Dutra	Frank Walsh	4 and 3
1931	Tom Creavy	Denny Shute	2 and 1
1930	Tommy Armour	Gene Sarazen	1 up
1929	Leo Diegel	Johnny Farrell	6 and 4
1928	Leo Diegel	Al Espinosa	6 and 5
1927	Walter Hagen	Joe Turnesa	1 up
1926	Walter Hagen	Leo Diegel	5 and 3
1925	Walter Hagen	William Mehlhorn	6 and 5
1924	Walter Hagen	James M. Barnes	2 up
1923	Gene Sarazen	Walter Hagen	1 up (38)
1922	Gene Sarazen	Emmet French	4 and 3
1921	Walter Hagen	James M. Barnes	3 and 2
1920	Jock Hutchison	J. Douglas Edgar	1 up
1919	James M. Barnes	Fred McLeod	5 and 4
1918–17	(No championship—World War I.)		
1916	James M. Barnes	Jock Hutchison	1 up

* Winner of playoff.

THE PGA HALL OF FAME

Golf's Hall of Fame was established by the PGA in 1940 to honor those who, by their lifetime playing ability, made outstanding contributions to the game. The original group of twelve included three amateurs.

Player	Year Elected	Player	Year Elected
Anderson, Willie	1940	Hutchison, Jock, Sr.	1959
Armour, Tommy	1940	Jones, Bob	1940
Barnes, Jim	1940	Little, Lawson	1961
Brady, Mike	1960	Mangrum, Lloyd	1964
Burke, Billy	1966	McDermott, John	1940
Cooper, Harry	1959	McLeod, Fred	1960
Cruickshank, Bobby	1967	Nelson, Byron	1953
Demaret, Jimmy	1960	*Ouimet, Francis	1940
Diegel, Leo	1955	Picard, Henry	1961
Dudley, Ed	1964	Revolta, Johnny	1963
Dutra, Olin	1962	Runyan, Paul	1959
*Evans, Chick	1940	Sarazen, Gene	1940
Farrel, Johnny	1961	Shute, Denny	1957
Ghezzi, Vic	1965	Smith, Alex	1940
Guldahl, Ralph	1963	Smith, Horton	1958
Hagen, Walter	1940	Smith, Macdonald	1954
Harbert, M. R. "Chick"	1968	Snead, Sam	1953
Harper, Chandler	1969	*Travers, Jerry	1940
Harrison, E. J. "Dutch"	1962	Travis, Walter	1940
Hogan, Ben	1953	Wood, Craig	1956

*Amateur

The Masters

The Masters tournament, played annually at the Augusta, Georgia, National Golf Club, has been one of the world's great links events since its very start in 1934. The event, like the course itself, is a dream come true for Bobby Jones, who started planning both after his retirement from the game in 1930. Participation is by invitation only.

Year	Winner	Score	Runner-up	Score
1970	*Bill Casper (69)	279	Gene Littler (74)	279
1969	George Archer	281	Bill Casper	282
			George Knudson	282
			Tom Weiskopf	282
1968	Bob Goalby	277	Roberto de Vicenzo	278
1967	Gay Brewer	280	Bobby Nichols	281
1966	*Jack Nicklaus (70)	288	Tommy Jacobs (72)	288
			Gay Brewer (78)	288
1965	**Jack Nicklaus	271	Gary Player	280
			Arnold Palmer	280
1964	Arnold Palmer	276	Jack Nicklaus	282
			Dave Marr	282
1963	Jack Nicklaus	286	Tony Lema	287
1962	*Arnold Palmer (68)	280	Gary Player (71)	280
			Dow Finsterwald (77)	280
1961	Gary Player	280	Arnold Palmer	281
			Charles Coe	281
1960	Arnold Palmer	282	Ken Venturi	283
1959	Art Wall, Jr.	284	Cary Middlecoff	285
1958	Arnold Palmer	284	Doug Ford	285
			Fred Hawkins	285
1957	Doug Ford	283	Sam Snead	286
1956	Jack Burke, Jr.	289	Ken Venturi	290
1955	Cary Middlecoff	279	Ben Hogan	286
1954	*Sam Snead (70)	289	Ben Hogan (71)	289
1953	Ben Hogan	274	Ed Oliver	279
1952	Sam Snead	286	Jack Burke, Jr.	290
1951	Ben Hogan	280	Skee Riegel	282
1950	Jimmy Demaret	283	Jim Ferrier	285
1949	Sam Snead	282	Lloyd Mangrum	285
			Johnny Bulla	285
1948	Claude Harmon	279	Cary Middlecoff	284
1947	Jimmy Demaret	281	Byron Nelson	283
			Frank Stranahan	283
1946	Herman Keiser	282	Ben Hogan	283
1945–43	(No championship—World War II.)			
1942	*Byron Nelson (69)	280	Ben Hogan (70)	280
1941	Craig Wood	280	Byron Nelson	283
1940	Jimmy Demaret	280	Lloyd Mangrum	284

375

Year	Winner	Score	Runner-up	Score
1939	Ralph Guldahl	279	Sam Snead	280
1938	Henry Picard	285	Ralph Guldahl	287
1937	Byron Nelson	283	Ralph Guldahl	285
1936	Horton Smith	285	Harry Cooper	286
1935	°Gene Sarazen (144)	282	Craig Wood (149)	282
1934	Horton Smith	284	Craig Wood	285

° Winner of playoff.
°° Record.

The British Open

The British Open is the oldest of the world's major golf tournaments and for many years was the most coveted title a golfer could capture. Most of the winners, naturally, have been English, but between 1921 and 1933 Americans took the title every year but one, with Walter Hagen a victor four times and Bobby Jones three. When Arnold Palmer won in 1961 and 1962, he was the first American to take the Open in consecutive years since Hagen did it in 1928 and 1929.

Year	Winner	Score	Year	Winner	Score
1969	Tony Jacklin	280	1952	Bobby Locke	287
1968	Gary Player	289	1951	Max Faulkner	285
1967	Roberto de Vicenzo	278	1950	Bobby Locke	279
1966	Jack Nicklaus, U.S.A.	282	1949	Bobby Locke	283
1965	Peter Thomson	285	1948	Henry Cotton	284
1964	Tony Lema, U.S.A.	279	1947	Fred Daly	293
1963	°Bob Charles	277	1946	Sam Snead, U.S.A.	290
1962	Arnold Palmer, U.S.A.	276	1945–40	(No championship—	
1961	Arnold Palmer, U.S.A.	284		World War II.)	
1960	Kel Nagle	278	1939	Richard Burton	290
1959	Gary Player	284	1938	Reginald A. Whitcombe	295
1958	°Peter Thomson	278	1937	Henry Cotton	290
1957	Bobby Locke	279	1936	Alfred Padgham	287
1956	Peter Thomson	286	1935	Alf Perry	283
1955	Peter Thomson	281	1934	Henry Cotton	283
1954	Peter Thomson	283	1933	°Denny Shute, U.S.A.	292
1953	Ben Hogan, U.S.A.	282	1932	Gene Sarazen, U.S.A.	283

376

Year	Winner	Score	Year	Winner	Score
1931	Tommy Armour, U.S.A.	296	1895	J. H. Taylor	322
1930	Robert T. Jones, Jr.,		1894	J. H. Taylor	326
	U.S.A.	291	1893	William Auchterlonie	322
1929	Walter Hagen, U.S.A.	292	1892	H. H. Hilton	305
1928	Walter Hagen, U.S.A.	292	1891	Hugh Kirkaldy	166
1927	Robert T. Jones, Jr.,		1890	John Ball	164
	U.S.A.	285	1889	°Willie Park, Jr.	155
1926	Robert T. Jones, Jr.,		1888	Jack Burns	171
	U.S.A.	291	1887	Willie Park, Jr.	161
1925	Jim Barnes, U.S.A.	300	1886	David Brown	157
1924	Walter Hagen, U.S.A.	301	1885	Bob Martin	171
1923	A. G. Havers	295	1884	Jack Simpson	160
1922	Walter Hagen, U.S.A.	300	1883	William Fernie	159
1921	Jock Hutchison, U.S.A.	296	1882	Bob Ferguson	171
1920	George Duncan	303	1881	Bob Ferguson	170
1919–15	(No championship—		1880	Bob Ferguson	162
	World War I.)		1879	Jamie Anderson	170
1914	Harry Vardon	306	1878	Jamie Anderson	157
1913	J. H. Taylor	304	1877	Jamie Anderson	160
1912	Edward Ray	295	1876	Bob Martin	176
1911	Harry Vardon	303	1875	Willie Park	166
1910	James Braid	299	1874	Mungo Park	159
1909	J. H. Taylor	295	1873	Tom Kidd	179
1908	James Braid	291	1872	Tom Morris, Jr.	166
1907	Arnaud Massy	312	1871	(No championship.)	
1906	James Braid	300	1870	Tom Morris, Jr.	149
1905	James Braid	300	1869	Tom Morris, Jr.	157
1904	Jack White	296	1868	Tom Morris, Jr.	170
1903	Harry Vardon	300	1867	Tom Morris	170
1902	Alex Herd	307	1866	Willie Park	169
1901	James Braid	309	1865	Andrew Strath	162
1900	J. H. Taylor	309	1864	Tom Morris	167
1899	Harry Vardon	310	1863	Willie Park	168
1898	Harry Vardon	307	1862	Tom Morris	163
1897	H. H. Hilton	314	1861	Tom Morris	163
1896	°Harry Vardon	316	1860	Willie Park	174

° Winner of playoff.

The British Amateur

Although it consistently attracts the world's greatest amateurs, no one has ever come close to equaling the record of John Ball in the British Amateur. He won it eight times between 1888 and 1912.

Year	Winner	Year	Winner
1969	Michael Bonallack	1926	Jess W. Sweetser, U.S.A.
1968	Michael Bonallack	1925	Robert Harris
1967	Bob Dickson, U.S.A.	1924	E. W. E. Holderness
1966	Bobby Cole	1923	Roger H. Wethered
1965	Michael Bonallack	1922	E. W. E. Holderness
1964	Gordon Clarke	1921	Willie Hunter
1963	Michael Lunt	1920	Cyril Tolley
1962	Richard Davies, U.S.A.	1919–15	(No championship—
1961	Michael Bonallack		World War I.)
1960	Joe Carr	1914	J. L. Jenkins
1959	Deane Beman, U.S.A.	1913	Harold H. Hilton
1958	Joe Carr	1912	John Ball
1957	Reid Jack	1911	Harold H. Hilton
1956	John Beharrell	1910	John Ball
1955	J. W. Conrad, U.S.A.	1909	R. Maxwell
1954	D. W. Bachli	1908	E. A. Lassen
1953	Joe Carr	1907	John Ball
1952	Harvie Ward, U.S.A.	1906	James Robb
1951	Richard D. Chapman, U.S.A.	1905	A. G. Barry
1950	Frank Stranahan, U.S.A.	1904	Walter J. Travis, U.S.A.
1949	Max McCready	1903	R. Maxwell
1948	Frank Stranahan, U.S.A.	1902	C. Hutchings
1947	Willie Turnesa, U.S.A.	1901	Harold H. Hilton
1946	James Bruen	1900	Harold H. Hilton
1945–40	(No championship—	1899	John Ball
	World War II.)	1898	F. G. Tait
1939	Alex Kyle	1897	A. J. T. Allan
1938	Charles Yates, U.S.A.	1896	F. G. Tait
1937	Robert Sweeny, U.S.A.	1895	L. M. B. Melville
1936	Hector Thomson	1894	John Ball
1935	W. Lawson Little, Jr., U.S.A.	1893	Peter Anderson
1934	W. Lawson Little, Jr., U.S.A.	1892	John Ball
1933	Michael Scott	1891	J. E. Laidlay
1932	John DeForest	1890	John Ball
1931	Eric Martin-Smith	1889	J. E. Laidlay
1930	Robert T. Jones, Jr., U.S.A.	1888	John Ball
1929	Cyril J. H. Tolley	1887	Horace G. Hutchinson
1928	T. Philip Perkins	1886	Horace G. Hutchinson
1927	Dr. William Tweddell	1885	A. F. MacFie

378

The United States Women's Amateur

Just about every outstanding woman golfer in the United States has won the U. S. Women's Amateur at least once since this tournament was established in 1895, the same year the U. S. Open and the U. S. Amateur were launched. Top honors easily go to Glenna Collett Vare, a six-time winner.

Year	Winner	Runner-up	Score
1969	Catherine LaCoste	Shelley Hamlin	3 and 2
1968	Jo Anne Gunderson Carner	Anne Quast Welts	5 and 4
1967	Lou Dill	Jean Ashley	5 and 4
1966	Jo Anne Gunderson Carner	Marlene Stewart Streit	1 up
1965	Jean Ashley	Anne Quast Welts	5 and 4
1964	Barbara McIntire	Jo Anne Gunderson	3 and 2
1963	Anne Quast Welts	Peggy Conley	2 and 1
1962	Jo Anne Gunderson	Ann Baker	9 and 8
1961	Anne Quast Decker	Phyllis Preuss	14 and 13
1960	Jo Anne Gunderson	Jean Ashley	6 and 5
1959	Barbara McIntire	Jeanne Goodwin	4 and 3
1958	Anne Quast	Barbara Romack	3 and 2
1957	Jo Anne Gunderson	Ann Casey Johnstone	8 and 6
1956	Marlene Stewart	Jo Anne Gunderson	2 and 1
1955	Pat Lesser	Jane Nelson	7 and 6
1954	Barbara Romack	Mickey Wright	4 and 2
1953	Mary Lena Faulk	Polly Riley	3 and 2
1952	Jackie Pung	Shirley McFedters	2 and 1
1951	Dorothy Kirby	Claire Doran	2 and 1
1950	Beverly Hanson	Mae Murray	6 and 4
1949	Mrs. Mark Porter	Dot Kielty	3 and 2
1948	Grace Lenczyk	Helen Sigel	4 and 2
1947	Louise Suggs	Dorothy Kirby	2 up

Year	Winner	Runner-up	Score
1946	Babe Zaharias	Clara Sherman	11 and 9
1945–42	(No championship—World War II.)		
1941	Betty Hicks Newell	Helen Sigel	5 and 3
1940	Betty Jameson	Jane S. Cothran	6 and 5
1939	Betty Jameson	Dorothy Kirby	3 and 2
1938	Patty Berg	Estelle Lawson Page	6 and 5
1937	Estelle Lawson Page	Patty Berg	3 and 2
1936	Pamela Barton	Maureen Orcutt Crews	4 and 3
1935	Glenna Collett Vare	Patty Berg	3 and 2
1934	Virginia Van Wie	Dorothy Traung	2 and 1
1933	Virginia Van Wie	Helen Hicks	4 and 3
1932	Virginia Van Wie	Glenna Collett Vare	10 and 8
1931	Helen Hicks	Glenn Collett Vare	2 and 1
1930	Glenna Collett	Virginia Van Wie	6 and 5
1929	Glenna Collett	Leona Pressler	4 and 3
1928	Glenna Collett	Virginia Van Wie	13 and 12
1927	Miriam Burns Horn	Maureen Orcutt	5 and 4
1926	Mrs. G. Henry Stetson	Mrs. W. D. Goss, Jr.	3 and 1
1925	Glenna Collett	Mrs. W. G. Fraser	9 and 8
1924	Dorothy Campbell Hurd	Mary K. Browne	7 and 6
1923	Edith Cummings	Alexa Stirling	3 and 2
1922	Glenna Collett	Mrs. W. A. Gavin	5 and 4
1921	Marion Hollins	Alexa Stirling	5 and 4
1920	Alexa Stirling	Mrs. J. V. Hurd	5 and 4
1919	Alexa Stirling	Mrs. W. A. Gavin	6 and 5
1918–17	(No championship—World War I.)		
1916	Alexa Stirling	Mildred Caverly	2 and 1
1915	Mrs. C. H. Vanderbeck	Mrs. W. A. Gavin	3 and 2
1914	Mrs. Arnold Jackson	Elaine Rosenthal	1 up
1913	Gladys Ravenscroft	Marion Hollins	2 up
1912	Margaret Curtis	Mrs. R. H. Barlow	3 and 2
1911	Margaret Curtis	Lillian B. Hyde	5 and 3
1910	Dorothy Campbell	Mrs. G. M. Martin	2 and 1
1909	Dorothy Campbell	Mrs. R. H. Barlow	3 and 2
1908	Katherine C. Harley	Mrs. T. H. Polhemus	6 and 5
1907	Margaret Curtis	Harriot S. Curtis	7 and 6
1906	Harriot S. Curtis	M. B. Adams	2 and 1
1905	Pauline Mackay	Margaret Curtis	1 up
1904	Georgiana M. Bishop	Mrs. E. F. Sanford	5 and 3
1903	Bessie Anthony	J. A. Carpenter	7 and 6
1902	Genevieve Hecker	Louisa A. Wells	4 and 3
1901	Genevieve Hecker	Lucy Herron	5 and 3
1900	Frances G. Griscom	Margaret Curtis	6 and 5
1899	Ruth Underhill	Mrs. Caleb Fox	2 and 1
1898	Beatrix Hoyt	Maud Wetmore	5 and 3
1897	Beatrix Hoyt	N. C. Sargent	5 and 4
1896	Beatrix Hoyt	Mrs. Arthur Turnure	2 and 1
1895	*Mrs. Charles S. Brown (132)	N. C. Sargent (134)	

* Medal play.

The United States Women's Open

As golf tournaments go, the United States Women's Open is still a baby. It was played for the first time in 1946. But the event has won the esteem of both players and spectators as the top tournament for women.

Year	Winner	Score	Runner-up	Score
1969	Donna Caponi	294	Peggy Wilson	295
1968	Susie Berning	289	Mickey Wright	292
1967	Catherine LaCoste	294	Susie Maxwell	296
			Beth Stone	296
1966	Sandra Spuzich	297	Carol Mann	298
1965	Carol Mann	290	Kathy Cornelius	292
1964	°Mickey Wright (70)	290	Ruth Jessen (72)	290
1963	Mary Mills	288	Louise Suggs	292
			Sandra Haynie	292
1962	Murle McKenzie Lindstrom	301	Joann Prentice	303
			Ruth Jessen	303
1961	Mickey Wright	293	Betsy Rawls	299
1960	Betsy Rawls	292	Joyce Ziske	293
1959	Mickey Wright	287	Louise Suggs	289
1958	Mickey Wright	290	Louise Suggs	295
1957	Betsy Rawls	299	Patty Berg	305
1956	°Kathy Cornelius (75)	302	Barbara McIntire (82)	302
1955	Fay Crocker	299	Louise Suggs	303
			Mary Lena Faulk	303
1954	Babe Zaharias	291	Betty Hicks	303
1953	°Betsy Rawls (71)	302	Jackie Pung (77)	302
1952	Louise Suggs	284	Marlene Bauer	291
			Betty Jameson	291
1951	Betsy Rawls	293	Louise Suggs	298
1950	Babe Zaharias	291	Betsy Rawls	300
1949	Louise Suggs	291	Babe Zaharias	305
1948	Babe Zaharias	300	Betty Hicks	308
1947	Betty Jameson	295	Sally Sessions	301
			Polly Riley	301
1946	Patty Berg	5 and 4	Betty Jameson	

° Winner of playoff.

The Ladies PGA Championship

Mickey Wright, a four-time winner, is the outstanding champion of the Ladies Professional Golfers Association tournament, which dates back only to 1955.

Year	Winner	Score	Runner-up	Score
1969	Betsy Rawls	293	Carol Mann	297
			Susie Berning	297
1968	*Sandra Post	294	Kathy Whitworth	294
1967	Kathy Whitworth	284	Shirley Engelhorn	285
1966	Gloria Ehret	282	Mickey Wright	285
1965	Sandra Haynie	279	Clifford Ann Creed	280
1964	Mary Mills	278	Mickey Wright	280
1963	Mickey Wright	294	Mary Lena Faulk	296
			Mary Mills	296
			Louise Suggs	296
1962	Judy Kimball	282	Shirley Spork	286
1961	Mickey Wright	287	Louise Suggs	296
1960	Mickey Wright	292	Louise Suggs	295
1959	Betsy Rawls	288	Patty Berg	289
1958	Mickey Wright	288	Fay Crocker	294
1957	Louise Suggs	285	Wiffi Smith	288
1956	*Marlene Bauer Hagge	291	Patty Berg	291
1955	Beverly Hanson	220	Louise Suggs	223

* Winner of playoff.

International Matches

Golfers in the United States have won most of the laurels in team competition with Great Britain. The oldest of these matches is for the amateur Walker Cup, started in 1922. The professional Ryder Cup matches were begun in 1927, and the Curtis Cup, for amateur women, in 1932. The matches are played every two years.

WALKER CUP

Year	Result
1969	United States 10, Great Britain 8
1967	United States 13, Great Britain 7
1965	United States 11, Great Britain 11
1963	United States 12, Great Britain 8
1961	United States 11, Great Britain 1
1959	United States 9, Great Britain 3
1957	United States 8, Great Britain 3 (One match halved.)
1955	United States 10, Great Britain 2
1953	United States 9, Great Britain 3
1951	United States 6, Great Britain 3 (Three matches halved.)
1949	United States 10, Great Britain 2
1947	United States 8, Great Britain 4
1938	Great Britain 8, United States 4
1936	United States 9, Great Britain 0 (Three matches halved.)
1934	United States 9, Great Britain 2 (One match halved.)
1932	United States 8, Great Britain 1 (Three matches halved.)
1930	United States 10, Great Britain 2
1928	United States 11, Great Britain 1
1926	United States 6, Great Britain 5 (One match halved.)
1924	United States 9, Great Britain 3
1923	United States 6, Great Britain 5 (One match halved.)
1922	United States 8, Great Britain 4

RYDER CUP

Year	Result
1969	United States 16, Great Britain 16 (Tie)
1967	United States 23½, Great Britain 8½
1965	United States 19½, Great Britain 12½
1963	United States 23, Great Britain 9
1961	United States 14½, Great Britain 9½
1959	United States 8½, Great Britain 3½
1957	Great Britain 7½, United States 4½

1955	United States 8, Great Britain 4
1953	United States 6½, Great Britain 5½
1951	United States 9½, Great Britain 2½
1949	United States 7, Great Britain 5
1947	United States 11, Great Britain 1
1937	United States 8, Great Britain 4
1935	United States 9, Great Britain 3
1933	Great Britain 6½, United States 5½
1931	United States 9, Great Britain 3
1929	Great Britain 7, United States 5
1927	United States 9½, Great Britain 2½

CURTIS CUP

Year	Result
1968	United States 10½, Great Britain 7½
1966	United States 13, Great Britain 5
1964	°United States 10½, Great Britain 7½
1962	United States 8, Great Britain 1
1960	United States 6½, Great Britain 2½
1958	United States 4½, Great Britain 4½ (Tie.)
1956	Great Britain 5, United States 4
1954	United States 6, Great Britain 3
1952	Great Britain 5, United States 4
1950	United States 7½, Great Britain 1½
1948	United States 6½, Great Britain 2½
1938	United States 5½, Great Britain 3½
1936	United States 4½, Great Britain 4½ (Tie.)
1934	United States 6½, Great Britain 2½
1932	United States 5½, Great Britain 3½

° Scoring changed to 18 points. Two 18-hole rounds for 12 points; one Scotch-foursome for 6 points.

384

WORLD CUP

The World Cup, formerly the Canada Cup, is a comparatively new international tournament. The matches are held yearly throughout the world. There are two men to a team. Their combined scores for 72 holes determine the winner.

Year	Site	Winner	Score	Runner-up	Score
1969	Singapore	United States	552	Japan	560
1968	Rome	Canada	569	United States	571
1967	Mexico City	United States	557	New Zealand	570
1966	Tokyo	United States	548	South Africa	553
1965	Madrid	South Africa	571	Spain	579
1964	Hawaii	United States	554	Argentina	564
°1963	France	United States	482	Spain	485
1962	Argentina	United States	557	Argentina	559
1961	Puerto Rico	United States	560	Australia	572
1960	Ireland	United States	565	England	573
1959	Australia	Australia	563	United States	573
1958	Mexico	Ireland	579	Spain	582
1957	Japan	Japan	557	United States	566
1956	England	United States	567	South Africa	581
1955	United States	United States	560	Australia	569
1954	Canada	Australia	556	Argentina	560
°°1953	Canada	Argentina	287	Canada	297

° Cut off because of rain.
°° Finals at 36 holes.

EISENHOWER CUP

Another fairly new international competition, the Eisenhower Cup matches are played every two years with competitors from all over the world. Four men compete on each team but only the low three scores count. Competition is at 72 holes.

Year	Site	Winner	Score	Runner-up	Score
1968	Melbourne	United States	868	Britain-Ireland	869
1966	Mexico City	Australia	877	United States	879
1964	Rome	Great Britain	895	Canada	899
1962	Japan	United States	854	Canada	862
1960	United States	United States	834	Australia	876
1958	Scotland	*Australia	918	United States	918

* Won playoff, 222–224.

Ice Hockey

The History of Ice Hockey

A noted sports writer, describing his reaction to the sport of ice hockey, once wrote, ". . . for speed and pep and action, there is only one attraction."

And so it is for so many who see ice hockey in person or have the ability to play it.

Ice hockey is indeed full of action. Skaters flash down the ice like track sprinters. The players pass the puck with blinding speed. And the shot at goal comes so quickly it's a wonder the goalie ever gets into position to stop a score.

Canada has been established as the birthplace of ice hockey. But there is still some debate about where the sport actually originated. Some sources feel that the first game of ice hockey was played on Christmas Day in 1855 in Kingston, Ontario, between members of the Royal Canadian Rifles. However, other historians have suggested that the sticks used in this game had been loaned by the Halifax Garrison, which would imply that the game actually originated in Halifax, Nova Scotia.

The first organized playing league, however, was a four-team unit in Kingston in 1885. And the Stanley Cup, which is awarded to the year's top team, was first presented to a league champion eight years later.

Hockey in the United States has cropped up almost everywhere but in the Deep South. In 1893 it appeared simultaneously in New Haven, Connecticut, and Baltimore, Maryland. The first league (amateur) was organized in 1896 in New York and consisted of four teams. The sport then spread to other cities. Teams were organized in Philadelphia, Washington, Pittsburgh, Chicago, and (in 1914) Portland, Oregon.

Ice hockey is played on natural or artificial ice. Many of the northern colleges play on natural ice, and some prep and

The Boston Bruins halt the New York Rangers.

United Press International

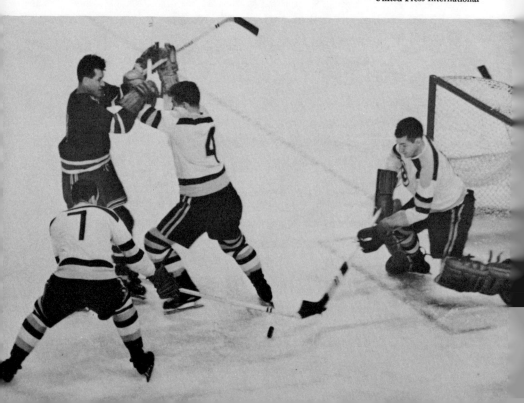

high schools play outdoors on rinks, frozen ponds and lakes, or on tennis courts which have been flooded.

A center, two forwards or wings, two defensemen, and a goalie make up the six-man hockey team. There are usually six or seven substitutes (called spares) on the bench, and they play almost as many minutes as the starters. Because of the excessive speed and body contact, no man plays at full tempo in professional hockey for more than two or three minutes, although some players, particularly defensemen, stay on much longer. That is why the spares are as important as the starters.

A game consists of three periods, each lasting twenty minutes. A goal is scored when the puck, or disk, is driven by a stick into the opponent's goal. The puck is a flat, round

Toronto Maple Leafs stop a New York Ranger's scoring attempt.

Associated Press

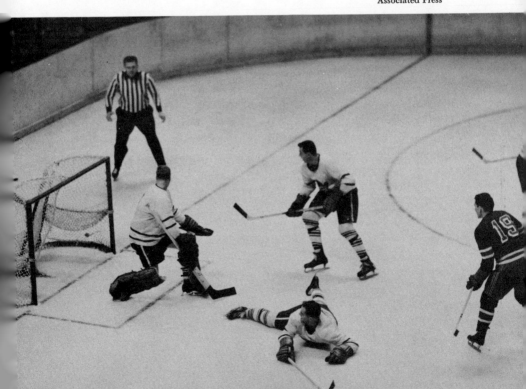

United Press International

Detroit Red Wing Sid Abel hooks the puck away from Ranger Reggie Sinclair as Red Wing star Gordie Howe skids along on the ice.

piece of black vulcanized rubber, 3 inches in diameter, 1 inch thick, weighing about six ounces. The goal is a mesh cage, 4 feet high and 6 feet wide.

The game begins with a face-off at a spot directly in the center of the ice. The referee drops the puck on the ice and the two centers attempt to hit it to one of their teammates. The face-off is similar to a center jump in basketball. The players carry the puck along the ice on the blade of their stick. The blade must be no more than 14 inches long or 3 inches high, and the shaft of the stick is limited to 53 inches. The object is to shoot the puck into the opponent's goal for a score.

In professional hockey, there are a center area and two attacking zones. Horizontal blue lines separate the center area from the attacking zones. In the center area, players can pass the puck from one to another. However, a pass cannot be made from the center area to a player in the attacking zone, although a player can follow the puck into the attacking zone and can pick up a pass in that zone, provided his skates are not over the blue line.

Once the offensive player has carried the puck into the attacking area, he may then pass to any of his teammates who are also inside it. Violation of this rule halts further play and results in another face-off between the two centers.

A penalty is given to a player who commits an infraction of the rules. Among the infractions that result in minor penalties are the following: checking into the boards, holding, hooking a player's arm or leg, tripping, or carrying a high stick. The penalized player is removed from the game and forced to sit in an area known as the "penalty box" for a

New York Ranger goalie Gump Worsley prevents score by Chicago Black Hawk forward Pete Conacher.

A Montreal Canadien and a New York Ranger come to a sudden halt against the sideboards.

period of two minutes. His team must play shorthanded for the two minutes of his penalty.

There are some penalties that are more severe. They cover such infractions as fighting, unsportsmanlike conduct, or a deliberate attempt to harm an opponent. For these infractions a player may draw a major penalty ranging from a minimum of five minutes to a match penalty. However, his team is forced to play shorthanded for two minutes only, although the penalized player himself is not allowed to return to action until his full penalty has been served. When a goal is scored on a team that is shorthanded, that team is allowed to return to full strength immediately, despite any penalty time that may remain.

The standard hockey rink is 180 feet long (divided into three equal sections); this dimension includes 10 feet of playing area behind each goal. The rink is 75 feet wide. However, these dimensions vary according to the size of the indoor arena.

The National Hockey League is the leading professional league, just as the National and American Leagues are the big leagues in baseball. Although the sport is known to have started in Canada, there are more American than Canadian teams in the NHL. For years the NHL had six teams— Boston Bruins, Detroit Red Wings, Chicago Black Hawks, New York Rangers, Toronto Maple Leafs, and Montreal Canadiens—but the popularity of the sport has forced expansion to twelve teams.

This took place in 1968 when the new six—the Los Angeles Kings, the Minnesota North Stars, the Oakland Seals, the Philadelphia Flyers, the Pittsburgh Penguins and the St. Louis Blues—were added. Two divisions were formed, with the new clubs all grouped into the Western Division, and the schedule for each team was extended to seventy-four games.

Under the six-team setup, each team played seventy scheduled games in a season that started in mid-October and ended in mid-March. Games were generally played on Wednesday, Saturday, and Sunday nights. Saturday afternoon games were started in 1957 for network television, and many people in the southern and western regions of the United States were able to see this major sport for the first time. With the national interest came the inevitable expansion.

At the conclusion of the season, the first four teams in the league standings engaged in a playoff competition. The eventual survivor was acknowledged as champion and awarded the Stanley Cup.

The NHL began play the winter of 1917÷18, with the first games on December 19, 1917. The infant league consisted of four teams—the Montreal Canadiens, the Montreal Wanderers, the Ottawa Senators, and the Toronto Arenas. The Quebec Bulldogs entered the league in 1919 and were replaced the following season by the Hamilton Tigers.

The league was confined to Canadian teams until 1924, when the Boston Bruins became the first team from the United States to acquire a franchise. The New York Americans, the Pittsburgh Pirates, the Chicago Black Hawks, and the New York Rangers became members during the next two seasons.

In 1926 there were ten teams in the NHL, five Canadian and five American. From 1927 through 1937, the league remained divided into these two sections, with no individual team dominating either division.

The Ottawa Senators, the New York Rangers, and the Boston Bruins were winners in 1927, 1928, and 1929. Ottawa had a low-scoring unit and depended on the fine defensive play of goalie Alex Connell and defenseman King Clancy. The Rangers were so colorful and popular that they took most of the New York fans' affection from the other Manhattan team, the Americans.

First coach of the Rangers and the developer of their early

great teams was Lester Patrick, who, because of his white hair, became famous as the "Silver Fox." Two of his sons, Lynn and Murray, played with later Ranger teams and went on to become top executives in hockey. Murray became manager of the Rangers, and Lynn manager of the Bruins.

The finest of the early championship Rangers were Frank Boucher, the Cook brothers, Bill and Bun, and Ching Johnson, a sterling defenseman.

Frank Boucher, later the coach and manager of the Rang-

Ching Johnson

The Toronto Maple Leaf "Kid Line" of the thirties—
Charley Conacher, Joe Primeau and Harvey Jackson.

ers, was a center who set up many of the goals scored by
the Cook brothers. He was an expert passer and stick-han-
dler and one of the game's most sportsmanlike performers.

Bill Cook was noted for his hard shot; Bun Cook was outstanding at breaking up the opponents' attack and stealing
the puck.

Johnson was the "god of the gallery." The fans loved him.
His hatchetlike face, partly bald head, and broad shoulders
made him an easy target to single out on the ice. He loved
body contact and was a popular figure throughout the
league.

Dit Clapper, Cooney Weiland, and Dutch Gainor were
among the fastest skaters and top scorers for the Bruins.
Goalie Tiny Thompson and defenseman Eddie Shore made it
difficult for the other teams to score on the Boston sextet.

The champion Montreal Canadiens of 1931 were among
the most famous and spectacular of all teams. The great

Howie Morenz, fearless skater and feared goal-getter, was the wizard of the Canadiens, who had other excellent players in Aurel Joliat, Johnny Gagnon, and Pit Lepine.

The Rangers and the Toronto Maple Leafs shared honors for the next two years. The Cook brothers, Boucher, and Johnson were still at the height of their careers for the Rangers. The Leafs came up with a high-powered scoring unit of center Joe Primeau and wings Charley Conacher and Harvey (Busher) Jackson. Also, King Clancy of the old Ottawa Senators was now a Maple Leaf and still an outstanding defenseman.

In the 1933–34 season the Detroit Red Wings didn't land a player among the top ten scorers, but were good enough to win the NHL title. However, the Chicago Black Hawks beat them in the Stanley Cup playoffs, largely through the efforts of their great goalie, Chuck Gardiner, who held the Wings to two scores in three games.

Conacher and Jackson paced the Leafs to the 1934–35 title, and the Red Wings came back to win championships in 1935–36 and 1936–37. Marty Barry, Larry Aurie, and Herbie Lewis were among the fleetest of the Red Wings who whipped the Maple Leafs and Rangers in the Stanley Cup finals.

Perhaps the greatest come-from-behind victory in Stanley Cup play was registered in 1937–38. This was the last season that the NHL was divided into two divisions. That season there were two divisions, Canadian and American. In the Canadian Division were the Toronto Maple Leafs, St. Louis Senators, Montreal Canadiens, Montreal Maroons and New York Americans. In the American Division were the Boston

Bruins, New York Rangers, Chicago Black Hawks, Detroit Cougars and Pittsburgh Pirates. By 1942 there were only six teams in the NHL: the Montreal Canadiens, Toronto Maple Leafs, Boston Bruins, New York Rangers, Detroit Red Wings and Chicago Black Hawks. The Chicago Black Hawks finished third in the regular season but came on to triumph in the playoffs, upsetting the Canadiens. Paul Thompson was the best scoring Hawk, and Johnny Gottselig and Doc Romnes were clever playmakers. Outstanding on defense was Earl Siebert. Coach of this team was Bill Stewart, who had been an NHL referee and whose name will be recognized by some baseball fans as a former National League umpire.

From 1937–38 through 1940–41 the Boston Bruins were the league's powerhouse—the first team in league history to win four straight titles. But the Bruins were to taste defeat in two Stanley Cup playoffs in these four seasons.

There were many Bruin heroes during the streak of titles. The indestructible Eddie Shore, one of the greatest of all defensemen, was closing out a star-studded career, and Bill Cowley was still scoring goals and setting up plays that led to many goals.

But the three best reasons for the Bruins' success were Milt Schmidt, Woody Dumart, and Bobby Bauer. They were the high-scoring first line and were nicknamed the "Kraut Line." In 1939–40, they were at their mightiest. Schmidt led the NHL scorers, and Dumart and Bauer tied for second place. No other team ever had three men capture the top scoring positions in the league.

After the Rangers had won the 1941–42 title (and lost the Stanley Cup to the Toronto Maple Leafs), the Canadiens became the second team to win four straight league crowns.

400

They were victors from 1942–43 through 1946–47, when Elmer Lach, Bill Durnan, Toe Blake, Emile (Butch) Bouchard, and a fiery black-haired skater named Maurice Richard proved to be demons on ice.

The Maple Leafs swept all honors in 1947–48—and then the Detroit Red Wings began a reign that can be compared with the pennant victories of the New York Yankees in baseball. The Wings finished on top of the NHL for seven consecutive seasons, finally yielding to the Canadiens in the 1955–56 season.

Every player on the Detroit team was a hero during the Wings' record-shattering march. Bill Quackenbush, Jack Stewart, and Red Kelly were great defensemen. The scoring power was generated by Gordie Howe, Ted Lindsay and center Sid Abel, and the man who tended goal in the early 1950's was Terry Sawchuk, certainly one of the best of all time.

Detroit bounced back to win in the 1956–57 season, but then the Canadiens, from the 1957–58 season through the 1961–62 season, went on to win the league title each year and, more important, added five straight Stanley Cup triumphs for an all-time record.

The Canadiens most responsible for this streak were the Richard brothers (Maurice and Henri), Jean Beliveau, Bernie Geoffrion, high-scorer Dickie Moore, and defenseman Doug Harvey.

The Toronto Maple Leafs ended the streak in the 1962–63 season, Montreal won the league title back the next year, and Detroit picked it up in 1964–65. Montreal won it back in 1965–66.

In winning the 1966–67 regular-season championship, the

Chicago Black Hawks were led by Golden Jet Bobby Hull and Stan Mikita. Hull once more scored more than 50 goals (52); Mikita won the scoring championship with 97 points on 35 goals and 62 assists. The Stanley Cup went, however, to Toronto.

Almost immediately after the 1967–68 season, which saw Montreal dethrone Toronto, the NHL doubled its size to twelve teams, with the new clubs each paying $2 million for the privilege of joining. In return, each new club received twenty players from the established six teams.

After expansion, a familiar name led all the rest—the Montreal Canadiens. The Frenchmen finished first in the East Division and then conquered the tough Boston Bruins in six games to annex the Stanley Cup. The series marked the end of one of hockey's most illustrious careers. Toe Blake, Montreal coach, retired with a record of nine first-place finishes and eight Stanley Cups in thirteen years.

Great Names in Ice Hockey

JEAN BELIVEAU

Jean Beliveau of the Montreal Canadiens stands head and shoulders above most of today's competitors, physically and mentally. Bigger than most NHL players, at 6 feet 3 inches and 205 pounds, he also does things better than most players in the league. In his eighteen seasons he has scored an average of better than one point a game.

Quiet and unassuming almost to the point of shyness, Beliveau has been called "Hockey's Humble Giant." From his earliest days of prominence with the Victoriaville Juniors, Jean has graciously and modestly accepted stardom and the praise that goes with it. Today he is regarded as the perfect player and recognized as an all-time center.

Before big Jean ever signed a pro contract with the Canadiens, the Three Rivers (Quebec) terror was regarded by Detroit's Jack Adams as one of the three best players in the world. He named Gordie Howe, Maurice Richard, and Jean Beliveau, and added, "And I'm not sure which of the three is the best."

403

Beliveau, who has suffered a broken jaw and a break in the small bone in the lower leg, twice led the league in goals scored with 45 and 47. He shares with Maurice Richard the playoff record of most goals in a series—12.

Despite his size, he is regarded as a "clean" player—one who will not take physical advantage of a smaller opponent. There are faster men in the league than Jean, but his long strides cover the ice quickly and he moves easily. He is a fine playmaker, a throwback to the days of deft stick-handling and passing, and a very intelligent performer. He possesses a booming slapshot—a wrist shot of accuracy and great velocity.

PHIL ESPOSITO

Admittedly, Phil Esposito is a bit young to be listed with the greats of hockey, but after his magnificient 1968–69 season, how could he be denied? The soft-spoken center skated off with almost everything that season: the Art Ross Trophy; the Hart Trophy; a record for assists in a regular season (77), and a record for total points (126).

Esposito was born in Sault Ste. Marie, Ontario, on Feb. 20, 1942. He is a left-handed shooter and stands 6 feet 1 inch with 195 pounds of solid muscle. Phil broke in with Sault Ste. Marie in 1961 and moved to St. Louis the next two years. He joined the National Hockey League in 1963–64 with Chicago.

He was traded to Boston in 1967–68. That year Esposito set the NHL record for assists (49). He broke his own record the next season by 28.

405

Jean Beliveau

DOUG HARVEY

It's always tough to be a sports star in your home town. Nobody was more aware of this than Doug Harvey, one of hockey's finest and most durable defensemen.

Doug's first few seasons with the Montreal Canadiens were unhappy ones. Success, which had come easily to him as an amateur, first eluded him in pro ranks in Montreal. But in thirteen seasons with the Canadiens, he progressed to the point where a nationwide poll placed him alongside Eddie Shore as one of the two greatest defensemen of all time. He won the Norris Trophy, awarded to the National Hockey League's best defenseman, a record seven times.

Doug grew up in the west end of Montreal and played football, baseball, and hockey. He soon advanced to pro football, Class B baseball, and hockey prominence with the senior Royals. Montreal sports authorities still maintain that Harvey, as a ball carrier, was capable of national pro ranking had he stayed with football. As for his baseball talent, the old Boston Braves saw much promise in him as a slugging outfielder. However, Doug decided on a hockey career and turned pro in 1947, when he joined the Canadiens.

It wasn't until 1951–52 that Harvey gained ranking on the All-Star first team of the NHL, but he remained there for seven straight years, building a reputation as a superb ice general, playmaker, and defender. Through 1969 he had been a first-team All-Star selection ten times.

In 1954–55 Harvey set a record for most assists by a defenseman in one season with 43. Two seasons later he topped that mark with 44.

406

Doug Harvey

David Bier, Montreal

GORDIE HOWE

Greatest of all Detroit Red Wings, and to many the greatest hockey player of all time, is Gordie Howe.

The Saskatchewan sensation has already written his name in records of both the NHL and his team perhaps more times than any other single player.

Howe ranks as the highest goal scorer in NHL history. When Gordie rammed the puck into the net against the Rangers on March 14, 1962, it was the 500th goal of his career and put him within reach of Maurice Richard's 544. At the end of the 1968–69 season, his twenty-third year as a pro, Gordie had 732 goals. His lifetime totals for assists, 954, and points, 1,686, are the highest in the league.

Howe, through 1968, was named the league's most valuable player five times, more than any other player in the history of the game. In addition, he has been named to the All-Star team seventeen times, ten times to the first team.

Included in Howe's achievements have been five seasons in which he led the league in point scoring; four of these, 1950 to 1954, were consecutive. His best point-making season was 1968–69, when he scored 103. He also holds an unchallenged mark of 20 playoff points, set in 1954–55.

Gordie Howe

Detroit Red Wings

BOBBY HULL

Bobby Hull of the Chicago Black Hawks is the greatest single-season scorer in hockey history.

Hull is the only man ever to score 50 or more goals in more than one season. He did it four times, and his record of 58 for the 1968–69 season is considered fantastic. Bobby first reached the magic figure when he tied Maurice Richard and Bernie Geoffrion's old record of 50 in 1961–62. In 1965–66 Hull slammed in 54; he scored 52 the following season.

He slipped to 44 in 1967–68, but 1968–69 was a very good year because Bobby skyrocketed to 58.

Hull was born in Point Anne, Ontario, on January 3, 1939. He is a left-handed shooter who plays center without anyone near him. At 5 feet 10 inches and 195 pounds, he has exceptional speed and enough heft to defend himself.

Bobby has always been a good scorer; in his rookie year he slammed home 13 goals for the Black Hawks. Accordingly, honors have been heaped upon him almost from the start. He won the Art Ross Trophy three times, the Lady Byng Trophy and the Hart Trophy.

At the end of the 1968–69 season, his twelfth in the NHL, Bobby had played 819 games and had scored 472 goals and 425 assists for a total of 897 points. He had also been in 82 playoff games and scored 44 goals and 40 assists for a total of 84 points.

410

Bobby Hull

RED KELLY

One of the oldest defensemen in point of service in the NHL, Leonard Patrick Kelly will always rank as one of Detroit's all-time greats. Before being traded to the Toronto Maple Leafs in 1960, the red-haired tobacco farmer from Simcoe, Ontario, won ranking as the fifth highest point scorer in Red Wing history and had won more honors than any other rear guard in Detroit annals. He returned at the end of the 1966–67 season.

His list of achievements in the NHL is indeed a mark for any young player. He was the original winner of the Norris Memorial Trophy in 1953–54, four times captured the Lady Byng Award for sportsmanship, and won All-Star recognition eight times, being named to the first team on six occasions. Had he not been available to play center as well, he might have won even more All-Star honors.

His greatest single feat was a "hat trick" (scoring three goals in one game) against the Boston Bruins. This is the only hat trick that a defenseman has scored in modern history.

TED LINDSAY

Fiery Ted Lindsay played with the Detroit Red Wings and the Chicago Black Hawks. One of the smallest players, yet one of the fiercest competitors in the NHL, Lindsay ranked as the third highest goal scorer of all time with 379 goals at the close of the 1964–65 season, his eighteenth, when he retired.

The battling competitor made his way through the hockey wars the hard way. He had to overcome a series of injuries to win a place on the Toronto St. Michael's junior team, and then made the big jump directly from junior ranks to the Red Wings.

In his first season in the big time, 1944–45, Ted was tabbed as a penalty killer and defensive forward, yet he wound up scoring 17 goals and was soon the most feared left-winger in the league. He went on to average better than 24 goals a season, and he was heralded as a model for young hockey players.

A hard-going, spirited player, Lindsay asked no quarter and gave none. The most penalized forward in the game, he earned the dubious honor of accumulating the most penalty minutes in 1958–59. However, he was selected as a first-team All-Star forward for eight seasons and once as a second-team forward.

HOWIE MORENZ

They called him the "Stratford Streak," and until Maurice Richard burst on the hockey scene in the 1940's, no other player had so thoroughly captured the attention of fans everywhere as did No. 7—Howie Morenz.

Even in the late 1920's and early 1930's, when radio and press coverage of pro hockey was a spotty thing at best, Morenz' name was a household word. Although he died in 1937, he is still remembered as one player who contributed a great deal to the game. He took it out of the horse-and-buggy era and brought it international prominence.

A daring, reckless center with blinding speed and without fear, Morenz was idolized in every city in the league. He was the top gate attraction on both sides of the border. His skating momentum was so great and his balance so unusual that he was often able to crash two or three men to the ice, remaining upright to score.

Morenz played with no regard for his personal safety. Scoring goals and winning games were all that mattered. As a boy he possessed this trait, and as a fading veteran it was this desire to excel that caused his death.

In January of 1937, nearing the end of his career, Morenz tried to hurdle Chicago's Earl Seibert. They collided, and Howie was thrown heavily to the ice and into the boards. His leg snapped and two months later he died as a result of complications from the injury. Those who knew him best claimed Morenz died of a broken heart because he knew he could never strap on a skate again.

Morenz came to the Canadiens in 1923 when he was twenty-one. Within a year he was a star, and in two seasons he was recognized as the best in the game. He toiled brilliantly for the Canadiens until 1933–34, when he was traded to the Chicago Black Hawks.

Morenz scored 270 goals in the NHL, won the Hart Trophy three times, twice led the league in scoring and three times was selected to the All-Star team. His was one of the first names enshrined in the Hockey Hall of Fame.

MAURICE RICHARD

Maurice (Rocket) Richard, the Montreal Canadiens' dynamic right-winger, enjoyed eighteen seasons unmatched in the annals of ice hockey. He had scored a record 544 goals when he retired in 1960.

Maurice, the second of seven children, played organized hockey at eleven and graduated to park league hockey, where he could play four and five nights a week. When he reached his late teens, it was apparent that Richard possessed a natural scoring talent. But his skating and checking were below accepted standards, and it was with some difficulty that he obtained a position with the junior Verdun Maple Leafs.

As he matured, his hockey ability improved and in the early days of his first senior season, 1940–41, he began to show signs of definite all-around improvement. His success was short-lived, however, for before many games had been played, he fell into the boards and broke his ankle. He played no more that season.

He had shown promise, though, and started his NHL career with the Canadiens in the 1942–43 season. He was an immediate sensation, but a broken right ankle closed out his first NHL year after sixteen games.

Two seasons later, Richard catapulted to international hockey fame by scoring 50 goals in as many games in 1944–1945.

The scoring of 50 goals was hailed by some as the work of a master scorer. Others maintained it was a fluke, or a result of weak, wartime opposition. The cry was heard on many sides that Richard was strictly a wartime star and that when the NHL "big guns" returned from the armed services his goal totals would drop.

The stars returned, but Richard remained the greatest scorer of them all, scoring his 200th NHL goal in 1948–49, his seventh season; hitting the 300 mark three seasons later; and setting a new all-time mark of 325 shortly after the opening of the 1952–53 season. Rocket scored the 400th on December 18, 1954, and three years later he registered number 500.

415

TERRY SAWCHUK

Senior goalkeeper, in point of service in the NHL, Terry Sawchuk played his twentieth regular season (1968–69) in the big time. He was back with Detroit that year after three years with Toronto and one with Los Angeles.

Terry was drafted by Toronto on July 10, 1964. He continued his great play the following season and ended the year sharing the Vézina Trophy with Johnny Bower.

Sawchuk has one of the most impressive goalkeeping records in hockey history. A product of the Detroit junior farm club, the Windsor Spitfires, he turned professional at seventeen with the Omaha Knights of the old United States League in 1947. In his freshman season he topped the circuit in shutouts and won the league's rookie of the year award. Sawchuk was then advanced to Indianapolis, where he again was chosen the outstanding rookie.

Terry started with the Wings in 1950. He played on five consecutive league championship teams, won the Vézina Trophy four times, led the league in shutouts three times, and won All-Star recognition each year. Three times he was the first-team All-Star goalie. His "goals against" average never rose above 1.98.

Terry wrote his name into the record books in the 1952 playoffs when he equaled a league record by turning in four consecutive home-ice shutouts as his team swept to the Stanley Cup in eight straight games.

Traded to Boston in 1955, he performed in outstanding fashion until stricken with a nervous disorder in 1956. A year later, Detroit Manager Jack Adams, believing him "the greatest goalie in the world in a Detroit uniform," bought him from the Bruins.

Terry was regarded by many observers as the smartest goalie in the game.

Married and the father of three children, Sawchuk maintains year-round residence in the Detroit suburbs and heads a small sales agency.

MILT SCHMIDT

Art Ross, former Bruins' coach and general manager, calls Milt Schmidt the greatest center of all time, and even Ross' foes are inclined to agree. A fierce competitor, Schmidt played his entire NHL career with the Bruins, starting in 1936 when only eighteen years old. Milt retired as an active player in 1954 and immediately stepped into the role of Bruin coach.

Schmidt was center of the Bruins' famed Kraut Line with his two hometown buddies from Kitchener, Ontario—Woody Dumart and Bobby Bauer. This line, regarded as one of hockey's greatest, sparked the Bruins to Stanley Cup triumphs in 1939 and 1941.

Because he played with such zest, he was prone to injuries. During his career he suffered a broken jaw, had his nose fractured several times, and wound up with two bad knees. Once during a playoff series, Schmidt had to have both knees strapped so he could play. Before the strapping had been put on, somebody asked team physician Thomas A. Kelly if Schmidt would play. Knowing Milt's spirit, the doctor replied, "If he can breathe, he'll play."

Schmidt lasted several years longer than his teammates. He won many NHL honors during his career and would have won more except for his injuries and a three-year period during World War II in which he served with the Royal

417

Canadian Air Force. He won the league scoring title in 1939–40, the Hart Trophy as most valuable player in 1950–51, and was named center on the NHL All-Star team three times.

EDDIE SHORE

Eddie Shore, the Edmonton Express, played for the Boston Bruins from 1926 through the start of 1940, when he was traded to the Brooklyn Americans. During his career with the Bruins he is credited with making hockey a popular pro sport in Boston. His electrifying rink-length rushes and repeated arguments with visiting players made him a magnet all around the circuit.

Some circles called him the "Babe Ruth of Hockey." He is credited with "building" the Boston Garden, because the Boston Arena became too small for hockey crowds once he attained stardom. In 1934 Shore was in a collision with Toronto's Ace Bailey, and the Maple Leaf right wing suffered a fractured skull that almost cost him his life. Shore was suspended for a month but returned to action later in the season, and in the next few years he went on to play his greatest hockey. He played with the Bruins' Stanley Cup champions in 1928–29 and 1938–39. He was chosen to the NHL All-Star team as a defenseman seven times and won the Hart Trophy as the most valuable player to his team four times.

All-Time Records

STANLEY CUP CHAMPIONS

The National Hockey League championship is won by the team that finishes first at the end of regular season's play. The team that wins the playoffs is awarded the Stanley Cup.

The present system of the two final playoff survivors playing a best-of-seven series for the Stanley Cup began in 1938–39. From 1930–31 through 1937–38 the two survivors played a best-of-five series. From 1917–18 through 1925–26 the cup was given to the team scoring the most goals in playoff competition.

Season	Champion (Runner-up)	Team Coach
1968–69	Montreal Canadiens (Boston) 4–2	Blake, Toe
1967–68	Montreal Canadiens (St. Louis) 4–0	Blake, Toe
1966–67	Toronto Maple Leafs (Montreal) 4–2	Imlach, Punch
1965–66	Montreal Canadiens (Detroit) 4–3	Blake, Toe
1964–65	Montreal Canadiens (Chicago) 4–3	Blake, Toe
1963–64	Toronto Maple Leafs (Detroit) 4–3	Imlach, Punch
1962–63	Toronto Maple Leafs (Detroit) 4–1	Imlach, Punch
1961–62	Toronto Maple Leafs (Chicago) 4–2	Imlach, Punch
1960–61	Chicago Black Hawks (Detroit) 4–2	Pilous, Rudy
1959–60	Montreal Canadiens (Toronto) 4–0	Blake, Toe

Season	Champion (Runner-up)	Team Coach
1958–59	Montreal Canadiens (Toronto) 4–1	Blake, Toe
1957–58	Montreal Canadiens (Boston) 4–2	Blake, Toe
1956–57	Montreal Canadiens (Boston) 4–1	Blake, Toe
1955–56	Montreal Canadiens (Detroit) 4–1	Blake, Toe
1954–55	Detroit Red Wings (Montreal) 4–3	Skinner, Jimmy
1953–54	Detroit Red Wings (Montreal) 4–3	Ivan, Tommy
1952–53	Montreal Canadiens (Boston) 4–1	Irvin, Dick
1951–52	Detroit Red Wings (Montreal) 4–0	Ivan, Tommy
1950–51	Toronto Maple Leafs (Montreal) 4–1	Primeau, Joe
1949–50	Detroit Red Wings (Rangers) 4–3	Ivan, Tommy
1948–49	Toronto Maple Leafs (Detroit) 4–0	Day, Hap
1947–48	Toronto Maple Leafs (Detroit) 4–0	Day, Hap
1946–47	Toronto Maple Leafs (Montreal) 4–2	Day, Hap
1945–46	Montreal Canadiens (Boston) 4–1	Irvin, Dick
1944–45	Toronto Maple Leafs (Detroit) 4–3	Day, Hap
1943–44	Montreal Canadiens (Chicago) 4–0	Irvin, Dick
1942–43	Detroit Red Wings (Boston) 4–0	Adams, Jack
1941–42	Toronto Maple Leafs (Detroit) 4–3	Day, Hap
1940–41	Boston Bruins (Detroit) 4–0	Weiland, Cooney
1939–40	New York Rangers (Toronto) 4–2	Boucher, Frank
1938–39	Boston Bruins (Toronto) 4–1	Ross, Art
1937–38	Chicago Black Hawks (Toronto) 3–1	Stewart, Bill
1936–37	Detroit Red Wings (New York) 3–2	Adams, Jack
1935–36	Detroit Red Wings (Toronto) 3–1	Adams, Jack
1934–35	Montreal Maroons (Toronto) 3–0	Gorman, Tommy
1933–34	Chicago Black Hawks (Detroit) 3–1	Gorman, Tommy
1932–33	New York Rangers (Toronto) 3–1	Patrick, Lester
1931–32	Toronto Maple Leafs (New York) 3–0	Irvin, Dick
1930–31	Montreal Canadiens (Chicago) 3–2	Hart, Cecil
1929–30	Montreal Canadiens (Boston) 2–0	Hart, Cecil
1928–29	Boston Bruins (New York) 2–0	Denneny, Cy
1927–28	New York Rangers (Canadiens) 3–2	Patrick, Lester
1926–27	Ottawa Senators (Boston) 2–0	Gill, Dave
1925–26	Montreal Maroons	Gerard, Eddie
1924–25	Victoria Cougars (Canadiens)	Patrick, Lester
1923–24	Montreal Canadiens	Dandurand, Leo
1922–23	Ottawa Senators	Green, Pete
1921–22	Toronto St. Pats	Powers, Eddie
1920–21	Ottawa Senators	Green, Pete
1919–20	Ottawa Senators	Green, Pete
1918–19	No decision	
1917–18	Toronto Arenas	Carroll, Dick

Hart Trophy

The Hart Memorial Trophy was presented by the NHL in 1960, after the original Hart Trophy was retired to the Hockey Hall of Fame. The original trophy was donated to NHL in 1923 by Dr. David A. Hart, father of Cecil Hart, former manager-coach of Montreal. The winner is selected by a poll of sports writers and broadcasters in six NHL cities.

Hockey's most valuable team player is awarded the Hart Trophy and a $1,000 bonus. This trophy is the game's most significant award, since it is usually presented to the best performer in the NHL.

Gordie Howe of the Red Wings has won the trophy five times. Eddie Shore, Boston's great defenseman of the 1930's, was a four-time winner.

Season	Player	Team	Season	Player	Team
1968–69	Esposito, Phil	Boston	1944–45	Lach, Elmer	Canadiens
1967–68	Mikita, Stan	Chicago	1943–44	Pratt, W. "Babe"	Toronto
1966–67	Mikita, Stan	Chicago	1942–43	Cowley, Bill	Boston
1965–66	Hull, Bobby	Chicago	1941–42	Anderson,	
1964–65	Hull, Bobby	Chicago		Tommy	Americans
1963–64	Beliveau, Jean	Canadiens	1940–41	Cowley, Bill	Boston
1962–63	Howe, Gordie	Detroit	1939–40	Goodfellow,	
1961–62	Plante, Jacques	Canadiens		Ebbie	Detroit
1960–61	Geoffrion, Bernie	Canadiens	1938–39	Blake, Toe	Canadiens
1959–60	Howe, Gordie	Detroit	1937–38	Shore, Eddie	Boston
1958–59	Bathgate, Andy	Rangers	1936–37	Seibert, "Babe"	Canadiens
1957–58	Howe, Gordie	Detroit	1935–36	Shore, Eddie	Boston
1956–57	Howe, Gordie	Detroit	1934–35	Shore, Eddie	Boston
1955–56	Beliveau, Jean	Canadiens	1933–34	Joliat, Aurel	Canadiens
1954–55	Kennedy, Ted	Toronto	1932–33	Shore, Eddie	Boston
1953–54	Rollins, Al	Chicago	1931–32	Morenz, Howie	Canadiens
1952–53	Howe, Gordie	Detroit	1930–31	Morenz, Howie	Canadiens
1951–52	Howe, Gordie	Detroit	1929–30	Stewart, Nels	Montreal
1950–51	Schmidt, Milt	Boston	1928–29	Worters, Roy	Americans
1949–50	Rayner, Chuck	Rangers	1927–28	Morenz, Howie	Canadiens
1948–49	Abel, Sid	Detroit	1926–27	Gardiner, Herb	Canadiens
1947–48	O'Connor,		1925–26	Stewart, Nels	Montreal
	"Buddy"	Rangers	1924–25	Burch, Billy	Hamilton
1946–47	Richard, Maurice	Canadiens	1923–24	Nighbor, Frank	Ottawa
1945–46	Bentley, Max	Chicago			

Art Ross Trophy

The leading scorer in the NHL is awarded the Art Ross Trophy and a $1,000 bonus from the league. Each goal counts as one point, as does each assist.

Arthur Howie Ross, former manager-coach of Boston, presented the trophy to the NHL in 1947.

Phil Esposito of the Boston Bruins holds the all-time one-season scoring mark of 126 points, established in 1968–69. He scored 49 goals and had 77 assists in that season. Bobby Hull holds the all-time record of 58 goals in one season (1968–69).

Season	Player	Team	Games	Goals	Assists	Points
1968–69	Esposito, Phil	Boston	74	49	77	126
1967–68	Mikita, Stan	Chicago	72	40	47	87
1966–67	Mikita, Stan	Chicago	70	35	62	97
1965–66	Hull, Bobby	Chicago	65	54	43	97
1964–65	Mikita, Stan	Chicago	70	28	59	87
1963–64	Mikita, Stan	Chicago	70	39	50	89
1962–63	Howe, Gordie	Detroit	70	38	48	86
1961–62	Hull, Bobby	Chicago	70	50	34	84
1960–61	Geoffrion, Bernie	Canadiens	64	50	45	95
1959–60	Hull, Bobby	Chicago	70	39	42	81
1958–59	Moore, Dickie	Canadiens	70	41	55	96
1957–58	Moore, Dickie	Canadiens	70	36	48	84

Season	Player	Team	Games	Goals	Assists	Points
1956–57	Howe, Gordie	Detroit	70	44	45	89
1955–56	Beliveau, Jean	Canadiens	70	47	41	88
1954–55	Geoffrion, Bernie	Canadiens	70	38	37	75
1953–54	Howe, Gordie	Detroit	70	33	48	81
1952–53	Howe, Gordie	Detroit	70	49	46	95
1951–52	Howe, Gordie	Detroit	70	47	39	86
1950–51	Howe, Gordie	Detroit	70	43	43	86
1949–50	Lindsay, Ted	Detroit	69	23	55	78
1948–49	Conacher, Roy	Chicago	60	26	42	68
1947–48	Lach, Elmer	Canadiens	60	30	31	61
1946–47	Bentley, Max	Chicago	60	29	43	72
1945–46	Bentley, Max	Chicago	47	31	30	61
1944–45	Lach, Elmer	Canadiens	50	26	54	80
1943–44	Cain, Herbie	Boston	48	36	46	82
1942–43	Bentley, Doug	Chicago	50	33	40	73
1941–42	Hextall, Bryan	Rangers	48	24	32	56
1940–41	Cowley, Bill	Boston		17	45	62
1939–40	Schmidt, Milt	Boston		22	30	52
1938–39	Blake, Toe	Canadiens		24	23	47
1937–38	Drillon, Gordie	Toronto		26	26	52
1936–37	Schriner, Dave	Americans		21	25	46
1935–36	Schriner, Dave	Americans		19	26	45
1934–35	Conacher, Charley	Toronto		36	21	57
1933–34	Conacher, Charley	Toronto		32	20	52
1932–33	Cook, Bill	Rangers		28	22	50
1931–32	Jackson, Harvey	Toronto		28	25	53
1930–31	Morenz, Howie	Canadiens		28	23	51
1929–30	Weiland, Cooney	Boston		43	30	73
1928–29	Bailey, Ace	Toronto		22	10	32
1927–28	Morenz, Howie	Canadiens		33	18	51
1926–27	Cook, Bill	Rangers		33	4	37
1925–26	Stewart, Nels	Montreal		34	8	42
1924–25	Dye, Babe	Toronto		38	6	44
1923–24	Denneny, Cy	Ottawa		22	1	23
1922–23	Dye, Babe	Toronto		26	11	37
1921–22	Broadbent, Punch	Ottawa		32	14	46
1920–21	Lalonde, Newsy	Canadiens		33	8	41
1919–20	Malone, Joe	Quebec		39	6	45
1918–19	Lalonde, Newsy	Canadiens		23	9	32
1917–18	Malone, Joe	Canadiens		44	0	44

(Number of games not recorded until 1941–42.)

Vézina Trophy

The goaltender who allows the fewest number of goals a season is presented with the Vézina Trophy and a bonus of $1,000.

Leo Dandurand, Louis Letourneau and Joe Cattarinich, former owners of the Montreal Canadiens, presented the trophy to the league in 1926–27 in memory of Georges Vézina, outstanding Montreal goalkeeper who died in 1926. The winner is selected by poll of sports writers and broadcasters.

Jacques Plante of the Canadiens won the trophy for the seventh straight season in 1961–62, an all-time record.

Season	Goalie	Team	Season	Goalie	Team
1968–69	Hall, Glenn	St. Louis	1948–49	Durnan, Bill	Canadiens
	Plante, Jacques		1947–48	Broda, W.	
1967–68	Worsley, Gump	Canadiens		"Turk"	Toronto
	Vachon, Rogatien		1946–47	Durnan, Bill	Canadiens
1966–67	DeJordy, Denis	Chicago	1945–46	Durnan, Bill	Canadiens
	Hall, Glenn		1944–45	Durnan, Bill	Canadiens
1965–66	Worsley, Gump	Canadiens	1943–44	Durnan, Bill	Canadiens
1964–65	Sawchuk, Terry		1942–43	Mowers,	
	Bower, Johnny	Toronto		Johnny	Detroit
1963–64	Hodge, Charlie	Canadiens	1941–42	Brimsek, Frank	Boston
1962–63	Hall, Glenn	Chicago	1940–41	Broda, W.	
1961–62	Plante, Jacques	Canadiens		"Turk"	Toronto
1960–61	Plante, Jacques	Canadiens	1939–40	Kerr, Dave	Rangers
1959–60	Plante, Jacques	Canadiens	1938–39	Brimsek, Frank	Boston
1958–59	Plante, Jacques	Canadiens	1937–38	Thompson, C.	
1957–58	Plante, Jacques	Canadiens		"Tiny"	Boston
1956–57	Plante, Jacques	Canadiens	1936–37	Smith, Normie	Detroit
1955–56	Plante, Jacques	Canadiens	1935–36	Thompson, C.	
1954–55	Sawchuk, Terry	Detroit		"Tiny"	Boston
1953–54	Lumley, Harry	Toronto	1934–35	Chabot, Lorne	Chicago
1952–53	Sawchuk, Terry	Detroit	1933–34	Gardiner,	
1951–52	Sawchuk, Terry	Detroit		Chuck	Chicago
1950–51	Rollins, Al	Toronto	1932–33	Thompson, C.	
1949–50	Durnan, Bill	Canadiens		"Tiny"	Boston

424

Calder Memorial Trophy

The best rookie player in the NHL is awarded the Calder Memorial Trophy and $1,000. To be eligible for this trophy a player cannot have participated in more than twenty games in any preceding season.

From 1936–37 until his death in 1943, Frank Calder, NHL president, presented his own trophy to the outstanding rookie. The NHL made the presentation from 1943 on.

Season	Player	Team	Season	Player	Team
1968–69	Grant, Dan	Minnesota	1951–52	Geoffrion,	
1967–68	Sanderson, Derek	Boston		Bernie	Canadiens
1966–67	Orr, Bobby	Boston	1950–51	Sawchuk, Terry	Detroit
1965–66	Selby, Brit	Toronto	1949–50	Gelineau, Jack	Boston
1964–65	Crozier, Roger	Detroit	1948–49	Lund, Pentti	Rangers
1963–64	Laperriere,		1947–48	McFadden,	
	Jacques	Canadiens		Jimmy	Detroit
1962–63	Douglas, Kent	Toronto	1946–47	Meeker, Howie	Toronto
1961–62	Rousseau,		1945–46	Laprade, Edgar	Rangers
	Bobby	Canadiens	1944–45	McCool, Frank	Toronto
1960–61	Keon, Dave	Toronto	1943–44	Bodnar, Gus	Toronto
1959–60	Hay, Bill	Chicago	1942–43	Stewart, Gaye	Toronto
1958–59	Backstrom,		1941–42	Warwick,	
	Ralph	Canadiens		Grant	Rangers
1957–58	Mahovlich,		1940–41	Quilty, Johnny	Canadiens
	Frank	Toronto	1939–40	MacDonald,	
1956–57	Regan, Larry	Boston		Kilby	Rangers
1955–56	Hall, Glenn	Detroit	1938–39	Brimsek, Frank	Boston
1954–55	Litzenberger,		1937–38	Dahlstrom,	
	Eddie	Chicago		Cully	Chicago
1953–54	Henry, Camille	Rangers	1936–37	Apps, Syl	Toronto
1952–53	Worsley, Lorne	Rangers			

Lady Byng Memorial Trophy

"Clean" playing performance is recognized in the form of the Lady Byng Memorial Trophy and a $1,000 bonus awarded to the player "adjudged to have exhibited the best type of sportsmanship and gentlemanly conduct combined with a high standard of playing ability during the season."

Frank Boucher, center of the Rangers in the late 1920's and early 1930's, was awarded the trophy a record seven times.

Season	Player	Team	Season	Player	Team
1968–69	Delvecchio, Alex	Detroit	1957–58	Henry, Camille	Rangers
			1956–57	Hebenton, Andy	Rangers
1967–68	Mikita, Stan	Chicago			
1966–67	Mikita, Stan	Chicago	1955–56	Reibel, Earl	Detroit
1965–66	Delvecchio, Alex	Detroit	1954–55	Smith, Sid	Toronto
			1953–54	Kelly, Red	Detroit
1964–65	Hull, Bobby	Chicago	1952–53	Kelly, Red	Detroit
1963–64	Wharram, Ken	Chicago	1951–52	Smith, Sid	Toronto
1962–63	Keon, Dave	Toronto	1950–51	Kelly, Red	Detroit
1961–62	Keon, Dave	Toronto	1949–50	Laprade, Edgar	Rangers
1960–61	Kelly, Red	Toronto	1948–49	Quackenbush, Bill	Detroit
1959–60	McKenney, Don	Boston			
1958–59	Delvecchio, Alex	Detroit	1947–48	O'Connor, "Buddy"	Rangers

Season	Player	Team	Season	Player	Team
1946–47	Bauer, Bobby	Boston	1935–36	Romnes, "Doc"	Chicago
1945–46	Blake, Toe	Canadiens	1934–35	Boucher, Frank	Rangers
1944–45	Mosienko,		1933–34	Boucher, Frank	Rangers
	Billy	Chicago	1932–33	Boucher, Frank	Rangers
1943–44	Smith, Clint	Chicago	1931–32	Primeau, Joe	Toronto
1942–43	Bentley, Max	Chicago	1930–31	Boucher, Frank	Rangers
1941–42	Apps, Syl	Toronto	1929–30	Boucher, Frank	Rangers
1940–41	Bauer, Bobby	Boston	1928–29	Boucher, Frank	Rangers
1939–40	Bauer, Bobby	Boston	1927–28	Boucher, Frank	Rangers
1938–39	Smith, Clint	Rangers	1926–27	Burch, Billy	Americans
1937–38	Drillon, Gordon	Toronto	1925–26	Nighbor, Frank	Ottawa
1936–37	Barry, Marty	Detroit	1924–25	Nighbor, Frank	Ottawa

National Hockey Hall of Fame

The all-time stars of the NHL are many. But only the greatest have been elected to the game's Hall of Fame. Going into the 1969–70 season, there were 171 members, including 124 players, 40 builders, and 7 referees.

PLAYERS

Abel, Sid
Adams, John
Apps, Charles
Bain, Donald H.
Baker, Hobart
Barry, Martin J.
Benedict, Clinton S.
Bentley, Douglas W.
Bentley, Maxwell
Blake, Hector
Boon, Richard R.
Bouchard, Emile
Boucher, Frank
Boucher, George
Bowie, Russell
Brimsek, Francis C.
Broadbent, Harry L.

Broda, Walter
Cameron, Harold H.
Clancy, Francis M.
Clapper, Aubrey
Cleghorn, Sprague
Colville, Neill
Conacher, Charles W.
Connell, Alex
Cook, William Osser
Cowley, William
Crawford, Samuel R.
Darragh, John P.
Davidson, Allan M.
Day, Clarence H.
Denneny, Cyril
Drinkwater, Charles G.
Durnan, William R.

427

PLAYERS (Continued)

Dutton, Mervyn A.
Farrell, Arthur F.
Foyston, Frank
Fredrickson, Frank
Gardiner, Charles R.
Gardiner, Herbert M.
Gardner, James H.
Gerard, Eddie
Gilmour, Hamilton L.
Goheen, Frank X.
Goodfellow, Ebenezer R.
Grant, Michael
Green, Wilfred
Griffis, Silas S.
Hainsworth, George
Hall, Joseph H.
Hay, George
Hern, William M.
Hextall, Bryan
Hooper, Charles T.
Horner, George R.
Howe, Sydney H.
Hutton, John B.
Hyland, Harry M.
Irvin, James D.
Johnson, Ernest
Johnson, Ivan
Joliat, Aurel
Keats, Gordon
Kelly, Red
Kennedy, Ted
Lach, Elmer
Lalonde, Edouard C
Laviolette, Jean B.
Lehman, Hugh
LeSueur, Percy
Lindsay, Robert T.
MacKay, Duncan
Malone, Joseph
Mantha, Sylvio
Marshall, John
Maxwell, Fred G.
McGee, Frank
McGimsie, William G.
McNamara, George

Moran, Patrick J.
Morenz, Howie
Mosienko, William
Nighbor, Frank
Noble, Edward R.
Oliver, Harold
Patrick, Lester
Phillips, Tommy
Pitre, Didier
Pratt, Walter
Primeau, A. Joseph
Pulford, Harvey
Rankin, Frank
Reardon, Kenneth
Richard, Joseph H. M.
Richardson, George T.
Ross, Arthur H.
Russell, Blair
Russell, Ernest
Ruttan, J. D.
Scanlan, Fred
Schmidt, Milton C.
Schriner, David
Seibert, Earl W.
Seibert, Oliver L.
Shore, Edward W.
Siebert, Albert C.
Simpson, Harold E.
Smith, Alfred E.
Stanley, Russell
Stewart, John S.
Stewart, Nelson
Stuart, Bruce
Stuart, Hod
Taylor, Frederic
Thompson, Cecil R.
Trihey, Col. Harry J.
Vézina, Georges
Walker, John Phillip
Walsh, Martin
Watson, Harry E.
Westwick, Harry
Whitcroft, Fred
Wilson, Gordon Allan
Worters, Roy

428

BUILDERS

Adams, Charles F.
Ahearn, Thomas F.
Allan, Sir Montague
Brown, George V.
Brown, Walter A.
Calder, Frank
Campbell, Angus D.
Campbell, Clarence S.
Dandurand, Joseph V.
Dilio, Francis P.
Dudley, George S.
Dunn, James A.
Gorman, Thomas P.
Hendy, James
Hewitt, Foster
Hewitt, William A.
Hume, Fred J.
Kilpatrick, Gen. John Reed
Leader, George A.
Lockhart, Thomas F.

Loicq, Paul
McLaughlin, Major Frederic
Nelson, Francis
Norris, Bruce A.
Norris Sr., James
Norris, James D.
Northey, William M.
O'Brien, John A.
Patrick, Frank
Pickard, Allan W.
Raymond, Sen. Donat
Robertson, John R.
Robinson, Claude C.
Selke, Frank J.
Smith, Frank D.
Smythe, Conn
Stanley of Preston, Lord
Sutherland, Capt. James T.
Turner, Lloyd
Waghorne, Fred C.

REFEREES

Chadwick, William L.
Elliotte, Chaucer
Hewitson, Robert W.
Ion, Fred J.

Rodden, Michael J.
Smeaton, J. Cooper
Storey, Roy Alvin

Surfing

The History of Surfing

The first recorded history of surfing was made two centuries ago in the South Pacific Islands. And the first surfers were the ancient Polynesians, who supposedly introduced surfing to Hawaii as early as 1778.

It is said that the first American to ride a board was George Freeth, who rode a wave off Redondo Beach in 1907. But the man generally accepted as introducing the comparatively new sport to the United States is Hawaiian Duke Kahanamoku, who started the sport in Australia and later helped bring it to California.

Most of the surfing breed are young and daring. They are youngsters with a language of their own, and up till a few years ago they were all but chased from the beaches. Swimmers constantly complained that the surfboards were dangerous and responsible for many accidents.

For several years, as the sport spread from the West Coast to the East, surfing was in general disrepute. The youngsters who first practiced the sport, in the fifties and early sixties, were disorganized. A few wild beach parties and some

Surfer rushing to get a good spot at Gilgo Beach, Long Island.

vandalism turned adult sentiment against them. They were called "beatniks on ironing boards."

It wasn't until the United States Surfing Association was formed that the sport gained respectability. In 1961 a group of surfing board manufacturers, lifeguards, and top surfers met in Southern California to try to save the sport before it was legislated out of existence. Committees and subcommittees were set up with strict rules for each district, and areas on beaches were set aside solely for the surfers. The sport survived, took root, and started to grow.

By 1968 surfing had kicked off its growing pains and was determined to gain acceptance as a respectable sport. Indeed, 1968 could be called the year surfing became an institution.

Various organizations, formerly operating on their own, joined forces to exchange ideas and fight for acceptance. Surfers refused to be typecast as beach bums, and they won their battle. The sport was no longer downcast as amateurism; professionalism surged to the foreground with a world's champion and United States champion crowned.

More important, new ideas burst forth. The products of these varied efforts were numerous: short boards, new shapes, speed concepts, lightweight foams, stronger glass, fins, shaping machines, and the introduction of the catamaran as a full-fledged surfing vehicle that was economically within reach of many surfers the world over.

With this universal growth, it appeared the next step for surfing would be inclusion as part of the Olympics.

Surfing had developed its own personalities, too, much in the same way that baseball had developed its Mickey Mantle

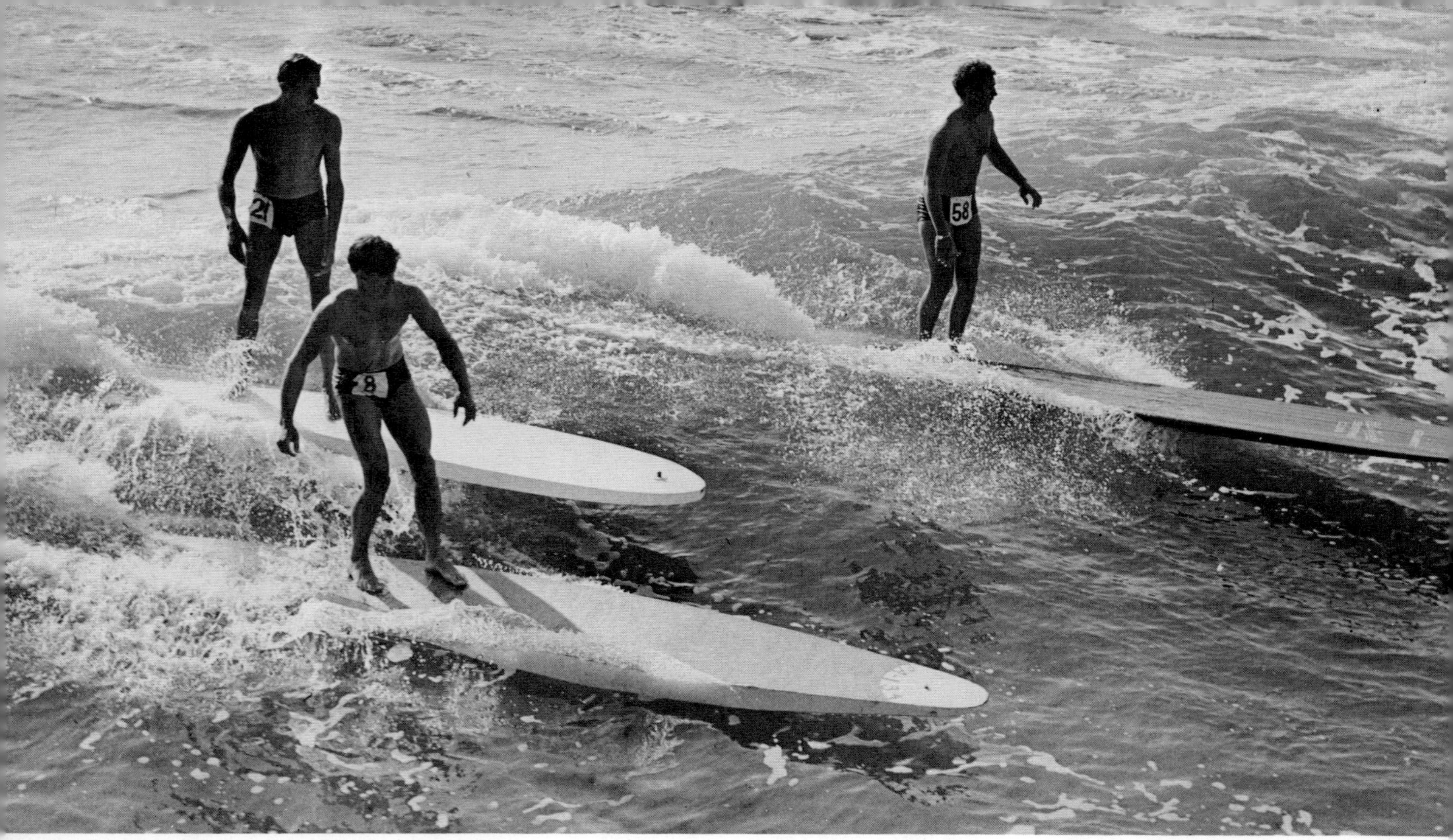

Acme Photo

and football its Joe Namath. There were Nat Young of Australia; Mike Doyle of California; Fred Hemmings, the world's champion who lived in Hawaii. And the women took their share of the spotlight, most notably Margo Godfrey, women's world champion, and Linda Benson, U.S. champion.

Today the sport has spread from the South Pacific, Hawaii, and California to Long Island's Gilgo Beach and beyond: Peru, France, Portugal, South Africa, and even Ceylon have their surfers.

Southern California is still the capital of surfdom. In 1965 a crowd of 10,000 turned out to watch the International Surf Festival with competitors from all over the world. In the United States alone, it is estimated there are more than a million surfers, and the number keeps rising as better surfboards are made.

During the early days of the sport there was no room for 97-pound weaklings. The surfboards, made of redwood, often weighed as much as 150 pounds and were up to 18 feet long. They were unwieldy and hard to control and the only people courageous enough to ride the surf did so on their stomachs. Then came the pioneers.

Bob Simmons, a former student at Cal Tech, experimented with a combination of balsa wood and varnish. He later turned to balsa with Fiberglas, and had developed a styrofoam board before he drowned off La Jolla in 1954.

One of the most popular boards used in the early '60's, still in use today, is a core of polyurethane foam covered with Fiberglas and resin. It is 8 feet 6 inches long and weighs from 13 to 15 pounds. The boards generally cost

437

Photo by Stanley Wolfson

Coming in on a wave.

around $90, but custom craftsmen charge anywhere from $125 to $175 to shape a board to the buyer's specifications.

Surfing is not without its dangers, such as crashing into several tons of water or slamming against submerged reefs and boulders. In 1964 eighteen surfers, all novices, drowned off the coast of California. But surfing has its splendid moments too, and a surfer is never more joyful than when he is standing on his board, skimming the crest of a swell at 30 to 40 miles an hour.

For novices it is like learning to walk on skis. At first it seems awkward and almost impossible, but after mastering the fundamentals a novice should experience the kick of riding a wave by the end of his first day in the surf.

With practice, a surfer can then master a "hot curl" by "hanging ten" (the toes of both feet gripping the front edge of the board), coast "goofyfoot" (the right leg in front of the left leg), and learn to keep cool while "pearling" (when the nose of the board dips below the water).

This sounds fine but no one should attempt surfing unless he can swim 100 yards at good speed, at least 500 yards at a relaxed speed, and a minimum of 50 yards underwater. It is also important that a surfer be able to float on the surface or to tread water for three minutes and to stay submerged for one-half to one minute. And he should keep his eyes open at all times.

If you can do all this you are qualified to try to ride the waves.

439

RIDING THE WAVES

In the United States we have "small wave" surfing. It is most popular in Southern California, where the waves are consistently shaped the best and the water is the warmest the year round. Storms far out at sea, the varying depths and composition of the surface beneath the water, and the shape of the shoreline contribute to the form of a wave.

The face of the wave is called a wall; the lip of the breaking wave, a hook; the cavern under the lip, a tube; and foam from a breaking wave is called soup. The ideal surfing wave is one that does not break all along its length at once. Small waves of 8 feet or less give the longest and steadiest rides; waves of 10 feet or more offer the fastest, most exciting rides.

THE GUNS

The old wooden surfboards, as noted earlier, were too long and too heavy. The new boards, or "guns," are made of fiberglass polyurethane, are 7 to 12 feet long, and weigh 20 to 40 pounds. They are streamlined and have fins to the rear. A thin board is best in small surf; a thick board is best in heavy surf. It is important to select a board to support your weight. The chart shows what board length is best according to body weight:

Body Weight	Board Length
85 pounds	8 feet 8 inches
100 pounds	8 feet 10 inches
115 pounds	9 feet
130 pounds	9 feet 2 inches
145 pounds	9 feet 4 inches
160 pounds	9 feet 6 inches
180 pounds	9 feet 8 inches
200 pounds	9 feet 11 inches
220 pounds	10 feet 2 inches

440

Competition

Surfing contests have recently reached international pro-
portions, with most of the activity taking place, naturally, on
the West Coast. This area of the sport, aside from attracting
large aggregations of spectators, is also of vital importance
to the science of lifesaving.

During the late summer of 1965, the Australian Lifeguard
Association arrived at Montauk Point, L.I., and tested its col-
lective skills in the crashing sea against various lifeguard
teams from twelve states along the East and West coasts.

Aside from the rather unusual method of amassing points
in the lifeguard contests, there are two methods of determining surfing skills:

In one, the contestants attempt to catch as many waves as
possible within a 90-minute span.

There are five judges who usually sit on 15-foot observa-
tion stands. With paper and pencil in hand, they observe
the individual performance, awarding points for wave size,
coordination, and the distance attained on single wave carries.

The final tally includes only the top scores made on the

441

best five waves ridden by each surfer. A perfect score for a single wave is 20 points. Such aspects as poise in mounting the board, balance, style, and length of the ride are of paramount concern. Among surfing enthusiasts it is generally agreed that a perfect score is not possible—just as a perfect score is rarely, if ever, achieved by figure skaters.

The other criterion for determining ability in surfing has been labeled "hot dogging." This contest is intended for top performers only, because of its high level of risk. It involves mounting a board, riding a wave, and performing acrobatic moves while skimming the top of a shifting crest of sea. Surfers do somersaults and handstands, and occasionally a girl and boy negotiate balancing feats amid the foam. This is definitely not advocated for persons who want to be around to collect their social security.

Listed below are the results of the 1968 United States Championships at Huntington Pier, Huntington Beach, California, and the World Championships at Rincon, Puerto Rico.

Huntington Beach

MEN'S DIVISION

1. David Nuuhiwa, Hermosa Beach
2. Mike Tabeling, Florida
3. Corky Carroll, Dana Point
4. Rolf Arness, Pacific Palisades
5. Mike Purpus, Hermosa Beach

WOMEN'S DIVISION

1. Linda Benson, Hermosa Beach
2. Shelly Merrick, Santa Monica
3. Margo Godfrey, Santa Barbara
4. Joyce Hoffman, San Diego
5. Joey Hamasaki, Venice

JUNIORS' DIVISION

1. Brad McCaul, Newport Beach
2. Bobby Michel, Hermosa Beach
3. Randy Lewis, Huntington Beach
4. Roger Adams, Santa Cruz
5. Jack Riddle, Santa Monica

Wildest surfing in the world: on the winter waves at Oahu, Hawaii.

BOYS' DIVISION

1. Chris Schlichenmeyer, Hermosa Beach
2. Bobby Burnside, Malibu
3. Leonard Foster, Newport Beach
4. Niles Osborne, Los Alamitos
5. John Meier, Los Alamitos

SENIOR MEN

1. Phil Vedder, Dana Point
2. Bob Holland, Virginia
3. Les Williams, Dana Point
4. LeRoy Grannis, Hermosa Beach
5. Fred Ashley, Encinatas

MIXED TANDEM

1. Ron Ball (San Jose) and Debbie Gustavson (Santa Cruz)
2. Steve Bochne (Fountain Valley) and Barrie Algau (Venice)
3. Bob Moore (Hawaii) and Patti Young (Glendale)
4. Hal Sachs (Capistrano Beach) and Sally Reid (Dana Point)
5. Jack Iverson (Newport Beach) and Ester Algau (Venice)

DORY RACING

1. LONG BEACH: Rick Hose, Scott Agee
2. LOS ANGELES COUNTY: Chick Mcllory, Paul Mathus
3. CARPENTERIA: Kenn Lynn, Frank Brooks
4. LONG BEACH: Bill Starr, Hank Bowell
5. LOS ANGELES COUNTY: Bob Burnside, Herb Barthels

PADDLEBOARD RACING

1. Bill Mount, Santa Monica
2. Corky Carroll, Dana Point
3. Bobby Burnside, Malibu

ALL-ROUND SURFER AWARD

(Duke Kahanamoku Perpetual Trophy)

Corky Carroll, Dana Point, Calif.

World Championships

MEN'S DIVISION

1. Fred Hemmings, Hawaii
2. Bernard (Midget) Farrelly, Australia
3. Russell Hughes, Australia
4. Nat Young, Australia
5. Mike Doyle, California
6. Reno Abellira, Hawaii

WOMEN'S DIVISION

1. Margo Godfrey, California
2. Sharron Weber, Hawaii
3. Phyllis O'Donnell, Australia
4. Martha Sunn, Hawaii
5. Candy Chase, Puerto Rico
6. Janice Domorski, East Coast

5,000-METER PADDLING RACE

Winning Team: West Coast (Bill Mount, Kenny Linn, Jerry Bennette, Mike Doyle).
Second Place: Australia (Midget Farrelly, Ted Spencer, Peter Drouyn, Nat Young).

MIXED TANDEM

1. Ron Ball-Debbie Gustafon, California
2. Dr. Robert Scott-Liz Herd, California & East Coast
3. Rodney Sumpter-Annete Hughes, Ireland & England
4. Fred Hemmings-Leslie Scott, Hawaii & California
5. Mike Doyle-Margo Godfrey, California

1968 MEN'S WORLD SURFING CHAMPION

Fred Hemmings, Hawaii

1968 WOMEN'S WORLD SURFING CHAMPION

Margo Godfrey, Santa Barbara, Calif.

The Surfer's Dictionary

BACKWASH: The water that rolls off the sand back into the ocean.

BAGGIES: A pair of loose-fitting bathing trunks usually made of canvas with a wild design in loud colors.

BEACH BUNNY: A girl who hangs around a beach where there are surfers, but who never goes surfing herself.

BELLYBOARD: A small board similar to a surfboard but no more than 5 feet long. Used for riding waves in a prone position.

BIG GUN: A large, narrow surfboard with a pintail used for riding big surf. Allows maximum speed on a wave.

CAKED ON: When a surfer gets carried away waiting for a lull and puts too much wax on his board.

CHEATING FIVE: Said of a surfer who reaches out with one foot to hang five toes over the nose of the surfboard while the rest of his body is toward the center of the board.

446

CLOSED OUT: When the waves have no foam and break the length of the beach at once. Usually occurs in a very large surf.

CRITICAL SECTION: The part of a perfectly formed wave that starts to break ahead of the curl.

CURL: The part of a wave that is breaking, usually hollow and crisp. It is the best part of the wave while riding.

CUT BACK: When a surfer has to change his direction on a wave.

DING: A dent or hole made in a surfboard.

DROP IN: When one surfer takes off on a wave and cuts in front of the path of another surfer who has already caught the wave.

FOAM: The core, or inside, of a surfboard.

GLASSY: A condition of the surf that occurs when there is no wind, causing the ocean and waves to look like green or blue glass.

GO LEFT: The cry a surfer gives when he wishes to go left on a wave.

GOOFYFOOT: Stance with the right foot forward on a surfboard.

GO RIGHT: Opposite of Go Left.

GREMMIE ACTION: Bad behavior on part of nonsurfers.

GRAB A RAIL: When the surfer bends down and grabs the side of the surfboard with one hand.

HANG FIVE: Movement of holding or hanging the toes of one foot over the nose of a surfboard.

HANG TEN: Holding or hanging the toes of both feet over the nose of a surfboard.

HEAVIES: Big surf.

HIGHWAY SURFER: Someone who drives around with a surfboard sticking out of his car window but who never surfs.

HODAD: A person who never surfs but who is constantly pointing out mistakes made by others.

HOTDOGGER: Surfer who is always doing tricks on the board.

JETTY: Rocks extending out into the water.

KAHUNA: Name given to leader of a surfing club.

KICKOUT: Action of riding to the end of a wave and turning the board to go out to sea again.

KILLERBOARD: A surfboard ending up on a wave without its rider.

KUK: A rookie surfer who is constantly getting into the way of others.

LULL: The calm surfers wait for so they may paddle out through the heavies.

NOSE: The front of a surfboard.

OUTSIDE: Cry heard when someone spots a large swell coming in from the ocean.

PEARL: When a surfboard dives down into the water instead of riding the wave.

PINTAIL: The pointed tail of a surfboard.

RAILS: The sides of surfboards.

ROLLERS: Waves that look like glassy humps in the water.

SEMI-GUN: Surfboard larger than a "hotdogger's" board but smaller than a "big gun."

SET: Waves come in from the ocean in groups of three. Usually the first wave is smallest, second wave medium-sized, third wave the largest.

448

SHOOTING THE PIER: Riding a wave through the piling of a pier.

SKEG: The rudder of a surfboard.

SLIDE: When a surfer rides the face of a wave.

SOUP: White water of a wave.

SPINNER: When a surfer spins or turns himself in a complete circle while riding a wave.

STRINGER: Wooden support in the middle of a surfboard extending from the nose to the tail. Usually made of redwood or balsa.

SWELL: The glassy hump that starts in deep water and later, upon entering shallow water, becomes a breaking wave.

TAIL: Rear part of a surfboard.

TANDEM: Two riders on a surfboard.

TUBE: Rolling of a wave in a hollow, pipelike formation.

WIPE-OUT: When a surfer falls or gets knocked off his surfboard.

Swimming

The History of Swimming

"C'mon in, the water's fine!"

It is not necessary to have a set of statistics to back up the statement that more people, in all parts of the world, engage in swimming than in any other sport.

People swim at all ages, from twenty months or younger to eighty years and over. They swim in oceans, rivers, lakes, streams, brooks, backyard pools, and old-fashioned mudholes. Many swim because it's fun, others because it offers the best exercise of all sports.

Swimming is the one sport that requires the use of all the muscles of the body. It teaches you how to breathe properly and how to make the best use of your arms and legs. It is highly recommended by doctors as an excellent all-round developer of the body.

You certainly have read of the back ailment of the late President John F. Kennedy. He was advised by his doctor to swim daily to build up the strength in his back muscles. President Franklin D. Roosevelt also swam regularly, to strengthen legs weakened by paralysis.

When did swimming begin? Probably the caveman found out how to swim by watching animals in the water. He may also have had to learn in order to escape from wild animals and hostile neighbors. The Old Testament mentions swimming, and it is known that the ancient gladiators swam during their training periods.

Early Middle Eastern drawings clearly show men and women using a stroke similar to a dog paddle, and several history books mention that Caesar was a swimmer of great endurance. Plato, the Greek philosopher, held that one who swam or dived was a person of great education.

The first country to recognize the competitive nature of the sport was England. In 1837, London had several indoor pools, and there were occasional competitive exhibitions of speed swimming.

Perhaps the first swimming tour for the purpose of competition occurred about 1845. At that time a group of American Indians went to London to compete against the English. History tells us that the Indians, particularly one by the name of Flying Gull, were clearly superior.

The swimming style of the Indians was something never before witnessed in Engand. They refused to use the "proper" strokes of the British, which were the breaststroke and the sidestroke. Instead, the invaders used strokes described as "uncivilized" because of the free manner in which they churned through the water.

Formal rules for competition were first established in England in 1869, when several clubs formed the Amateur Swimming Association. The contestants were more interested in distance than in speed. This resulted in several at-

Breaststroke competition in the 1960 Olympic Games at Rome, Italy.

tempts to swim the English Channel from England to France, a feat first performed by Captain Matthew Webb in 1875.

It was not until 1878 that the first world record was recognized. The honor fell to E. T. Jones, who swam 100 yards in 68.5 seconds, a snail's pace compared with the average time of 50 seconds in major competition nowadays.

All in all, swimming in the late 1870's was not particularly exciting as a competitive sport. The strokes used in those

days kept the arms and legs beneath the surface of the water, and it was difficult to improve greatly on speed.

A turning point came at this time, however, when an English family, the Cavills, emigrated to Australia. Frederick Cavill, a swimming enthusiast, was fascinated by the style employed by some Australian natives. He noticed that they were extremely fast swimmers because of the kicking action of their legs. It was a technique he had never seen, but he was quick to adopt it.

Cavill and his six sons built several swimming pools in their new country and taught this unusual method of swimming—the "Australian crawl"—to other Britons who had settled in Australia.

Encouraged by the enthusiastic response of their first pupils, the Cavills exported the Australian technique to England and the United States. One son, Richard, went back to England and won a number of championships, using the Australian crawl. He later coached many British international teams. A second son, Sydney, came to the United States and was a coach for twenty-five years.

Another Englishman, J. Arthur Trudgen, also is credited with giving the sport great impetus. Trudgen is generally recognized as the man who introduced the idea of lifting the arms *above* the surface of the water. This, combined with the kicking action of the legs, was the forerunner of the free style, the most popular of all swimming strokes.

Interest in swimming became so keen as a result of the Cavill and Trudgen innovations that the sport was made a part of the first modern Olympic Games in 1896.

The first American to swim 100 yards in 60 seconds was

Olympic divers practice for the 1960 competition in Rome.

J. Scott Leary, who employed the Australian crawl to turn the trick on July 18, 1905. Leary went on to win seventeen consecutive races. He became something of a national hero among American swimming devotees, and this in turn inspired others to take up competition in the United States.

Another influential figure in American swimming was Charles M. Daniels. He developed the "American crawl" by the simple trick of timing the kick to the stroking of the arms.

On March 23, 1906, Daniels set a world record of 56 seconds for 100 yards. He won a total of thirty-three national championships, from the 50-yard to the one-mile swim, captured four Olympic titles, and reached his peak on April 7, 1910, when he lowered his world mark for 100 yards to 54.8 seconds.

Since 1904, when Daniels won the 440-yard race to give the United States its first Olympic swimming crown, the country has been an aquatic leader. Today, competition in the States exists at almost every level, and some of our most popular athletic stars are young men and women who can, as the saying goes, swim like fish.

Great Names in Swimming

Swimmers should not be rated strictly on speed. They must be grouped according to the stroke used and the quality of competition.

Swimming records seldom last even a full year because techniques and coaching methods are constantly being improved. New theories on diet and food values also contribute to the development of the swimmer. Thus, the record of a standout performer of the early 1900's compares poorly with the speed marks of today.

Yet, as in other sports, swimmers—and divers, too—have entered fine performances in the record books through the years. They belong to a permanent part of the sport's history, even though their skills have been, or will be, surpassed.

The Olympic Games have provided the setting for many, perhaps most, of swimming's heroes. The first American swimmer to become a glamour figure was a native Hawaiian, the bronzed and flashy Duke Kahanamoku. He scored international free-style victories in both 1912 and 1920, high

459

points of a career in which he seemed to set a record every time he hit the water.

Then there was Johnny Weissmuller, whose name for years was on the lips of every American youngster who entered swimming competition. Handsome and smiling—the personification of the perfect athlete—Johnny, too, was a consistent record-smasher. In 1924 he became the first American to win two free-style events in the Olympics, at 100 and 400 meters. Weissmuller later went to Hollywood and won international fame as Tarzan in the movies.

Other outstanding American free-stylers have included Alan Ford, Wally Ris, Jimmy McLane, Steve Clark, and Don Schollander. Australia—a country as famous for its swimming stars as for its tennis greats—has contributed John Marshall, Murray Rose, and Jon Konrads.

Rose, who was graduated from the University of Southern California, was prepared for swimming greatness as a child. His parents believed in a revolutionary nonmeat diet, which consisted of fruits, nuts, and vegetables. It developed him into an aquatic dynamo who won three events in the 1956 Olympics and many national titles.

Konrads, with the help of his sister, Ilsa, practically monopolized the swimming scene for a time. In 1958, when Jon was fifteen and Ilsa thirteen, the brother-sister combination set sixteen of the thirty-one new world records reported for the year. Jon broke twenty world marks between January, 1958, and February, 1959. Ilsa, in a two-month period in 1958, set records for 800 meters, 880 yards, 1,500 meters and 1,650 yards.

But the most persistent record-breaker of all time was a

Dane, Ragnhild Hveger. From 1936 to 1942 he established new standards in a total of forty-one free-style and back-stroke events.

At the breaststroke, John Higgins, Leonard Spence, Joe Verdeur, and Australia's Terry Gathercole have been among the best. Bill Yorzyk and Mike Troy are rated all-time butterfly stroke leaders, and Adolph Kiefer, Al Stack, Frank Mc-Kinney, Charles Bittick, and Australia's John Monckton have been backstroke greats.

Kiefer must be considered the finest backstroke exponent America has ever produced. He was the king of this style for nine years, taking all national laurels from 1935 to 1943.

The women, too, have made swimming history. Ask grandfather about Gertrude Ederle, and he'll smile and recall how this daughter of a New York City butcher became famous in 1926 as the first woman to swim the English Channel.

Twenty-four years later Florence Chadwick won recognition as the greatest of all women distance swimmers. She not only became the first woman to swim the English Channel in both directions, but she was the first to navigate the treacher-

Duke Kahanamoku

Australia's Murray Rose (left) and Alan Somers (right) of Bloomington, Indiana.

ous waters of the Catalina Channel off the coast of California.

For sheer speed, no one ever performed more spectacularly than Helene Madison in the early 1950's, Ann Curtis in the mid-1940's, or Chris von Saltza in 1960.

Miss Madison was eighteen years old when she held fifteen indoor and outdoor marks; Miss Curtis helped wipe out all of Miss Madison's records, and sixteen-year-old Chris von Saltza was the first woman swimmer to win three Olympic gold medals—at the 400-meter free style and as a member of the United States team in the 400-meter free-style and 400-meter medley relays.

For both speed and versatility, Dawn Fraser of Australia demonstrated that she was in a class by herself. As an eighteen-year-old in 1956, she won the 100-meter Olympic free-style. In 1960 she became the first woman to defend successfully an Olympic swimming crown.

In 1962, at the age of twenty-five, when most swimmers have retired from competition, Dawn made her mightiest assault on the record books. In October she became the first woman to break the one-minute barrier in the 100-meter free style, doing it in 59.9 seconds. A month later she swam it in 59.5. On February 29, 1964, Dawn lowered the mark to 58.9.

In diving events, American men and women have been su-

Chris von Saltza

U. S. Olympic Association

preme. From the springboard, American men have won every Olympic test since 1920. From the high platform, the United States has produced nine of the thirteen champions since 1904. Albert White, in 1924, and Pete Desjardins, in 1928, were double winners.

Among women divers, eight of the nine springboard events and seven of the ten high platform competitions have been won by the United States. Pat McCormick is the queen of this realm, having won both events in 1952 and again in 1956.

The United States scored a swimming triumph at the 1964 Olympic Games when Don Schollander, at eighteen, became the first swimmer in the history of the Games to win four gold medals in a single Olympiad. The youngster was hailed as the greatest Olympian since Jesse Owens, the fabulous track star of the thirties.

At Tokyo, Schollander set an Olympic record when he was clocked in 53.4 seconds for the 100-meter free syle. In the 400-meter free style, Schollander set a world record of 4 minutes 12.2 seconds. In addition, he helped the United States to world records in the 400- and 800-meter free-style relays.

Schollander, who became a Yale student in 1965, has received numerous athletic awards, including the Grand Award of Sports, which designated him as the world's foremost athlete.

He was born Donald Arthur Schollander on April 30, 1946, in Charlotte, North Carolina; then the family moved to Lake Oswego, a suburb of Portland, Oregon. Young Don, who was introduced to swimming at the age of nine, has always coveted an Olympic gold medal. When he was fifteen he joined the Santa Clara (California) Swim Club, headed by George

Don Schollander

United Press International

Haines, one of the best swimming coaches in the United States. He had moved from Oregon, with his parents' consent, and attended Santa Clara High School, where he became active in swimming and water polo.

In April 1962, when he was sixteen, Don set a United States record of 4 minutes 18.3 seconds for the 440-yard free style at an AAU indoor meet at Bartlesville, Oklahoma. In August of that year he tied the world record for the 200-meter free style at 2 minutes 4 seconds. He really gained fame when he swam the 200-meter free style in 1 minute 58.8 seconds, the first swimmer in recorded competition to do it in less than 2 minutes.

Among his victories in 1963 was an American citizens' record of 4:17.7 in the 400-meter free style. He was a member of the Santa Clara Swim Club's team in the 800-meter free-style relay when the team was clocked at 8 minutes 7.6 seconds, then a world record. While touring Japan Schollander twice bettered his own record for the 200-meter free style, covering the distance in 1:58.5 and in 1:58.4.

Don kept moving ahead in 1964. He set an American standard of 1:42.6 for the 200-yard free style and 4:44.5 for the 500-yard free style; he crashed the world record with his 1 minute 57.6 seconds for 200 meters. He also set the world standard of 4:12.7 for 400 meters. The world had never seen anything like him.

Then in 1965, after winning a 200-meter free-style race at Bern, Switzerland, Schollander was stricken with mononucleosis, a glandular fever that frequently hits young people of college age. This knocked him out of any further competition.

Schollander, however, refused to give up. He said: "Swimming is my life. I want to continue. To compete on a high level of swimming you have to devote your life to it. Were I to retire now and succumb to the pressure of the public, look what I would miss."

It was a long, hard grind back. Through constant practice and determination, Schollander started to regain his form. And by 1967 Don had set two more records. He turned in 1:55.7 for a 200-meter free style record and 1:57 flat for the 220-yard free style. He was also a member of the record-breaking 800-meter free style U.S. relay team which turned in a 7:52.1 clocking. Also on that team were Steve Clark, Roy Saari, and Gary Ilman. Don went on to the 1968 Olympics but though he set no records he did pick up some medals as part of relay teams.

Don is 5 feet 11 inches tall, weighs 175 pounds, and has blond hair and brown eyes. A great swimmer and a courageous young man, he deserves every honor he gets.

In the pre-Olympic year of 1967, the world's best swimmers were Americans, mostly youngsters from California. Of the 32 world records for men, 16 were broken, 10 by Americans. Of the 30 world records for women, 21 were shattered, 14 by Americans.

The most productive of the Americans were seventeen-year-old Mark Spitz of Santa Clara, Calif., fifteen-year-old Catie Ball of Jacksonville, Fla., and fourteen-year old Debbie Meyer of Sacramento, Calif. They all won Amateur Athletic Union outdoor and indoor titles and Pan American Games championships.

Spitz was fantastic. He broke three world butterfly

records and for a short time held the world record for the 400-meter free style. Catie shattered four breaststroke records for women, and Debbie bettered world free style records for 400 meters, 800 meters, 880 yards, and 1,500 meters.

Another teenager, this one on the other side of the ocean, who began making great strides was Roland Matthes, a sixteen-year-old East German. He broke three world backstroke records. European teenage girls were not to be denied, either. Ada Kok of Holland set the butterfly mark and fourteen-year-old Karen Muir of South Africa became the new backstroke titleholder.

It seemed the swimming world was getting ready for the Olympics in 1968.

By 1968 the Americans were almost unbeatable. There were 16 world records for men up for grabs; 14 were broken, 8 by Americans. There were 15 world records for women; 12 were broken, 11 by Americans.

The year's best swimmers were Meyer, twenty-one-year-old Mike Burton of Carmichael, Calif., and twenty-one-year-old Charles Hickcox of Phoenix, Ariz.

Debbie won the women's 200, 400 and 800-meter freestyles in the Olympics. Five weeks before the Olympic trials she set a world record of 17:31.2 for 1,500 meters.

In one race Burton set world free style records of 8:34.3 for 800 meters and 16:08.5 for 1,500 meters, and he won Olympic titles at 400 and 1,500 meters.

Hickcox established world individual medley records of 2:10.6 for 200 meters and 4:39 for 400 meters, and he then won both gold medals in the Olympics.

468

The American swimmers were magnificent, and the rest of the world at those Mexico City Olympics applauded wildly at the accomplishments of these youngsters.

Swimming and Diving Techniques

Fastest of all swimming strokes is the free style. It is done with the body prone in the water, alternating the arms in a pulling motion while the feet kick in a steady flutter. The stroke provides a maximum of speed because there is little wasted motion.

The backstroke is the opposite of the free style. Swimming is done on the back, and the arms are pulled horizontally instead of vertically. The kicking action is almost the same, the power being provided by the upward, instead of the downward, motion of the feet.

The breaststroke is popular for enjoyment and relaxation. Since it demands less arm and leg action, it is a good stroke for distance swimming and very easy for beginners. The arms are moved together, forward and out, and the legs are kicked in a froglike manner—all of this action under the surface of the water.

The butterfly is the most recent of all strokes, coming along quite by accident in the early 1930's. Dissatisfied with the slow pace of the conventional breaststroke, various swimmers

Judges watch a diver enter the water in perfect form at the 1960 Olympic Games in Rome.

started to experiment by bringing the arms *over* the water. This stroke resembles the flapping wings of the butterfly, thus its name.

In diving, there are required dives for the 1-meter springboard, the 3-meter springboard, and the 10-meter platform. The six required dives are the forward, back, reverse, inward, twist, and handstand. Each of these can be performed in one of three positions—the pike (body in jackknife position), the layout (body almost rigid), and the tuck (body bunched) —and each carries a specific value of scoring points.

Point values vary according to the difficulty of the dive and the height from which it is made.

The optional dives are the same as the compulsory, but the diver has many choices within each group. For example, there are at least nine varieties of forward dives, seven of back and reverse, six of inward, and approximately twenty-five of twist and handstand dives.

All-Time Records

WORLD RECORDS

(As of January 1, 1969)

Separate world records for men and women are approved by the International Amateur Swimming Federation, known as FINA, which stands for Federation Internationale Natation Amateur. Records may be set indoors in fresh water or salt water pools. Until October of 1968, FINA abolished all records for distances in yards, retaining only those for corresponding distances in meters. Following are records in meters and yards.

METERS—MEN

Event and Record	Holder	Date
100-free style 52.2	Wenden, Mike (Australia)	10/19/68
200-free style 1:54.3	Schollander, Don (U.S.A.)	8/30/68
400-free style 4:06.5	Hutton, Ralph (Canada)	8/1/68
800-free style 8:34.3	Burton, Mike (U.S.A.)	9/3/68

Event and Record	Holder	Date
1,500-free style 16:08.5	Burton, Mike (U.S.A.)	9/3/68
100-breaststroke 1:06.2	Pankin, Nikolai (U.S.S.R.)	4/18/68
200-breaststroke 2:27.4	Kosinsky, Vladimir (U.S.S.R.)	4/3/68
100-butterfly 55.6	Spitz, Mark (U.S.A.)	8/30/68
200-butterfly 2:05.7	Spitz, Mark (U.S.A.)	10/8/67
100-backstroke 58.0	Matthes, Roland (E. Germany)	10/26/68
200-backstroke 2:07.5	Matthes, Roland (E. Germany)	8/14/68
200-individual medley 2:10.6	Hickcox, Charles (U.S.A.)	8/31/68
400-individual medley 4:39.0	Hickcox, Charles (U.S.A.)	8/30/68
400-free style relay 3:31.7	U.S.A. (Zorn, Rerych, Spitz, Walsh)	10/17/68
800-free style relay 7:52.1	U.S.A. (Clark, Saari, Ilman, Schollander)	10/18/64
7:52.1	Santa Clara S.C. (Ilman, Wall, Spitz, Schollander)	8/12/67
400-medley relay 3:54.9	U.S.A. (Hickcox, McKenzie, Russell, Walsh)	10/26/68

METERS—WOMEN

Event and Record	Holder	Date
100-free style 58.9	Fraser, Dawn (Australia)	2/29/64
200-free style 2:06.7	Meyer, Debbie (U.S.A.)	8/24/68
400-free style 4:24.5	Meyer, Debbie (U.S.A.)	8/25/68
800-free style 9:10.4	Meyer, Debbie (U.S.A.)	8/28/68
1,500-free style 17:31.2	Meyer, Debbie (U.S.A.)	7/21/68
100-breaststroke 1:14.2	Ball, Catie (U.S.A.)	8/25/68
200-breaststroke 2:38.5	Ball, Catie (U.S.A.)	8/26/68

474

Event and Record	Holder	Date
100-butterfly 1:04.5	Kok, Ada (Holland)	8/14/65
200-butterfly 2:21.0	Kok, Ada (Holland)	8/25/67
100-backstroke 1:06.2	Hall, Kaye (U.S.A.)	10/23/68
200-backstroke 2:23.8	Muir, Karen (South Africa)	7/21/68
200-individual medley 2:23.5	Kolb, Claudia (U.S.A.)	8/25/68
400-individual medley 5:04.7	Kolb, Claudia (U.S.A.)	8/24/68
400-free style relay 4:01.0	Santa Clara S.C. (Gustavson, Watson, Carpinelli, Henne)	7/6/68
400-medley relay 4:28.1	U.S.A. (Hall, Ball, Danie, Pedersen)	9/14/68

YARDS—MEN

Event and Record	Holder	Date
110-free style 53.5	McGregor, Robert (England)	9/10/68
220-free style 1:57	Schollander, Don (U.S.A.)	8/27/66
440-free style 4:12.2	Charlton, Greg (U.S.A.)	8/26/66
880-free style 8:55.5	Rose, Murray (Australia)	9/5/64
1,650-free style 17:11.0	Konrads, Jon (Australia)	2/27/60
110-breaststroke 1:08.2	O'Brien, Ian (Australia)	8/12/66
220-breaststroke 2:28	O'Brien, Ian (Australia)	8/6/66
110-butterfly 56.3	Spitz, Mark (U.S.A.)	10/30/67
220-butterfly 2:08.4	Berry, Kevin (Australia)	1/12/63
110-backstroke 1:00.1	Matthes, Roland (E. Germany)	9/20/67
220-backstroke 2:12	Reynolds, Peter (Australia)	8/9/66
440-individual medley 4:46.8	Holthaus, Michael (W. Germany)	8/20/68

Event and Record	Holder	Date
440-free style relay 3:35.6	Australia (Wenden, Dickson, Ryan, Windle)	8/11/66
880-free style relay 7:59.5	Australia (Wenden, Dickson, Ryan, Windle)	8/5/66
440-medley relay 4:03.2	Australia (Reynolds, O'Brien, Dunn, Wenden)	8/12/66

YARDS—WOMEN

Event and Record	Holder	Date
110-free style 59.5	Fraser, Dawn (Australia)	11/24/62
220-free style 2:11.6	Fraser, Dawn (Australia)	2/27/60
440-free style 4:38.8	Wainwright, Kathy (Australia)	8/12/66
880-free style 9:44.1	Meyer, Debbie (U.S.A.)	9/30/67
1,650-free style 18:47.8	Coughlan, Angela (Canada)	7/27/68
110-breaststroke 1:17	Ball, Catie (U.S.A.)	9/25/68
220-breaststroke 2:46.9	Ball, Catie (U.S.A.)	9/30/67
110-butterfly 1:05.1	Kok, Ada (Holland)	5/30/67
220-butterfly 2:21	Kok, Ada (Holland)	8/25/67
110-backstroke 1:06.7	Muir, Karen (South Africa)	1/30/68
220-backstroke 2:24.1	Muir, Karen (South Africa)	1/29/68
440-individual medley 5:25.1	Olcese, Mary Ellen (U.S.A.)	8/21/65
440-free style relay 4:10.8	Canada (Tanner, Hughes, Kennedy, Lay)	8/6/66
440-medley relay 4:37.4	U.S.A. (Watson, Ball, Daniel, Barkman)	9/30/67

Olympic Records

The Olympic Games, held every four years, not only provide the true international competition in swimming but produce records that have some degree of durability. Because the 1968 games were staged in Mexico City with its 7,350-foot altitude and 25 percent thinner air, it was doubtful any swim marks would fall. But they did, a tribute to the fine conditioning of the athletes. Americans won 11 of the 17 gold medals for men and 12 of the 16 for women.

MEN

Event and Record	Holder	Country
100-meter free style 52.2	Wenden, Michael	Australia
200-meter free style 1:55.2	Wenden, Michael	Australia
400-meter free style 4:09	Burton, Michael	United States
1,500-meter free style 16:38.9	Burton, Michael	United States
100-meter breaststroke 1:07.7	McKenzie, Don	United States
200-meter breaststroke 2:27.8	O'Brien, Ian	Australia
100-meter butterfly 55.9	Russell, Doug	United States
200-meter butterfly 2:06.6	Berry, Kevin	Australia
100-meter backstroke 58.7	Matthes, Roland	E. Germany
200-meter backstroke 2:09.6	Matthes, Roland	E. Germany
200-meter individual medley 2:12	Hickcox, Charles	United States

Event and Record	Holder	Country
400-meter free style relay 3:31.7	Zac Zorn, Steve Rerych, Mark Spitz, Ken Walsh	United States
400-meter individual medley 4:45.4	Roth, Dick	United States
400-meter medley relay 3:54.9	Charles Hickcox, Don McKenzie, Doug Russell, Ken Walsh	United States
800-meter free style relay 7:52.1	Steve Clark, Roy Saari, Gary Ilman, Don Schollander	United States

WOMEN

Event and Record	Holder	Country
100-meter free style 59.5	Fraser, Dawn	Australia
100-meter butterfly 1:04.7	Stouder, Sharon	United States
400-meter free style 4:31.8	Meyer, Debbie	United States
100-meter backstroke 1:06.2	Hall, Kaye	United States
100-meter breaststroke 1:15.8	Bjedov, Djurdjica	Yugoslavia
200-meter individual medley 2:24.7	Kolb, Claudia	United States
400-meter free style 4:02.5	Jane Barkman, Linda Gustavson, Sue Pedersen, Jan Henne	United States
200-meter butterfly 2:24.7	Kok, Ada	Holland
200-meter free style 2:10.5	Meyer, Debbie	United States
200-meter backstroke 2:24.8	Watson, Pokey	United States
800-meter free style 2:10.5	Meyer, Debbie	United States
400-meter individual medley 5:08.5	Kolb, Claudia	United States
200-meter breaststroke 2:44.4	Wichman, Sharon	United States
400-meter medley 4:28.3	Kaye Hall, Catie Ball, Ellie Daniel, Sue Pedersen	United States

478

College Champions

The annual swimming championships of the National Collegiate Athletic Association are held each March, with competition limited to men. Although this meet has been conducted since 1924, no team champion was recognized until 1937.

The coaching record of Yale's Bob Kiphuth is very likely the most outstanding ever put together by any coach in any area of sports. Kiphuth, who believed in a full-scale series of training drills on land before permitting his athletes to enter the water, became Yale coach in 1918 and retired in 1959. In those forty-two years his teams won 527 dual meets and lost only 12.

At one time or another, Kiphuth, Michigan's Matt Mann, and Ohio State's Mike Peppe coached American teams to glittering victories in the Olympic Games.

Year	Champion	Year	Champion
1970	Indiana	1953	Yale
1969	Indiana	1952	Ohio State
1968	Indiana	1951	Yale
1967	Stanford	1950	Ohio State
1966	Southern California	1949	Ohio State
1965	Southern California	1948	Michigan
1964	Southern California	1947	Ohio State
1963	Southern California	1946	Ohio State
1962	Ohio State	1945	Ohio State
1961	Michigan	1944	Yale
1960	Southern California	1943	Ohio State
1959	Michigan	1942	Yale
1958	Michigan	1941	Michigan
1957	Michigan	1940	Michigan
1956	Ohio State	1939	Michigan
1955	Ohio State	1938	Michigan
1954	Ohio State	1937	Michigan

479

Tennis

The History of Tennis

Millions of Americans, young and old, play or follow tennis with great enthusiasm today; and no other sport, except for track and field, has developed such keen competition among the nations of the world. But tennis did not always enjoy such widespread popularity.

For many years tennis was a game enjoyed only by the rich and the socially prominent. The majority of Americans looked upon it as a sissy sport.

Today, however, tennis knows no such limitations. Towns and cities throughout the country have their public as well as their private tennis courts. The game is played in high school and college. Clinics are held to teach boys and girls the fine points of the game at an early age.

According to some records, a form of lawn tennis, which is the kind of tennis we know today, was played as early as the 2nd century. Court tennis, played on a court enclosed by four walls, has a history that dates back to the 13th century.

It is generally agreed that the modern game of tennis was

Court tennis, as played in the 17th century.

born in England in 1873 and reached the United States the following year.

Credit for introducing the game goes to a British army major, Walter C. Wingfield. Some believe he merely took the features of court tennis, which usually was played indoors, and moved them to the outdoors. But the major himself said he got the idea after reading about a game that was popular among the ancient Greeks.

Major Wingfield tried out his new version of tennis at one of his lawn parties in 1873. It was an immediate hit, not only among the young men who played it but also among the older folks who watched while sipping their tea.

The playing area and the equipment were crude, but the action was swift. Major Wingfield's invention produced far

Tennis reaches Staten Island, New York.

more excitement than the British were accustomed to at their parties.

A few weeks later, one of Major Wingfield's fellow officers took a supply of rackets and balls with him to Bermuda for the amusement of the British regiment stationed there, and it was in Bermuda that the game attracted the attention of an American.

Mary Ewing Outerbridge, member of a wealthy Staten Island, New York, family, watched a contest while vacationing in Bermuda and became fascinated by it. She learned the rules, acquired some rackets and balls, and set sail for home.

A court was laid out on the grounds of the Staten Island Cricket and Baseball Club, and the first match on record in

485

the United States was played by Mary Outerbridge's brothers. Oddly, her sisters thought the game too "unladylike."

Word of the doings at the Cricket and Baseball Club spread rapidly, and it wasn't long before the entire social set on Staten Island was playing tennis. Within a year the new game was adopted by private clubs in New York, Philadelphia, Boston, Newport, and other cities where socialites gathered.

One of those most active in the early development of the game was Dr. James Dwight, later known as "the father of American lawn tennis." Dr. Dwight and F. R. Sears, Jr., elder brother of Richard Sears, our first national champion, laid out a court in Nahant, Massachusetts, during the summer of 1875. It was there that the first tournament in the United States was played in 1876.

By 1879 tennis was being played on crudely marked courts as distant as California. Controversy over rules and scoring made it evident that an organization to supervise the game was needed. In 1881 E. H. Outerbridge, an older brother of Mary, called a meeting in New York of representatives of Eastern clubs, and the United States Lawn Tennis Association was established.

R. S. Oliver was elected the first president of the USLTA, today the most important tennis body in the world. Dr. Dwight succeeded him in 1882 and went on to serve a total of twenty-one years in that office.

It was under Dr. Dwight's leadership that tennis in this country developed its strongest roots. He made a number of visits to England, where the famed Wimbledon tournament had been started in 1877, and brought back informa-

Richard D. Sears *James Dwight*

tion on rules and organization and on the leading players'
methods of play.

The first U. S. national tournament was played at Newport
Casino from August 31 to September 3, 1881, the singles
championship going to Richard Sears and the doubles to F.
W. Taylor and Clarence M. Clark.

Attendance at this event was small, and interest was limited largely to players and their friends, but tennis nevertheless had a firm footing. The national women's singles tourna-

ment was started in 1887, the doubles in 1890, and the mixed doubles in 1892.

The game not only flourished here and in England, but also started to gain participants in countries all over the globe. It began, for instance, in Brazil and India in 1875, in France in 1877, in Australia, Sweden, Italy, Hungary, and Peru in 1878, in Argentina in 1881, in Greece and Turkey in 1885, in Egypt in 1890, and in South Africa in 1892.

America's first great star was Sears, who won the U. S. singles championship seven straight years starting in 1881— a record never equaled. England's first immortal of the courts was William Renshaw, who won the British crown seven times, six in succession.

With the rapid growth of the game on a worldwide basis, it was only natural that an international competition should be set up, and in 1900 the Davis Cup, donated by Dwight F. Davis, was brought out for challenge.

Like the sport itself, Davis Cup competition was slow to gain momentum. In the first four years, only the United States and Great Britain competed for it, and even in 1920 only six countries took part. In 1921, however, the number of competing countries increased to twelve, and in 1928 there were thirty-three.

Little Bill Johnston

European

Fred Perry (right) and Bunny Austin

The 1920's brought with them the unforgettable Golden Era of Sports, and tennis came up with stars as famous and as idolized as those of baseball and football.

Big Bill Tilden, Little Bill Johnston, and Vinnie Richards were America's kingpins—colorful figures who featured a slashing, booming type of play that produced thrilling victories and put tennis up front on the sport pages.

Tilden, Johnston, and Richards kept the United States supreme in Davis Cup competition for seven years in a row, and Tilden ruled as our national champion for six years.

Next it was France's turn. With Jean René Lacoste, Henri Cochet, and Jean Borotra romping through championship after championship, France seized the Davis Cup from the United States in 1927 and held it for six straight years.

Then Britain came to the fore. Fred Perry and Henry (Bunny) Austin were the names in the headlines as England swept to four straight cup victories.

Don Budge and Frank Parker regained the cup for the United States in 1937, and Budge teamed with Bobby Riggs to keep it here in 1938. Since that year the Davis Cup challenge round has been mainly a duel between the United States and Australia, and the honors have been largely with Aussies, for whom tennis is almost a national disease.

Women, too, have played major roles in developing the popularity of the sport. Premier event for the girls is the Wightman Cup, placed in competition between the United States and Britain in 1923 by Hazel Hotchkiss Wightman.

A significant development in 1968 was the inception of open competition, meaning amateurs and professionals could compete in the same tournaments.

Great Britain was the first to establish an open—on the hallowed courts of Wimbledon, no less—and the United States followed suit with an open tournament at historic Forest Hills in New York.

The opens were just what tennis needed, giving a lift to both the amateur and professional games at a time when interest in the sport was sagging badly.

Great Names in Tennis

ARTHUR ASHE

The time may come when the color of a man's skin will not call for special mention, but as the final paragraphs of the decade of the 1960's were written in sports, it was still appropriate to refer to "firsts" scored by Negroes.

In the game of tennis, Arthur Ashe stood alone. He was the first Negro to win innumerable titles, but outstanding among them were the national amateur and the first United States Open, both in 1968. He also was the first Negro to represent the United States in Davis Cup competition, joining the team for the first time in 1963 and turning in his most impressive performance in 1969 with two singles victories in the challenge round.

Ashe, born on July 10, 1943, in Richmond, Virginia, was still in his teens when he first served notice of his talents on the tennis court. During the tournament season of 1960–61, he captured eighteen junior indoor singles titles and capped the sweep by being crowned national schoolboy champion.

491

In 1965, wearing the colors of the University of California at Los Angeles, he won the national intercollegiate singles tournament and shared the doubles championship.

He perfected his game despite the fact that he did little playing in his hometown. Most courts were denied him because of his race. This only strengthened his determination to make good, and he was not yet twenty years old when his name was well-known on the amateur tennis circuit.

By 1963, Ashe was ranked sixth in the national ratings. The next year he climbed to third, and in 1965 he was second. Then it seemed that Ashe had reached a point of arrested development, for he remained second in 1966 and 1967. But 1968 saw him come into full flower.

Playing in twenty-two tournaments and four Davis Cup zone matches that year, he compiled an average of .878 on 72 wins against only 10 losses, at one point winning 27 matches in a row. He was the victor in ten tournaments and split the two matches he played in the Davis Cup challenge round.

Arthur Ashe

Associated Press

Ashe provided the biggest American tennis thrills of '68 with his two proudest—and toughest—triumphs. In the finals of the national amateur, the tall, slim powerhouse outlasted Californian Bob Lutz, 4–6, 6–3, 8–10, 6–0, 6–4. And in the final match of the United States Open, he overcame Tom Okker of the Netherlands, 14–12, 5–7, 6–3, 3–6, 6–3.

DON BUDGE

Red-haired J. Donald Budge, a slim fireball with a flaming competitive spirit, is generally rated the best tennis player the United States has had since the immortal Bill Tilden.

In 1937 and 1938 Budge stood without challenge as the top amateur netman of the world. A recital of his victories is enough to prove that he deserved that high position.

In 1937 Don won the U. S. singles championship and was runner-up in the doubles. He won both the British singles and doubles and scored three Davis Cup victories, two in the singles and one in the doubles, as America crushed Great Britain in the challenge round. In 1938 the singles and doubles championships of both this country and Britain fell to his brilliant play, and he again was the hero of the Davis Cup final, beating both of Australia's aces in his singles matches.

Budge was ranked our number one amateur for three straight years (1936, 1937, and 1938)—something no other player has achieved since—and then startled the tennis world by turning professional.

As a professional player, Budge was no less exciting than he was as an amateur, for he brought with him the same

493

sizzling service and fluid-motion forehand and backhand that had beaten the world's best amateurs.

He won the pro singles championship in 1940 and 1942 and was runner-up to Bobby Riggs in 1946, 1947, and again in 1949. In the doubles, he was even more powerful, winning the tandem crown five times (with three different partners) and finishing as runner-up once between 1940 and 1949.

It was in 1933 that Budge first served notice of his tennis prowess by winning the national junior singles. He was named to our Davis Cup team in 1935 and lost both of  his singles matches to the British. But when he got to the U. S. singles final in 1936, America knew it had another great, even though he lost the title to England's Fred Perry.

Don was voted into the Hall of Fame in 1964.

Don Budge

Associated Press

PANCHO GONZALES

Boys and girls who feel they can't play tennis unless they take lessons should find ample inspiration in Richard Alonzo (Pancho) Gonzales.

Gonzales played the game for the first time at the age of twelve, after his mother had given him a fifty-cent racket for Christmas. He didn't have a formal lesson then and has never had one. But if a poll were taken among tennis experts to name the world's best player of recent years, many votes surely would go to Pancho.

The 6-foot-3 Californian was the world's finest amateur when he turned professional in 1949, and for twenty years was rated among the top pros.

A natural-born master of the game, Gonzales won the U. S. singles championship for the first time in 1948, when he was twenty years old.

Pancho Gonzales

United Press International

The following year brought even greater success. His most notable 1949 victory was in the U. S. singles. After losing the first two sets in the championship final to Ted Schroeder, 16–18, 2–6, he turned on the steam to win the next three, 6–1, 6–2, 6–4.

That same year Gonzales also won the indoor crown, shared in the Wimbledon doubles championship, was runner-up in the U. S. indoor doubles, and scored two victories for the United States in the Davis Cup challenge round against Australia.

Gonzales moved into command of the professionals in 1953 by beating every challenger.

Strange as it may seem, Pancho has long felt his all-round game could have been a lot better. But his serve has been clocked at 112.88 miles an hour, and his power, combined with his ability to cover the court, has been enough to make him supreme.

BILL JOHNSTON

William M. (Little Bill) Johnston, as short as Bill Tilden was tall, was Big Bill's keenest rival and finest partner on the amateur tennis court.

These two great champions met for the U. S. singles crown six times between 1919 and 1925. Johnston won only once, in 1919, but every battle between them was a rousing affair. Before 1919, Johnston had defeated Maurice McLoughlin for the title in 1915 and lost to him in 1916, so that in all, Little Bill was champion twice and runner-up six times.

In Davis Cup play he and Tilden gave the United States

its greatest reign. He was a member of our cup team every year from 1920 through 1927, and lost only three singles matches out of fourteen in the challenge round. He played two doubles matches and won both.

Although Johnston spent most of his career in the shadow of Tilden, he was a mighty figure in his own right. He was one of the greatest volleyers the game has known and had a wicked forehand drive.

The first "mighty mite" to attain prominence in the sports world, Little Bill ranked among the first ten netmen in the country twelve times in fourteen years, starting in 1913.

In addition to his achievements in the U. S. singles and in the Davis Cup matches, he won the national doubles with Clarence J. Griffin in 1915, 1916, and 1920 and was national clay court champion in 1919.

A particular tribute came his way when he was elected to the Hall of Fame in 1958, a year before the honor was conferred on Tilden—but twelve years after his death in 1946 at the age of fifty-one.

JACK KRAMER

In 1947 John A. (Jack) Kramer posted a record that is without equal in the history of tennis. He won every major championship in sight. The U. S. singles, the U. S. doubles, the indoor singles, the indoor doubles, the Wimbledon singles, the Wimbledon doubles—all of these titles were swept up by Jack the Giant. And he topped off the remarkable year by winning both of his singles matches against Australia in the Davis Cup challenge round.

With a smashing brand of play very much like Tilden's, Kramer won the U. S. singles title twice, the U. S. doubles four times, and the Wimbledon doubles twice. He played on our Davis Cup team in both 1946 and 1947, winning two singles matches in the challenge round each time without the loss of a set.

Kramer turned pro after his grand-slam year of 1947 and promptly became king of the professionals by winning both the singles and doubles in 1948. Jack might have continued as pro champ for many years, but he was more interested in the business side of tennis and took over promotion of professional tournaments.

Jack Kramer

VINCENT RICHARDS

Vinnie Richards began playing tennis at the age of eight, entered his first tournament at twelve, was a national champion (boys' singles) at fifteen, and became a member of the Davis Cup team at nineteen. Before his playing days were over, he won twenty-seven national titles in singles, doubles, and mixed doubles, and seven professional championships.

Richards never won the U. S. singles, chiefly perhaps because he turned professional in 1926, when he was only twenty-three and at his best.

A tremendous volleyer, the sandy-haired Vinnie teamed with Bill Tilden to win his first national doubles title in 1918. They triumphed again in 1921 and 1922, but then a bitter rivalry set in between these two greats, and Richard Norris Williams II was Richards' partner when he became doubles champ again in 1925 and 1926.

Richards' decision to turn pro was a blow to the amateur game, especially since he had helped the United States win the Davis Cup in 1924, 1925, and 1926. At the same time, however, he gave pro tennis the boost it needed and was its singles king in 1927, 1928, 1930, and 1933. He died in 1959.

BOBBY RIGGS

Robert L. (Bobby) Riggs proved that in tennis, as in other sports, a good little man can beat a good big man when his ability is backed up by a fighting heart.

The small, chunky Riggs made a habit, both as an amateur and as a professional, of winning championships by defeating opponents who were a full head taller than himself. He had a fine all-round game, legs that carried him around the court like a rabbit, and a will to win that was superb.

When Riggs won the national singles title in 1939, he defeated the towering Welby Van Horn. Don McNeill, a player nearer Riggs' own size, beat him in the 1940 final, but in 1941 it was big Frankie Kovacs who fell before Riggs.

If Bobby was a giant killer as an amateur, he was a David felling Goliaths in professional competition, to which he turned in 1942.

He and the powerful Don Budge went at each other tooth and nail as pros, and Budge came off second best. Bobby was world champion three times, in 1946, 1947, and 1949, and each time his victim was Budge. The only time Budge defeated him with a title at stake was in the 1942 final, and it took another big man, Jack Kramer, to conquer him in the 1948 final.

In the pro doubles, Riggs and Budge made a whale of a team. They were champions in 1942 and 1947 and runners-up in 1948. With other partners, Riggs finished second in the doubles again in 1946 and 1951.

Riggs' collection of amateur titles also included the Wimbledon singles and doubles (with Elwood Cooke) of 1939, the same year he won the U. S. singles, and the indoor singles and doubles of 1940. From 1936 through 1941, Bobby never ranked lower than 4th nationally and was top-ranked in 1939 and 1941.

BILL TILDEN

William Tatum (Big Bill) Tilden II was the greatest tennis player the world has ever known. Consider these achievements:

He won thirty-one national championships, outdoors and indoors, in singles, doubles, and mixed doubles.

He won the national singles title seven times, 1920 through 1925 and again in 1930, and was runner-up three times.

He was the first American to win the British Crown at Wimbledon, in 1920, and repeated in 1921 and 1930.

He was ranked number one player in the United States for ten consecutive years, beginning in 1920.

He played on the U. S. Davis Cup team eleven successive years, starting in 1920, and won a record thirteen singles matches in a row in the Challenge Round between 1920 and 1926.

After leaving the amateur ranks in 1930, the towering Tilden went on to reach new heights among the pros. Though he was past the age of forty, he captured the world singles title in 1931 and 1935, and continued as a headline attraction until he was almost fifty.

Bill Tilden

Like Babe Ruth in baseball, Jack Dempsey in boxing, and Bobby Jones in golf, Big Bill was a true monarch of his sport.

In 1928 he was the central figure of a crisis without parallel in the history of tennis. Tilden was captain of the team that went to France seeking to regain the Davis Cup for the United States. American tennis officials suddenly announced he would not be permitted to play. It was said that he had violated the amateur code. Tilden was under fire because he had written a series of articles for a San Francisco newspaper, a violation of the by-laws of the United States Lawn Tennis Association. This particular violation is known as the Amateur Rule. The violation came under paragraph four, Section B, which reads: "By writing for pay or a consideration current newspaper articles covering a tournament or match in which he is entered as a competitor."

The ruling set off an uproar on both sides of the Atlantic and threatened to upset relations between this country and France. Finally, the American ambassador stepped in and had Tilden reinstated. Big Bill scored the only victory for the United States in the Cup series, but was prevented that year from playing in the national championships back home.

Born in 1893, Tilden was playing tennis when he was barely old enough to hold a racket. By 1910 he had captured national attention in boys' competition. By 1920 he was the ace of aces.

Tilden died at the age of sixty in 1953, after having devoted his last years to teaching youngsters how to play the game he loved.

Lewis Hoad

Associated Press

OUTSTANDING FOREIGN PLAYERS

Besides the United States, three countries, Australia, Great Britain, and France, have produced the world's greatest tennis players.

In Australia, tennis is considered the national sport just as baseball is in this country. As a result, Australia has been in the Davis Cup Challenge Round every year but one between 1936 and 1965, has won the cup fourteen times in that span and has been the most consistent of all countries in the world in developing top-notch players.

503

Ken Rosewall

Frank Sedgman

In the early part of this century, Norman Brookes and Anthony Wilding were the tennis heroes of that distant land. Since 1936, when Australia returned to the heights after a lapse of some years, the Aussies have never lacked for stars.

Jack Crawford, Adrian Quist, John Bromwich, and Dinny Pails were the players who brought Australia back to international fame in the thirties and kept her there through the forties. The record of Bromwich was particularly outstanding. In addition to playing in six Davis Cup Challenge Rounds, he helped win three U. S. doubles titles and two Wimbledon doubles crowns.

In 1949 a new wave of Aussie greats began to sweep world tennis honors, and such superb players as Frank Sedgman, Lewis Hoad, Ken Rosewall, Ken McGregor, Rex Hartwig,

Malcolm Anderson, Ashley Cooper, Neale Fraser, and Rod Laver became as familiar to American net fans as our own stars.

Sedgman was number one amateur in the world when he turned professional in 1953. He won nine straight Davis Cup Challenge Round matches—six singles and three doubles —in 1950, 1951, and 1952, and fought his way to two championships in the U. S. singles, two in the U. S. doubles, one in the Wimbledon singles, and three in the Wimbledon doubles.

Hoad and Rosewall, who also turned pro, teamed up to deal the United States 5–0 defeats in the Davis Cup finals in 1955 and 1956, and Hoad went on to become Wimbledon champion twice in the singles and twice in the doubles.

How thoroughly the Aussies have ruled the game in recent years can be verified by the fact that they won seven U. S. and six Wimbledon singles titles from 1956 through 1962, losing only in 1959 to Alex Olmedo at Wimbledon. In 1962, Rod Laver captured every major singles title and then joined his fellow Australians on the pro tour.

As Laver left, Roy Emerson and Fred Stolle came in to keep the Australian supremacy alive. Emerson was the British singles champ in 1964 and 1965, with Stolle runner-up both times. Emerson was the player of the year in 1964, dethroning America's Chuck McKinley at Wimbledon and at Forest Hills, and was instrumental in bringing back the Davis Cup to Australia that year.

Laver, who had reached world heights as an amateur in 1962, performed the same feat as a professional in 1969 with another grand slam: the open championships of the United States, England, Australia and France.

As 1969 went into the record books, the left-handed wizard from Australia had the following notation placed alongside his name: "Without a doubt one of the great players of all time."

In the early years of tennis, Great Britain had most of the stars. She hasn't been able to reach the Davis Cup Challenge Round since 1937, and hasn't had a truly outstanding player since that time, but in the early and middle thirties two Englishmen—Fred Perry and Henry (Bunny) Austin—were the game's masters.

They gave the British a four-year sweep of the Davis Cup from 1933 through 1936, and Perry was the acknowledged world amateur king at a time when America and Australia had some of their greatest players. Perry still ranks as the

Jean Borotra

only foreigner to have won the U. S. singles title three times (1933, 1934, and 1936) and the only player since World War I to have captured the Wimbledon singles crown three years in a row (1934, 1935, and 1936).

In Davis Cup challenge play, Perry won nine out of ten singles matches, the last eight in a row, while Austin lost only three out of ten. Austin, further, was runner-up for the Wimbledon singles title in 1932 and 1938.

France, like Great Britain, has seen the tennis parade pass her by in the last quarter century, but between 1925 and 1933, three Frenchmen—Henri Cochet, Jean Borotra and Jean René Lacoste—were almost in a class by themselves. Not only did they keep the Davis Cup in France for six successive years, but they gathered up many individual honors at the same time.

Most durable of the three was Borotra, who played in nine Davis Cup Challenge Rounds between 1925 and 1933, winning four singles and two doubles matches, and who won a major title (the U. S. indoor doubles) as late as 1948.

Borotra was a fierce competitor on both outdoor and indoor courts. Outdoors, he was Wimbledon singles champion in 1924 and 1926, and was runner-up to fellow Frenchmen in 1925, 1927, and 1929. He won three Wimbledon doubles titles, the first in 1925 and the last eight years later. Indoors, Borotra captured four U. S. singles and three U. S. doubles championships—a record for a foreign entrant.

OUTSTANDING WOMEN

Many women hold places of honor in the history of tennis, but there is only one Helen Wills. Miss Poker Face, as she was affectionately known, brought with her a record beyond compare when she was voted into the Tennis Hall of Fame in 1959.

Seven times winner of the U. S. singles, eight times winner of the Wimbledon crown, Helen Wills (Mrs. Helen Wills Moody Roark) captured the American championship for the first time in 1923 and reigned as queen of the world's courts up to her retirement from tournament play in 1938.

Some of Miss Wills' fiercest battles were with her rival, Helen Jacobs, herself one of the game's all-time stars. They met for the Wimbledon title three times and the U. S. title twice. Only once was Miss Jacobs the winner—in 1933, when Miss Wills defaulted in the midst of their match for the U. S. crown because of a back injury.

Miss Jacobs did, however, win four U. S. titles—in four successive years—and one at Wimbledon, and compiled a record of fourteen victories in twenty-two Wightman Cup singles matches.

Another famous foe of Helen Wills was Molla Bjurstedt Mallory, the woman who comes closest to challenging her as all-time queen of the nets.

Mrs. Mallory won her first U. S. singles title in 1915 and her last in 1926. Her 1921 victory was over the famous French star, Suzanne Lenglen. They met again the following year in the final at Wimbledon; this time Miss Lenglen was the winner.

Actually, there was never a time when America lacked for great women players, and the crop has been especially abundant in recent years.

Since the heyday of Helen Wills and Helen Jacobs, the United States has produced such feminine stars as Alice

508

Marble, Sarah Palfrey Cooke, Pauline Betz, Louise Brough, Margaret Osborne duPont, Maureen Connolly, Doris Hart, Shirley Fry, Althea Gibson, Darlene Hard, Billie Jean Moffitt King, and Nancy Richey. Champions both here and abroad, they are among the reasons why the United States has almost monopolized the Wightman Cup.

Miss Marble, Miss Betz, Mrs. duPont, and Miss Connolly share the distinction of having won the U. S. singles championship three years in a row. Miss Brough and Mrs. duPont as a team won the U. S. doubles title a record twelve times, including nine years without a break, and the Wimbledon doubles five times. Miss Brough also is a three-time singles champion at Wimbledon.

Maureen (Little Mo) Connolly was only sixteen years old when she won her first U. S. singles in 1951, and the following year she began a string of three straight singles championships at Wimbledon.

In 1959, Althea Gibson became the first Negro to play in the U. S. championships at Forest Hills. By 1957 she was the greatest woman player in the world, winning both at Forest Hills and at Wimbledon—a feat she repeated in 1958. After that she turned to a singing career, and late in 1959 she joined the professional ranks of tennis.

Great Britain, too, has had top-flight women players through the years, including Kathleen McKane, Betty Nuthall, Dorothy Round, Kay Stammers, Angela Mortimer, Angela Buxton, and Christine Truman.

America's top star of the late 1960's was Billie Jean Moffitt King, who turned pro in 1968 after a blazing amateur career in which she won 31 national championships, 14 of them American.

All-Time Records

THE DAVIS CUP

The most famous tennis trophy in the world—and one of the most famous in all sports—is the Davis Cup, for which the tennis-playing nations of the world have competed since 1900.

The winner of the cup automatically defends it the following year after a series of eliminations to determine the challenger. Since 1902, the challenge round has consisted of four singles matches and one doubles match. Each match is decided by three out of five sets.

Year	Winner	Runner-up	Score
1969	United States	Romania	5–0
1968	United States	Australia	4–1
1967	Australia	Spain	4–1
1966	Australia	India	4–1
1965	Australia	Spain	4–1
1964	Australia	United States	3–2
1963	United States	Australia	3–2
1962	Australia	Mexico	5–0

Year	Winner	Runner-up	Score
1961	Australia	Italy	5–0
1960	Australia	Italy	4–1
1959	Australia	United States	3–2
1958	United States	Australia	3–2
1957	Australia	United States	3–2
1956	Australia	United States	5–0
1955	Australia	United States	5–0
1954	United States	Australia	3–2
1953	Australia	United States	3–2
1952	Australia	United States	4–1
1951	Australia	United States	3–2
1950	Australia	United States	4–1
1949	United States	Australia	4–1
1948	United States	Australia	5–0
1947	United States	Australia	4–1
1946	United States	Australia	5–0
1945–40	No competition—World War II.		
1939	Australia	United States	3–2
1938	United States	Australia	3–2
1937	United States	Great Britain	4–1
1936	Great Britain	Australia	3–2
1935	Great Britain	United States	5–0
1934	Great Britain	United States	4–1
1933	Great Britain	France	3–1
1932	France	United States	3–2
1931	France	Great Britain	3–2
1930	France	United States	4–1
1929	France	United States	3–2
1928	France	United States	4–1
1927	France	United States	3–2
1926	United States	France	4–1
1925	United States	France	5–0
1924	United States	* Australasia	5–0
1923	United States	Australasia	4–1
1922	United States	Australasia	4–1
1921	United States	Japan	5–0
1920	United States	Australasia	5–0
1919	Australasia	British Isles	4–1
1918–15	No competition—World War I.		
1914	Australasia	United States	3–2
1913	United States	British Isles	3–2
1912	British Isles	Australasia	3–2
1911	Australasia	United States	5–0
1910	Australasia	—	Default

Year	Winner	Runner-up	Score
1909	Australasia	United States	5–0
1908	Australasia	United States	3–2
1907	Australasia	British Isles	3–2
1906	British Isles	United States	5–0
1905	British Isles	United States	5–0
1904	British Isles	Belgium	5–0
1903	British Isles	United States	4–1
1902	United States	British Isles	3–2
1901	United States	—	Default
1900	United States	British Isles	3–0

* Australasia represented Australia and New Zealand.

THE WIGHTMAN CUP

Since 1923 the top women tennis players of the United States and England have competed annually for the Wightman Cup. American girls hold an overwhelming margin in the series.

Five singles and two doubles matches are played each year, with victory in two sets out of three deciding a match.

Year	Winner	Score	Year	Winner	Score
1969	United States	5–2	1954	United States	*6–0
1968	Great Britain	4–3	1953	United States	7–0
1967	United States	6–1	1952	United States	7–0
1966	United States	4–3	1951	United States	6–1
1965	United States	5–2	1950	United States	7–0
1964	United States	5–2	1949	United States	7–0
1963	United States	6–1	1948	United States	6–1
1962	United States	4–3	1947	United States	7–0
1961	United States	6–1	1946	United States	7–0
1960	Great Britain	4–3	1945–40	No competition—	
1959	United States	4–3		World War II.	
1958	Great Britain	4–3	1939	United States	5–2
1957	United States	6–1	1938	United States	5–2
1956	United States	5–2	1937	United States	6–1
1955	United States	6–1	1936	United States	4–3

Year	Winner	Score	Year	Winner	Score
1935	United States	4–3	1928	Great Britain	4–3
1934	United States	5–2	1927	United States	5–2
1933	United States	4–3	1926	United States	4–3
1932	United States	4–3	1925	Great Britain	4–3
1931	United States	5–2	1924	Great Britain	6–1
1930	Great Britain	4–3	1923	United States	7–0
1929	United States	4–3	* One match canceled by rain.		

The Hall of Fame

The National Tennis Hall of Fame, together with its museum, was established in 1954 in the Casino at Newport, Rhode Island, where the first U. S. championships were played in 1881. Members are elected by officers and directors of the National Tennis Hall of Fame and Tennis Museum.

MEN

Member	Year Elected	Member	Year Elected
Adee, George T.	1964	Kramer, John A.	1968
Alexander, Fred B.	1955	Larned, William A.	1956
Allison, Wilmer L.	1963	Larsen, Arthur	1969
Behr, Karl H.	1969	Lott, George M., Jr.	1964
Budge, J. Donald	1964	McLoughlin, Maurice E.	1957
Campbell, Oliver S.	1955	McNeill, W. Donald	1965
Chace, Malcolm G.	1961	Murray, R. Lindley	1958
Clark, Joseph S.	1955	Myrick, Julian S.	1963
Clothier, William J.	1956	Parker, Frank A.	1966
Danzig, Allison	1968	Pell, Theodore R.	1966
Davis, Dwight F.	1956	Richards, Vincent	1961
Doeg, John H.	1962	Riggs, Robert L.	1967
Dwight, Dr. James	1955	Schroeder, Frederick R.	1966
Garland, Charles S.	1969	Sears, Richard D.	1955
Gonzalez, Richard A.	1968	Shields, Frank	1964
Hackett, Harold H.	1961	Slocum, Henry W., Jr.	1955
Hunt, Joseph R.	1966	Talbert, William F.	1967
Hunter, Francis T.	1961	Tilden, William T., II	1959
Johnston, William M.	1958	Van Alen, James H.	1965

Van Ryn, John	1963	Williams, Richard Norris, II	1957
Vines, H. Ellsworth, Jr.	1962	Wood, Sidney, Jr.	1964
Ward, Holcombe	1956	Wrenn, Robert D.	1955
Washburn, Watson	1965	Wright, Beals C.	1956
Whitman, Malcolm	1955		

WOMEN

Member	Year Elected	Member	Year Elected
Addie, Pauline Betz	1965	Hart, Doris	1969
Allerdice, Ellen H.	1965	Jacobs, Helen Hull	1962
Brinker, Mrs. Maureen		Mallory, Molla B.	1958
Connolly	1968	Marble, Alice	1964
Browne, Mary K.	1957	Roark, Helen Wills Moody	1959
Bundy, May Sutton	1956	Sears, Eleanora	1968
Clapp, Mrs. Louise Brough	1967	Wagner, Marie	1969
Danzig, Sarah P.	1963	Wallach, Maud Barger	1958
DuPont, Mrs. Margaret		Wightman, Hazel Hotchkiss	1957
Osborne	1967		

United States Rankings

Each year, after all of the sanctioned tournaments have been played, the U. S. Lawn Tennis Association ranks the country's best men and women players. The men have been ranked since 1885; women's rankings started in 1913.

MEN

Year	Leading Player	Year	Leading Player
1969	Stan Smith	1961	Whitney Reed
1968	Arthur Ashe	1960	Barry MacKay
1967	Charles Pasarell	1959	Alejandro Olmedo
1966	R. Dennis Ralston	1958	Hamilton Richardson
1965	R. Dennis Ralston	1957	E. Victor Seixas, Jr.
1964	R. Dennis Ralston	1956	Hamilton Richardson
1963	Charles R. McKinley	1955	Tony Trabert
1962	Charles R. McKinley	1954	E. Victor Seixas, Jr.

Year	Leading Player	Year	Leading Player
1953	Tony Trabert	1918	R. Lindley Murray
1952	Gardnar Mulloy	1917	No ranking made.
1951	E. Victor Seixas, Jr.	1916	R. N. Williams II
1950	Arthur D. Larsen	1915	William M. Johnston
1949	Richard A. Gonzales	1914	Maurice E. McLoughlin
1948	Richard A. Gonzales	1913	Maurice E. McLoughlin
1947	John A. Kramer	1912	Maurice E. McLoughlin
1946	John A. Kramer	1911	William A. Larned
1945	Frank A. Parker	1910	William A. Larned
1944	Frank A. Parker	1909	William A. Larned
1943	Joseph R. Hunt	1908	William A. Larned
1942	Frederick R. Schroeder, Jr.	1907	William A. Larned
1941	Robert L. Riggs	1906	William J. Clothier
1940	W. Donald McNeill	1905	Beals C. Wright
1939	Robert L. Riggs	1904	Holcombe Ward
1938	J. Donald Budge	1903	William A. Larned
1937	J. Donald Budge	1902	William A. Larned
1936	J. Donald Budge	1901	William A. Larned
1935	Wilmer L. Allison	1900	Malcolm D. Whitman
1934	Wilmer L. Allison	1899	Malcolm D. Whitman
1933	Frank X. Shields	1898	Malcolm D. Whitman
1932	H. Ellsworth Vines, Jr.	1897	Robert D. Wren
1931	H. Ellsworth Vines, Jr.	1896	Robert D. Wren
1930	John H. Doeg	1895	Fred H. Hovey
1929	William T. Tilden II	1894	Robert D. Wren
1928	William T. Tilden II	1893	Robert D. Wren
1927	William T. Tilden II	1892	Oliver S. Campbell
1926	William T. Tilden II	1891	Oliver S. Campbell
1925	William T. Tilden II	1890	Oliver S. Campbell
1924	William T. Tilden II	1889	Henry W. Slocum, Jr.
1923	William T. Tilden II	1888	Henry W. Slocum, Jr.
1922	William T. Tilden II	1887	Richard D. Sears
1921	William T. Tilden II	1886	Richard D. Sears
1920	William T. Tilden II	1885	Richard D. Sears
1919	William M. Johnston		

WOMEN

Year	Leading Player	Year	Leading Player
1969	Nancy Richey	1965*	Billie Jean Moffitt
1968	Nancy Richey		Nancy Richey
1967	Billie Jean Moffitt King	1964	Nancy Richey
1966	Billie Jean Moffitt King	1963	Darlene R. Hard

Year	Leading Player	Year	Leading Player
1962	Darlene R. Hard	1937	Alice Marble
1961	Darlene R. Hard	1936	Alice Marble
1960	Darlene R. Hard	1935	Helen Jacobs
1959	Beverly Baker Fleitz	1934	Helen Jacobs
1958	Althea Gibson	1933	Helen Jacobs
1957	Althea Gibson	1932	Helen Jacobs
1956	Shirley J. Fry	1931	Helen Wills Moody
1955	Doris Hart	1930	Anna McC. Harper
1954	Doris Hart	1929	Helen Wills Moody
1953	Maureen Connolly	1928	Helen N. Wills
1952	Maureen Connolly	1927	Helen N. Wills
1951	Maureen Connolly	1926	Molla Bjurstedt Mallory
1950	Margaret O. duPont	1925	Helen N. Wills
1949	Margaret O. duPont	1924	Helen N. Wills
1948	Margaret O. duPont	1923	Helen N. Wills
1947	A. Louise Brough	1922	Molla Bjurstedt Mallory
1946	Pauline Betz	1921	Molla Bjurstedt Mallory
1945	Sarah P. Cooke	1920	Molla Bjurstedt Mallory
1944	Pauline Betz	1919	Hazel Hotchkiss Wightman
1943	Pauline Betz	1918	Molla Bjurstedt
1942	Pauline Betz	1917	No ranking made.
1941	Sarah P. Cooke	1916	Molla Bjurstedt
1940	Alice Marble	1915	Molla Bjurstedt
1939	Alice Marble	1914	Mary K. Browne
1938	Alice Marble	1913	Mary K. Browne

* Shared top ranking.

U. S. and British Champions

The outstanding tennis tournaments in the world are those played annually for the American and British championships.

The list of players who have won these titles reads like a Who's Who of tennis, and when a player wins both the American and British crowns in the same year, he (or she) gains a special place in the game's history.

The British tournaments are known as the Wimbledon championships because they are played on the most famous courts in the world—at Wimbledon, England. The U. S. championships are played at Forest Hills, New York.

Both the American and British tournaments were made open events beginning in 1968, with professionals as well as amateurs competing.

U. S. Champions—Men

OUTDOOR SINGLES

Year	Winner	Runner-up
1969	Rodney Laver	Tony Roche
1968	Arthur Ashe	Tom Okker
1967	John Newcombe	Clark Graebner
1966	Fred Stolle	John Newcombe
1965	Manuel Santana	Cliff Drysdale
1964	Roy Emerson	Fred Stolle
1963	Rafael Osuna	Frank Froehling
1962	Rodney Laver	Roy Emerson
1961	Roy Emerson	Rodney Laver
1960	Neale Fraser	Rodney Laver
1959	Neale Fraser	Alejandro Olmedo
1958	Ashley J. Cooper	Malcolm J. Anderson
1957	Malcolm J. Anderson	Ashley J. Cooper
1956	Kenneth Rosewall	Lewis Hoad
1955	Tony Trabert	Kenneth Rosewall
1954	E. Victor Seixas, Jr.	Rex Hartwig
1953	Tony Trabert	E. Victor Seixas, Jr.
1952	Frank Sedgman	Gardnar Mulloy
1951	Frank Sedgman	E. Victor Seixas, Jr.
1950	Arthur Larsen	Herbert Flam
1949	Richard A. Gonzales	Frederick R. Schroeder, Jr.
1948	Richard A. Gonzales	Eric W. Sturgess
1947	John A. Kramer	Frank A. Parker
1946	John A. Kramer	Tom P. Brown, Jr.
1945	Frank A. Parker	William F. Talbert
1944	Frank A. Parker	William F. Talbert

Year	Winner	Runner-up
1943	Joseph R. Hunt	John A. Kramer
1942	Frederick R. Schroeder, Jr.	Frank A. Parker
1941	Robert L. Riggs	Francis L. Kovacs II
1940	Donald McNeill	Robert L. Riggs
1939	Robert L. Riggs	S. Welby Van Horn
1938	J. Donald Budge	C. Gene Mako
1937	J. Donald Budge	Baron Gottfried von Cramm
1936	Fred J. Perry	J. Donald Budge
1935	Wilmer L. Allison	Sidney B. Wood, Jr.
1934	Fred J. Perry	Wilmer L. Allison
1933	Fred J. Perry	Jack Crawford
1932	H. Ellsworth Vines, Jr.	Henri Cochet
1931	H. Ellsworth Vines, Jr.	George M. Lott, Jr.
1930	John H. Doeg	Francis X. Shields
1929	William T. Tilden II	Francis T. Hunter
1928	Henri Cochet	Francis T. Hunter
1927	Jean René Lacoste	William T. Tilden II
1926	Jean René Lacoste	Jean Borotra
1925	William T. Tilden II	William Johnston
1924	William T. Tilden II	William Johnston
1923	William T. Tilden II	William Johnston
1922	William T. Tilden II	William Johnston
1921	William T. Tilden II	Wallace F. Johnson
1920	William T. Tilden II	William Johnston
1919	William Johnston	William T. Tilden II
1918	R. Lindley Murray	William T. Tilden II
1917	R. Lindley Murray	Nathaniel W. Niles
1916	R. N. Williams II	William Johnston
1915	William Johnston	Maurice E. McLoughlin
1914	R. N. Williams II	Maurice E. McLoughlin
1913	Maurice E. McLoughlin	R. N. Williams II
1912	Maurice E. McLoughlin	Wallace F. Johnson
1911	William A. Larned	Maurice E. McLoughlin
1910	William A. Larned	Thomas C. Bundy
1909	William A. Larned	William J. Clothier
1908	William A. Larned	Beals C. Wright
1907	William A. Larned	Robert Le Roy
1906	William J. Clothier	Karl H. Behr
1905	Beals C. Wright	Clarence Hobart
1904	Holcombe Ward	William J. Clothier
1903	Hugh L. Doherty	William J. Clothier
1902	William A. Larned	Reginald F. Doherty
1901	William A. Larned	Beals C. Wright
1900	Malcolm D. Whitman	William A. Larned

OUTDOOR DOUBLES

Year	Winners
1969	Kenneth Rosewall—Fred Stolle
1968	Stan Smith—Bob Lutz
1967	John Newcombe—Tony Roche
1966	Roy Emerson—Fred Stolle
1965	Roy Emerson—Fred Stolle
1964	Charles R. McKinley—R. Dennis Ralston
1963	Charles R. McKinley—R. Dennis Ralston
1962	Rafael Osuna—Antonio Palafox
1961	Charles R. McKinley—R. Dennis Ralston
1960	Neale Fraser—Roy Emerson
1959	Neale Fraser—Roy Emerson
1958	Alejandro Olmedo—Hamilton Richardson
1957	Ashley J. Cooper—Neale Fraser
1956	Lewis Hoad—Kenneth Rosewall
1955	Kosei Kamo—Atsushi Miyagi
1954	E. Victor Seixas, Jr.—Tony Trabert
1953	Rex Hartwig—Mervyn Rose
1952	Mervyn Rose—E. Victor Seixas, Jr.
1951	Kenneth McGregor—Frank Sedgman
1950	John Bromwich—Frank Sedgman
1949	John Bromwich—Billy Sidwell
1948	Gardnar Mulloy—William F. Talbert
1947	John A. Kramer—Frederick P. Schroeder, Jr.
1946	Gardnar Mulloy—William F. Talbert
1945	Gardnar Mulloy—William F. Talbert
1944	W. Donald McNeill—Robert Falkenburg
1943	John A. Kramer—Frank A. Parker
1942	Gardnar Mulloy—William F. Talbert
1941	John A. Kramer—Frederick R. Schroeder, Jr.
1940	John A. Kramer—Frederick R. Schroeder, Jr.
1939	Adrian K. Quist—John E. Bromwich
1938	J. Donald Budge—C. Gene Mako
1937	Baron Gottfried von Cramm—Henner Henkel
1936	J. Donald Budge—C. Gene Mako
1935	Wilmer L. Allison—John Van Ryn
1934	George M. Lott, Jr.—Lester R. Stoefen
1933	George M. Lott, Jr.—Lester R. Stoefen
1932	H. Ellsworth Vines, Jr.—Keith Gledhill
1931	Wilmer L. Allison—John Van Ryn
1930	George M. Lott, Jr.—John H. Doeg
1929	George M. Lott, Jr.—John H. Doeg

Year	Winners
1928	George M. Lott, Jr.—John F. Hennessey
1927	William T. Tilden II—Francis T. Hunter
1926	Vincent Richards—R. N. Williams II
1925	Vincent Richards—R. N. Williams II
1924	Howard O. Kinsey—Robert G. Kinsey
1923	William T. Tilden II—Brian I. C. Norton
1922	William T. Tilden II—Vincent Richards
1921	William T. Tilden II—Vincent Richards
1920	William Johnston—Clarence J. Griffin
1919	Norman E. Brooks—Gerald L. Patterson
1918	William T. Tilden II—Vincent Richards
1917	Fred B. Alexander—Harold A. Throckmorton
1916	William Johnston—Clarence J. Griffin
1915	William Johnston—Clarence J. Griffin
1914	Maurice. E. McLoughlin—Thomas C. Bundy
1913	Maurice E. McLoughlin—Thomas C. Bundy
1912	Maurice E. McLoughlin—Thomas C. Bundy
1911	Raymond D. Little—Gustave F. Touchard
1910	Harold H. Hackett—Fred B. Alexander
1909	Harold H. Hackett—Fred B. Alexander
1908	Harold H. Hackett—Fred B. Alexander
1907	Harold H. Hackett—Fred B. Alexander
1906	Holcombe Ward—Beals C. Wright
1905	Holcombe Ward—Beals C. Wright
1904	Holcombe Ward—Beals C. Wright
1903	Reginald F. Doherty—Hugh L. Doherty
1902	Reginald F. Doherty—Hugh L. Doherty
1901	Holcombe Ward—Dwight F. Davis
1900	Holcombe Ward—Dwight F. Davis

U. S. Champions—Women

OUTDOOR SINGLES

Year	Winner	Runner-up
1969	Margaret Smith Court	Nancy Richey
1968	Margaret Smith Court	Maria Bueno
1967	Billie Jean Moffitt King	Ann Haydon Jones
1966	Maria Bueno	Nancy Richey
1965	Margaret Smith	Billie Jean Moffitt
1964	Maria Bueno	Carole Graebner

Year	Winner	Runner-up
1963	Maria Bueno	Margaret Smith
1962	Margaret Smith	Darlene R. Hard
1961	Darlene R. Hard	Ann Haydon
1960	Darlene R. Hard	Maria Bueno
1959	Maria Bueno	Christine Truman
1958	Althea Gibson	Darlene R. Hard
1957	Althea Gibson	A. Louise Brough
1956	Shirley J. Fry	Althea Gibson
1955	Doris Hart	Patricia Ward
1954	Doris Hart	A. Louise Brough
1953	Maureen Connolly	Doris Hart
1952	Maureen Connolly	Doris Hart
1951	Maureen Connolly	Shirley Fry
1950	Margaret Osborne duPont	Doris Hart
1949	Margaret Osborne duPont	Doris Hart
1948	Margaret Osborne duPont	A. Louise Brough
1947	A. Louise Brough	Margaret E. Osborne
1946	Pauline M. Betz	Doris Hart
1945	Sarah Palfrey Cooke	Pauline M. Betz
1944	Pauline M. Betz	Margaret E. Osborne
1943	Pauline M. Betz	A. Louise Brough
1942	Pauline M. Betz	A. Louise Brough
1941	Sarah Palfrey Cooke	Pauline M. Betz
1940	Alice Marble	Helen Jacobs
1939	Alice Marble	Helen Jacobs
1938	Alice Marble	Nance Wynne
1937	Anita Lizana	Jadwiga Jadrzejowska
1936	Alice Marble	Helen Jacobs
1935	Helen Jacobs	Sarah Palfrey Cooke
1934	Helen Jacobs	Sarah Palfrey
1933	Helen Jacobs	Helen Wills Moody
1932	Helen Jacobs	Carolin Babcock
1931	Helen Wills Moody	Eileen Bennett Whittingstall
1930	Betty Nuthall	Anna McCune Harper
1929	Helen N. Wills	Phoebe Watson
1928	Helen N. Wills	Helen Jacobs
1927	Helen N. Wills	Betty Nuthall
1926	Molla Bjurstedt Mallory	Elizabeth Ryan
1925	Helen N. Wills	Kathleen McKane
1924	Helen N. Wills	Molla Bjurstedt Mallory
1923	Helen N. Wills	Molla Bjurstedt Mallory
1922	Molla Bjurstedt Mallory	Helen N. Wills
1921	Molla Bjurstedt Mallory	Mary K. Browne
1920	Molla Bjurstedt Mallory	Marion Zinderstein
1919	Hazel Hotchkiss Wightman	Marion Zinderstein
1918	Molla Bjurstedt	Eleanor Goss
1917	Molla Bjurstedt	Marion Vanderhoef
1916	Molla Bjurstedt	Louise Hammond Raymond
1915	Molla Bjurstedt	Hazel Hotchkiss Wightman

Year	Winner	Runner-up
1914	Mary K. Browne	Marie Wagner
1913	Mary K. Browne	Dorothy Green
1912	Mary K. Browne	Eleanora Sears
1911	Hazel V. Hotchkiss	Florence Sutton
1910	Hazel V. Hotchkiss	Louise Hammond
1909	Hazel V. Hotchkiss	Louise Hammond
1908	Maud Barger-Wallach	Marie Wagner
1907	Evelyn Sears	Carrie B. Neely
1906	Helen Homans	Maud Barger-Wallach
1905	Elisabeth H. Moore	Helen Homans
1904	May G. Sutton	Helen Homans
1903	Elisabeth H. Moore	Carrie B. Neely
1902	Marion Jones	Carrie B. Neely
1901	Elisabeth H. Moore	Marion Jones
1900	Myrtle McAteer	Edith Parker

OUTDOOR DOUBLES

Year	Winners
1969	Francoise Durr—Darlene R. Hard
1968	Margaret Smith Court—Maria Bueno
1967	Billie Jean Moffitt King—Rosemary Casals
1966	Maria Bueno—Nancy Richey
1965	Carole Graebner—Nancy Richey
1964	Billie Jean Moffitt—Karen Hantze Susman
1963	Margaret Smith—Robyn Ebbern
1962	Darlene R. Hard—Maria Bueno
1961	Darlene R. Hard—Lesley Turner
1960	Darlene R. Hard—Maria Bueno
1959	Jeanne M. Arth—Darlene R. Hard
1958	Jeanne M. Arth—Darlene R. Hard
1957	A. Louise Brough—Margaret Osborne duPont
1956	A. Louise Brough—Margaret Osborne duPont
1955	A. Louise Brough—Margaret Osborne duPont
1954	Shirley Fry—Doris Hart
1953	Shirley Fry—Doris Hart
1952	Shirley Fry—Doris Hart
1951	Shirley Fry—Doris Hart
1950	A. Louise Brough—Margaret Osborne duPont
1949	A. Louise Brough—Margaret Osborne duPont
1948	A. Louise Brough—Margaret Osborne duPont
1947	A. Louise Brough—Margaret E. Osborne
1946	A. Louise Brough—Margaret E. Osborne
1945	A. Louise Brough—Margaret E. Osborne

Year	Winners
1944	A. Louise Brough—Margaret E. Osborne
1943	A. Louise Brough—Margaret E. Osborne
1942	A. Louise Brough—Margaret E. Osborne
1941	Sarah Palfrey Cooke—Margaret E. Osborne
1940	Sarah Palfrey Cooke—Alice Marble
1939	Sarah Palfrey Fabyan—Alice Marble
1938	Sarah Palfrey Fabyan—Alice Marble
1937	Sarah Palfrey Fabyan—Alice Marble
1936	Marjorie G. Van Ryn—Carolin Babcock
1935	Helen Jacobs—Sarah Palfrey Fabyan
1934	Helen Jacobs—Sarah Palfrey
1933	Betty Nuthall—Freda James
1932	Helen Jacobs—Sarah Palfrey
1931	Betty Nuthall—Eileen Bennett Whittingstall
1930	Betty Nuthall—Sarah Palfrey
1929	Phoebe Watson—Mrs. L. R. C. Michell
1928	Hazel Hotchkiss Wightman—Helen N. Wills
1927	Kathleen McKane Godfrey—Ermyntrude Harvey
1926	Elizabeth Ryan—Eleanor Goss
1925	Mary K. Browne—Helen N. Wills
1924	Hazel Hotchkiss Wightman—Helen N. Wills
1923	Kathleen McKane—Mrs. B. C. Covell
1922	Marion Zinderstein Jessup—Helen N. Wills
1921	Mary K. Browne—Mrs. R. H. Williams
1920	Marion Zinderstein—Eleanor Goss
1919	Marion Zinderstein—Eleanor Goss
1918	Marion Zinderstein—Eleanor Goss
1917	Molla Bjurstedt—Eleanora Sears
1916	Molla Bjurstedt—Eleanora Sears
1915	Hazel Hotchkiss Wightman—Eleanora Sears
1914	Mary K. Browne—Mrs. R. H. Williams
1913	Mary K. Browne—Mrs. R. H. Williams
1912	Dorothy Green—Mary K. Browne
1911	Hazel V. Hotchkiss—Eleanora Sears
1910	Hazel V. Hotchkiss—Edith E. Rotch
1909	Hazel V. Hotchkiss—Edith E. Rotch
1908	Evelyn Sears—Margaret Curtis
1907	Marie Weimer—Carrie B. Neely
1906	Mrs. L. S. Coe—Mrs. D. S. Platt
1905	Helen Homans—Carrie B. Neely
1904	May G. Sutton—Miriam Hall
1903	Elisabeth H. Moore—Carrie B. Neely
1902	Juliette P. Atkinson—Marion Jones
1901	Juliette P. Atkinson—Myrtle McAteer
1900	Edith Parker—Hallie Champlin

British Champions

MEN'S SINGLES

Year	Winner	Runner-up
1969	Rodney Laver	John Newcombe
1968	Rodney Laver	Tony Roche
1967	John Newcombe	Wilhelm Bungert
1966	Manuel Santana	R. Dennis Ralston
1965	Roy Emerson	Fred Stolle
1964	Roy Emerson	Fred Stolle
1963	Charles R. McKinley	Fred Stolle
1962	Rodney Laver	Martin Mulligan
1961	Rodney Laver	Charles R. McKinley
1960	Neale Fraser	Rodney Laver
1959	Alejandro Olmedo	Rodney Laver
1958	Ashley J. Cooper	Neale Fraser
1957	Lewis Hoad	Ashley J. Cooper
1956	Lewis Hoad	Kenneth Rosewall
1955	Tony Trabert	Kurt Nielsen
1954	Jaroslav Drobny	Kenneth Rosewall
1953	E. Victor Seixas, Jr.	Kurt Nielsen
1952	Frank Sedgman	Jaroslav Drobny
1951	Richard Savitt	Kenneth McGregor
1950	Budge Patty	Frank Sedgman
1949	Frederick R. Schroeder, Jr.	Jaroslav Drobny
1948	Robert Falkenburg	John Bromwich
1947	John A. Kramer	Tom P. Brown, Jr.
1946	Yvon Petra	Geoff Brown
1945–40	No tournament.	
1939	Robert L. Riggs	Elwood T. Cooke
1938	J. Donald Budge	H. W. Austin
1937	J. Donald Budge	Gottfried von Cramm

Year	Winner	Runner-up
1936	Fred J. Perry	Gottfried von Cramm
1935	Fred J. Perry	Gottfried von Cramm
1934	Fred J. Perry	Jack H. Crawford
1933	Jack H. Crawford	H. Ellsworth Vines, Jr.
1932	H. Ellsworth Vines, Jr.	H. W. Austin
1931	Sidney B. Wood, Jr.	Frank X. Shields
1930	William T. Tilden II	Wilmer L. Allison
1929	Henri Cochet	Jean Borotra
1928	Jean René Lacoste	Henri Cochet
1927	Henri Cochet	Jean Borotra
1926	Jean Borotra	Howard Kinsey
1925	Jean René Lacoste	Jean Borotra
1924	Jean Borota	Jean René Lacoste
1923	William M. Johnston	F. T. Hunter
1922	G. L. Patterson	R. Lycett
1921	William T. Tilden II	Brian I. C. Norton
1920	William T. Tilden II	Zenzo Shimizu
1919	G. L. Patterson	A. R. F. Kingscote
1918–15	No tournament.	
1914	N. E. Brookes	O. Froitzheim
1913	A. F. Wilding	Maurice E. McLoughlin
1912	A. F. Wilding	A. W. Gore
1911	A. F. Wilding	H. R. Barrett
1910	A. F. Wilding	Beals C. Wright
1909	A. W. Gore	M. J. G. Ritchie
1908	A. W. Gore	H. R. Barrett
1907	N. E. Brookes	A. W. Gore
1906	Hugh L. Doherty	F. L. Riseley
1905	Hugh L. Doherty	N. E. Brookes
1904	Hugh L. Doherty	F. L. Riseley
1903	Hugh L. Doherty	F. L. Riseley
1902	Hugh L. Doherty	M. J. G. Ritchie
1901	A. W. Gore	C. P. Dixon
1900	R. F. Doherty	S. H. Smith

MEN'S DOUBLES

Year	Winners	Year	Winners
1969	John Newcombe—Tony Roche	1965	John Newcombe—Tony Roche
1968	John Newcombe—Tony Roche	1964	Robert Hewitt—Fred Stolle
1967	Robert Hewitt—Fred McMillan	1963	Rafael Osuna—Antonio Palafox
1966	Kenneth Fletcher—John Newcombe	1962	Robert Hewitt—Fred Stolle

Year	Winners	Year	Winners
1961	Neale Fraser—Roy Emerson	1930	Wilmer L. Allison—John Van Ryn
1960	R. Dennis Ralston—Rafael Osuna		
1959	Neale Fraser—Roy Emerson	1929	Wilmer L. Allison—John Van Ryn
1958	Sven Davidson—Ulf Schmidt		
1957	Gardnar Mulloy—Budge Patty	1928	Henri Cochet—J. Brugnon
1956	Lewis Hoad—Ken Rosewall	1927	William T. Tilden II—Francis T. Hunter
1955	Rex Hartwig—Lewis Hoad		
1954	Rex Hartwig—Mervyn Rose	1926	Henri Cochet—J. Brugnon
1953	Lewis Hoad—Ken Rosewall	1925	Jean Borotra—Jean René Lacoste
1952	Kenneth McGregor—Frank Sedgman	1924	Vincent Richards—Francis T. Hunter
1951	Kenneth McGregor—Frank Sedgman	1923	R. Lycett—L. A. Godfree
		1922	R. Lycett—J. O. Anderson
1950	John Bromwich—Adrian Quist	1921	R. Lycett—M. Woosnam
1949	Richard Gonzales—Frank Parker	1920	R. N. Williams II—C. S. Garland
1948	John Bromwich—Frank Sedgman	1919	R. V. Thomas—P. O'Hara Wood
		1918–15	No tournament.
1947	John A. Kramer—Robert Falkenburg	1914	N. E. Brooks—A. F. Wilding
		1913	H. R. Barrett—C. P. Dixon
1946	John A. Kramer—Tom Brown	1912	H. R. Barrett—C. P. Dixon
1945–40	No tournament.	1911	M. Decugis—A. H. Gobert
1939	Robert L. Riggs—Elwood T. Cooke	1910	A. F. Wilding—M. J. G. Ritchie
		1909	A. W. Gore—H. R. Barrett
1938	J. Donald Budge—C. Gene Mako	1908	A. F. Wilding—M. J. G. Ritchie
1937	J. Donald Budge—C. Gene Mako	1907	N. E. Brooks—A. F. Wilding
1936	G. P. Hughes—C. R. D. Tuckey	1906	S. H. Smith—F. L. Riseley
1935	Jack H. Crawford—Adrian Quist	1905	R. F. Doherty—H. L. Doherty
		1904	R. F. Doherty—H. L. Doherty
1934	G. M. Lott, Jr.—L. R. Stoefen	1903	R. F. Doherty—H. L. Doherty
1933	Jean Borotra—J. Brugnon	1902	S. H. Smith—F. L. Riseley
1932	Jean Borotra—J. Brugnon	1901	R. F. Doherty—H. L. Doherty
1931	John Van Ryn—George M. Lott, Jr.	1900	R. F. Doherty—H. L. Doherty

WOMEN'S SINGLES

Year	Winner	Runner-up
1969	Ann Haydon Jones	Billie Jean Moffitt King
1968	Billie Jean Moffitt King	Judy Tegart
1967	Billie Jean Moffitt King	Ann Haydon Jones
1966	Billie Jean Moffitt King	Maria Bueno
1965	Margaret Smith	Maria Bueno
1964	Maria Bueno	Margaret Smith
1963	Margaret Smith	Billie Jean Moffitt
1962	Karen Hantze Susman	Vera Sukova
1961	Angela Mortimer	Christine Truman
1960	Maria Bueno	Sandra Reynolds
1959	Maria Bueno	Darlene R. Hard

Year	Winner	Runner-up
1958	Althea Gibson	Angela Mortimer
1957	Althea Gibson	Darlene R. Hard
1956	Shirley J. Fry	Angela Buxton
1955	A. Louise Brough	Beverly B. Fleitz
1954	Maureen Connolly	A. Louise Brough
1953	Maureen Connolly	Doris Hart
1952	Maureen Connolly	A. Louise Brough
1951	Doris Hart	Shirley J. Fry
1950	A. Louise Brough	Margaret Osborne duPont
1949	A. Louise Brough	Margaret Osborne duPont
1948	A. Louise Brough	Doris Hart
1947	Margaret Osborne	Doris Hart
1946	Pauline Betz	A. Louise Brough
1945–40	No tournament.	
1939	Alice Marble	Kay E. Stammers
1938	Helen Wills Moody	Helen Jacobs
1937	Dorothy E. Round	Jadwiga Jadrzejowska
1936	Helen Jacobs	Mrs. Svend Sperling
1935	Helen Wills Moody	Helen Jacobs
1934	Dorothy E. Round	Helen Jacobs
1933	Helen Wills Moody	Elizabeth Ryan
1932	Helen Wills Moody	Helen Jacobs
1931	Cecile Aussen	Elia de Alvarez
1930	Helen Wills Moody	Dorothy E. Rounds
1929	Helen Wills	Helen Jacobs
1928	Helen Wills	H. Krahwinkel
1927	Helen Wills	Elia de Alvarez
1926	Kathleen McKane Godfrey	Elia de Alvarez
1925	Suzanne Lenglen	J. Fry
1924	Kathleen McKane	Helen Wills
1923	Suzanne Lenglen	H. McKane
1922	Suzanne Lenglen	Molla Bjurstedt Mallory
1921	Suzanne Lenglen	Elizabeth Ryan
1920	Suzanne Lenglen	Dorothy Douglass Chambers
1919	Suzanne Lenglen	Mrs. Satterthwaite
1918–15	No tournament.	
1914	Dorothy Douglass Chambers	Ethel W. Larcombe
1913	Dorothy Douglass Chambers	Mrs. McNair
1912	Ethel W. Larcombe	Charlotte Cooper Sterry
1911	Dorothy Douglass Chambers	Dorothea Boothby
1910	Dorothy Douglass Chambers	Miss Johnson
1909	Dorothea Boothby	A. M. Morton
1908	Charlotte Cooper Sterry	A. M. Morton
1907	May G. Sutton	C. M. Wilson
1906	Dorothy K. Douglass	Charlotte Cooper Sterry
1905	May G. Sutton	C. M. Wilson
1904	Dorothy K. Douglass	Charlotte Cooper Sterry
1903	Dorothy K. Douglass	Miss Thompson
1902	M. E. Robb	A. M. Morton
1901	Charlotte Cooper Sterry	Miss Martin
1900	Blanche Bingley Hillyard	Charlotte Cooper

WOMEN'S DOUBLES

Year	Winners
1969	Margaret Smith Court—Judy Tegart
1968	Billie Jean Moffitt King—Rosemary Casals
1967	Billie Jean Moffitt King—Rosemary Casals
1966	Maria Bueno—Nancy Richey
1965	Maria Bueno—Billie Jean Moffitt
1964	Margaret Smith—Lesley Turner
1963	Maria Bueno—Darlene R. Hard
1962	Karen Hantze Susman—Billie Jean Moffitt
1961	Karen Hantze—Billie Jean Moffitt
1960	Darlene R. Hard—Maria Bueno
1959	Jeanne M. Arth—Darlene R. Hard
1958	Maria Bueno—Althea Gibson
1957	Althea Gibson—Darlene R. Hard
1956	Angela Buxton—Althea Gibson
1955	Angela Mortimer—Anne Shilcock
1954	A. Louise Brough—Margaret Osborne duPont
1953	Shirley Fry—Doris Hart
1952	Shirley Fry—Doris Hart
1951	Shirley Fry—Doris Hart
1950	A. Louise Brough—Margaret Osborne duPont
1949	A. Louise Brough—Margaret Osborne duPont
1948	A. Louise Brough—Margaret Osborne duPont
1947	Doris Hart—Patricia Canning Todd
1946	A. Louise Brough—Margaret Osborne
1945–40	No tournament.
1939	Alice Marble—Sarah Palfrey Fabyan
1938	Alice Marble—Sarah Palfrey Fabyan
1937	René Mathieu—A. M. Yorke
1936	Katherine E. Stammers—Freda James
1935	Katherine E. Stammers—Freda James
1934	Elizabeth Ryan—René Mathieu
1933	Elizabeth Ryan—René Mathieu
1932	D. Metaxa—J. Sigart
1931	Mrs. D. C. Shepherd Barron—Phyllis Mudford King
1930	Elizabeth Ryan—Helen Wills Moody
1929	Phoebe Watson—Peggy Saunders Michell
1928	Phoebe Watson—Peggy Saunders
1927	Elizabeth Ryan—Helen Wills
1926	Elizabeth Ryan—Mary K. Browne
1925	Suzanne Lenglen—Elizabeth Ryan
1924	Hazel Hotchkiss Wightman—Helen Wills

Year	Winners
1923	Suzanne Lenglen—Elizabeth Ryan
1922	Suzanne Lenglen—Elizabeth Ryan
1921	Suzanne Lenglen—Elizabeth Ryan
1920	Suzanne Lenglen—Elizabeth Ryan
1919	Suzanne Lenglen—Elizabeth Ryan
1918–15	No tournament.
1914	Elizabeth Ryan—A. M. Morton
1913	Mrs. McNair—Dorothea Boothby

Track and Field

The History of Track and Field

If it's continuous action you like best, you can't beat a track meet. The sprinters dash headlong to provide the close finishes. The hurdlers, combining speed and grace, add precision, beauty, and excitement. The milers, beginning with easy strides, furnish lung-bursting, heart-pounding final efforts as they strain to hit the tape.

The field events—high and broad jumps, javelin and discus, pole vault and shot-put—are just as spectacular to watch. So you can see that a track meet is a rather exciting show, especially with two or three events going on at the same time.

These activities are popular all over the world and are the main events in the Olympic Games. In the United States, competition begins in school and continues in college. For those who wish to continue the sport longer, there are athletic clubs and organizations that are members of the Amateur Athletic Union, the AAU.

We can trace the origins of some track and field events back to primitive man, who chased animals and ran from

533

those that turned on him. Primitive man was therefore a "runner." To capture animals he had to track them down and kill them by throwing a stone or club. Thus primitive man was a crude "shot-putter," or maybe a "javelin thrower" if the object he hurled was a piece of wood with a sharp point.

Often he had to jump over obstacles and leap from rock to rock to escape unfriendly tribes or man-eating animals. These were the first forms of high jumping, broad jumping, and hurdling—necessary functions of day-to-day living that survived through the centuries down to the early civilizations.

In ancient Greece athletes were greatly admired, especially runners and jumpers. But the mightiest of all sports heroes were those who hurled the discus. And competitive athletics in ancient Greece were as popular as they are in the world today. A series of running and throwing events, begun in the 8th century B.C., was the forerunner of the modern Olympic Games. The Games, conducted every four years, bring together amateur athletes from all over the world for the purpose of competition.

Athletes from the United States have dominated most of the runs from 100 meters through 800 meters, most of the jumps, the pole vault, discus throw, and shot-put. The metric system of measurement is used in Olympic competition, but all school racing in the United States is measured in yards. A meter is approximately 1.094 yards. Thus the 100-meter dash is longer than the 100-yard dash by about 9⅓ yards.

Track and field in America is held both indoors and outdoors and is a year-round sport. The major school meets are

An Olympic champion drives his chariot through a throng of admirers in ancient Greece. Victory in the Olympics made a Greek a national hero, and the populace showered him with gifts.

held outdoors in the spring; the athletic clubs stage their top outdoor meets in early summer.

Indoor events are limited according to the facilities and space available. The major event on most indoor programs is the mile run, and the same competitors will clash week after week in different cities. Some of the better known indoor meets are those of the Millrose Athletic Association, New York Athletic Club, Knights of Columbus, Boston Athletic Association, and the AAU.

Although marks set indoors are called world records, they are not officially recognized as such by the International Amateur Athletic Foundation, which approves only outdoor records.

To indicate the difference between competing indoors and outdoors: As of September 1, 1962, the outdoor mile had been run in under 4 minutes seventy-odd times by more than thirty men. But not until February 10, 1962, did anyone (Jim Beatty, 3:58.9, at Los Angeles) ever break 4 minutes indoors. Indoor races are run on boards, and the tracks, which vary in size and contour, are not as fast as outdoor cinder tracks.

The more popular outdoor meets are conducted by the Intercollegiate Association of Amateur Athletes of America (IC4A), the AAU, the NYAC, the National Collegiate Athletic Association (NCAA), and the various college conferences that hold their own championships.

The running events draw the greatest number of entrants and, along with the high jump, hold the most interest for spectators. Time records for the dashes and runs have been lowered over a period of years. Many credit improved coach-

XVth Olympic Games, Helsinki 1952—the U. S. team parades.

ing methods and stronger competition for the better marks. But no matter how it has come about, it is a fact that every running record set a generation ago has since been broken.

Many years ago a 100-yard-dash man was top flight when he ran the distance in a bit better than 10 seconds. This is no longer true. The world record is now 9.1 seconds, established in 1963 by Bob Hayes.

A 220-yard-dash man who could run it in about 22 seconds was of championship quality. But in 1956 Dave Sime of Duke did it in the world-record time of 20 seconds. Frank Budd of Villanova tied it in 1962. Tommie Smith broke the record of 1966 when he was clocked in 19.5.

Running the 440 in 47 seconds and the 880 in 1 minute 50 seconds were headline achievements a generation ago.

In fact, Ben Eastman, one of the great middle-distance runners of the 1930's, held records for both events. In 1932 he did the 440 in 46.4 seconds, and in 1934 he ran the 880 in 1:49.8. Compare these records with the present world marks of 44.8 in the 440 (by Tommie Smith in 1967) and 1:44.9 in the 880 (by Jim Ryun in 1966). These are amazing performances when we consider that men, not machines, have bettered the records.

Over the years, the event that has attracted the most attention has been the mile run. America has had its share of great milers, and in recent years most of the top competitors have had only one thought in mind when starting their run—to break the 4-minute barrier.

The first miler of reputation was Walter George of England. In 1882 his time of 4 minutes 20 seconds was hailed throughout the sports world. Four years later, he ran the mile in slightly over 4 minutes 12 seconds, slicing almost 8 seconds from his previous record. Then the milers of the world set their sights on running the distance in 4 minutes 10 seconds.

From Finland, where track men are trained for endurance runs instead of sprints, came an athlete who revolutionized the method of running the mile. He was Paavo Nurmi, a tireless competitor who introduced the system of "level-pace" running. Level-pace running is a theory based on running each quarter of a mile (440 yards) in about the same time. Nurmi's system of perfect pacing paid off in 1923, and he shattered most existing running records—from the mile (which he ran in 4:10.4), to the one-hour-run record of better than 11 miles.

Nurmi was an outstanding member of the colorful sporting picture of the Golden Twenties. Golf had Bobby Jones; boxing, Jack Dempsey; baseball, Babe Ruth; tennis, Bill Tilden; and track had Paavo Nurmi.

During the 1930's and 1940's many milers achieved the 4:10 mile. Among the outstanding milers of this era were Glenn Cunningham, Bill Bonthron, and Gene Venzke from America; Jack Lovelock of New Zealand; and Luigi Beccali of Italy.

Paavo Nurmi
United Press International

Now milers frequently were hitting around 4 minutes 5 seconds, and during the mid-1940's it was apparent that the 4-minute barrier would be broken some day. Two of Sweden's fastest—Gunder Hagg and Arne Andersson—were regarded as the ones to do it, and both almost succeeded.

Andersson did the distance in 4:1.6; later, Hagg lowered it to 4:1.4.

During the next nine years, Wes Santee of Kansas, Roger Bannister of England, and John Landy of Australia attempted to better Hagg's time. Finally Bannister, a medical student from Oxford University, did the distance in 3:59.4—on May 6, 1954—seventy-two years after his countryman had established a world record of 4 minutes 20 seconds.

But the Englishman's mark stayed in the record books for only a little over a month. John Landy, the

Glenn Cunningham

United Press International

Australian, attained a 3:58 mark at Turku, Finland, on June 21. Two men had now broken the elusive barrier in less than forty-five days! But the track world was yet to receive its greatest surprise.

Bannister and Landy were scheduled to compete against each other for the first time. Their historic meeting at the British Empire games in Vancouver, British Columbia, received worldwide attention. It was covered by television and movie cameras, radio, and the press.

Landy led for half a mile, but Bannister, running the sounder race under the Nurmi level-pace system, came from behind to win.

Bill Bonthron
Princeton University

The first race in history in which two runners ran the mile in less than four minutes. England's Roger Bannister crosses the finish line ahead of Australia's John Landy during the 1954 British Empire Games at Vancouver, B. C.

No new records were set, but for the first time two athletes covered the distance in less than four minutes in the same race. Bannister's time was 3:58.8; Landy was clocked at 3:59.6.

There have been electrifying moments and sparkling achievements in every sport. But never has there been so dramatic an event as the one that took place on August 6, 1958, in Dublin. Herb Elliott of Australia ran what was then the fastest mile in history. But Elliott was not the only man to crack the barrier that day. No fewer than five runners ran the mile in less than four minutes, and a barrier that athletes

542

had sought to conquer for more than twenty years suddenly crumbled.

Elliott's record time was 3:54.5. Right on his heels were Merv Lincoln of Australia (3:55.9), Ron Delaney of Ireland and Murray Halberg of New Zealand (3:57.5), and Al Thomas, also of Australia (3:58.6).

Herb Elliott of Australia sets a new world record for the mile at Dublin in 1958 in a race that saw five men finish in well under four minutes.

United Press International

As remarkable as it was, Elliott's record could not survive. A twenty-two-year-old New Zealander, Peter Snell, lowered the time to 3:54.4 on January 27, 1962, in a race at Wanganui, New Zealand—and he did it on a grass track, which is considered slower than other surfaces.

Snell broke his own record when he was clocked at 3:54.1 in November 1964 in Auckland, New Zealand. Then France's Michel Jazy lowered the mark to 3:53.6 on June 9, 1965, in Rennes, France. America's Jim Ryun lowered that by a little better than two seconds when he did 3:51.1 in 1967 at Bakersfield, California.

Track and field championships in which a clear-cut winner in each event could be recognized first began in America in 1876. Since 1888 these championships have been held annually under the sponsorship of the AAU of the United

States. The winners of these annual meets are given recognition as American champions.

Although almost all the running events are measured in yards, an exception is made during an Olympic year, when all major outdoor meets in our country are under the metric system. This is to help qualify members for the Olympic team that will represent our country in the Games.

To compete in the Olympics is the dream of American boys and girls who excel in some form of track and field. They practice their special events for years, hoping some day to represent our country in this most famous of all international sports competitions. To compete is an honor; to win is perhaps the most exciting moment of an athlete's career.

The first Olympics were held in 776 B.C. They took place every four years until they were abolished in A.D. 393 by the Roman emperor Theodosius I. For 1,500 years the world had no Olympics. Then Pierre, Baron de Coubertin, decided to revive the glory of the Golden Age of Greece. Through his efforts an international conference of nine nations met in 1894 and voted to resume athletic competition among the nations of the world. The first modern Olympics were held in Athens in 1896, marking the start of I Olympiad (the four-year interval between Olympic Games). Except for the war years 1916, 1940, and 1944, they have been held as planned.

Olympic Games Highlights

American athletes demonstrated their prowess in the first modern Olympics in 1896. Tom Burke (100- and 400-meter dashes), Ellery Clark (running high and broad jumps), and Bob Garrett (shot put and discus throw) each scored double triumphs.

In the Games of the II Olympiad at Paris in 1900, Alvin Kraenzlein took four events (110- and 200-meter hurdles, running broad jump, and 60-meter dash), and Ray Ewry won all three standing jumps (broad, high, and hop, step, and jump).

The third Olympics in 1904 were the first held in the United States, and only ten other countries decided to send squads to St. Louis, Missouri. Ewry again won his three standing jump specialties. Other triple winners were Archie Hahn (60-, 100-, and 200-meter dashes), Jim Lightbody, an Indian (800- and 1,500-meter runs and 2,500-meter steeplechase), and Harry Hillman (400-meter run, 200- and 400-meter hurdles).

International disputes marked the Games at London in

1908. Finishes were unusually close and officials' decisions were not accepted with good grace. Athletes from the United States and Great Britain won twenty-three of the twenty-seven events. The 60-meter run, 200-meter hurdles, and standing hop, step, and jump were dropped from the Games that year. It was the last Olympic appearance for Ewry, who won two more gold medals to bring his Olympic record total to eight. Mel Sheppard (800- and 1,500-meter runs) and Marty Sheridan (discus, American and Greek styles) were double winners for the United States.

Stockholm was the site of the fifth Olympics in 1912 and the scene of the greatest one-man performance by an American. Jim Thorpe, later an All-American football player, won the two most grueling events—the pentathlon (200- and 1,500-meter runs, discus and javelin throws, and broad jump) and decathlon (100-meter run, broad jump, shot put, high jump, 400-meter run, 110-meter hurdles, discus, pole vault, javelin, and 1,500-meter run)—only to be denied entrance in the record books when he was later disqualified for being a professional athlete. (He had once accepted money for playing in a baseball game.) However, other U. S. athletes took fourteen of the thirty-one events, and Ralph Craig won both the 100-meter and 200-meter runs. Finland, which won six events, had a triple winner in Hannes Kolehmainen, who took the 5,000-meter and 10,000-meter runs and the 8,000-meter cross-country.

The First World War canceled the Games of the VI Olympiad, and it was not until 1920, in Antwerp, that the Games were resumed. This meeting marked the debut of Paavo Nurmi of Finland, one of the great distance runners.

548

Nurmi won the 10,000-meter and cross-country events. Of the twenty-nine track and field events, Finland won nine, as did the United States.

Nurmi was at his peak in the 1924 Olympics at Paris. In one day he won the 1,500- and 5,000-meter runs, an unparalleled performance. He put the icing on the cake by win-

The great Indian athlete—Jim Thorpe.

United Press International

A dramatic moment in the 1936 Olympic Games in Berlin. Wearing the laurels of victory, winners in the broad jump are shown saluting officials. Jesse Owens, whose leap broke the previous Olympic record, stands in the center. In front is Naoto Tajina of Japan (third); behind is Lutz Long of Germany, who placed second.

ning the cross-country run. For the United States, Hal Osborn (high jump and decathlon) and Clarence Houser (shot put and discus) were outstanding.

The Games of the IX Olympiad at Amsterdam in 1928 saw American runners turn in their poorest performance. Outside of team victories in the 400-meter and 1,600-meter relays, the only track winner was Ray Barbuti in the 400-meter run. In 1928 track and field events for women appeared for the first time, and Elizabeth Robinson of the United States won a gold medal in the 100-meter run.

Los Angeles was host to the 1932 Olympics. Mildred (Babe) Didrikson, the greatest of all women athletes, took honors in the 80-meter hurdles and the javelin throw. Of the six events in track and field for women that year, American girls won five. Eddie Tolan set two new Olympic marks with his 100- and 200-meter victories.

The city of Berlin was the solemn background for the 1936 Games, which produced a three-event champion—Jesse Owens. Owens, an American Negro from Ohio State University, couldn't have achieved his success under more dramatic conditions. Adolf Hitler had hoped to use the Games to prove German racial superiority to the rest of the world. Instead, Owens' activities made the headlines. He set two new Olympic records (broad jump and 200 meters), tied a third (100 meters), and won a fourth gold medal in the 400-meter relay.

The outbreak of World War II canceled the Games of the XII and XIII Olympiads; but the 1948 Games, held in London's White City Stadium, heralded the start of the XIV Olympiad. Bob Mathias, a seventeen-year-old Californian who won the decathlon, and Emil Zatopek of Czechoslovakia, who set a record in the 10,000-meter event, were individual standouts among the men. But it was a woman who took triple honors: Fanny Blankers-Koen of the Netherlands won the 100-meter and 200-meter runs and the 80-meter hurdles. France had a double champion in Micheline Ostermeyer (discus and shot put).

World records were made in seven events at Helsinki in 1952, and Zatopek set three of them. By winning the 5,000- and 10,000-meter events and the marathon, he proved to be the all-time best in the distance runs. American men won fourteen events, and Mathias became the first ever to take two consecutive decathlons. Soviet athletes, competing in the women's discus and shot put.
the Olympics for the first time, won no men's events, but took

The Games of the XVI Olympiad, held at Melbourne in 1956, saw nineteen records shattered and one tied as U.S.S.R.

men scored their first victories in international competition.

Only one American had a double triumph—Bobby Morrow of Abilene Christian—but ten shattered existing marks. Morrow won the 100- and 200-meter dashes, running the 200 in 20.6 seconds to break Jessie Owens' twenty-year-old record by one-tenth of a second. Other Americans to establish new standards were Tom Courtney in the 800-meter run, Lee Calhoun in the high hurdles, Glenn Davis in the low hurdles, Charley Dumas in the high jump, Bob Richards in the pole vault, Al Oerter in the discus, Parry O'Brien in the shot put, Harold Connolly in the hammer throw, and Milt Campbell in the decathlon.

Soviet Russia produced one of the greatest of all distance runners in Vladimir Kuts, who scored memorable triumphs in the grueling 5,000- and 10,000-meter runs, erasing records established by Emil Zatopek.

The 1960 Olympics in Rome were the most fantastic of all. Of the thirteen track events, records were set in ten; of the nine field events, new standards were established in eight; also a new record was made in the 50,000-meter walk.

Most significant of the new marks was in the broad jump. Ralph Boston recorded a leap of 26 feet 7¾ inches to erase the last of Jesse Owens' memorable Olympic records of twenty-four years earlier. Rafer Johnson was a spectacular performer in the decathlon, bettering Campbell's 1956 record by 455 points.

But it remained for a college girl to provide the biggest thrills. Wilma Rudolph of Tennessee State, who had conquered polio at the age of eight, became a triple gold medal winner at the age of twenty. Wilma, the seventeenth child of poverty-stricken parents in Clarksville, Tennessee, took the 100-meter dash in record time (11 seconds flat), won the 200-meter dash, and anchored the victorious 400-meter relay quartet.

Tokyo was the scene of the summer Games of the XVIII

Wilma Rudolph winning the 100-meter dash at the 1960 Olympics.

U. S. Olympic Association

Olympiad, in 1964, and the Japanese spent $2 billion on new roads, facilities, and sports arenas. It was a magnificent setting for magnificent performances.

The United States won twelve of the twenty-four track and field events for men (and sixteen of the twenty-two swimming and diving events for men and women) and stole the show with such exciting competitors as Billy Mills, Bob Schul, Bob Hayes, and Al Oerter. Americans regained sprint supremacy with Bob Hayes and Henry Carr, and won both the 5,000-meter and the 10,000-meter runs for the first time.

Nothing in the Olympics was more stunning than Mills' victory in the 10,000. A comparative unknown, the twenty-six-year-old Marine survived two last-lap shoving incidents and came from third place with a spectacular sprint in the last 60 yards to win in 28:24.4 for an Olympic record. Schul, incidentally, was the only one who thought Mills could win. Most people thought Schul could win the 5,000-meter run and he did. His time of 13.48.8 was good, considering rain and a wet track.

Bob Hayes set the stands on fire as he blazed the 100-meter dash in 10 seconds flat to tie the world record. What was amazing was his winning margin of three yards. Later he anchored the U. S. 400-meter relay to victory in the world-record time of 0:39.

Al Oerter, hampered all year by a bruised neck disc, had a torn cartilage in Tokyo. But his one good throw of the discus sailed 200 feet 1½ inches, broke his 1960 Olympic record, and earned him his third gold medal.

Fred Hansen, Mike Larrabee, and John Thomas were also among the standouts. Hansen, down to his last attempt, won

555

the pole vault at 16 feet 9 inches (an Olympic record) after nine hours of competition. Larrabee won the 400 meters over a brilliant field in 0.45.1. Thomas, up against old foe Valery Brumel of Russia, refused to back down and lost the high jump only on a count of misses. Both men turned in Olympic record leaps of 7 feet 1¾ inches.

Of the American athletes, the swimmers and divers were the biggest winners, with the men winning nine of the twelve events. Don Schollander, only 18½, won four gold medals, the most in a single Olympics for any American since Jesse Owens won four in track in 1936.

Never in modern times did the Olympic Games face so many obstacles as did the XIX Olympiad in October of 1968 in Mexico City. Early in the year, the Games were threatened by an Afro-Asian boycott if South Africa, despite her racial policies, were allowed to compete (South Africa eventually was barred). The Games were also threatened by Mexican youths protesting their government's policies.

Through it all, the Olympics prospered; there were no serious incidents and no serious boycotts. The only significant incident came during the victory-staging ceremony when Tommie Smith and John Carlos of the United States, both militants, raised black-gloved fists in a Black Power gesture during the playing of "The Star Spangled Banner." Both black runners were sent home, but they had already completed their competition.

Competitively, it was a glorious Olympics for the United States. American athletes dominated the three sports they are most interested in: track and field, swimming and basketball. In track and field the U.S. won twelve of the twenty-four events for men and three of the twelve for women. The U.S. stars included Jim Hines, Tommy Smith and Lee Evans in the sprints, Bob Beamon in the long jump, Dick Fosbury in the high jump, Bob Seagren in the pole vault, Al Oerter in the discus and Bill Toomey in the decathlon.

Beamon set a world record of 29 feet 2½ inches in the long jump, almost two feet better than man had ever jumped before. Fosbury won the high jump with an eye-opening, head-first backward leap. Oerter won the discus for his fourth straight Olympics victory.

In swimming Americans won eleven of the seventeen gold medals for men and twelve of the sixteen for women. The U.S. went undefeated in basketball.

Sixteen recognized track and field records were shattered and a seventeenth was tied at the glorious '68 Olympics. Beamon's record jump was most noteworthy. Meanwhile, five other Americans ran, jumped or threw their way into the record book. Jim Hines tied the 100-meter record of 9.9; Tommie Smith knocked his 200-meter (turn) time down to 19.8 and Lee Evans did 43.8 for the 400-meter record.

En route to the Olympics, Bob Seagren pole vaulted 17 feet 9 inches and Jay Silvester spun the discus 224–5.

World records also were set by Dave Hemery, an Englishman, who raced the 400-meter hurdles in 48.1; Viktor Saneyev of Russia, who triple-jumped 57 feet ¾ inch; and by the United States 400-meter and 1,600-meter relay teams, 38.6 seconds and 2 minutes 56.1 seconds, respectively.

Great Names in Track and Field

JIM BEATTY

Jim Beatty, a pint-sized capsule of determination and confidence, has proved that the United States *can* produce a runner who can go the distance. But he might not have gone so far so fast if a Hungarian coach had not decided to live in the West.

In 1956 Jim was a promising miler at the University of North Carolina when he met the man who was to help him attain two world records and four American marks.

Mihail Igloi, the head coach of the Hungarian track and field squad at the 1956 Olympics, defected to the United States after the games. Igloi taught Beatty the European method of training and pacing. "He gave me schedules to follow," says Jim, "and then he would change them for no apparent reason. It was like working on several problems in mathematics and not getting any answers, until one day all of them came at once."

Beatty's assault on the record book was launched when he began to run for the Los Angeles Track Club, coached, of course, by Igloi. No other American ever established so many distance records as did this 128-pound dynamo in 1962. He became the first to shatter the four-minute indoor mile (3:58.9) and created a world standard for the outdoor two-mile (8:29.8).

Jim Beatty

Associated Press

Beatty followed these achievements by making the most successful American invasion of Europe since D-day. Here's what he did in the summer of 1962: ran the mile in 3:56.5 at London; the 3,000-meter in 7:54.2 at Paris; the 1,500-meter in 3:39.4 at Oslo, Norway; the mile in 3:56.3 at Helsinki, Finland, and the 5,000-meter in 13:45 at Turku, Finland— all the fastest times ever recorded by an American.

GLENN DAVIS

One of the best of all the quarter-milers, hurdles or flat, was barrel-chested Glenn Davis, a superb runner who made Ohio State a track power in the mid-1950's. Davis, who won the Sullivan Award in 1958, held Olympic and world records in the 400-meter hurdles, a rare double accomplishment. He also held the world's record in the 440-yard run (45.7), until Tommie Smith did it in 44.8.

Davis first streaked to international acclaim in the 1956 Olympics when he sped over the 400-meter hurdles in 50.1. Two years later he ran his specialty in 49.2 to break his own world record.

Davis returned to Olympic glory in 1960. He not only retained his hurdles title with another record (49.3), but also helped the United States capture the 1,600-meter relay in the record time of 3:02.2.

Glenn seemed to thrive on international competition. He had perhaps the finest day of his career in Oslo, Norway, in July 1958, when he won four events in two days—the 100-, 200- and 400-meter runs and the 400-meter hurdles.

RON DELANY

As a rule, runners are careful clock-watchers. But Ron Delany, who must be regarded as one of the greatest ever to run, didn't seem to care about the ticking of the stopwatch.

Ron was born in Ireland. He set all kinds of records at Villanova University. In 1956 he ran the Olympic's fastest 1,500-meter race in its sixty-year history, 3:41.2, a mark eclipsed by Herb Elliott's 3:35.6 in the 1960 Games. He also held the one-mile indoor record (4:01.4) until Jim Beatty bettered it in 1962, and he ran the mile in less than four minutes on three occasions.

Delany always had one thought when in competition: winning the race no matter what the time. He refused to quicken his pace for the sake of breaking records. Did it pay off? Well, he took three straight IC4A mile titles and four AAU indoor miles, and he had a string of thirty-four indoor mile victories when he halted competition—except for relay running—in 1961.

BOB HAYES

Perhaps the greatest race in Bob Hayes' life was run in the 1964 Olympics in Tokyo. The event was the 400-meter relay against the Russians, and it was especially important because the Americans in an earlier Olympic race had been penalized for passing the baton out of zone.

As the anchor man, Hayes turned out to be the most important man on the team. The United States had been extra careful in the early stages of the race, not wanting to be penalized for illegal passing. As a result, after the first three legs of the race, they were trailing the Russians by several yards.

Hayes took the baton about five yards behind the Soviet anchor man and turned on the juice. When he completed his leg of the run the U. S. team had its victory. Unofficial clockers had him timed in 8.8 seconds flat, which would be equal to running 100 yards in 8 seconds!

If anyone questioned Bob's being "the world's fastest human," that race answered him. He first laid claim to the title on June 21, 1963, when he set a world record 9.1 in the 100-yard dash in the AAU championships in St. Louis.

Hayes won another 1964 Olympics gold medal with a record-tying 10 seconds in the 100 meters. As a sophomore, he won the NAIA 100- and 200-yard championships. As a junior he captured the 220 and 200 meters in the NCAA championships.

Bob set an indoor record of 5.9 seconds for the 60-yard dash in the AAU championships in Madison Square Garden on February 22, 1964. The mark has since been tied.

The chunky 5-foot-11-inch 192-pounder from Jacksonville, Florida, has never had a smooth running form. He has thickly muscled arms and legs and runs a bow-legged, wobbly gait. Actually, he runs like a football player, which he is.

Hayes starred as a halfback at Florida A&M and then became a standout with the Dallas Cowboys in the National Football League.

JESSE OWENS

Long before the Atlas and the Jupiter, America had a missile in the person of Jesse Owens, a bolt of lightning who blazed through the record books as no other runner has.

During the mid-1930's, this supremely conditioned athlete was the world's fastest dash man, the nation's outstanding low hurdler, and the broad-jump champion of all the hemispheres. Though none of his records still stand, his name will always occupy a special place in sports annals.

No one ever thinks of Owens without recalling his epic feats in the 1936 Olympic Games, but his fame was widespread even before then. So fabulous had been some of his performances, in fact, that the other nations preparing for the Olympics were inclined to dismiss them. They were soon to realize that everything they had heard about Owens was true.

The 1936 Olympics in Berlin were staged at a time when Adolf Hitler was determined to prove the Nazi theory of Aryan race supremacy. Owens had only his brown legs and a champion's heart to reply to the Hitler propaganda machine. But how well he used them!

Owens humbled the competition in the 100- and 200-meter dashes and in the broad jump, and he was the leadoff man on the winning 400-meter-relay team. It was the first time in a single Olympics that a male contestant won four gold medals.

JIM RYUN

His parents called him "slowpoke" when he was growing up on a farm outside of Wichita, Kansas, but Jim Ryun grew up to become famous as the "Kansas Tornado."

Ryun was a nineteen-year-old freshman at the University of Kansas when he thrilled the world with an incredible 3:51.3 record-shattering time for the mile. The scene was an AAU invitational meet at Berkeley, Calif., on July 17, 1966. The old mark was set by Michel Jazy of France on June 9, 1965.

For Ryun it was the ninth time he had broken four minutes in his young career, which had started so brilliantly while he was still in Wichita East High School. As a high school sophomore, he clocked miles at 4:20, 4:16.2, and 4:07.8 in 1963.

At 6 feet 2 inches and 165 pounds, James Ronald Ryun is a firm believer in hard work. As a boy he would run constantly through the Kansas corn fields. As a college freshman he practiced running anywhere from 70 to 100 miles a week to keep his skinny legs strong. The hard work has paid off not only in the mile record, which Ryun lowered to 3:51.1 in 1967, but in the world marks as well for the 880-yard run (1:44.9) and 1,500 meters (3:33.1).

In the 1968 Olympics in Mexico City, Ryun, bothered by the thin air, ran a disappointing second to Kenya's Kip Keino. Jim was clocked in 3:37.8, well above his world record, while Keino won in 3:34.9 for a new Olympic mark.

565

Ryun's style is deceptive. He usually starts a race slowly, but he has a tremendous finishing kick. For example, in his 3:51.3 world record race, he raced the final 440 yards in a remarkable 56.3 seconds.

JOHN THOMAS

"Seven feet," announced the official, and the listeners strained their ears, not believing that such a mark was possible. But it was, and John Thomas is the youth who jumped that high. Some observers considered it a fluke. So thirty days later young Thomas made believers of all the doubters of Thomas when he jumped not 7 feet, but 7 feet 1¼ inches, a height never before attained by any other American high jumper.

Thomas is, by any measurement, a remarkable young man. In March 1959 his left foot, or "takeoff" foot, was severely injured in an accident. Yet less than a year later, in his first competitive meet since the accident, he scaled 7 feet ½ inch.

He went on to set a world record of 7 feet 3¾ inches (since bettered by 2 inches by Russia's Valery Brumel) and was considered a certain winner in the 1960 Olympics. But his leap of 7 feet ¼ inches was only good enough for third place. In the 1964 Olympics he and Brumel both cleared 7 feet 1¾ inches.

Jim Ryun in a familiar role—breasting the tape.

All-Time Records

WORLD RECORDS

(As of January 1, 1969; asterisk denotes pending record)

A world record can be approved only by the International Amateur Athletic Federation, which meets at least once a year to determine those records which should be officially recognized. Only those made in outdoor meets are considered.

All countries which are members of the IAAF submit records they believe eligible. The federation then investigates the conditions under which the event was held. If they meet the federation's rigid specifications, the record is approved.

RUNNING (YARDS)

Event and Record	Holder	Date
100 yards 09.1	Bob Hayes (U.S.A.)	6/21/63
220 yards 19.5	Tommie Smith (U.S.A.)	5/7/66
220 yards (turn) 20.0	Tommie Smith (U.S.A.)	6/11/66
440 yards 44.8	Tommie Smith (U.S.A.)	5/20/67
880 yards 1:44.9	Jim Ryun (U.S.A.)	6/10/66
1 mile 3:51.1	Jim Ryun (U.S.A.)	6/23/67
2 miles 8:19.6	Ron Clarke (Australia)	6/27/67
3 miles 12:50.4	Ron Clarke (Australia)	7/10/65
6 miles 26:47.0	Ron Clarke (Australia)	7/14/65
10 miles 47:02.2	Ron Hill (England)	4/6/68
15 miles 1 hr. 12:48.2	Ron Hill (England)	7/21/65

RUNNING (METERS)

Event and Record	Holder	Date
100 meters 09.9	Jim Hines (U.S.A.)	10/14/68
200 meters 19.5	Tommie Smith (U.S.A.)	5/7/66
200 meters (turn) 19.8	Tommie Smith (U.S.A.)	10/16/68
400 meters 43.8	Lee Evans (U.S.A.)	10/18/68
800 meters 1:44.3	Peter Snell (New Zealand) Ralph Doubell (Australia)	2/3/62 10/15/68
1,000 meters 2:16.2	Jurgen May (East Germany) Franz-Jozef Kemper (W. Germany)	7/20/65 9/21/66
1,500 meters 3:33.1	Jim Ryun (U.S.A.)	7/8/67
2,000 meters 4:56.2	Michel Jazy (France)	10/12/66
3,000 meters 7:39.6	Kipchoge Keino (Kenya)	8/27/65

Event and Record	Holder	Date
3,000 meters (chase) 8:24.2	Juoko Kuha (Finland)	7/17/68
5,000 meters 13:16.6	Ron Clarke (Australia)	7/5/66
10,000 meters 27:39.4	Ron Clarke (Australia)	7/14/65
15,000 meters 44:54.6	Emil Zatopek (Czechoslovakia)	9/21/51
20,000 meters 58:06.2	Gaston Roelants (Belgium)	10/28/66
25,000 meters 1 hr. 15:22.6	Ron Hill (England)	7/21/65
30,000 meters 1 hr. 32:25.4	Jim Hogan (England)	11/12/66
3,000 meter steeplechase 8:26.4	Gaston Roelants (Belgium)	8/7/65

HURDLES

Event and Record	Holder	Date
120-yard high	Martin Laver (W. Germany)	7/7/59
13.2	Lee Calhoun (U.S.A.)	8/21/60
	Earl McCullouch (U.S.A.)	7/16/67
220-yards low 21.9	Don Styron (U.S.A.)	4/2/60
440 yards 43.9	Gert Potgieter (South Africa)	4/16/60
110-meter high	Martin Lauer (W. Germany)	7/7/59
13.2	Lee Calhoun (U.S.A.)	8/21/60
	Earl McCullouch (U.S.A.)	7/16/67
200-meter low 21.9	Don Styron (U.S.A.)	4/2/60
200 meters	(straight)—	
22.5	Martin Lauer (W. Germany)	7/7/59
	(turn)—	
	Glen Davis (U.S.A.)	8/20/60
400 meters 49.1	Rex Cawley (U.S.A.)	9/13/64

RELAYS

Event and Record	Holder	Date
400 meters 38.2	U.S.A. (Charlie Greene, Mel Pender, Ronnie Ray Smith, Jim Hines)	10/20/68

Event and Record	Holder	Date
440-yards 38.6	Southern California (Earl McCullouch, Fred Kuller, O. J. Simpson, Lennox Miller)	6/17/67
800 meters 880 yards 1:22.1	San Jose State (Ken Shackelford, Bob Talmadge, Lee Evans, Tommie Smith)	5/13/67
1,600 meters 2:56.1	U.S.A. (Vince Matthews, Ron Freeman, Larry James, Lee Evans)	10/20/68
One mile 3:02.8	Trinidad (Lennox Yearwood, Kent Bernard, Edwin Roberts, Wendell Motteley)	8/13/66
3,200 meters 7:08.6	West Germany (Manfred Kinder, Walter Adams, Dieter Bogatzki, Franz-Josef Kemper)	8/13/66
Two miles 7:14.6	West Germany (Bodo Tummler, Walter Adams, Harald Norpoth, Franz-Josef Kemper)	6/13/68
6,000 meters 14:49.0	France (Pierre Vervoort, Claude Nicolas, Michel Jazy, Jean Wadoux)	6/25/65
Four miles 16:05.0	Oregon T.C. (Roscoe Divine, Wade Bell, Arne Kvalheim, Dave Wilborn)	5/31/68

FIELD EVENTS

Event and Record	Holder	Date
High jump 7 ft. 5¾ in.	Valery Brumel (U.S.S.R.)	7/21/63
Pole vault 17 ft. 9 in.	Bob Seagren (U.S.A.)	9/21/68
Long jump 29 ft. 2½ in.	Bob Beamon (U.S.A.)	10/18/68
Triple jump 57 ft. ¾ in.	Viktor Saneyev (U.S.S.R.)	10/17/68
Shot put 71 ft. 5½ in.	Randy Matson (U.S.A.)	4/22/67
Discus 224 ft. 5 in.	Jay Silvester (U.S.A.)	9/18/68
Hammer throw 242 ft.	Gyula Zsivotzky (Hungary)	9/14/68
Javelin 307 ft. 9½ in.	Janis Lusis (U.S.S.R.)	6/23/68
Decathlon 8.319 points	Kurt Bendlin (West Germany)	5/14/67

Event and Record	Holder	Date
Pole vault 17 ft. 4 in.	Fred Hansen (U.S.A.)	7/25/64
17 ft. 5½ in.°°	Bob Seagren (U.S.A.)	5/21/66
16-lb. shot put 70 ft. 7¼ in.	Randy Matson (U.S.A.)	5/8/65
Discus throw 211 ft. 9½ in.	Ludvik Danek (Czechoslovakia)	8/2/64
213 ft. 11½ in.°	Ludvik Danek (Czechoslovakia)	10/12/65
Javelin throw 300 ft. 11 in.	Terje Pedersen (Norway)	9/2/64
16-lb. hammer throw 233 ft. 9½ in.	Harold Connolly (U.S.A.)	6/20/65
241 ft. 11 in.°	Gyula Zsivotzky (Hungary)	9/9/65
Decathlon 8,089 points°° 9,121 points°°°	C. K. Yang (Taiwan)	4/27–28/63

°° New scoring system.
°°° Old scoring system.

Olympic Records

These records can be set only in the Olympic Games, which are held every four years. Americans hold records in sixteen events. Russia, which entered the competition for the first time in 1952, has four.

MEN

Event and Record	Holder	Country	Year
100 meters 9.9	Jim Hines	U.S.A.	1968
200 meters 19.8	Tommie Smith	U.S.A.	1968
400 meters 43.8	Lee Evans	U.S.A.	1968
800 meters 1:44.3	Ralph Doubell	Australia	1968
1,500 meters 3:34.9	Kipchoge Keino	Kenya	1968

Event and Record	Holder	Country	Year
5,000 meters 13:39.6	Vladimir Kuts	U.S.S.R.	1956
10,000 meters 28:24.4	Billy Mills	U.S.A.	1964
Marathon 2 hr. 12 min. 11.2 sec.	Adebe Bikala	Ethiopia	1964
50,000-meter walk 4 hr. 11 min. 12.4 sec.	Abdon Pamich	Italy	1964
110-meter hurdles 13.3	Willie Davenport	U.S.A.	1968
400-meter hurdles 48.1	Dave Hemery	England	1968
3,000 meter steeplechase 8:30.8	Gaston Roelants	Belgium	1964
High jump 7 ft. 4½ in.	Dick Fosbury	U.S.A.	1968
Long jump 29 ft. 2½ in.	Bob Beamon	U.S.A.	1968
Triple jump 57 ft. ¾ in.	Victor Saneev	U.S.S.R.	1968
Pole vault 17 ft. 8½ in.	Bob Seagren	U.S.A.	1968
Discus 212 ft. 6½ in.	Al Oerter	U.S.A.	1968
Javelin 295 ft. 7¼ in.	Yanis Lusis	U.S.S.R.	1968
Shot put 67 ft. 4¾ in.	Randy Matson	U.S.A.	1968
Hammer throw 240 ft. 8 in.	Gyula Zsivotsky	Hungary	1968
Decathlon 8,193 points	Bill Toomey	U.S.A.	1968
400-meter relay 38.2	Charlie Greene, Mel Pender, Ray Smith, Jim Hines	U.S.A.	1968
1,600-meter relay 2:56.1	Vince Matthews, Ron Freeman, Larry James, Lee Evans	U.S.A.	1968

WOMEN

Event and Record	Holder	Country	Year
100 meters 11.0	Wiomia Tyus	U.S.A.	1968
200 meters 22.5	Irena Szewinska	Poland	1968
400 meters 52.0	Betty Cuthbert Collette Besson	Australia France	1964 1968
800 meters 2:09	Madeline Manning	U.S.A.	1968
80-meter hurdles 10.3	Maureen Caird	Australia	1968
High jump 6 ft. 2⅞ in.	Iolanda Balas	Romania	1964
Long jump 22 ft. 4½ in.	Vera Viscopoleanu	Romania	1968
Discus 191 ft. 2½ in.	Lia Manoliu	Romania	1968
Javelin 198 ft. 7½ in.	Mihaela Penes	Romania	1964
Shot put 64 ft. 4 in.	Margarita Gummel	East Germany	1968
Pentathlon 5,246 points	Irena Press	U.S.S.R.	1964
400-meter relay 42.8	Ferrell, Bailes, Netter, Tyus	U.S.A.	1968

Sullivan Trophy Winners

The outstanding amateur athlete of the year is awarded the James E. Sullivan Memorial Trophy by the AAU. Outstanding sports authorities vote annually for the amateur athlete "who by performance, example, and good influence did the most to advance the cause of good sportsmanship."

Year	Holder	Where From	Sport
1969	Bill Toomey	Santa Barbara, Calif.	Decathlon
1968	Debbie Meyer	Sacramento, Calif.	Swimming
1967	Randy Matson	Pampa, Texas	Shot put
1966	Jim Ryun	Wichita, Kan.	Running
1965	William Bradley	Crystal City, Mo.	Basketball
1964	Donald Schollander	Tacoma, Wash.	Swimming
1963	John Pennel	Hollywood, Fla.	Pole vault
1962	James Beatty	Los Angeles A.C.	Running
1961	Wilma Rudolph	Tennessee State	Running
1960	Rafer Johnson	UCLA	Decathlon
1959	Parry O'Brien	So. Calif. Striders	Shot put
1958	Glenn Davis	Ohio State University	Running, hurdles
1957	Bobby Joe Morrow	Abilene Christian Coll.	Running
1956	Patricia McCormick	Los Angeles A.C.	Diving
1955	Harrison Dillard	Cleveland, Ohio	Running, hurdles
1954	Malvin G. Whitfield	Los Angeles A.C.	Running
1953	Sammy Lee	U.S. Army Med. Corps	Diving
1952	Horace Ashenfelter	New York A.C.	Running

Year	Holder	Where From	Sport
1951	Robert E. Richards	Illinois A.C.	Pole vault
1950	Fred Wilt	New York A.C.	Running
1949	Richard T. Button	Englewood, N.J.	Figure skating
1948	Robert B. Mathias	Tulare, Calif.	Decathlon
1947	John B. Kelly, Jr.	Philadelphia, Pa.	Rowing
1946	Y. Arnold Tucker	U.S. Military Academy	Football, track
1945	Felix Blanchard	U.S. Military Academy	Football, shot put
1944	Ann Curtis	San Francisco	Swimming
1943	Gilbert Dodds	Boston A.A.	Running
1942	Cornelius Warmerdam	San Francisco Olympic Club	Pole vault
1941	Leslie MacMitchell	New York University	Running
1940	J. Gregory Rice	South Bend (Ind.) A.C.	Running
1939	Joseph W. Burk	Pennsylvania A.C.	Rowing
1938	Donald Lash	Indiana State Police	Running
1937	J. Donald Budge	Oakland, Calif.	Tennis
1936	Glenn Morris	Denver A.C.	Decathlon
1935	W. Lawson Little, Jr.	California	Golf
1934	William R. Bonthron	New York A.C.	Running
1933	Glenn Cunningham	University of Kansas	Running
1932	James Bausch	Kansas City, Mo.	Decathlon
1931	Bernard E. Berlinger	Philadelphia, Pa.	Decathlon
1930	Robert T. Jones, Jr.	Atlanta, Ga.	Golf

Winter Skiing

The History of Skiing

To supposedly sensible people, the skier is an enigma. What drives a young man or young woman out into the snow and cold every weekend? Why do they leave the comfy confines of their homes for chilblains, or worse, broken bones? Are these trips necessary?

Does it make sense to spend a vacation in Denver, Colorado, waiting for a chair lift at 10 below zero? Does it make sense to risk your neck plunging down the side of a mountain then wait in line to take the same risk again? The answer is yes to a growing band of adventurers in the United States and the rest of the world.

Skiing has a language, a history and traditions all its own which fascinate the novice from the moment he tries on his first pair of skis. The sport has a unique intangible appeal with dozens of special ingredients. If you don't ski, you will never know the feeling; if you do ski, only you can understand the beauty of fighting the bitter cold for a chance to glide down a slope.

Ski historians believe one of Leif Ericson's Vikings introduced skiing to America. Scandinavian archeologists have proved Ericson's ancestors in Norway had used wooden skis since Stone Age times. Archeologists have also proved that skis date back to 2500 B.C. because planks bearing a startling resemblance to today's skis have been found in the Altai Mountains of Siberia.

The Norwegians, of course, have taken skiing to their hearts . . . and their battlefields. In 1747 a Norwegian general, Hans Jacob Amholdt, formed the first ski troops. His troops had fancy helmets, fancy uniforms and fancy skis. The left ski was three feet longer than the right, which was seven feet long. The short ski was the pusher and the longer right one was the slider. The equipment also included one long pole with a sharp iron spike on the end, to be used on the enemy or unfriendly bears. The pole was also used to slow down their flight.

Between battles, around 1820, the imaginative Norwegians brought skiing into the sports picture. It was great going down hills at great speeds but, in order to race, it was necessary to change direction. A lad from Telemark, Sondre Nordheim, developed a graceful but extremely difficult method of turning in deep snow which he called the Telemark. It involved placing the tip of one ski against the boot of the other.

Two rivals, youngsters from the town of Christiania— Torjus and Mikke Hemmestviet—came up with a skidded turn that kept the skis wide apart and more or less parallel. This became known as the Christiania.

Meanwhile, other adventurous Norwegians were propelling themselves off bumps to see how far they could go, and with that, ski-jumping was born.

The first authentic record of skiing in America dates back to 1850 when settlers and frontiersmen began pushing out to the Northwest Territories. Among them were many immigrants from Scandinavia; they taught the American frontiersmen the use of skis and introduced the sport of skiing.

Along about 1856 or '57 a Scandinavian named John Thompson had a small farm in the California-Sierra Nevada mountains. Hearing that the United States was having difficulty delivering mail to snowbound mining camps during the winter, Thompson contracted to carry the mail from Placerville to Carson Valley and return, a route that lay under three to twenty feet of snow. By today's standards, Thompson's skis were less than primitive. They were nine feet long and over four inches wide. But he trekked across the Sierra, crossing 10,000-foot passes on his skis, and became a legend. He also taught the miners how to ski-jump and race.

Before long, each mining camp had its own team of expert skiers, and in 1867 the town of La Porte formed a winter sports association, the first ski club ever formed in America. Thousands of dollars in bets rode on the racers between each mining town.

The ski club idea spread, and in 1872 a group of Norwegians in Berlin, New Hampshire, formed the Nansen Ski Club. In the 1880's several Midwest jumping clubs were formed, and in 1887, the Ishpeming, Michigan, Ski Club organized the first formal ski jumping tournament ever held in the United States.

Those early jumps, achieved on natural hills with a small takeoff platform built half-way down, were never more than 50 feet long, and the jumper landed in a rather upright position. But as jumping became more popular, innovations were made, with better platforms to increase the speed of the jumpers, and bigger and better records were established.

In 1904 the first national jumping championship was held at Ishpeming and was won by Conrad Thompson with a leap of 82 feet. In 1913 Anders Haugen soared 169 feet. As the jumping hills grew bigger and ski equipment improved, the "riders" altered their style to accommodate the tremendous speed they were achieving on the in-run and in the air. Today's jumper reaches close to 75 miles per hour at the takeoff and he may land more than 300 feet away.

Eventually, the jumpers and cross-country skiers banded together in the Midwest to form the Central Ski Association. The cross-country skiers were called "langlaufers." Thus, with ski jumping and cross-country races (downhill racing was out of the question on the wooded hills of the East and Midwest), the two events became known as Nordic events. Later the name of the organization was changed to the National Ski Association, which numbers seven regional divisions and encompasses every aspect of the ski sport in America.

Some of the outstanding early jumpers were Lars and Anders Haugen, Barney Riley, Henry Hall and Ole Mangseth in the 1920's. Anders Haugen placed fourth in the first Winter Olympics at Chamonix, France, in 1924. Four years later, Rolf Monsen was sixth at St. Moritz. In 1932, when the U.S. hosted the third winter games at Lake Placid, New York, Casper Oimen was fifth in the jumping.

The Lake Placid games were the last in which the Olympic ski championships were limited to Nordic events. In 1936, the Olympics were held at Garmisch-Partenkirchen, Germany, and included new Alpine events: downhill and slalom racing. A young American named Dick Durrance became a hero for his exploits on the downhill trail and slalom (skiing between poles) slope. Durrance learned to ski in Germany but wore the colors of Dartmouth College when he competed.

Downhill racing was practiced in the Sierras as early as 1860 but downhill racing in its modern form was first introduced in Switzerland by a group of British skiers, led by Arnold Lunn. The first modern American downhill was staged in 1927 on a carriage road on Mt. Moosilauke, New Hampshire, by some racers from Dartmouth College. Charles Procter was the first winner. The race had been the inspiration of Colonel Anton Dietrich, Dartmouth ski coach, who was the first of many foreign ski coaches to turn Dartmouth College into the most important single factor in Alpine skiing in America.

In 1930 a Bavarian ski teacher named Otto Schniebs took over as Dartmouth coach. He soon saw that if his skiers were to compete against the best of Europe they would have to have downhill and slalom practice. Before long he supervised the cutting of a trail down Mt. Moosilauke, a trail designed only for racing. He also helped introduce the low-crouching, wide-stanced style which revolutionized downhill racing in America. Schniebs coached Dartmouth to six successive national championships and produced such stars as Ted Hunter, Durrance and Ed Wells.

Other European skiing teachers came to the United States, and with each new coach came new ideas for the downhill racers. One of the last teachers to arrive, and one of the very best, was Hannes Schneider, the revered "skimeister" of the Arlberg. Taken prisoner by the Nazis in his beloved St. Anton, Schneider was released through the intervention of prominent Americans and settled in North Conway, New Hampshire, where he taught a new generation of skiers.

With World War II came the American 10th Mountain Division, the famed ski troops whose veterans came back

Gretchen Fraser

from Europe to spark the great post-war ski boom. They were the ones who built the magnificent ski hotels and luxurious ski resorts and ski lodges. And the men of the 10th competed against the world's best in downhill and jumping. Gordon Wren won fifth place in Olympic jumping at St. Moritz in 1948. Racers like Steve Knowlton, Dev Jennings and Leon Goodman competed successfully against Europe's Alpine elite.

France's Jean-Claude Killy sails over a bump en route to victory in the men's downhill event in the Winter Olympics on February 9, 1968.

By 1950, when the world ski championships were staged at the newly created resort of Aspen, Colorado, American skiing had definitely come of age.

Though American men have never won an Olympic gold medal in skiing, one of our girls did the trick. She was Gretchen Fraser, who got the coveted gold in 1948. American men like Billy Kidd, John Bower, Dennis McCoy and Rick Chaffee were making great strides, but the Europeans were still the best.

Dramatic evidence of this came in the 1968 Winter Olympics, at Grenoble, France, where France's Jean-Claude Killy accomplished something never done before. He captured the gold medal in three nerve-wracking events: the slalom, the giant slalom and the downhill.

The world-wide ruling body of skiing is the Fédération Internationale de Ski (FIS), founded in 1924. In America, the major organization is the United States Ski Association, which takes in more than five hundred clubs with a total membership exceeding 50,000.

Skiing Records

1968 WINTER OLYMPICS CHAMPIONS
At Grenoble, France
SKIING (ALPINE)
Men's Slalom (Two Runs)

		Time
1. Jean-Claude Killy	France	1:39.73
2. Herbert Huber	Austria	1:39.82
3. Alfred Matt, Austria	Austria	1:40.09

Men's Giant Slalom (Two Runs)

1. Jean-Claude Killy	France	3:29.28
2. Willy Favre	Switzerland	3:31.50
3. Heinrich Messner	Austria	3:31.83

Men's Downhill

1. Jean-Claude Killy	France	1:59.85
2. Guy Perillat	France	1:59.93
3. Daniel Daetwyler	Switzerland	2:00.32

Women's Slalom (Two Runs)

1. Marielle Goitschel	France	1:25.86
2. Nancy Greene	Canada	1:26.15
3. Annie Famose	France	1:27.89

Women's Giant Slalom

1. Nancy Greene	Canada	1:51.97
2. Annie Famose	France	1:54.61
3. Fernande Bochatay	Switzerland	1:54.74

Women's Downhill

1. Olga Pall	Austria	1:40.87
2. Isabelle Mir	France	1:41.33
3. Christl Haas	Austria	1:41.82

SKIING (NORDIC)

Men's 15-Kilometer

1. Harald Groenningen	Norway	47:54.2
2. Eero Maentyranta	Finland	47:56.1
3. Gunnar Larsson	Sweden	48:33.7

Men's 50-Kilometer

1. Ole Ellefsaeter	Norway	2:28:45.8
2. Viatches Venedine	U.S.S.R.	2:29:02.5
3. Josef Haas	Switzerland	2:29:14.8

Men's 30-Kilometer

1. Franco Nones	Italy	1:35:39.2
2. Odd Martinsen	Norway	1:36:28.9
3. Eero Maentyranta	Finland	1:36:55.3

Men's 40-Kilometer Relay

1. Norway	2:08:33.5	4. U.S.S.R.		2:10:57.2
2. Sweden	2:10:13.2	5. Switzerland		2:15:32.4
3. Finland	2:10:56.7	12. United States		2:21:30.4

(United States team: Mike Gallagher, Mike Elliott, Robert Gray and John Bower.)

Women's Five-Kilometer

1. Toini Gustafsson	Sweden	16:45.2
2. Galina Koulakova	U.S.S.R.	16:48.4
3. Alevtina Koltchina	U.S.S.R.	16:51.6

Women's 10-Kilometer

1. Toini Gustafsson	Sweden	36:46.5
2. Berit Moerdre	Norway	37:54.6
3. Inger Aufles	Norway	37:59.9

Women's 15-Kilometer Relay

1. Norway	57:30.0	4. Finland	58:45.1
2. Sweden	57:51.0	5. Poland	59:04.7
3. U.S.S.R.	58:13.6		

Men's 70-Meter Jump

		Points
1. Jiri Raska	Czechoslovakia	216.5
2. Reinhold Bachler	Austria	214.2
3. Baldur Preiml	Austria	212.6
33. John Balfanz	United States	189.7

Men's 90-Meter Jump

1. Vladimir Beloussov	U.S.S.R.	231.3
2. Jiri Raska	Czechoslovakia	229.4
3. Lars Grini	Norway	214.3
34. William Bakke	United States	175.5

1968 WORLD CUP LEADERS

MEN'S DIVISION

1. Jean-Claude Killy	France	200
2. Dumeng Giovanoli	Switzerland	119
3. Hans Huber	Austria	112
4. Gerhard Nenning	Austria	102
5. Guy Perillat	France	83

(Billy Kidd of the United States was seventh with 73 points.)

1. Nancy Greene	Canada	191
2. Isabelle Mir	France	159
3. Florence Steurer	France	153
4. Marielle Goitschel	France	128
5. Fernande Bochatay	Switzerland	128

(Judy Nagel of the United States was 11th with 53 points.)

UNITED STATES ALPINE CHAMPIONSHIPS
(March 8–10, 1968, at Seattle)

Men's Downhill		Time
1. Scott Henderson	Banff, Can.	1:46.51
2. Rod Hebron	Vancouver, B.C.	1:48.05
3. Billy Kidd	Stowe, Vt.	1:48.34
4. Wayne Henderson	Banff, Can.	1:48.42
5. Jerry Rinaldi	Kimberley, B.C.	1:48.43

Men's Giant Slalom		
1. Rick Chaffee	Rutland, Vt.	2:20.78
2. Scott Henderson	Banff, Can.	2:21.06
3. Rod Hebron	Vancouver, B.C.	2:22.17
4. Jere Elliott	Steamboat Springs, Colo.	2:22.53
5. Spider Sabich	Kyburz, Calif.	2:22.67

Men's Slalom		
1. Rick Chaffee	Rutland, Vt.	1:37.19
2. Jere Elliott	Steamboat Springs, Colo.	1:39.08
3. Jim Huega	Squaw Valley, Calif.	1:39.39
4. Scott Henderson	Banff, Can.	1:39.40
5. Ken Sheppard	Lake Louise, Calif.	1:40.19

Women's Downhill		
1. Ann Black	Seattle	1:54.04
2. Erica Skinger	Stowe, Vt.	1:54.31
3. Cathy Nagel	Enumclaw, Wash.	1:54.70
4. Karen Dokka	Vancouver, B.C.	1:54.82
5. Felicity Field	Britain	1:55.57

	Women's Giant Slalom		Time
1. Marilyn Cochran	Richmond, Vt.		2:16.30
2. Nancy Greene	Rossland, B.C.		2:16.37
3. Judy Nagel	Enumclaw, Wash.		2:18.42
4. Louise Sparks	Stowe, Vt.		2:23.13
5. Karen Dokka	Vancouver, B.C.		2:23.19

	Women's Slalom	
1. Judy Nagel	Enumclaw, Wash.	1:37.68
2. Sherry Blann	Bend, Ore.	1:38.88
3. Judi Leinweber	Canada	1:40.47
4. Penny McCoy	Bishop, Calif.	1:41.82
5. Kathy Korfanta	Pinedale, Wyo.	1:42.83

UNITED STATES VETERANS CHAMPIONSHIPS
(March 15–17, 1968, Waterville Valley, New Hampshire)

Men's Downhill: Tom Corcoran, Waterville Valley	1:57.56
Women's Downhill: Mrs. Cricket Mackinley, Orinda, Calif.	2:12.01
Men's Slalom: Al Hobart, Waitsfield, Vt.	1:23.3
Women's Slalom: Mrs. Cricket Mackinley, Orinda, Calif.	1:44.18
Men's Giant Slalom: Tom Corcoran, Waterville Valley	1:42.75
Women's Giant Slalom: Mrs. Cricket Mackinley, Orinda, Calif.	2:01.75

UNITED STATES JUNIOR CHAMPIONSHIPS
(March 12–16, 1968, at Bozeman, Montana)

Men's Team Cross Country: Eastern Relay No. 1—Bruce Cunningham (Mexico, Me.), Larry Poulin (Mexico, Me.), Joseph McNulty (Tilton, N.H.), Scott Broomhall (Brumford, Me.)

Girl's Cross Country: Inter-Mountain—Trudy Owen (Wilson, Wyo.), Deeda Johnson (Wilson, Wyo.), Karol Hanson (Pinedale, Wyo.)

Men's Giant Slalom: Eric Poulsen, Olympic Valley, Calif.
Men's Slalom: Eric Poulsen, Olympic Valley, Calif.
Men's Downhill: Dan Bell, Ketchum, Idaho
Men's Cross Country: Malcolm Hunter, Canada
Special Jumping: Tim Kingsfield, Racine, Wis.
Jumping: George Perry, Mexico, Me.

590

Girl's Downhill: Cheryl Bechdolt, Tahoe City, Calif.
Girl's Slalom: Jan Harvey, Englewood, Colo.
Girl's Giant Slalom: Julie Walcott, Underhill Center, Vt.
Girl's Cross Country: Shirley Firth, Canada.
Nordic Combined: George Perry, Mexico, Me.

NATIONAL COLLEGIATE CHAMPIONSHIPS
(March 21–23, 1968, at Steamboat Springs, Colo.)

Downhill: Barney Peet, Ft. Lewis	Time:	1:37.30
Downhill Team: Colorado	Points:	99.5
Cross Country (15 kilometers): Clark Matis, Colorado	Time:	0:56.21
Cross Country Team: Ft. Lewis	Points:	99.1
Slalom: Dennis McCoy, Denver	Time:	1:36.32
Slalom Team: Dartmouth	Points:	95.9
Alpine Combined: Dennis McCoy, Denver	Points:	194.7
Jumping: Peter Robes, Wyoming	Points:	221.2
Jumping Team: Wyoming	Points:	99.8
Nordic Combined: Jim Miller, Ft. Lewis	Points:	437
Team Champion: Wyoming	Points:	383.9
Skimeister: Eric Piene, Wyoming	Points:	338.8

AMERICAN SKI JUMPING RECORDS

Year	Skier	Site	Feet
1950	Gorden Wren	Steamboat Springs, Colo.	297
1950	Billy Olson	Iron Mountain, Mich.	297
1951	Ansten Samuelstuen	Steamboat Springs, Colo.	316
1960	James Brennan	Iron Mountain, Mich.	316
1962	John Balfanz	Westby, Wis.	317
1962	Pekka Tirkkonen	Iron Mountain, Mich.	317
1963	Eugene Kotlarek	Steamboat Springs, Colo.	318–322
1965	Toraif Engan	Leavenworth, Wash.	324
1965	John Balfanz	Iron Mountain, Mich.	325
1967	Bjorn Wirkola	Leavenworth, Wash.	335